FLASHBACKS

Pat Nolan comes from Baltimore, County Cork.
A graduate of University College Cork,
he spent some time teaching in Nigeria before settling in
Ballycastle, County Antrim. Now retired, he spends his time
writing, attending matches and visiting west Cork.
His previous book, *When we were Young,*
was reprinted in 1998.

Flashbacks
A Half Century of Cork Hurling

Pat Nolan

The Collins Press

PUBLISHED BY
The Collins Press, West Link Park, Doughcloyne, Wilton, Cork, 2000

© Pat Nolan

British Library Cataloguing in Publication data.

Photographs in picture section courtesy of *The Irish Examiner*

ISBN: 1-898256-99-3

Printed in Ireland by ColourBooks

Cover design by Jackie Raftery.

Main cover photograph Fergal McCormac and Peter Barry,
compliments Mark Condren.
Secondary sover photographs source/compliments Pat Nolan

INTRODUCTION

It is a great privilege to be asked to write the introduction to *Flashbacks: A Half Century of Cork Hurling*, which is a fascinating and individualistic story of one man's recollections of 50 years of supporting Cork teams. It is, of course, a book that will rekindle memories of different eras, players, selectors, controversies from the famous 1950 Cork versus Tipperary Munster Final in Killarney, to the most recent victory at the end of the last millennium (1999). This is a comprehensive review of all the great games of that period and people will have their own special memories of the many great hurlers and footballers who have represented Cork in that time and helped keep Cork to the forefront in the quest for All-Ireland glory.

All the great names of the past are recalled, such as Jack Lynch in his final game for the county in 1950, bringing to an end a magnificent career in which he achieved the extraordinary feat of winning six All-Irelands in a row, five hurling and one football. I think we can safely assume this is a feat which will not be equalled in the modern game.

Of course the great three-in-a-row teams of the 1950s are recalled and from a personal viewpoint, as a very young boy, my first recollections of the household names of Cork hurling at that time are Willie John Daly, Mattie Fuohy, Johnny Clifford who scored the winning goal in 1954 and, of course, the incomparable Christy Ring. His presence both as a player and selector on subsequent Cork teams in the 1970s was such a huge influence on so many Cork triumphs in that period. One of my own special memories of this era is the 1966 final, as this was my first occasion in Croke Park when Cork, as complete outsiders, defeated the old enemy, Kilkenny. I will never forget the roar when Gerald McCarthy raised the cup aloft at the end of the game.

All these great occasions are relived through the eyes of

the author, as are the days when Cork had to endure the agony of defeat. Many great players from other counties are also given due credit, as are the author's recollections of the huge social and cultural changes in society during that time. In what was obviously a massive undertaking, the author deserves great credit and I am certain *Flashbacks* will bring great enjoyment to sports followers everywhere.

JIMMY BARRY-MURPHY
CORK, OCTOBER 2000

1950

On the long winter nights when I weary of catnapping in front of the television, what a joy it is to retire to 'my study'. 'My study' is really a spare bedroom with a desk, a chair, a word processor and a few book shelves. On the shelves, neatly filed under various headings is my most treasured memorabilia. Yes, that's where I store the match programmes, the newspaper cuttings, the magazines, the autographs and the photographs, all of which are my favourite source of nostalgia. It all brings back memories of glorious summer days spent watching my idols display rare craft and sportsmanship at Gaelic Athletic venues throughout the country. As I sit there reading and reflecting, I relive the excitement and the enormous pleasure derived from the feats of men and boys who over the years wielded the caman and played Gaelic football with amazing skill and artistry. I am sometimes touched by sadness and emotion as I ponder on the great deeds of the men who graced the Gaelic arena with such panache but, alas, who are no longer with us. How the transient nature of life is brought home!

My earlier recollections are of the stalwarts whose athleticism and command of caman and sliotar thrilled a nation. Not all were privileged to witness the deftness of play but many like myself were introduced to the magic of Gaelic games by the equally magic voice of Micheál O'Hehir on Radio Éireann.

The west Cork village I grew up in didn't have any great GAA tradition. I'm told a Gaelic football club did exist in the 1940s. I have no recollection of any such club or associated teams. In fact one could say that my love affair with Gaelic games began at the top because for many years I knew very little of club activities.

It was the county hurling teams of the era which caught my imagination. I became a Cork fan simply because of folklore and the magnificent Sunday radio commentaries. Slowly but surely the hurling stars of the mid-1940s became household names. Few were better known than the Cork players, who had won every honour hurling could bestow. As a child, I was filled with pride when over the airwaves came the names of those men in the famous red jerseys.

The mere mention of players such as Tom Mulcahy, Alan Lotty, Jim Young, Jack Lynch, Mossie O'Riordan, Fr Con Cottrell, Paddy O'Donovan, and the greatest of them all, Christy Ring, thrilled fans young and old alike. Paddy was a distant in-law of my own and because of that I felt I deserved some plaudits for the wonderful exhibitions of top class hurling he gave. In fact I referred to him as a cousin rather than an in-law for the benefit of those gathered around the radio on Sunday afternoons. I felt that enhanced my claim to fame considerably.

My memory of Cork's opponents up to 1949 is very sketchy. All I knew was that teams from different counties played one another but never thought beyond that. The idea of a county having to win a provincial final in order to qualify for the All-Ireland series never dawned on me. It was not until 1947 that I began to understand the system. I was then ten years of age. Cork had won five out of the six previous All-Ireland hurling finals.

My perception was that Cork teams were unbeatable, and it came as no surprise, to me at any rate, when in 1947 the Munster championship became the most recent conquest. Between Cork and another All-Ireland championship stood the hurlers of Antrim and Kilkenny. In August, Antrim were disposed of, and in my mind it was a case of Kilkenny next. How wrong I was, and perhaps for the first time I realised that my idols were not invincible. They were mortal after all! The name of Terry Leahy of Kilkenny became indelibly fixed in my mind. In what I'm told was probably the greatest hurling classic of them all, Cork led by a point with time almost up, when scores from Terry in the closing stages gave Kilkenny victory. It was a salutary reminder that all good things come to an end. Cork did not appear in an All-Ireland final again until 1952!

Five years is a long long time in a young boy's life. However, all was not doom and gloom because in the 1949 Munster championship it took a replay between Cork and Tipperary to separate the sides. Tipperary won a dramatic game which made a lasting impression on me. The names of some great, never to be forgotten Tipperary players came to the fore – Tony Reddin, Tommy Doyle, Pat Stakelum, Phil Shanahan, Seamus Bannon and many others – all giants of the game of hurling. Everyone was talking about the match which started a few minutes after three o'clock on one of the hottest days ever recorded in Ireland, and finished at six o'clock. With the scores level at the end of normal time, extra time was played. Among the questions being asked next day was, why before extra time did the Cork players lay out in the scorching sun while their Tipperary counterparts cooled off with water brought in churns? The newspapers made much of the Cork 'goal that never was'. It was a Mossie O'Riordan shot from 25 yards out which caused the controversy. Some observers said the ball hit the support at the back of the net and that Tipperary goalkeeper Tony Reddin cleared it on the rebound. Others observers, including some Tipperary players, said the ball did not go into the net. Half-a-century later the topic is still open for discussion.

OBLIVIOUS OF WORLD AFFAIRS IT ALL BEGAN FOR ME AT KILLARNEY

With the arrival of 1950 my hour was nigh. I had been agitating for a few years to get to a hurling match and all the talk about the Cork/Tipperary encounter of the previous year heightened my craving even more. Some time in June – I think it was the day I got my summer holidays from school – I was told that, all going well, I would be taken to the Munster final in Killarney on Sunday, 23 July.

Had I been asked to move mountains to go to the match, I would have been more than willing to try. All the time I kept asking myself, am I really going to see all those Cork and Tipperary players in the flesh? From what I had heard and read about them, a picture of supermen had formed in my mind. I wondered what it was going to be

3

like when they ran on to the field. For me, June and July of that year seemed never ending.

I was totally oblivious to what was going on outside my own little world. Nobody told me or maybe I wasn't listening, that for instance, India became a democratic republic or, that in the United States President Truman, gave the green light for the development of the hydrogen bomb. Unknown to me too, the United States government agreed to admit Alaska as the forty-ninth state. I did however read in the newspaper that Edgar Rice Burroughs, the novelist creator of *Tarzan of the Apes*, had died. Perhaps I was too young to take note of a significant medical breakthrough in the United States – on 17 June the first kidney transplant was carried out. Those happenings took place before my trip to Killarney.

On the morning of Sunday, 23 July 1950, I was a nervous wreck. A car load of us set out for Killarney at about nine o'clock. The weather was pleasant and a light balmy breeze made it feel warm. On the way one could not fail to be impressed by the wonderful scenery. Bantry Bay was resplendent, Glengarriff a picture, and the mountain road which took us through Moll's Gap and on to Kenmare was breathtaking. Once out of Kenmare, with Killarney now only twenty miles further on, traffic movement was reduced to the proverbial snail's pace. The narrow, winding, approach road to our destination was chock-a-block with cars. We were almost there!

By then I was blind with anticipation. The spectacular beauty of the Lakeland was lost on me. I scarcely noticed Ladies' View, the more distant Gap of Dunloe, or arguably Ireland's most famous landmark, the lakes of Killarney.

I had been to Killarney previously but not on match day. It seemed an entirely different town. I had never seen so many people in one place. The streets were thronged with good humoured Cork and Tipperary supporters. It seemed to me as if the entire male population of Ireland had come to Killarney.

Once inside the grounds we bought a few bars of chocolate and some minerals. Then we made our way to what we thought were the best available seats. There was still a long time to wait before the start of play. I had never seen a match programme before so I read it from cover to cover, which helped to contain my exuberance somewhat.

I remember nothing of the curtain-raiser. Perhaps it was because I didn't know anything about the players. I have vivid memories of a beautiful smooth, green, playing surface. I recall too that by the time the senior match began a very strong breeze was blowing down the pitch. At some point the enormity of the crowd struck me. No one was surprised when word spread that some entrance gates had been broken down and that walls were being scaled. Later we were to learn of an estimated attendance of 50,000 as opposed to official attendance records of 39,600.

The senior match was magnificent and my heroes lived up to all expectations. Cork played into the breeze in the first-half and were losing by seven points at the interval. The general opinion was that with wind advantage in the second-half, Cork would fight back. That assessment proved correct. The speed, the man-to-man combat and the sheer intensity of play lifted the game to new heights. True to form Christy Ring was the one to show the way. Christy had the crowd on their feet every time the ball even went near him. However, Tipperary were in no mood to give in and clearly the Cork players had a real battle on their hands. As the second-half wore on spectators around the sideline began to interrupt play. It was Cork supporters who seemed to be the culprits. They did their team no favours by running on to the field-of-play after every score. Then major confusion developed as supporters crowded the pitch around the goal area defended by Tipperary. The scene became chaotic and play was held up for about ten minutes before players managed to clear the pitch.

The last minutes of the game were very tense as Cork players did their utmost in an all-out effort to score. Again the supporters, not realising that their enthusiasm was hindering rather than helping, were instrumental in the referee not seeing one of the umpires signal a 70-yard free for Cork. The free could have been crucial to the outcome. Instead the final whistle went with the score reading,

Tipperary 2-17; Cork 3-11, a three point victory for the gallant Tipperarymen who went on to win the All-Ireland final.

One thing was certain. I had seen a match that had every ingredient imaginable. It was a very special day in my life. I had experienced excitement, passion, skill, atmosphere, tension and a well-being hitherto unknown to me. I couldn't wait for another day like it.

Apart from Christy Ring, two other Cork players made a lasting impression on me. One was Jack Lynch who had worn the county jersey with rare distinction since 1934. I didn't fully realise what a legend Jack had become in his own lifetime. I knew he was one of a number of top-class Cork players of the era but was later to learn that he was exceptional. By winning six successive All-Ireland senior medals, Jack achieved a record that will never be surpassed. Alas, the match in Killarney that day was the last outing on which the distinguished Glen Rovers man was to wear the jersey he had adorned for so long. The other player who impressed me was Matty Fouhy – maybe it was because the name sounded unusual.

At Fitzgerald Stadium, Killarney, on 23 July 1950, I was introduced not just to a game, but to a culture, a way of life, that was to become an obsession. The magic, the thrill-a-minute of those wonderfully exciting occasions surpassed all else.

Now as I sit alone in my 'study' and browse through those items of memorabilia which had their origin on that wonderful day in Killarney, I am briefly transported back to heady days at Semple Stadium, Thurles; the Gaelic Grounds, Limerick; Fitzgerald Stadium, Killarney; Pairc Ui Chaoimh, on the Banks of the Lee; Casement Park, Belfast; or to Croke Park itself. In my mind the sun is shining brilliantly, the stadium is animated with colour and ebullient supporters, the players, while locked in combat are displaying skills and artistry unparalleled in other games, the distinguished red jerseys, and the men who wore them fill me with ardent pride. To have been part of it is a joy forever.

While I remained enthralled by the Killarney experience,

the first world motor racing championship was held in
Monza, Italy. It was won by Nino Farina. In other developments, the first automatic telephone answering
machine was tested, a new cartoon strip called Peanuts
appeared, and Al Jolson, singer and entertainer, who
gained instant cinema immortality as the star of the first
talking picture, died.

1951

A SWELTERING HOT DAY AT THE GAELIC GROUNDS

With the excitement of the 1950 encounter at Killarney fresh in my mind, I prayed that the same counties would meet in the 1951 Munster hurling final. When Cork beat Clare in the semi-final by a score line of 5-7 to 3-5, I jumped for joy. I was determined to see the decider at the Gaelic Grounds, Limerick, in July.

Around the world the year so far had seen Second World War hero General Douglas McArthur stripped of all his commands by an incensed President Truman, and the hanging of the last Nazi condemned by the Nuremberg court for crimes against humanity. Shortly before Munster final day the worst floods in the history of the United States left 41 people dead and hundreds of thousands homeless.

Back in Ireland when the great day arrived it was sweltering hot. I was among the west Cork contingent who regardless of temperature travelled to Limerick donned in Sunday suit, shirt and tie. Tipperary, captained by the magnificent Jimmy Finn, were red hot favourites. A crowd of 42,337 gathered to see the match. Tipperary supporters were looking forward to three Munster championships in a row while those of the Rebel county were hoping that would not be the case. There was great craic among rival fans as we walked along Ennis Road towards the venue. Tipperary riding on the crest of a wave had a well established, settled side. Cork on the other hand had made several positional changes and no less than seven personnel changes from the team beaten in Killarney the previous year. It was very much a transitional time with stalwarts like Tom Mulcahy, Jack Lynch, Paddy O'Donovan and Mossie O'Riordan calling it a day. The newcomer to the team who impressed me most was Vincie Twomey playing at left-corner back.

The first half was very close, scribbles on a match pro-gramme show that Tipperary led by two points at half-time. Christy Ring lined out at midfield for Cork. His opposite number was the great Seamus Bannon. Ring seemed to be here, there and everywhere. As the game wore on his prominence became remarkable. Indeed many informed observers regard his play that day as his greatest Munster final – not an easy choice to make where the mae-stro was concerned.

In spite of the efforts of Ring and those of his team-mates, Tipperary were not to be denied and edged out their arch rivals after a tremendous struggle. What an afternoon of excitement it was! As the temperature soared every man on the pitch played as if his life depended on it. The enthralled spectators absorbed for one hour in the magic of the men in the red jerseys of Cork and the blue and gold of Tipperary gave scant thought to the fact that earlier in the year the first film to receive an X-rating was shown in London, or that the United States tested a dozen small nuclear weapons and four large atomic bombs in the Nevada desert. With ten minutes left to play Tipperary led by three points but again the extraordinary hurling genius Christy Ring struck back with two glorious points. The final score was Tipperary 2-11; Cork 2-9.

TIPP UNSTOPPABLE? GRAND ENTRANCES, A SUPERMARKET AND A FIRE!

From my point of view the only missing ingredient on that brilliant July afternoon was a Cork victory. The loss was considerably numbed by the performance of my all-time idol, Christy Ring, who finished the game in his bare feet.

Cork had now lost three Munster finals in a row to Tipperary. I had witnessed two defeats. There was really nothing to suggest that things would be any different the following year. A Tipperary team laden with hurling talent seemed unstoppable. Indeed there was talk of this excep-tional side dominating Munster for the entire decade. The one ray of hope that shone eternal was the presence of Christy Ring. Christy was undoubtedly the deadliest for-ward around at the time. Tipperary players, mentors and followers were well aware of his ability to turn a game with a flick of his stick. Could it be that his uncanny ability and fierce enthusiasm would somehow save Cork from years of humiliation at the hands of Tipperary? It remained to be seen!

As we made our way back to west Cork on that most beautiful of July evenings there was little in the way of red and white flags on display en route. Passing through the various towns, people on the street corners and standing at front doors just shook their heads as we passed by. The silence was deafening but screaming forth from all and sundry was the one question, how are Tipperary going to be stopped?

In September there was no consolation for Cork folk when Tipperary went on to beat Wexford convincingly in the All-Ireland final by a score of 7-7 to 3-9. It all happened in a year that two renowned international soccer players, Kevin Keegan (England), and Kenny Dalglish (Scotland) were born. Likewise, rock musician, Phil Collins, and Russian chess champion, Anatoly Karpov, first made their grand entrances. It was in 1951 too that the Abbey Theatre in Dublin burnt down and the first supermarket opened in London.

1952

REGARDLESS OF ALL THE UNACCEPTABLE HAD TO STOP!
In the early months of 1952 those close to Cork county senior hurling were more than a little concerned. The unacceptable had happened! In the past three championship campaigns Tipperary had beaten Cork. They had to be stopped! But how was it going to be done? The declaration by Pope Pius XII, in January, that television was a threat to family life, or the fact that jet-age travel was born when in May a de Havilland Comet airliner with 36 passengers aboard took off from London to Johannesburg, faded into insignificance when placed in the context of how Cork were going to halt the march of Tipperary. I was reliably informed that throughout the early months of 1952 Christy Ring was obsessed by that very challenge.

For the second year running the Cork selectors made wholesale changes in an effort to boost morale and at the same time redress the balance of power in Munster hurling. The combined efforts of the selectors and players were put to the test when Cork met Limerick in the championship at Thurles. The new-look Cork side won the match with a score of 6-6 to 2-4. A comfortable win you might say, so perhaps we were in with a chance against Tipperary! Not a bit of it. According to the pundits, Cork continued to be rank outsiders to dethrone the current Munster and All-Ireland champions.

Surely I was not destined to see my team beaten for a third time. I wondered what was going wrong! Long ago when I listened to matches on the radio, Cork always seemed to win. Was I somehow mistaken?

However, come July I was Limerick bound once again. It was backs to the wall time for all concerned. I read every bit of literature I could lay hands on relating to Cork's preparation and I literally prayed for a victory. The atmosphere, excitement and tension experienced in 1950 and 1951 were all very well, but this time, please God, let us have the all-important extra dimension – a win.

On Sunday 13 July 1952 Munster final day was not as fine or as warm as it had been for the corresponding fixture on the two previous occasions. It was overcast with a stiff breeze blowing. Followers of Cork and Tipperary hurling once again thronged Limerick.

The Cork team selected for the match had nine changes in personnel from the side beaten by Tipperary in 1951. I was hugely disappointed to find that one of my favourite players, Matty Fouhy, by then an established team member, was to miss the game through injury. Among the 'newcomers' to the team was 33-year-old goalkeeper Dave Creedon. It must have brought a smile to the faces of Tipperary folk when they learned that beleaguered Cork selectors, because of circumstances beyond their control, enticed Dave out of retirement to fill the all-important position between the posts. For the first time too the names of Corkmen John Lyons, Tony O'Shaughnessy, Joe Twomey, Gerald Murphy, Paddy Healy, Liam Dowling and team captain Paddy Barry were to appear on a Munster final hurling programme. The question was, could they blend with Gerry O'Riordan, Willie John Daly, Vincie Twomey, Seanie O'Brien, Mossie O'Riordan, Joe Hartnett, and you know who, the one and only Christy? Could the fifteen players possibly form a unit good enough to beat Tipperary?

It was talked about in bars, in public toilets, on street corners, outside chapels after Mass, on Limerick-bound trains and in the hackney cars as they headed north through Mallow and Buttevant. It too was the main topic of conversation in the Gaelic Ground before the match. Conclusions ranged from, at worst, 'they couldn't beat their way out of a paper bag, never mind Tipp', to at best, 'they look sound enough, you never know boy'. In my mind I believed it we would win because we had Christy. I was, and still am of the opinion that in many matches his contribution equalled that of any two other mortals on a hurling field.

THE MOMENT OF TRUTH

As the Cork and Tipperary teams ran on to the pitch that afternoon the prognostication of most observers was that Cork had little chance of beating a particularly fine, tried and trusted Tipperary fifteen. Before the sliotar was thrown in I felt a shiver down my back as if there was a chill in the air. I suppose it could have been the dull, overcast sky that was responsible. But surely not on a mid-July afternoon. No, it was the nervous tension manifesting itself. Tension had built up in the Cork supporters and now that the moment of truth was at hand it spread among them like a contagious disease.

From the throw in of the sliotar the slick Tipperary side assisted by the wind quickly notched up three points without reply. The contributors Pat Stakelum, Paddy Kenny and Mick Ryan were all household names in the world of hurling. It got worse; it took fifteen minutes for Cork to register a score, a point by Ring. The arrival of half-time did little to steady the nerves of most Cork supporters. Tipperary led by six points. The shrewder observers noted that the Cork defence had played well, Ring was prominent and inspirational, and Liam Dowling at full forward was troubling Tipperary.

Soon after the resumption Cork had narrowed the score gap to four points and were beginning to look good. The relief in the air was perceptible. Cork's followers sensed what was happening and when Liam Dowling put a great shot past Tony Reddin in the Tipperary goal it was as if all the doom and gloom generated by the past three championship defeats evaporated as a result of that one stroke. Was I to see Cork win for the first time? Was it to happen on the year that war-time rationing ended and a pacemaker to control heartbeat was first fitted to a human being? In the final minutes the Rebel County took control of the match and when Seanie O'Brien scored a glorious point from fully 80 yards out the ecstatic Cork supporters went wild. Revenge was about to be extracted and importantly the critics were about to be silenced.

I simply couldn't contain myself and I remember that in the midst of all the elation someone reminded me that the match was not yet won. That brought me to my senses! Suddenly I realised even though Cork seemed to be dominant for a long time the scoreboard read Cork 1-11, Tipperary 2-6 – just a two point lead! However the match was entering the closing stages and Cork looked safe.

Then Tipperary were awarded a sideline cut which would take the sliotar in the direction of the Cork goal. It was unthinkable that a late score would give Tipperary victory. Pat Stakelum stepped up to take the cut. The sliotar sailed towards the packed goal area, a Cork defender appeared to have things under control but then lost possession. Fortunately Gerald Murphy was at hand for Cork and made a relieving clearance. Then came the sweetest sound I had ever heard – the sound of the final whistle blown by the referee.

Relief mixed with emotion and jubilation was evident wherever Cork's supporters gathered after the match. It was a marvellous sensation as bursting with pride, along with my fellow travellers, we moved along ever so slowly with the tightly packed crowd from the Grounds and on to the Ennis Road. Tipperary supporters assured us they would be back again next year. No problem, we'll be waiting, came the reply from the now cocky Corkmen.

BACK IN THE BIG TIME AND IT'S THE FIRST NUMBER ONE
I had not given a lot of thought to the All-Ireland campaign which Cork would now pursue as Munster representatives. The chances of me getting to Croke Park in Dublin were absolutely nil. I had no hope of seeing either the semi-final or the final. Indeed that was to be the case until 1960 and then it was a football final I went to. Not seeing those matches didn't bother me too much. I lived for the Munster final and somehow I must have regarded following the fortunes of the team at All-Ireland level through newspapers and radio as part of the natural order of things. Strangely, I have no recollection of listening to the broadcast of the All-Ireland semi-final against Galway in 1952 but I do recall reading about a low scoring match which Cork won with little to spare. I did, however, listen very intently to the broadcast on the first Sunday of September, when

through the eloquence of Micheál O'Hehir I could imagine every stroke as it was played. I had a picture of each Cork player fixed in my mind. As for the Dublin team, their opponents on the day, I had no such insight but thought they might look a bit like the Tipperary players. The name to catch my fancy more than any other that afternoon was Tony O'Shaughnessy. Tony seemed to be doing wonders in the stonewall-like last line of defence which had served Cork so well in Limerick against Tipperary. The names of Gerry O'Riordan, John Lyons and Tony O'Shaughnessy were set to become well known. I never met Tony, but I knew his brother Denis, a St Finbar's man, who ran a butcher shop on Evergreen Road in Cork.

That September Sunday in 1952 was Cork's first appearance in Croke Park since 1947. They made no mistake and trounced Dublin 2-14 to 0-7.

Cork hurling was back in the big time – All-Ireland champions! The question now was who was going to depose them? It's amazing what can happen in a year!

The outcome of the All-Ireland final was history when later in the year, John Cobb, world waterspeed record holder, lost his life. It happened in Lough Ness, Scotland, as his boat broke up after hitting a wave at a speed in excess of 200 miles per hour.

About mid-November music lovers found a new interest. They were able to follow the relative popularity of tunes because Britain published its first pop chart. The first Number One to appear was, 'Here in My Heart', by Al Martino.

Births, in 1952, of those who were to become famous included Elaine Page, musical star of *Cats* and *Evita* fame; Jimmy Connors, tennis star; Christopher Reeve, 'Superman'; and Jenny Agutter, actress, who first came to prominence in a film called 'The Railway Children'.

1953

In March, 1953, Joseph Stalin, the man who galvanised the Soviet Union into a global superpower died of a brain haemorrhage. The demise of one responsible for creating oppression which resulted in the deaths of millions was unlikely to cause much grief in Cork.

Potential for grief though would have been the inability of the county hurlers to galvanise themselves for another championship campaign. The early signs were good. The National League campaign had gone well and in the process a few new faces had been introduced into the team. Guess who Cork met in the final at Croke Park? None other than Tipperary! According to newspaper reports Cork had a reasonably comfortable win though Tipperary scored two late goals through Paddy Kenny. Tony O'Shaughnessy and Gerry O'Riordan were credited with outstanding displays.

One of the hit songs of early 1953 was 'Don't Let The Stars Get In Your Eyes', sung by Perry Como. Cork's hurlers must have taken heed of the title because they made no mistake when they played Clare in the championship. They registered a 2-11 to 4-2 victory. For Cork followers it was once again a case of planning the annual pilgrimage to Limerick where our now customary opponents, Tipperary, would be waiting.

By then I was sixteen years of age and it would have been unthinkable for me not to see the Munster hurling final. Why did it take me so long to go and see an All-Ireland final? Perhaps there were various reasons. For example it would have been difficult to travel from west Cork to Dublin and back in one day; it would have been expensive to stay overnight in Dublin; Dublin was still a bit of an unknown quantity to country boys.

In May, New Zealand-born Edmund Hillary and the

Sherpa guide Tensing Norgay scaled Mount Everest, the world's highest peak. For 30 years men had tried and failed to conquer Chomolungma, as it is called in Tibetan, but finally it succumbed.

The Tipperary hurling team was not exactly Mount Everest, yet Cork, captained by Christy Ring, could not afford to underestimate the effort that would be required to conquer them at the Gaelic Grounds, Limerick on Sunday, 26 July. The thousands of Cork followers including myself who made their way on foot from the Treaty City centre towards the residential Ennis Road for the third year in a row were more confident and relaxed this time round. Cork were playing well, Christy was captain, they had just beaten Tipperary in the National League final and were current All-Ireland champions. Hadn't we come a long way in a short time? There was every reason for optimism.

ANOTHER TITANIC BATTLE

By three o'clock a crowd of 46,265 had assembled to witness yet another titanic battle between the current giants of Munster hurling. Each individual present harboured his own thoughts and expectations. A glance at the Cork team line-out on the match programme confirmed what had been reported during the week. Matty Fouhy was to play at right- half back. That made me very happy. There were only two newcomers on the team, Derry Hayes and Terry Kelly. Seanie O'Brien and Paddy Healy were the absentees from last year's side.

So here we were again. The atmosphere was electric, powered by anticipation of the drama about to unfold before our eyes. No one knew how the game would go but we could be assured of a battle royal, fought out midst a combination of stamina, skill, artistry, courage, determination, man-to-man combat and superior sportsmanship. While we waited for the teams to come on to the park a nervous Cork supporter seated beside me hummed the tune of a current popular song. The song was a top twelve hit for four weeks in March/April and was called, 'She Wears Red Feathers', made famous by a chap called Guy Mitchell.

From the throw in of the sliotar Christy Ring was extremely prominent. How Tipperary followers must have loved to hate the man. While he was admired by all, he was a real thorn in the side of opponents and he kept coming back year after year to inflict maximum punishment.

In spite of a Ring goal in less than a minute after the throw-in, Tipperary played well and at times looked as if they were having the better of things. The half-time discussion among Cork supporters was a little subdued and there was an element of surprise in that their team had not dominated as expected. Tipperary led by 1-8 to 1-4.

After the interval again it was Ring who starred for Cork. He scored some wonderful points to give his team the edge. As in the previous year Liam Dowling scored a well-taken goal for the Leesiders.

Shortly after that came a sequence of action which has remained vividly stored in my mind. From my vantage point Tipperary were playing from right to left - towards the Ennis Road end of the pitch. The 21-yard line closest to the Cork goal was slightly to my left as I looked straight across the park. Tipperary were awarded a 21-yard free; Ring, a forward, ran back to join his defence in the goal. That in itself was unusual as defending such a free is normally left to the backs. Paddy Kenny the Tipperary free taker-in-chief hit a bullet-like shot towards the Cork goal; Ring, who by then had moved out from the goal, cleanly grabbed the sliotar and cleared it up-field to Joe Hartnett who shot it past Tony Reddin in the Tipperary goal. This sequence of events became all the more amazing when it later came to light that before Ring went to face the free he told Joe Hartnett, 'You stay there, I'm going to get it and I'll drop it into your hand'. It was uncanny, and furthermore as soon as Ring took up position to defend the free I believe everyone in the Ground, including the free taker, knew that he was going to make the save. Such was the magic surrounding the man on the hurling pitch. Who can argue that he was not uniquely the most influential player of all time?

Tipperary seemed stunned by what had happened. Phil Shanahan scored a point later on but by then Ring had scored three further points to give Cork a 3-10 to 1-11 victory. At the end of the game, Christy, then almost 33 years of age, had scored a personal tally of 1-8.

A HURLER APART AND JFK WEDS

As we left Limerick that evening it seemed clear that Cork had indeed curtailed the dominance of Tipperary. The sting had been taken out of a tail that two years earlier threatened to kill off all-comers in the foreseeable future. Would we be back again next year or would another Munster county come to the fore? Well, we would just have to wait and see.

The exploits of Ring continued to be the main topic of conversation in the car as we made our way home. There was general agreement that his status as a hurler was that of the best ever. His supreme confidence in his own ability and the manner in which he dictated all that went on around him was awesome. He was a real showman. His arrogance on occasions intimidated even match officials. Ring was certain in his own mind that he was the best.

Often as I sit here and reflect on the happenings of the day, I study a picture of Christy Ring given to me by a County Antrim man who came across it while demolishing an old house. It shows the upper body with arms folded across the chest. There is a suggestion of a smile on the face but real determination is evident in the steely blue eyes. The head is crowned with thinning, fair hair. He is wearing a white-collared, red jersey bearing the Munster provincial emblem – the three crowns. Inscribed below the emblem is '1952', and on his right shoulder the words 'Sports Star of the Year' are enclosed in a star-like shape. As I look at the picture it is not so much the face or the sports star sign which catches my eye. No, it is the massive forearms. The solid, sturdy, brawny, strength and power of the man is conveyed through those limbs in an unmistakable way.

In September 1953 a new record attendance of 71,195 for an All-Ireland final was created at Croke Park. Cork beat Galway in what was described as a tempestuous encounter. Yes, while the attention of many around the world was turning to Newport, Rhode Island in the USA, where the marriage of Senator John Fitzgerald Kennedy to

Jacqueline Lee Bouvier was about to take place, a Ring inspired Cork team became All-Ireland hurling champions for the second year in succession. The score was Cork 3-3; Galway 0-8.

Who was unstoppable now? Maybe the Frankie Lane hit song 'Answer Me' which topped the charts for eight weeks in November/December 1953 was inspired by that very question.

1954

A Sad Bikini but We Make Hay While Roger, Lester and Jimmy Excel

In February 1954, American actor, John Travolta, star of the films 'Grease' and 'Saturday Night Fever', was born.

In April, a song called 'Rock Around The Clock', which set the dancing world crazy, was recorded by Bill Haley and the Comets. Between times in early March the USA exploded the most powerful bomb ever made – the Hydrogen Bomb. The tiny island of Bikini Atoll in the Pacific Ocean completely vanished in an explosion which was the equivalent of 15,000,000 tons of TNT. The test was declared a complete success and the immense mushroom cloud formed was captured on film to be shown around the world as the symbol of our post-war era.

In Ireland, as yet another Munster championship loomed, there was not a bomb in sight, but a few counties were hoping that by now Cork might be battle weary. The belief was that the winning of two Munster championships, two All-Ireland finals and a National League in two years must have taken its toll. Maybe they could be caught 'on the hop' in the first round this year.

Alas when Waterford took on the Rebels in Thurles it was business as usual. Cork won by a score of 7-8 to 4-5. It looked as if the men in red were on their way to seek a third successive title! Ring was again captain, he had seven All-Ireland medals to his credit, he was almost 34 years of age and as if to remind him of that fact a gentleman called Eddie Calvert blasted out on a trumpet a hit tune called 'Oh Mein Papa'.

It was a year when nothing seemed impossible. In May a 25-year-old medical student, Roger Bannister, confounded the experts when he ran a mile in three-fifths of a second less than four minutes. In the world of sport too an eighteen-year-old won the Derby on a horse called 'Never Say

Die'. The jockey's name was Lester Piggott.

Before we knew where we were, July was once again with us. The post-war, green, Ford V8, a luxury car by standards of the day, was destined for another trip to Limerick. The crowd was eager and hopes were high that Cork would make it three wins-in-a-row over old rivals Tipperary. The hurlers and followers of both counties had great respect for one another.

I remember having a particularly strenuous week leading up to the game. I was helping with hay and was one of three who found myself in a stuffy, warm, humid, corrugated iron shed where our job was to trample the stuff into submission. It was the most energy-sapping activity imaginable. The only thing which kept us going was the match on Sunday.

Topical at the time was the feat of great Clare hurler, Jimmy Smyth, who in the Munster senior hurling championship of that year scored a personal tally of 6-4 against Limerick. A record for a Munster championship match! Newspaper reports on the achievement also brought attention to the fact that Jimmy had played Munster minor championship hurling on five successive years which has to be a unique minor career!

TIPPERARY LEFT WONDERING!
The mid-July Sunday dawned beautifully. It was a case of an early breakfast, first Mass and then we were on our way north. The elation brimmed over as we travelled through the various towns. Ahead lay a day filled with excitement, intrigue, the unexpected ...

We found Limerick brimming with followers. The matches between Cork and Tipperary had grown in stature year by year as the new record attendance of 52,449 on that day showed. Hurling supporters came from all over Ireland to see the match. The Munster hurling final, thanks to the mighty men of Tipperary and Cork in the 1950s had become a showpiece that no one wanted to miss.

The Cork team showed just two changes from the previous year. Mick Cashman replaced Joe Twomey at centrefield and Johnny Clifford came in at corner-forward for

Terry Kelly. The match inevitably took the pattern we had now come to expect. Tipperary, as in 1951 was captained by Jimmy Finn. The Premier Countymen hurled Cork hard and dominated the game at times. Ring again thwarted much of what Tipperary tried to do and troubled them sufficiently for their selectors to move the great Mickey Byrne from his customary corner-back position to right-half in an effort to curtail the scheming Cork forward. Byrne did not have a great deal of success and eventually John Doyle, was switched on to Ring. Ring continued to excel and soon after the interval he crashed a 21-yard free past Tony Reddin and his defence. It seemed inevitable again that in spite of the best efforts of Tipperary the influence of Ring was about to engineer another Cork victory.

Points by Joe Hartnett, Willie John Daly and Ring left Cork trailing by just a single point. The score stood at 1-7 to 1-8. It was nail-biting stuff with time running out. Added-on time was being played when Ring fought his way past two Tipperary defenders and shot for goal. Tony Reddin, arguably the best goalie of all-time, fumbled the sliotar and it rebounded to Cork's Paddy Barry who crashed it into the net. Cork were two points in the lead. Christy scored a point from a free a few seconds later and when the final whistle sounded the score board read Cork 2-8; Tipperary 1-8. Tipperary were once again left wondering what had gone wrong.

Cork had achieved three wins in-a-row over Tipperary in successive Munster hurling finals.

YANKEE RELIC PLEASES BUT REBS EXCEL AS BOB, CHRIS AND ANNIE ARRIVE
One of the lads in the car had brought a radio with him from home that morning. I have a notion that the set came from America. Perhaps it was left behind by a Yankee visitor. The rather strange looking receiver set did not recognise any of the normal channels but it did play music from a foreign station. We were on top of the world as we headed south, waving flags at well-wishers, shouting at dancers at cross-road patterns, whilst coming from the radio, the tender words of the hit song, 'Secret Love' were sung by

Doris Day. Alternating with Doris was David Whitfield With Mantovani and his orchestra singing another hit song called, 'Cara Mia'.

Back home on Monday morning the papers were full of the deeds of the Corkmen. They were on their way to another All-Ireland semi-final. By now I was taking much more interest in the All-Ireland series and was well acquainted with the reported strengths and weaknesses of the opposition when Cork met Galway in August at Croke Park. That encounter ended in an easy 4-13 to 2-1 victory for the Leesiders. Jimmy Brohan, Eamon Goulding and Willie Moore came into the Cork side for that match. In the other semi-final a very good Wexford team beat Antrim convincingly. Nicky Rackard scored a personal tally of 7-7.

The All-Ireland final pairing of Cork and Wexford was unique. They had not met previously at that level. In the weeks that led up to the final it became clear that just as Ring was the symbol of Cork, the Rackard brothers, Nicky, Bobby and Billy were that of Wexford. It would have been mistaken though to think that Wexford's success was due to one family as over recent years a good team had been moulded in the Model County and names such as Nick O'Donnell, Ned Wheeler, Martin Codd, Jim English, Tim Flood, Padge Kehoe, Tom Ryan and Art Foley were by then well-known. Wexford badly needed to win an All-Ireland. While undoubtedly a good, talented team on paper, it had suffered a series of set backs in recent years, including an All-Ireland defeat at the hands of Tipperary in 1951. Another defeat could lead to self-doubt and frustration.

Cork on the other hand were overflowing with confidence. Christy Ring was seeking his eighth All-Ireland medal which would set him apart from all the other great hurlers in history. The Cork defence had a stone-wall like reputation with Gerry O'Riordan, John Lyons, Tony O'Shaughnessy, Matty Fouhy, Vincie Twomey and Derry Hayes playing out of their skins. Much was made of the fact that goalie Dave Creedon, at the age of 33, came out of retirement in 1952 when Cork were in dire straights. He was now on the verge of winning a third All-Ireland medal at the age of 36. We were also reminded that along with Christy Ring, Dave Creedon was the sole remaining link with the great 1946-7 Cork team on which he was a sub.

The attendance at Croke Park was 84,856, the largest on record. Accounts of a fine, clean, exciting game are on record. The final score was Cork 1-9; Wexford 1-6. The outcome could have been very different had it not been for an injury to renowned Wexford full-back Nick O'Donnell. The enforced reorganisation in defence did not by all accounts help Wexford's cause.

In the days that followed there was much public sympathy for the gallant Wexfordmen who had once again failed at the final fence. Widely reported later were remarks made by Christy Ring at a post-match dinner when he declared Bobby Rackard the most sporting of opponents and Wexford the cleanest team Cork had ever beaten. He hoped that 1955 would be Wexford's year. For the record Ring was then the proud holder of eight All-Ireland senior inter-county championship medals and Dave Creedon, whose long association with the county team began back in 1938 collected his third. Dave conceded only one solitary goal in the 1952, 1953 and 1954 All-Ireland finals. A fine record indeed!

What was left for this outstanding Cork team? From its humble beginnings in 1952 it had swept the board in championship hurling. It was inevitable that comparisons would be made between it and the 1946-7 team. My recollection of discussion and debate on the subject was that people felt the 1946-7 team was full of exceptionally skilful individuals while the 1952-4 side would have been hard pressed without the inspirational Ring. Maybe that was a bit harsh. I had seen them play and it had taken all fifteen players on the pitch to pull games out of the fire. Nevertheless Ring was a man apart by any standards and the question was, how long could he go on inspiring those around him? We would have to wait and see!

Did the world stand still in 1954 before and after the exploits of Cork on the hurling field? Well, not quite. In August Nigel Mansell, future world motor racing champion was born; in October Irish pop musician Bob Geldof of the Boomtown Rats and Live Aid concert fame was born; in December both American tennis star Chris Evert and singer Annie Lennox first saw the light of day.

Chart toppers as the year drew to a close were, 'Three Coins in the Fountain' sung by Frank Sinatra and 'This Ole House' by Rosemary Clooney.

1955

1955 started off very well for me since 10 March marked my eighteenth birthday. That was significant because I got a driving licence and I was also allowed to go to dances. Sunday night dances took on a new dimension at that time because of the advent of 'travelling bands'. Previously dance music was provided by one or two local lads who turned up at the same venue Sunday after Sunday. A 'travelling band' could have eight or nine members and played at various venues according to where bookings took it.

In 1955 popular music lovers who listened to radio were likely to hear a young man called Dickie Valentine singing 'Finger of Suspicion' or, possibly Belfast born Ruby Murray charming the nation with her special rendition of a love song called 'Softly, Softly'.

Before a sliotar was struck in championship hurling, Sir Alexander Fleming, discoverer of penicillin died and Mc Donald's were preparing to open their very first fast food outlet.

Could Cork win four Munster championships in a row? That was the question teasing the minds of hurling followers not only in Cork but nationwide. Could the American trip in late 1954 and the rigours of three championship campaigns prove too much for the mighty men in red? If they were to falter who was going to beat them? Surely not Clare in the first round of the Munster championship! There was no reason to believe that Tipperary would succeed where they had failed on three previous occasions.

For the followers of Christy and his men it looked very much like a return to Limerick in July. While nobody was saying, 'not Limerick again', clearly a visit to another venue would have been preferable. Thurles or Killarney would have been very acceptable alternatives. The reality was that as long as Cork and Tipperary dominated the hurling scene in Munster those other venues were unlikely to be used.

I had heard and read much about the Thurles Sportsfield. It was widely regarded as being the best hurling pitch in Ireland. I was very keen to see it for myself. I suggested to my fellow travellers that maybe we should consider a trip to Thurles for the first round match against Clare. On a Sunday morning in June we set out for Thurles certain that Cork were going to win.

On arrival in Thurles, the town where the Gaelic Athletic Association was born, the first thing that struck us was the lack of excitement and atmosphere. The streets were far from thronged and we had little difficulty in parking the car in Liberty Square directly opposite Hayes Hotel. What was to become Ireland's largest amateur sporting organisation was founded in that very premises in 1884. When we got out of the car our attention was drawn to a large monument of Dr Croke, a founder member and patron of the GAA.

As we made our way on foot towards the Sportsfield we had to keep reminding ourselves that today's match was only a first-round encounter. Hence the smaller crowds and the lack of atmosphere. The subdued but good humoured Clare supporters were obviously hoping that somehow against the odds their team would defeat the all conquering, three in-a-row All-Ireland champions.

Inside the grounds I tried to visualise what it had been like in 1910 when records show that local people purchased the grounds from Thurles Agricultural Show Committee. It was to be used for promoting our national games. Around 1920 major development work took place. The field was enclosed, embankments were raised and seating was provided. A few years later a timber stand was erected. The ambition of the north Tipperary people and the inherent love for our national games was further demonstrated in the 1930s and 1940s when the embankments were enlarged to make the Sportsfield the largest playing field in Ireland.

The Clare hurling team which ran on to the Sportsfield

that June Sunday was virtually unknown to me. The household name on the side was corner-forward Jimmy Smyth. His remarkable scoring feats endorsed all the superlatives used to describe his nifty stick-work. Fresh in the minds of Corkmen that day in Thurles was the hefty contribution of six goals and four points scored by Jimmy against Limerick in the championship just the year before.

The Cork team was captained by that great, gentleman hurler, Vincie Twomey. Two newcomers to the side Liam McGrath and Liam McAuliffe, replaced Paddy Barry and Willie Moore. Gerry O'Riordan, one-time forward and Dublin senior county player who later declared for Cork, his native county, and who subsequently put in umpteen sterling performances as a defender, had retired from inter-county hurling. Seanie O'Brien returned to the fold to take over Gerry's place on the team. Personnel on the Cork team were otherwise unchanged from 1954.

Before an official attendance of 25,256, a larger crowd than seemed likely earlier in the day, Clare started off playing much better hurling than Cork. Well into the first half, the Banner County led by eight points!

Albert Einstein, believed to be one of the most creative intellects of all time had died in April. Yet his intelligence would not have been required to conclude that Cork's hurlers were in deep trouble. At half-time the Rebels were trailing by seven points. The score was 3-6 to 2-2.

As the second-half got under way a balding, stocky, speedy, skilful, courageous man operating out on the wing for Cork was beginning to make an impression on the Clare defence. As the match wore on, more and more the question being asked was, 'Is he going to pull the game out of the fire for Cork again'? Of course, they were referring to the famous Christy. He was in outstanding form throughout the second-half. With ten minutes to go the sides were level! Cork had come back from the dead and when the magnificent Christy shot over the bar from 60 yards out to put Cork into the lead, the Rebel County supporters were already planning their Munster final outing. However, the Cork supporters forgot that Jimmy Smyth was playing for Clare and while we were dreaming of

Limerick in July, the Clare genius had scored two points for the Banner County and at the same time sent Cork tumbling out of the Munster championship.

Clare's supporters went wild, and why not! Their team had brought Cork and its supporters down to earth with a bang. The final score was Clare 3-8; Cork 2-10.

CLARE ABU! WEXFORD DO IT! ITS OLGA, ED AND STEVE AS A REBEL DIES

The jubilant Clare team and their loyal followers who had suffered disappointment on so many occasions were fully entitled to celebrate the toppling of the All-Ireland champions. Their day had come!

The Cork team had forgotten what losing was like. The feeling was one of disbelief! Clare could not have beaten us!

My first visit to Thurles was somewhat disappointing. Cork's defeat obviously did not fill me with joy but apart from that the day had little of the magic experienced at other venues. I have no doubt that Clare followers had a great day out and many of them travelling west that evening were humming or singing the hit song, 'Dreamboat' made popular at the time by a worldwide singing star, Alma Cogan.

Two weeks later Tipperary were beaten by a good up-and-coming Limerick team and consequently the Munster final of that year featured the unusual pairing of Clare and Limerick.

Wexford hurlers fulfilled their long-awaited dream when they became All-Ireland champions in September. A fine team captained by Nick O'Donnell beat Galway in the presence of 77,854 spectators at Croke Park.

Before Wexford's achievement in 1955, the births of two people destined for greatness had taken place. One was Soviet gymnast Olga Korbut who was to steal the hearts of the world with her performances at the Munich Olympics in 1972 while the other was American athlete Ed Moses who created a world record in the 400m hurdles at his first Olympic Games in 1976.

It was in 1955 too that the death of 24-year-old pin-up

actor James Dean, star of the film 'Rebel Without a Cause', generated widespread heartbreak, especially among teenagers. Notable also was the birth of British middle distance runner, Steve Ovett who won a gold medal at the Moscow Olympics in 1980.

As 1955 drew to a close Cork hurling enthusiasts were left to ponder on the happenings at Thurles in June and to wonder if the the good times were at least temporarily over.

1956

A LEGEND SPEAKS; CORK AND MONACO CHEER;
BOXERS COME AND GO

In January 1956 a young American made his first ever appearance on television and told the world, 'I don't know anything about music, in my line you don't have to'. A few months later his hit records, 'Heartbreak Hotel' and 'Love Me Tender' had hit the charts. Before the year was out the same man had his first film also called 'Love Me Tender' premiered in New York and Elvis Presley had most definitely arrived!

Following the defeat at the hands of Clare in 1955 and the retirement of outstanding veteran goalie Dave Creedon, changes to the Cork hurling team were inevitable. With the first round of the Munster championship looming and a constant reminder blaring from radios in the form of the popular song 'It's Almost Tomorrow', the search for replacements was well underway when on 14 April the first ever videotape was demonstrated in Chicago.

Waterford were Cork's immediate opponents in the championship. With high calibre players such as Phil Grimes, Frankie Walsh and Sean Power in the Decies ranks a Cork victory was far from a foregone conclusion. The match was played in Fermoy. Many pundits felt that the 5-9 to 2-12 win flattered the Rebel County men. The following day newspapers reported brilliant performances by Mick Cashman who had taken over from Dave Creedon, Willie John Daly who was switched to centre-half back at half-time to steady a jittery defence, new recruit Paddy Philpott at wing-back, Christy Ring in the half-forward line and, at midfield, Gerald Murphy who came on as a substitute. The same reports referred to poor or below par performances by some Cork players. Things didn't sound all that promising for the arduous campaign that undoubtedly lay ahead.

The event of 1956 which caught the imagination of the world was the marriage of the widely-admired screen actress Grace Kelly to Prince Rainier of Monaco. Another event to hit the headlines at the time was the retirement of Rocky Marciano as undisputed and undefeated heavy-weight boxing champion of the world. In 1956 another great American boxer Sugar Ray Leonard was born. Sugar Ray was destined to become world champion at welter-weight, light middleweight and middleweight.

THE MAGIC

A major decision for us in our west Cork village was whether or not to travel to Limerick for the Munster semi-final encounter between Cork and Tipperary. The magic associated with the meeting of those counties at any stage in a championship made the occasion so special as to be almost irresistible. Our visit was rewarded by a fine dis-play. Willie John Daly was outstanding and suddenly it dawned on me that I had taken this man for granted over the years as he always played well. At Limerick against Tipperary on that June day he was majestic at centre-back.

A highlight of the match was the half-time introduction of Pat Healy who had played brilliantly on the minor team in the curtain raiser. Desperate measures were needed. Tipperary led by the almost unbelievable score of 2-6 to 0-1. Ring was not his prominent self. Pat Healy played well and scored a vital point. Cork got themselves right back into the game and were leading by two points at the clos-ing stages when Paddy Kenny shot to the net for Tipperary. It looked like a one point victory for the Premier County men until the referee indicated that he had blown the whistle for a free before Paddy hit the sliotar. The 'goal' was disallowed and the free resulted in a point for Tipperary. Cork won by the narrowest of margins. The final score was Cork 4-6; Tipperary 3-8. A one point victo-ry was good enough to set us on the Munster final trail again. Thurles was the venue and Limerick the opponents.

THURLES IN JULY

As Cork prepared to meet a speedy, classy Limerick side known as Mick Mackey's greyhounds, five times Wimbledon men's singles tennis champion Bjorn Borg was born. At the same time Real Madrid had just won the first European Cup in Paris. In the final they beat Stade de Reims 4-3. That summer the world joined in with Ronnie Hilton as he sang 'No Other Love' whilst Doris Day was being philosophical with her rendering of the evergreen 'Whatever Will Be Will Be'.

No doubt the sentiment expressed by Doris in no way reflected the thinking in the Cork or Limerick camps as they prepared for the big showdown. A win was vital for both sides; Limerick wanted to show that last year's excursion to Croke Park and a semi-final appearance was not a fluke, while Cork were keen to demonstrate that they were back to their winning ways.

The outcome of the match between the Leesiders and the Shannonsiders at Thurles on Sunday 22 July would decide which county went on to the All-Ireland series.

My Thurles experience in 1956 was in total contrast to that of 1955. As we approached the outskirts of the town our driver was flagged down and we were directed into a field assigned as a car park for the day. All the Munster final pre-match buzz and carnival atmosphere we had come to expect was much in evidence. The idea of rioting fans or the likes was as remote as a man-on-the-moon. There was only one thing on the minds of the people who thronged Thurles and that was hurling. The craic and healthy rivalry between opposing supporters made the occasion a joy to be part of.

Limerick were reigning Munster champions and their followers were confident with good reason. Cork followers were uncertain about their team. A revamped 1955 team had performed poorly enough against Waterford, did better against Tipperary but were still an unknown quantity. A crowd of over 47,000 turned up to see the players of both counties exhibit their hurling skills. Could the Leesiders somehow counteract the speed of the Shannonsiders?

It wouldn't be Munster final day in Thurles without the

immaculately attired Sean Treacy – Moycarkey-Borris Pipe Band and 1956 was no exception. Melodious strains filled the air and the adrenalin flowed in torrents. All eyes were glued on the men of Limerick and Cork, the elite chosen to represent their respective counties. A few of the faces in the parade that day were not those of the seasoned veterans Cork followers had come to know so well. From the team that won the 1954 All-Ireland final Dave Creedon, Gerry O'Riordan, Tony O'Shaughnessy, Matty Fouhy, Derry Hayes, Willie Moore, Johnny Clifford and Eamonn Goulding were absent. Taking their places were Mick Cashman, Jimmy Brohan, Pat Dowling, Paddy Philpott, Mick O'Regan, Christy O'Shea, Florrie O'Mahony and Terry Kelly.

As the sliotar was thrown in at the start of the game I was less confident of a Cork victory than I had been for some years. Perhaps I had not fully recovered from the defeat by Clare at the same venue in 1955.

The first half was hard fought. The Cork defence, with Willie John Daly superb at centre-back, held out well against the highly-acclaimed Limerick attack. Just three points separated the sides at half-time. One still had the impression that Cork were holding on and that sooner rather than later Limerick would break free of the shackles. Yet full credit has to go to Willie John and his well mar-shalled wing-backs. Christy Ring was having a quiet game by his standards and much credit was given to Limerick's Donal Broderick for doing a good marking job. The pre-dicted Limerick dominance began to manifest itself even at an early stage in the second-half. With fifteen minutes to go the Shannonsiders were in command and the Leesiders looked devoid of ideas. Cork followers looked at one another and shook their heads. At the back of many minds, including my own, was the thought that Ring had let us down – how dare he not come to the rescue! Isn't fickleness a terrible thing? With about ten minutes of playing time left Limerick led by six points. Followers were cheering their team to victory. It was a question of how many points were they going to win by! Then all of a sudden Ring exploded into action! The first thing that registered with me was that he had the sliotar in his hand and was battling his way past two Limerick defenders. He seemed to stumble and fall. Yet from the reaction of Cork followers close to the action I realised that somehow he had scored. He had indeed palmed the sliotar into the net as he fell. Suddenly there was a ray of hope! From a position of certain defeat suddenly there were only three points between the teams. Could Ring at this late stage inject life back into the ailing Cork side? We had to wait only 60 seconds for the answer.

At the end of a solo run out on the left wing the same man shot a second goal. The scores were level! Limerick were unsettled, yet Tom McGarry and Vivion Cobbe combined to score a good goal. It looked as if Ring's magnificent efforts were in vain. Time was running out and Limerick were again a goal in front. The jubilation of the Limerick followers was short-lived because Christy refused to give in and scored another goal – his third in the space of five minutes. A further point by Ring and a late Terry Kelly goal left the score at 5-5 to 3-5 in favour of Cork. Yes, thanks to Ring, Cork plucked a most remarkable victory from the jaws of defeat.

The Limerick team and its supporters were visibly devastated. I don't know how the Cork team felt but on the terraces the followers could scarcely believe what they had just seen. The magic of Christy Ring had once again inspired a Cork team, as he had done for more than a decade. How the man endured! I will never forget that afternoon at the Thurles Sportsfield. At the end of the 1956 campaign he would have scored 6-13 in four championship matches. No one did better! Those who saw him play can never envisage another individual with a range of skills and qualities equal to those of the extraordinary native of Cloyne.

An added spice to Cork victories in Thurles was passing through the Tipperary towns of Cashel and Cahir on the way home. There was a certain satisfaction in flying the flag in 'enemy territory'. As we drove south that evening we did have some sympathy for those Limerick supporters in the village of Kilbeheny who in spite of the 'been robbed' feeling proudly displayed the green and white county colours. Many followers returning to Cork made their first stop for a drink or a meal in red-and-white decked Mitchelstown and Fermoy. There was plenty to talk about that evening and as the alcohol flowed Ring's goals were scored over and over again in pubs and snugs of Cork and beyond.

GAME, SET AND MATCH TO WEXFORD AS MARTINA ENTERS

I would have dearly loved to see the eagerly awaited All-Ireland final at Croke Park on 22 September, but it wasn't to be. The final was played a fortnight later than usual because of the Cork polio epidemic at the time. A crowd of over 83,000 attended the match and thousands more were turned away. During the week leading up to the match I digested all that was written about the strengths and weaknesses of the Cork and Wexford teams. Wexford were All-Ireland champions with a star-studded side. They were favourites to win but the warning from all quarters was, 'write off Cork at your peril'. Cork made a few personnel and positional changes from the team which lined out for the Munster final. Wexford, led by team captain, Jim English, fielded a virtually unchanged team from the previous year. It was hard to see them being beaten.

I listened to the match on the radio. It was an epic encounter with Wexford playing well but finding Cork a handful. At the closing stages Ring had a much-publicised shot saved by Wexford goalie, Art Foley. Had the sliotar found its way to the net a Cork win and a ninth All-Ireland senior hurling championship medal for Christy Ring was an almost certainty. It wasn't to be and Wexford became champions in successive years – their second in 46 years. It was Wexford's first victory over Cork in a senior hurling championship match but they were worthy champions and adorned themselves still further when team members Nick O'Donnell and Bobby Rackard lifted Christy on their shoulders after the game.

With All-Ireland hurling over for another year we turned our attentions to popular music and songs of the day. Ann Shelton was advising us to 'Lay Down Your Arms' while Frankie Laine was explaining some of the symptoms of 'A Woman in Love'. Meanwhile Johnnie Ray was getting soakin' wet, 'Just Walkin' in the Rain'.

On a sporting note, a Czechoslovakian baby girl was born on 18 October. In addition to winning numerous Grand Slam tennis events she was to become a nine times women's Wimbledon singles champion. She was named Martina Navratilova.

1957

WITH HALF THE MUNSTER TEAM CORK WENT FORWARD
BUT THEN LOST RING

Was January 1957's most popular hit tune 'Singing the Blues' a premonition of how followers of Cork hurling might feel before the year was out? I don't think so, in spite of the fact that two separate recordings of the song were made, one by Guy Mitchell, the other by Tommy Steele and the Steelmen. A sense of confidence throughout the county was reinforced by the presence of no less than eight Corkmen on the winning Railway Cup Munster hurling team. They were Mick Cashman, Jimmy Brohan, John Lyons, Tony O'Shaughnessy, Paddy Philpott, Terry Kelly, Christy Ring and Paddy Barry. Furthermore the team narrowly beaten by Wexford in the 1956 All-Ireland final was virtually intact and would go forward confidently when championship time came around. The belief was further reinforced when Cork dismissed Clare in the opening round of the Munster championship by a score of 4-10 to 2-7.

Once again my friends and I succumbed to the intrigue of a Cork versus Tipperary Munster semi-final and travelled to Limerick on 30 June. Somehow that match has not remained etched on my mind to the same extent as many others. I remember that the score was close at half-time and that Sarsfield's Paddy Barry was outstanding. In spite of the best efforts of the great Tipperary defender John Doyle, Barry scored 3-1. Cork looked the better side and victory for the Rebels always seemed the likely outcome.

It was not to be Tipperary's day. A goal decision went against them before half time and a soft goal given away after the interval had a devastating effect. The one incident I recall vividly was the sight of Christy Ring leaving the field injured during the second half. We were later to learn that as a result of a heavy tackle he sustained a wrist fracture. The final score was 5-2 to 1-11 in favour of the

Leesiders with Paddy Barry, Christy Ring and Terry Kelly being the main contributors.

Cork's supporters were not deliriously happy that afternoon. Was it Ring's injury that took away from what should have been another memorable victory over Tipperary? Could it be that winning had become the norm and we were beginning to take it for granted? Perhaps it was a bit of each.

Even though the extent of the injury was not known immediately it was clear that Ring, who left the field with his right arm in a sling, was unlikely to play in the Munster final clash with Waterford a few weeks later. Ring's injury was indeed a matter of grave concern for the Cork team mentors and followers but it's an ill wind that doesn't do some good. No doubt it brought smiles to the faces of Waterford folk and who could blame them. A Cork team without Ring at Thurles on Munster final day was going to be a much easier proposition to deal with.

Back at home we couldn't make up our minds. Should we go to Thurles or not? The newspapers cast much doom and gloom and gave Cork only an outside chance without the 'maestro'.

When the big day came we were there at the Sportsfield among a crowd of close to 41,000 people. Derry Driscoll replaced Ring. The only other change I can detect from the Munster semi-final side was that Vincie Twomey came in for Gerald Murphy.

We were treated to a great game of hurling. Two fine teams locked in combat with no quarter given or asked. Mick Cashman in the Cork goal was outstanding. By what was regarded as one of the best saves of all time he denied Waterford's Johnny Kiely what would have been a memorable goal. Another man to shine was full-back John Lyons. John had been ever present in that key position right through the All-Ireland title campaigns from 1952-1954. He consistently gave sterling performances and was a great ambassador for Cork hurling.

Prominent too that day were Paddy Barry, Matty Fouhy and Paddy Philpott. I believe that Cork's one and only goal was scored by Mick O'Regan. The Leesiders played well but not as well as Waterford who took the advice given in a hit song by Lonnie Donegan called 'Putting on the Style'. They did just that and in the process dethroned the current Munster champions. Christy Ring had to content himself with watching from the sideline. One can only speculate on the difference his presence on the field would have made. On the way out of the Sportsfield late that afternoon many Cork followers were firmly of the opinion that had Ring been on the team we would have won. As it was there were few who could begrudge the good Waterford team a 1-11 to 1-6 victory.

AN INEVITABLE VACUUM, YET SOME 'NEW LOOK' AND A DOG CALLED LAIKA

The wind of change began to blow through the Cork team and as time went on followers were saddened to learn that we had seen Tony O'Shaughnessy, Willie John Daly, Gerald Murphy, Joe Hartnett and Matty Fouhy for the last time in inter-county hurling. A Cork senior hurling team without them was almost inconceivable. The question now was how and when would Cork recover from the loss of five players each of whom had been a vital ingredient of the great 1952-1954 side? Joe Hartnett like Matty Fouhy had played in the famous match at Killarney in 1950. To the best of my knowledge Joe was a half-back that day but in subsequent years it was as a half-forward that he became an integral part of all that was good in Cork county senior hurling. A vacuum had indeed been created in the Cork team. The selectors had the task of trawling the county's clubs for replacements.

A single point margin gave Kilkenny victory over Waterford when the counties met in the All-Ireland final in September.

So 1957 proved to be a disappointing year in the history of Cork hurling. It suffered the double blows of losing its champions of Munster status, and many of its most esteemed players.

What was happening elsewhere? Well, Irish-born writer Joyce Carey died; American Althea Gibson became the first black woman to become Wimbledon champion;

Oliver Hardy (Olly), of Laurel and Hardy fame died; world sporting personalities Steve Davis (snooker), Bernhard Langer (golf) and Jane Torville (ice-skating) were born; French Fashion designer Christian Dior died. After the Second World War he had transformed ladies-wear by introducing long hemlines and full skirts – the 'New Look'; Soviet satellite *Sputnik 2* with a dog on board, was launched into space. The dog Laika did not return to earth; famous Italian tenor Beniamino Gigli died; Gerry Lee Lewis recorded 'Great Balls Of Fire' and Harry Belafonte enhanced the Christmas atmosphere worldwide when he so beautifully combined the melody and lyrics of the song 'Mary's Boy Child'. What did 1958 hold in store for Cork hurling followers? Was our Munster final trip in doubt? We still had Ring and with him on our side all things were possible. Spring and early summer would reveal all.

1958

The first day of January 1958 marked the birth of the European Economic Community. The governments of France, Italy, West Germany, Belgium, Holland and Luxembourg formed an alliance that had long been envisaged. A few days later explorer Sir Edmund Hillary reached the South Pole. That achievement was quickly followed by the launch from Cape Canaveral of the first satellite to orbit the earth. It was called *Explorer 1*. An exciting start to the new year and February had not yet arrived! The new month had scarcely dawned when the world of sport was shocked by news of a tragic plane crash. Seven Manchester United Football Club players lost their lives on the runaway at Munich airport!

With winter beginning to give way to spring Michael Holliday told 'The Story of my Life' while Perry Como entertained with 'Magic Moments'. All the while Cork hurling followers were wondering how the selectors were coming to terms with selecting a 'new look' team for the Munster championship first round match against Clare. As Connie Francis gave vent to a song called 'Who's Sorry Now' Cork hurlers ignored the query and went on to beat Clare in Thurles. According to reports, a team built around the stalwarts of many championship matches gave a good account of themselves. I have no details of the line-out except that Liam Dowling returned to the fold at full-forward. A statistic from the game is that Clare led by ten points at half-time but were two goals adrift at full-time. The final score was Cork 5-9; Clare 3-9.

Heartened by that result we made our way to Limerick for the Munster semi-final clash with Tipperary. Ring was back on the team and Paddy Barry was captain. Tipperary had not beaten Cork since 1951 and last year's performance by the Premier Countymen gave no reason to believe that

that stranglehold would be broken. We had come to know the Treaty City well by then. Nothing much had changed over the years – the streets continued to be thronged with people coming from the railway station; we went to the same parking place in Dock Road; we joined the thousands as they made their way on foot to the Gaelic Grounds via Sarsfields Bridge; the three blind pipers were ever present; those not as well catered for as ourselves bought sandwiches at stalls; a mixture of good humour, excitement and expectation was evident everywhere. Getting a match programme on the way to the Grounds was a priority. I couldn't wait to get my hands on a copy that particular day. Even though the newspapers carried the Cork team line-out the previous Saturday it was not the same as seeing it set out in black and white on match day.

Inevitably many strange names appeared on the centre page! The full-back line was not too startling. Jimmy Brohan and John Lyons were still there but at left-corner-back the name of Stanley Roche did not ring a bell. Mick McCarthy, Phil Duggan and Paddy Philpott completed the defence. Mick and Phil were new to me but Paddy was a formidable and well-established left-half back. Eamonn Goulding and Mick O'Reagan filled the midfield positions. Eamonn had been in and out of the team in recent years and Mick, who had played a few games, was still relatively unknown to me. Tom Furlong, Terry Kelly and Paddy Fitzgerald made up the half-forward line. Terry was a veteran who had given Cork great service but Tom and Paddy were not household names where county hurling was concerned. A glance across the full-forward line personnel brought a smile to my face.

The names of Paddy Barry, Liam Dowling and Christy Ring erased all doubts from my mind.

A Premier Relief, Stars are Born and an Under Pole Voyage

Amid the usual excitement and tension the match got under way. Identifying the 'new' men and trying to assess how they were doing in what was an absorbing contest made the first-half pass in a flash. In spite of an early

Tipperary goal Cork did well and led by 2-3 to 1-1 at half-time. Ring and Dowling were the goal scorers. During the interval followers commented on the fact that Tipperary defender John Doyle was playing in the half-back line rather than his customary corner-back position. Much credit too was being given to Mick Mc Carthy for the fine marking job he was doing on Premier County scoring ace Jimmy Doyle.

In the second-half the Rebels continued to show great determination and were playing really well. The problem was that the Tipperary defence on that occasion was unyielding. The half-back line of John Doyle, team captain Tony Wall, and Jimmy Finn reached fortress like proportions whilst the full-back line was also proving rock solid with Mickey Byrne and Michael Maher outstanding. I was quickly identifying Tipperary players who had adorned their county team for some years but hitherto meant little to me. In addition to the aforementioned the names of Theo English, John Hough, Liam Devaney and Jimmy Doyle were to be firmly fixed on my mind from that day onwards. Among the forwards too was a lightly built, daring and dashing young man with tremendous skill named Donie Nealon.

Cork, undaunted by this spirited Tipperary side, did well. With five minutes of play remaining the scores were level. Intensity and tension were evident on the faces of followers from both counties. At the closing stages Cork were pressing and Tipperary folk with hearts in mouths prayed Ring would not deny them victory. Then Jimmy Doyle, and Liam Devaney scored a point apiece. Cork again caused Tipperary hearts to flutter, on and off the field, when Liam Dowling looked certain to score. A great save by Tipperary goalie John O'Grady was enough to give the proud wearers of the blue and gold the win they had waited so long for. Tipperary had finally eclipsed Cork's dominance over them in Munster championship hurling. The eclipse which had prevailed since 1951 had been removed. The final score was Tipperary 2-6; Cork 2-4.

All agreed that we had witnessed a well contested match. Tipperary followers in the midst of their immense

45

joy drew a huge sigh of relief. Tradition and pride had been sorely tested in recent years.

As Cork followers we had to accept that our side was no longer all conquering but the team which represented the county that day did it proud. We had more than our share of success. Cork teams over the years had delighted, thrilled and excited all who were in any way associated with them. One defeat by Tipperary was not going to stop us proudly flying the flag.

Tipperary went on to beat Galway in the All-Ireland hurling final by a score of 4-9 to 2-5 thereby regaining the magnificent Liam McCarthy Cup after a seven year interval.

As we travelled south from Limerick on the fine June evening a radio reminded us that the current chart topper was, 'On the Street Where You Live' sung by Vic Damone.

What else happened in 1958? In mid-summer Daley Thompson a man who was to gain gold at two Olympics was born. In August a nuclear powered submarine passed directly under the North Pole whilst on a five day 2000 mile underwater voyage. Into the world later that month came 1990s entertainers Madonna and Michael Jackson. In September the rousing voice of Connie Francis made its way back into the hit chart for a second time that year with a song called 'Carolina Moon'. 'It's Only Make Believe' sung by Conway Twitty was popular in December.

—— 1959 ——

WONDER MEN STOLE THE SHOW

On New Year's Day 1959 government leaders throughout the world were alerted to the fact that Cuban dictator Fulgencio Batista had been ousted from power. The revolutionary forces of 32-year-old Fidel Castro had ended the struggle against the hated Batista regime.

Another news item to hit the headlines in January was the launch of Soviet unmanned space rocket *Luna 1*. It was the first rocket to pass close to the moon. In January also the world was saddened by the death of film director, producer and screenwriter, Cecil B. de Mille.

Throughout the spring of 1959 there was nothing to suggest that Cork and Tipperary would not again contest the Munster championship final. The general opinion was that Waterford would give Tipperary a good game and that Cork would see-off Clare's challenge. The Cork Athletics Grounds was the venue for the Tipperary versus Waterford match. It was played on Sunday 12 July.

I remember the occasion well because it was the first championship match I had seen without Cork being involved. It was a windy, showery day, not at all what one might expect in July. As we stood on the embankment we were aware of a strong breeze blowing down the pitch. I was particularly interested in the Tipperary defence of Byrne, Maher, Carey, Finn, Wall and Doyle which had so impressed against Cork the previous year and indeed the whole team which later thrashed Galway in the All-Ireland final.

From the throw-in of the sliotar Waterford were on top. The team in white were rampant. To the amazement of all present Tipperary playing against the breeze, were swamped by the speed and class of their potent opponents. Waterford scored almost at will and the highly-acclaimed Tipperary defence was being torn to shreds. Surely this could not have been happening! It was. The goals kept going in and one wondered how or when it was going to stop. At half-time the score was Waterford 8-2; Tipperary 0-0. Not only were Tipperary followers and their team shattered but so also were those of Waterford.

Nobody expected the match to turn out like it did. Micheál O'Hehir who was commentating on the Leinster hurling final that day, reported the half-time score from the Athletic Grounds but advised listeners to ignore it – there had to be a mistake!

Over the years many have puzzled as to why Tipperary captain Tony Wall having won the toss, elected to play against the wind. No doubt it was not a decision taken solely by Tony.

The wind favoured Tipperary in the second-half but Waterford's lead was unassailable. What could the Tipperary team do? They tried hard from the throw-in but the score difference indicated that they had to go for goals. A few came but not enough and at the final whistle seventeen points separated the sides. Waterford had added 1-1 to their half time tally and Tipperary had scored 3-4. The final score was Waterford 9-3; Tipperary 3-4. It was incomprehensible!

So who were these Waterford wonder men? Remember, they were just supposed to give the current All-Ireland champions a good game! I cast my mind back to Thurles and to the July day in 1957 when virtually the same team beat a tired Cork side by five points. I recalled that in the opinion of many people Cork with Ring would have reversed the outcome. Maybe they were wrong! Waterford certainly had an easy victory over Galway in that year's All-Ireland semi-final but then a few weeks later whether through over anxiety or inexperience surrendered a two goal lead and gifted Kilkenny the All-Ireland championship. Maybe there was after all potential in the side but it had not yet fully matured. When the 1958 championship came around Tipperary beat them convincingly! Was the Waterford team which showed so much promise in 1957 on the slippery slope? It took the demolition of Tipperary at the Athletic Grounds on that windy 1959 day to restore confidence. All of a sudden hurling followers began to take note. Here was a well organised, talented, strong, speedy team with high calibre players such as Seamus Power, Phil Grimes, John Barron, team captain Frankie Walsh, Mick Flannelly, John Kiely, Larry Guinean and Charlie Ware.

THEY TOOK RING'S ADVICE AND WENT ALL THE WAY
As expected Cork beat Clare in the other semi-final. A re-run of the 1957 Munster hurling final was scheduled for Thurles on 23 July. Was there a hurling follower in the country who didn't want to be there?

Waterford were unlikely to repeat the performance they served up against Tipperary. Cork, who were not the settled, formidable outfit of the mid-1950s must have been a little nervous.

While a singing group called The Platters were having success in the charts with a song called 'Smoke Gets in your Eyes', and Buddy Holly was doing equally well with 'It Doesn't Matter Anymore', hurling followers prepared for the Thurles showdown. This time a few of us travelled in a brand new Ford Consul driven by yours truly.

That day in Thurles Waterford's magnificent win over Tipperary was the main talking point. Close on the heels of that topic were discussions on how the Decies men would fare against the Rebels. I couldn't wait for the match to begin. As the mighty men of Cork and Waterford marched behind the famous pipe band, followers were so focused that it was as if nothing else was happening in the world. The intensity of pride and passion brought a lump to the throat and close inspection might well reveal a little mois-ture welling up in the eyes. The strains of the 'Banks Of My Own Lovely Lee' at that moment would have left me per-sonally awash.

Once again the Cork team had an unfamiliar look to it. Gone were the days when near enough the same fifteen lined out on successive years. That day the injured Mick Cashman was replaced in goal by Seanie O'Brien. Jimmy Brohan (captain) along with John Lyons and Gerald Mulcahy formed the full-back line. There were seven or eight of the team making their championship debuts, among them were Noel O'Connell, Mick Quane, Noel Gallagher, Willie Walsh and Con Cooney.

At last the match got under way and Cork settled well. The fighting qualities and spirit we had come to expect from the proud wearers of those red jerseys was well in evidence. Waterford matched them all the way. They looked solid in defence and slick in attack. Cork were getting much joy from the fact that Paddy Barry, at centre-forward, was getting the better of his opposite number Martin Og Morrissey. Christy Ring, while doing well, was finding right full-back Joe Harney a handful. Barry's brilliance continued to bother the Waterfordmen and soon the mentors moved Phil Grimes from midfield to centre-back. Grimes effectively curtailed Paddy Barry's supremacy and gave a display of hurling that will be long remembered by followers of both counties. With the supply of ball to the Cork full-forward line virtually cut off, Ring and Barry changed positions. The Grimes stranglehold continued and the whole Waterford team began to play with more authority. By 5pm the fine Waterford team – all stars on the day - were crowned Munster champions. For the record Cork veterans Ring and Barry between them accounted for 2-8 of Cork's 2-9 total tally. Waterford scored 3-9.

Cork followers recognised that their men had been beaten by a very good Waterford team. A widely reported post-match gesture was that of Ring helping an exhausted Phil Grimes from the ground telling him as he did so to 'Go all the way this time', or words to that effect. That sentiment summed up the feelings of all Rebel County men on that late afternoon.

For the third year in a row Cork had failed to capture the premier Munster hurling crown. On each occasion the team representing the county gave a good account of itself and for that reason we were satisfied. Our day would come again!

On 6 September Waterford met Kilkenny at Croke Park in the All-Ireland final. A high-scoring thriller ensued. At the final whistle the scores were level at Waterford 1-17; Kilkenny 5-5. The replay took place on 4 October and the wishes of hurling followers in 31 counties were granted when the gallant and sometimes cavalier Waterfordmen emerged winners. The final score was Waterford 3-12; Kilkenny 1-10.

I have named some Waterford players but not to mention all of them would be a travesty. So let the names of Ned Power, Austin Flynn, Tom Cheasty, Mick Lacey, Jackie Condon, Donal Whelan, Tom Cunningham, Mickey O'Connor, Joe Coady, Paudie Casey, Tom Coffey and Freddie O'Brien be forever remembered for the enormous contribution they made in bringing the McCarthy Cup back to the Decies. It is widely accepted that Waterford were without doubt the best team in the 1959 championship.

THE END OF A DECADE IN WHICH SOME THOUGHT THE WORLD HAD GONE MAD

With all the excitement in Waterford that year I'm sure not many in the county noticed that childhood favourite Lou Costello, half the Abbott and Costello duo, departed this life. It is unlikely that the news of the launch of the first hovercraft at Cowes, Isle of Wight, or that Ingemar Johansson became the first Swedish heavyweight boxing champion of the world fared any better. Waterford folk had eyes only for the caman-wielding men in white. An event unknown to the country at large was the birth of fiery, talented tennis player John McEnroe.

In Waterford, like the rest of the country, singers and show bands were busy learning the several 'catchy' numbers in the charts. In July, Cliff Richard and the Drifters led the way with 'Livin' Doll'. In between the All-Ireland finals Craig Douglas made his mark with 'Only Sixteen'. In October, though untimely, Jerry Keller made it to the top with 'Here Comes Summer'. On a less frivolous note, Bobby Darin recorded 'Mack The Knife', while still in October Cliff Richard and the Shadows made 'Travellin Light' very popular. Then came what must have been the hit song of 1959, 'What do You want to Make Those Eyes at Me for'. It's singer Emile Ford and his band the Checkmates became almost as popular as Waterford hurlers in Waterford.

The decade which really began for me on a July day in Killarney was quickly drawing to a close. What a decade it had been for Cork hurling followers. I didn't have to rack my brain to recall that Cork had won four Munster championships and were finalists on four other occasions, missing out only in 1955 and 1958. Add three All-Ireland championships to that and there is not a follower of hurling in any county that would not give their eye teeth for a similar tally. The lads had indeed done the county proud.

The feats of some individual players were just incredible but it took all the players on any given day to make the magic. An enormous thanks to those still with us and may God rest those who have gone to hurl elsewhere.

As I now reflect on that decade of Cork hurling the joy match-days gave me are etched indelibly in my mind. The craic, the fun, the laughter, the tension, the passion, the pride, the intensity and the camaraderie were all ingredients of a heady period in my life.

It is worth reflecting too on the many changes experienced in everyday life during the course of the decade. When recalling the magnitude of those changes, strong words like 'momentous' and 'transfiguration' immediately spring to mind. Certainly there could not have been many people in Ireland who were not affected in some way by developments such as the nationwide availability of electricity and running water, new fashion trends in clothing, the arrival of synthetic materials on the market, the mass production of small cheap motor cars, the coming of commercial airlines and last but not least, the lightweight portable radio and record player. The new-found audio facilities which brought the stars of the day into kitchens and sitting rooms from Malin Head to Mizen Head probably made the greatest impact of all. Suddenly anyone with £10 to spare or those who could afford a ten shilling deposit and five shilling a week pay-back could become the owner of a completely self-contained record player. A slowly revolving 'long-playing' record provided 25 minutes of uninterrupted music per side – five or six tunes. With records stacked up to ten high and ready to drop automatically in sequence onto a turntable, an entire evening of music was possible. Furthermore one's favourite records could be played anywhere anytime. Record players powered by mains electricity or batteries and housed in a lightweight cases were transported on bicycles to parties, picnics, school-halls and dance-halls.

—— 1960 ——

AND A THRILLER AT THURLES

Ten years ago on a fateful July day in Killarney I experienced a phenomenon to which I quickly became addicted. As the decade progressed watching hurling championship matches involving Cork became an obsession. How I so looked forward to and enjoyed those match-days. Nothing surpassed getting up bright and early and heading off for Thurles, Limerick or Killarney. How I savoured the pre-match atmosphere and the magic of being absorbed by enthralling contests. Then to round it all off there was the craic on the journey home in the evening. But it was the red jerseys of Cork that stirred a dormant passion in me like nothing else did. By the time Cork and Tipperary met in the 1960 Munster final the new decade was well established and the Premier County men were desperately trying to forget the fiasco on that windy day at the Cork Athletic Grounds a year ago. With the War Years being little more than a memory people firmly believed that a new era was nigh.

Maybe that is why Michael Holliday had a song called 'Starry Eyed' in the charts! In South Africa the whites only parliament was told by British Prime Minister Harold Macmillan that 'a wind of change' was blowing through Africa. The clear message to disbelieving and astonished politicians was to accept racial equality. Anthony Newley was not a South African parliamentarian but a song sung by him titled 'Why' remained a chart topper for four weeks.

The results of early-summer Munster championship matches ensured that for the first time since 1954, the 1960 final would, dare I say it, see the 'big two', Cork and Tipperary, locked in combat once again. The Cork selectors must have been listening to Anthony Newley's second hit record of the year. It was called 'Do You Mind'. Whether they used those exact words or not the result was that a number of players who lined-out for the county in 1959 were not to be among the starting fifteen on the big-day at Thurles. In the meantime singer Lonnie Donegan continued to inform all and sundry, 'My Old Man's a Dustman'. In April the untimely accidental death of rock star Eddie Cochran virtually coincided with his hit single 'Three Steps To Heaven'.

The Munster final was played in Thurles on 31 July. Unlike all the other finals I travelled to over the years this time my journey began at Cork city. The morning was dull and overcast with intermittent rain. We hoped it wasn't an omen of things to come! Five students including myself paid a man called Dan Donovan who lived in Shandon Street a few pounds for the use of a car. It was an old Ford Prefect which had seen better days. Once we had gone through Mitchelstown a spiral of smoke rising up from a small hole in the dashboard signalled that something was wrong. With Thurles firmly fixed on our minds and, more importantly arriving there on time for the match, we at first ignored the ominous sign, but it got much worse, leaving us with no alternative but to stop and jump out. In a matter of minutes we were surrounded by the occupants of other cars who on becoming aware of our plight stopped to help. Someone discovered that the source of the trouble was a faulty windscreen-wiper motor. In no time he had us back on the road again. There was just one thing – the wipers were no longer functional. It was raining heavily but we were determined to continue the journey regardless of all. We arrived in Thurles in good time to savour the unrivalled pre-match atmosphere around Liberty Square.

Why is Thurles uniquely special on those big Munster hurling championship occasions? Is it because of it's location - situated as it is in the heart of a countryside steeped in hurling greatness? Does it have something to do with a November day in 1884? Do the ghosts of those who met in Hayes Hotel all those years ago cast a 'kind of spell' over the town? The music from the footpath near Hanifin's Corner was enough to let us know we were on the right road.

Once inside the stadium it was time to study the line-out of the teams. Both counties showed changes from the previous championship but the Tipperary team had the more settled look about it. Newcomers to the Cork team included Sean French at left-corner back and Denis O'Riordan at left-half back.

Joe Twomey returned to captain the side from the left-half-forward position. With the preliminaries over, throw-in time was fast approaching. The occasional torrential shower took some 'gloss' off the spectacle but not enough to dampen the spirits of fanatical followers. In the early stages of the match, perhaps even for the first fifteen minutes, Cork had the upper hand. Paddy Barry scored a goal in the first minute. A thrilling, high-scoring first-half followed. A tremendous exhibition of hurling was given by both teams. I still remember a great goal scored by Tipperary right-half forward Jimmy Doyle from fully 40 yards out. It was a fierce low shot which beat ace goalie Mick Cashman. Paddy Barry added a second goal for Cork but not before Connelly and McLoughlin had scored 'majors' apiece for Tipperary. As a ferocious, unyielding contest developed between the men of two proud hurling counties, Cork's Quane, Kelly and Ring exchanged points with Doyle, Devaney and Muloughney leaving the half-time score at 3-4 to 2-4, in favour of the men in blue and gold. To say that the first-half was very exciting would be a gross understatement. Clearly there was little between the teams.

The second-half got off to a flying start with Cork levelling the score for the third time in the match. Once again it was the maestro Ring who scored two points, bringing his total to four. Joe Twomey added the third. When Mick Quane put Cork into the lead the Rebels had scored four points without reply and things were looking good for the Leesiders. Undaunted, back came Tipperary with a McLoughlin goal. Excitement was at fever pitch when Devaney scored a well taken point. Tipperary had again opened up a three point gap between the teams. It was then that Jimmy Doyle showed the 49,670 patrons present the hurling wizardry he was capable of by knocking over three points in succession. Tipperary led by six points!

Were Cork beaten? No, not yet at least. It was not that kind of match and to prove it Liam Dowling set all Leesiders alight with a fine goal. The 'drama' continued, points were exchanged, two for Cork and two for Tipperary. Tipperary led by three points. Scores were coming so fast that it was necessary to check the scoreboard by the minute. Time was ebbing away and in spite of the best efforts of the Corkmen Tipperary seemed to be getting the better of things. At that crucial stage they scored a further three points to a single reply from Christy Ring. Cork were five points in arrears! Was there any way back for the gallant Leesiders?

Tipperary followers were far from complacent – they had seen it all before and knew Cork too well. How right they were – Cork weren't finished yet. A late goal by Mick Quane was a salutary reminder to anyone who might have thought otherwise. With two points between the teams and the final whistle about to be blown only a mere puck of the sliotar separated the sides. Regardless of the outcome those present that day had witnessed men from the counties of Cork and Tipperary give a whole new meaning to 'pride in the jerseys they wore'. And time did run out for Cork.

Tipperary had fought incredibly hard in order to register a first victory over Cork in a Munster final since 1951. The final score was Tipperary 4-13; Cork 4-11. I was honoured to have been present at such a magnificent sporting occasion. It was a fine victory for a fine Tipperary team but I was enormously proud of the men who represented Cork. Christy Ring, who would be 40 in October, seemed ageless. He was still 'king' where I was concerned and his confrontations with great Tipperary defender John Doyle that day were not for the faint hearted! Dan Donovan's Ford Prefect made it back to Cork without any further problems as Sir Francis Chichester made his solo round the world voyage – he had just arrived in New York having crossed the Atlantic in a record breaking 40 days.

WEXFORD CELEBRATES AS WE TAKE STOCK BUT IRELAND IS TRULY SADDENED

So Tipperary had beaten Cork but Rebel followers were in no way responsible for a Cliff Richard and the Shadows hit

'Please Don't Tease'. Tipperary fulfilled the all-important fixture in Croke Park on 4 September. They met Leinster hurling champions Wexford. The All-Ireland champions of 1955 and 1956 proved too strong for Tipperary on the day and ran out comfortable winners. The final score was Wexford 2-15; Tipperary 0-11. Rightly or wrongly it was claimed by some pundits that the epic encounter with Cork in the Munster final drained Tipperary to the extent that the players were subsequently unable to regain the stamina, sharpness, and fleetness of foot evident earlier in the year. With the All-Ireland final over for another year the shadows were lengthening as days got shorter. It was a time for taking stock of what was happening in other quarters.

In the world of popular music Ricky Valance was singing 'Tell Laura I Love Her', while Roy Orbison was entertaining with 'Only The Lonely'. In the world of literature, Penguin Books were charged with public obscenity while attempting to publish the naughty novel, *Lady Chatterley's Lover*. I'm sure there was no connection between that charge and the launch of the first nuclear-powered aircraft carrier. It took place on 24 September at Newport, Virginia. The big stories in the press during the early winter of 1960 related to such diverse happenings as the appearance of missiles in Moscow's Red Square for the first time and the instalment of John Fitzgerald Kennedy as United States president. As the year drew to a close it was a song which made the greatest impression on the population at large. The song, Elvis Presley's 'It's Now or Never', remained at the top spot in the charts for eight weeks. Prince, another American singer and musician, didn't figure in any hit chart that year because like Czechoslovakian tennis player Ivan Lendl he was not yet one year old. While hurling followers in the Model County were still celebrating the September victory at Croke Park, screen idol Clark Gable died. His portrayal of Rhett Butler in the film 'Gone With the Wind' has become a legend. Those who frequented the cinema in 1960 were certain to be among audiences screaming in terror as Norman Bates ran amok in the Alfred Hitchcock film 'Psycho'. With another year in the offing Cork hurling followers had two major questions on their minds, how much longer could the veteran players Ring, Barry and Dowling continue to give the outstanding performances we had become accustomed to and, was this good Tipperary team going to be too strong for Cork in the 1961 championship? We would have to wait and see.

One particular incident in 1960, and the circumstances surrounding it, has remained foremost in my mind. It was the Niemba ambush which took place in the Congo Republic. In July Irish soldiers were billeted in Albertville as part of a United Nations military back-up. On 8 November, while on a routine patrol, eleven of those young Irishmen were surrounded by Baluba warriors. Nine members of the patrol lost their lives in horrific circumstances. In Dublin 300,000 people were reported to have turned out to show their respects at the funeral of soldiers who died because, through no fault of their own, they were in the wrong place at the wrong time. It is with a heavy heart that I recall the grief and concern inflicted on the relatives, friends and people nationwide by the waste of such precious lives.

1961

HEADLINE MAKERS BUT EARLY ENCOURAGING SIGNS

LED TO LIMERICK FIASCO

In the early days of January 1961 those who had recovered from celebrating the arrival of the New Year might have noticed one or more of the following newspaper headlines: Millionth Minor; Cuba Severed; Longest Strike. Millionth Minor headed an article which informed us that by 3 January 1,000,000 Morris Minor motor cars would have been assembled. On the same date the United States broke-off diplomatic links with the Communist Castro-led Cuban administration. Castro had seized power on 1 January 1958. The heading 'Longest Strike' told the story of apprentice barbers in Copenhagen who took industrial action in 1938. It went on until 4 January 1961. For those not interested in world affairs Elvis Presley came to the rescue with yet another hit record, 'Are You Lonesome Tonight', which was to remain at number one in the charts for four weeks. The arrival of spring brought with it thoughts of the forthcoming Munster hurling championship.

Those close to the scene in Cork were concerned that again a county team with many debutantes and consequently inexperienced players would find it hard to overcome the more established sides. Cork's veteran and ultra reliable full-back John Lyons had decided to retire. He had become such a familiar figure that it was hard to imagine a Cork team without the tried and trusted stalwart. What service he gave to the Rebel County! In April, while John's replacement and players in several other positions were being tried-out, the birth of American comedian and actor Eddie Murphy almost coincided with the launch into space of Russian cosmonaut Major Yuri Gagarin, the first human to go where no man had gone before. It was a time when the Soviets and the United States were locked in a space superiority battle which came close to the rivalry between

Cork and Tipperary hurlers. Not to be outdone by the Soviets, three weeks after the Yuri Gagarin take-off the Americans blasted astronaut Alan Shepard into space. The fifteen minute part-orbit of the earth by the American as opposed to the 180 minute complete orbit by Gagarin left the Soviets well ahead on points.

Meanwhile a day of reckoning for Cork's hurlers was fast approaching. The Munster semi-final championship meeting with Waterford at Thurles before an attendance of over 42,000 caused no major problem. Suffice to say Christy Ring's personal scoring tally of three goals and four points equalled the total score registered by the opposing team. Once again the man who would be 41 in October mesmerised a Waterford team which included many of the stars of the 1959 All-Ireland winning side. The match which Paddy Barry missed through injury ended with a score of 5-7 to 2-7. That result and Ring's magical performance gave Rebel County followers reason for optimism. Not surprisingly Tipperary had filtered through the other side of the draw and couldn't wait to play Cork in the final at Limerick's Gaelic Grounds on 29 July.

With little more to go on other than the return of Paddy Barry and Ring's scintillating display against Waterford, Cork followers reckoned their team had a good chance of beating Tipperary. I suppose it had to be borne in mind too that the Rebels were only narrowly defeated in the bruising provincial final the previous year. Yes, all in all Cork had a 50-50 chance of toppling the champions. The fixture was looked forward to with extra relish not only by followers of the competing counties but by hurling enthusiasts nationwide. The mammoth appeal of the apparently ageless, intrepid and accomplished Ring was phenomenal. Few would argue against the widely-held view that his charisma swelled attendance at venues from Cork to New York. Nowhere was it more clearly demonstrated than on that warm July day in Limerick. With 61,000 packed into the stadium the gates closed long before the match started. It was a record attendance for a Munster final, beating the 1959 figure by 5,000.

I travelled from west Cork that morning along with a few

others and arrived in Limerick at about 11.30am. We spent an hour or so in the city before heading out for the Grounds in what we thought was plenty of time. As it turned out we were lucky to get in just before the gates were closed. By squeezing our way through the crowd we eventually found a vantage point from which to watch the match. I remember there was scarcely elbow-room as I tried to read the team line-outs in the match programme. Where the Cork team was concerned the now familiar trend of recent years pertained – names of players new to the Munster final appeared. Dan Brennan was selected to replace John Lyons and face a now very settled Tipperary team. Other newcomers were Johnny O'Connor, a half-back; Tim Walsh, a midfielder; and Richie Browne, a full-forward.

Somehow the atmosphere in the Grounds was more tense than usual. Perhaps that was because there were few present who did not anticipate a repeat of the ferocious, bruising battle which took place between the same counties in the 1960 provincial decider. In spite of a sweltering day the air of carnival was less evident than on other days. From the throw-in of the sliotar Tipperary controlled the match as was shown by the 3-3 to 0-1 half-time score. I couldn't take my eyes off the scoreboard during the interval and the incredible score-line was to become indelibly fixed on my mind. Indeed Tipperary had scored the three goals in the opening eighteen minutes – two by Donie Nealon and the third by Jimmy Doyle. Cork's sole score came from Christy Ring who started the match at left-corner forward. I watched incredulously as Theo English and Liam Devaney controlled the midfield sector.

When the Leesiders did manage to mount an attack an excellent Donie O'Brien, the Tipperary goalkeeper, foiled their best efforts. The Corkmen were indeed battling against a superb Tipperary team. A number of positional and personnel changes failed to make any real impression. Once again it was to Ring that Cork followers and mentors looked for salvation. He was moved to centre-forward where Paddy Barry was being given a torrid time by John Doyle.

Could Christy turn the match around as he had done so

many times in the past? Cork followers were hopeful, Tipperary followers became apprehensive! Try as he might the great man failed on that occasion to spark life into a lethargic Cork attack and for the first time some observers noted that the stamina and speed of old may have begun to desert the ageing genius. I watched the match from the embankment situated between the Hogan Stand and the Limerick city end of the pitch. Cork played towards the city end in the second-half and as such I had a good view of the Christy Ring/John Doyle altercations. Ring was playing his heart out but Doyle, backed up by a team firing on all cylinders, was matching the best efforts of the maestro. It began to look as if the task was too much even for Ring.

It may sound as if the great Cloyne man was the only Cork player doing his utmost to curb the might of Tipperary. That indeed was not the case but the emphasis on his performance illustrated the dependence of the Cork senior hurling team on him. The only hope of a Rebel victory that afternoon was through a bit of the old Ring 'magic'. The 'magic' failed to materialise! Christy Ring and John Doyle were noted adversaries and during the match that day the intensity in their play showed no signs of abating. It came to a head as the tension filled match entered the final quarter. Just about level with where I stood on the embankment, Ring and Doyle together ran some distance towards the sliotar. The two men, through a combination of shoulder contact, leaning-in and jostling tried to push each other off the direct line of the run. Doyle seemed to get slightly ahead of Ring as they neared the sliotar, hurleys were swung and the next thing both men were on the ground, Ring on his back with Doyle on top of him.

It saddened me greatly to see the two great hurlers ignominiously wrestling on the turf of Limerick's Gaelic Grounds. It had been a bad day for Cork and I'm sure Tipperary folk felt the balance of much that had gone on over the years between the county's hurlers had been well and truly restored. The Ring/Doyle incident led to further violence involving other players, all of which was extremely unfortunate. The final score was Tipperary 3-6; Cork 0-7.

It was with a heavy heart that I walked back into

Limerick. The Cork players had done their best against a superior team and all credit to them for that. Disappointment was evident among the Rebel County followers. The time had come to draw succour from all the wonderfully exciting and exhilarating days which Cork teams had given us just a short few years ago.

Tipperary's trip to Dublin and Croke Park on 3 September proved worthwhile. Victory over Dublin by the narrowest of margins was sufficient to crown the Munstermen All-Ireland hurling champions. The first-half of the match was almost completely dominated by Tipperary but Dublin made a great comeback in the second-half and in the end could have won. However, the score at the final whistle was Tipperary 0-16; Dublin 1-12.

SOMBRE MOOD AS BABIES OF 1961 COINCIDE WITH BERLIN WALL.

Cork hurling followers were in sombre mood. We had to go back five years for a Munster championship win to the day in Thurles when Ring denied Limerick with three late goals. The title of a hit song at the time was 'You're Driving Me Crazy' by the Temperance Seven – a sentiment experienced by many Leesiders who reflected on the current fortunes of our county's hurlers. Another hit 'Surrender' sung by Elvis Presley might well have been composed by a Tipperaryman. It was left to Helen Shapiro to raise our spirits when her lively number 'Walkin' Back to Happiness' topped the charts for three weeks in October. People destined to be famous who were born in 1961 included American athlete Carl Lewis who won three gold medals in the 1984 Olympic Games; Irish jockey Walter Swinburne who won the 1981 Derby on Shergar; Romanian gymnast Nadia Comaneci who won three Olympic gold medals; and British singer Sarah Brightman. Among the busiest people in 1961 must have been those 'employed' by the East German authorities to build a nine-feet high concrete barrier between the Eastern and Western sectors of Berlin.

The structure which was topped with barbed wire became known as the Berlin Wall. As the year drew to a close, Americans Elvis Presley and Danny Williams were respectively singing their way to the top of the hit parade with 'His Latest Flame' and 'Moon River'. Sadly at the other side of the world a young man of the same nationality, James Davis, became the first soldier to die in the Vietnam War. Once again the hurling fraternity of my beloved county were left to hope for better things in 1962.

1962

Mention of 1962 brings back memories of my graduation from University College Cork and taking up employment in Ballymena, County Antrim. Though not planned at the time I was never to return to Cork as a permanent resident. Employment was not easy to come-by in west Cork at the time. I could have emigrated but instead I chose to go to Ballymena. Initially my intention was to stay for a year but fate decided otherwise.

Sadly, Cork's involvement in the 1962 hurling championship occupies only a tiny percentage of my hurling memorabilia. There is an explanation for this. The Rebels made only the minimal appearance which saw them beaten in the first round. Cork had done well in the League. In early May they took on Kilkenny in the final. The match was played in Croke Park and by all accounts the standard of hurling shown by both teams was extremely high. There was no reason to suspect that Cork would not do well in the championship. Newcomers to the side were Denis Murphy, Sean Kennifeck, Donal Sheehan and Mick Mortell. For the lone Munster championship outing against Waterford, some changes in personnel took place. I note that John Barry, Tom Corbett, Denis O'Riordan and Tim Walsh replaced Mick Quane, Sean Kennifeck, Phil Duggan and Mick Mortell. The match was played at Thurles. A snippet from a report which has survived over the years mentions Patsy Harte as having accounted for 1-6 of Cork's total score. Terry Kelly, Denis O'Riordan and Gerry O'Sullivan were also recorded as having played well. The ultimate superlative, excelled, was reserved for Ring! The team did not have the all-round strength to bother Waterford. The final score was Waterford 4-10; Cork 1-16.

The Rebels were in the doldrums where championship

hurling was concerned! Gone were the days of the 1950s when followers of the Leesiders took winning for granted. It was a far cry from when we were complaining at having to return to the same venue year after year for the Munster final. By 1962 we would have been more than pleased to go anywhere. The epic game in Thurles in 1956 now seemed a lifetime away. The dominance of Tipperary in Munster hurling continued. Evidence of an easy victory over Waterford is to be found in the final score which reads Tipperary 5-14; Waterford 2-3.

The Premier County was back on the All-Ireland trail yet again. For the second year running Tipperary, captained by Jimmy Doyle made no mistake thus ensuring that the McCarthy Cup stayed put for another year.

The All-Ireland hurling final was played on Sunday 2 September. Both the match and the date were to go down in GAA history because for the first time Gaelic sport was shown live on television. Yes, those fortunate enough to have a television witnessed the showpiece in which Tipperary beat Wexford 3-10 to 2-11. Regretfully I missed out on the highly acclaimed RTE presentation that afternoon. I had travelled to Ballymena, County Antrim the previous Saturday, and on the Sunday was bracing myself for Monday morning and my first day as a teacher of Chemistry.

OH FOR WEST CORK BUT WAS IT TO BE THE SAME?
I remember that September afternoon well. I was a stranger in a strange town! Some Ballymena people may well have been interested in the happenings at Croke Park but I had not met any of them.

As I sat alone on the side of a bed in the Clarence Hotel staring at the wall I kept asking myself, 'What am I doing here?' My only consolation was that come July, even though it seemed an eternity away at the time, I would return to people and a way of life familiar to me. Little did I know that was not to be!

In a year which saw the Rebel County hurlers fail to impress and I made my first career move, the world too had its share of good and bad. By February Cliff Richard and the Shadows may well have had some of those debutant Cork hurlers in mind when a song called 'The Young Ones' began a six week stint at the number one spot. In the same month American astronaut John Glenn circled the Earth three times in less than five hours. He was the first American to orbit the planet. For yet another year Elvis Presley continued to monopolise the popular music scene. His renditions of 'Rock-a-Hula-Baby', 'Can't Help Falling in Love' 'Good Luck Charm' 'She's Not You', and 'Return to Sender', collectively spent nineteen weeks in pole-position. However, other singers did manage to squeeze in a few hit numbers. Mike Sarne with Wendy Richard (now Eastenders star), made it to the top with, 'Come Outside', while Ray Charles did likewise with 'I Can't Stop Loving You'. Frank Ifield scored a double success with 'I Remember You' which shot him to fame in July whilst four months later it was the appeal of 'Love Sick Blues' which gave him his second chart topper. In August, news of the death of 36-year-old film star and sex symbol Marilyn Monroe shocked and saddened fans all over the world. In November 1962 a baby girl, later known to the world as Jodie Foster, Oscar-winner for her role in 'The Silence of the Lambs' was born.

Just before Christmas I made the long trip from Ballymena to west Cork for the festive break. By then I had acquired my first car, a secondhand Volkswagen. As the days went by I got the feeling that somehow things were not just the same and that I was regarded to some extent as a visitor. What I hadn't taken into account is that time doesn't stand still and change is continuously taking place. I find it a little sad. As I travelled the 300 miles back to Ballymena on a cold day in early January I had plenty of time to reflect on 1962, and to wonder what 1963 held in store! Maybe Cork hurlers would surprise us, as indeed they had done before, and give me the opportunity to see a first All-Ireland final. I vowed that regardless of whatever happened I would not be sitting alone in Ballymena come that special September Sunday.

—— 1963 ——

JANUARY SNOW, CROKE PARK IN MARCH,
ALCATRAZ CLOSES ITS DOORS

In January 1963 snow fell more generously than usual in the north of the country. Schools were forced to close and some roads remained impassable for a week or more. Meanwhile there was no sign of my red Volkswagen, which I had parked in a backyard in Ballymena but now the only evidence of its existence was a mound of snow occupying the space. As the days passed the snow became slush and normality returned.

Cliff Richard and the Shadows were first to have a number one hit in 1963 when 'Bachelor Boy' occupied top spot for three weeks. In an attempt to keep in touch with happenings in Cork, particularly on the hurling scene, I approached a Ballymena newsagent and asked if I could order the *Cork Examiner*. The gracious lady inside the counter explained that I might as well be trying to book a ticket to the moon. Eventually I had to arrange to have a copy of each Monday's newspaper posted to me. It usually arrived on the Wednesday but sometimes it was Thursday before I got to read about the previous weekend's activities.

I looked forward to the newspaper so much; it was the highlight of the week. I read virtually every word. The message coming through as regards Cork hurling was that no major breakthrough seemed imminent. The team continued to have an unsettled look about it with changes in personnel and erratic results being the order of the day.

Frank Ifield had a hit single called 'Wayward Wind' in February, but as far as Leeside hurling was concerned more than the wind was wayward. To add to its problems serious questions were being asked about how much longer Christy Ring could continue in top class hurling. Having made his debut on a Cork senior team in October

69

1939 he had devoted virtually every spare minute to the cause – an almost unbelievable 24 years of undying service to his county! He was now 42 years of age. Regardless of Ring's age the Munster Railway Cup hurling inter-provincial selectors of 1963 did exactly the same as their predecessors had done since 1942 – they named him among the starting fifteen. Munster easily dismissed Ulster in the semi-final of the competition. At the same stage Leinster overcame the Connacht challenge thereby setting up a Munster versus Leinster final at Croke Park on St Patrick's Day.

With the schools closed and little to do in Ballymena I decided to go to Dublin. I celebrated the feast of our patron saint in the capital and of course took in the hurling match at Croke Park. The Cork players on the Munster team were Mick Cashman, Jimmy Brohan and Christy Ring. Mick won a record sixth Railway Cup medal as a goalkeeper that day. Christy did not have one of his greatest matches. He was not as sharp as of old, appeared to lack fitness and retired injured. The signs were there that the great man might be slowing down. By 5pm on that St Patrick's Day he had won an incredible eighteen Railway Cup medals. The best of the rest, Kilkenny's Eddie Keher, had won nine.

Still, I left Croke Park somewhat disconsolate. The unthinkable continued to break into my thoughts. A doubt had established itself as to whether or not I had seen Ring grace a major hurling occasion for the last time. There were indications to suggest the his best days were past. There wasn't a radio in the red Volkswagen. Had there been, on the way back to Ballymena I could not have missed a Cliff Richard and the Shadows hit 'Summer Holiday'. Unseasonable though the title was it remained for two weeks at the top of the singles chart. Had I been able to tune into the world news I would most likely have heard that on 21 March, Alcatraz, the infamous island prison in San Francisco Bay, would close its doors for the last time. As spring merged into summer four young Liverpudlians called The Beatles took the popular music world by storm. In early April they secured the top five places in the United States singles charts with 'Can't Buy me Love', 'Twist And Shout', 'She Loves You', 'I Want To Hold Your Hand' and

'Please Please Me'. That achievement was followed by sixteen weeks on top in the UK charts with 'From Me to You', 'She Loves You' and 'I Want to Hold your Hand'. While hurling followers waited for the first round of the Munster championship, the film 'Lawrence of Arabia', starring Peter O'Toole, won seven Oscars. In the news too was the contraceptive pill which became available in the UK under the National Health Service.

RING-LESS CORK! WATERFORD SHOCK! KILKENNY BLINDER! JFK STUNNER!

All the while I was desperately trying to keep in touch with what was happening in Cork hurling. In the first round of the provincial championship the Rebels met Clare. With my ear 'glued' to the landlady's radio late on a Sunday night I managed to hear the result of the match in spite of wobbly airwaves and static interference. Cork won by 4-15 to 2-11. I was later to learn that Mick Cashman had retired from inter-county hurling and that Glen Rovers man Paddy Barry had made his debut in goal in the match against Clare. I was sad to see Mick go because he ranked amongst the greatest goalkeepers to wear the Cork jersey. Neither should his contribution in out-field positions be forgotten. His performance at midfield in 1954 when he partnered Gerald Murphy in Cork's third successive Munster final victory over Tipperary will long be remembered by those who were present on the day.

The Munster hurling semi-final of 1963 saw Cork pitted against old rivals Tipperary. On my way home for the summer holidays I stayed overnight with a friend in Mallow. The following morning we went to Limerick for the match. On so many occasions in the past Ring was the major post-match topic of conversation. On that day in Limerick it was different – it was before the match that the maestro was on the lips of hurling followers from both counties and beyond. The Treaty City was rife with the rumour that Ring did not travel with the Cork team. It was difficult to comprehend that Cork were about to play Tipperary in a championship match without the brightest star of so many past encounters.

The optimists among us believed he would make an appearance at some stage of the match. He didn't! The magic his presence would have brought was conspicuous by its absence. As a fanatical Ring supporter I was deeply saddened because his absence further reinforced the notion that indeed the end of an era was nigh. I couldn't come to terms with the fact that the man who had thrilled Cork followers for decades was unlikely to do so again. For Ring, the big-time was in the past and we were all left to ponder on what had been. There was an attendance of over 30,000 at the match. Tipperary hurling was on the crest of a wave. The county were All-Ireland champions in 1961 and 1962. Victory that day would have sent the men in blue and gold on their way to compete for a fourth successive Munster championship win. Cork, captained by Mick McCarthy, played well and held the champions to a two point lead at half-time. A feature of the game was the fine marking by the Cork captain on the brilliant Tipperary forward Jimmy Doyle.

A 'soft goal' by Tipperary's Tom Ryan early in the second-half left hardworking Cork with a lot of work to do. The Rebels, to their credit, did not give in and with Patsy Harte, Mick Mortell, substitute Christy O'Shea and Richie Browne all adding to the score, the Premier County's lead was reduced to two points. Things were looking good for Cork until up popped Sean McLoughlin to beat a somewhat static defence and shoot the sliotar to the net. Tipperary again had a comfortable lead to which Donie Nealon added a further point.

The Leesiders had indeed fought well and were not found wanting for commitment or effort but the best team won the match. The final score was Tipperary 4-7; Cork 1-11. A five point margin in what had been a tenacious performance by the Corkmen was far from a poor result. Make no mistake about it, the victorious Tipperary team were a star-studded side, steeped in talent and experience. The Premier County had lived up to its name by ruling the roost in the recent past. It would be amiss of me not to list some of the hurling giants who wore the blue and gold jerseys of their county with such distinction, arguably unparalleled. Names which come to mind are Michael Maher, Tony

Wall, John Doyle, Jimmy Doyle, Liam Devaney, Kieran Carey, Donie Nealon, Theo English, Tom Moloughney, Matt O'Gara, Tom Ryan, Sean McLoughlin, John Hough, Michael Burns, Michael Hassett, John 'Mackey' McKenna and Liam Connolly.

Just when Tipperary seemed invincible the factor which makes every match different from all others manifested itself. The factor is unpredictability and this time it was Waterford who caused the upset. In the Munster final the Decies men beat the champions in a low-scoring game. The score was Waterford 0-11; Tipperary 0-8. The newly-installed Munster champions met Kilkenny in the All-Ireland final on 1 September at Croke Park. The attendance of 73,123 would have been only 73,122 had it not been for my presence.

Yes, at long last I got to savour my first All-Ireland hurling final. It was my great privilege to experience the magnificent occasion and witness a superb game of hurling. Eddie Keher playing at left-half forward for Kilkenny gave an unforgettable performance. Waterford were a formidable side by any standards. That came as no surprise in view of the calibre of players on the team. The surnames of Power, Cunningham, Flynn, Byrne, Guinan, Morrissey, Condon, Flannelly, Cheasty, Walsh, Barron and Grimes were enough to make any opponents apprehensive. Yet it was Kilkenny and Keher, aided by outstanding midfield player Sean Clohosey, team captain Seamus Cleere, full-forward Billy Dwyer and the talents of Walsh, Larkin, Whelan, Treacy, Carroll, McGovern and Coogan that won the day for the Leinstermen. Above all, the dexterity, poise, skill and accuracy of Eddie Keher were the deciding factors as the fourteen points he contributed to Kilkenny's total score of 4-17 shows. The importance of his contribution becomes significant when you take into account that Waterford scored an impressive 6-8.

That afternoon of hurling at its best marked the end of my summer holidays. When I got out on to the Drumcondra Road it was north and to Ballymena the red Volkswagen was headed once more. Away from the ups and downs of hurling in 1963, the Beatles continued to virtually monopolise the popular music scene. Only Gerry and the Pacemakers with 'I Like It' and 'You'll Never Walk Alone' presented any real opposition for number one spot on the singles charts. Late August will be remembered by many for the oration by American civil rights leader Martin Luther King Junior. At a peaceful demonstration by 200,000 people he expressed his 'dream' for America – 'I still have a dream. It is a dream chiefly rooted in the American dream. I have a dream that one day this nation will rise up and live out the true meaning of its creed – we hold these truths to be self evident, that all men are created equal'.

While Mr King 'dreamed' a direct telephone line, a 'hot-line', between the White House and the Kremlin was established. Its purpose was to speed up diplomatic communication between the Soviet Union and the United States. Unfortunately no 'hot-line' could prevent a rock slide in the Italian Alps which resulted in the destruction of the Viaont Dam and the tragic loss of a staggering 3,000 lives. One tragedy followed another and on 22 November news which stunned the world broke on radio and television – John F. Kennedy, president of the United States, had been assassinated in Dallas, Texas.

On a lighter note, Doctor Who, the television science-fiction show was premiered by the BBC. As 1963 drew to a close the best news was that Christy Ring had not retired from hurling. Not many would have bet their life savings against the remarkable man defying logic by showing up again on the playing fields of Thurles or Limerick come high-summer. Would we see the magic touches again?

1964

On New Year's Night 1964 in the Glens of Antrim Hotel, Cushendall, County Antrim, I proposed to Una. Una accepted and there and then we made a decision that was to change our way of life. We decided to go to Nigeria where I would take up a teaching post after we were married. Our plans came to fruition on 12 August 1964 when at 7pm on our wedding day we joined a Liverpool bound ferry at Belfast. We were on the first stage of a voyage that would take us to the shores of West Africa.

By 1964 the 'swinging sixties' was well established. People in Ireland, especially teenagers and those in their twenties, were well aware that a 'spirit of change' prevailed worldwide. It was evident in almost every aspect of life. Young people were filled with an overwhelming desire to dismantle what was perceived as old rigid traditions and lifestyles, and to replace them with their concepts of freedom, permissiveness and liberalism. The will for change was coupled with new developments in the field of science, fabrics, materials, television, medical research, fashion, design and popular music.

Associated with the change was a non-violent anarchy youth movement known as 'flower power'. It identified itself with environmental concerns and rejection of materialism. The idealistic aim of hippies, as followers of 'flower power' were known, was to get people back to nature and to uncomplicated lives of peace and love.

To the casual viewer, Ireland in 1964 may seem to have been largely unaffected by the changing attitudes elsewhere. That perception proved to be wrong. The process of change was well in motion. In a short few years we too adopted the new-age trappings. It was a time of optimism, hope and a degree of economic prosperity previously unknown. It is also worth recalling that even in Ireland the institutions of Church, State and Universities had to come to terms with the changing attitudes of the 1960s.

HURLING HEARTBREAK, POP GROUPS FLOURISH AND PROMINENT ITEMS

Change was what Cork hurling supporters were looking for. It seemed an eternity since that day in Thurles when Ring shocked Limerick to win Cork's last Munster championship. It was an abysmal record for a county that had been dubbed as 'Cork of the champions'. How much longer were we going to have to wait for a Munster crown?

In 1964 as on other years in the recent past the league campaign did not go too badly for the Rebels. They reached the semi-final before losing to Wexford by a score of 2-9 to 2-7. Ring did not play throughout the 1963-4 league and the likelihood of a championship comeback became more remote. The county badly needed a settled side and, oh, for the inspiration of a Ring-like character. Could it be that the hit tune 'Glad All Over' by a group called Dave Clark Five was an omen of better things to come for the long suffering Rebel County followers? While Beatlemania swept the world a little known Liverpool girl called Cilla Black made it to the top with the song 'Anyone who had a Heart'. It remained at number one for three weeks in February/March. The Bachelors too made their mark with 'Diane'. Cilla Black was to feature again in May with 'You're my World'. Cheap records and maximum exposure on radio and television helped to make groups and individuals household names. Few were better known than The Rolling Stones who had a first hit 'It's All Over Now' in July, and went on to remain one of the most popular groups throughout the remainder of the decade. A concert given by the group in Belfast on 31 July lasted only twelve minutes before being stopped because of rioting fans. Earlier in the year 25,000 fanatical fans came to Kennedy Airport to welcome the Beatles on their first visit to the United States. Yes, the rock music and pop culture which was to become a worldwide phenomenon was in full-swing by late 1964.

While Cork hurlers and selectors once again strove to fashion a team that would bring silverware back to Leeside and joy to the hearts of followers, the media kept us informed of events from around the world. Prominent items included the marriage of widely admired, glamorous actress Elizabeth Taylor to film star Richard Burton; the death of Second World War commander of the Pacific Forces, General McArthur; the winning of an Oscar by Sidney Poitier, the first black actor to do so; and changing the course of the mighty River Nile to make way for the final stages of the Aswan Dam development in Egypt.

Cork had beaten Galway in the first round of the Munster championship (Galway in Munster championship since 1959), before we heard that a gentleman called Nelson Mandela had been sentenced to life imprisonment in South Africa for subversive activities. By all accounts Cork had an easy win over Galway. The final score of 4-14 to 2-7 would suggest as much. Noteworthy was the contribution of Avondhu's Richie Browne who scored all of Cork's four goals. So the Rebels were through to the Munster semi-final. Waterford were to be the opponents.

My departure to Nigeria was looming and should Cork falter in the semi-final the chances were that I would not see my county hurlers in action for a long time again. With that prospect in mind I travelled south for the meeting with Waterford at Thurles. We arrived in Thurles around midday on Sunday. The renowned hurling name of Stakelum remained prominent on business fronts and all the other landmarks were in place. The aura that belonged to a tradition based on the greatest hurling occasions was in evidence all round. Even though it was only a semi-final, Waterford, always well supported, were current Munster champions, and many Cork followers like myself were no longer assured of our team reaching the final. Hence the reasons for a large attendance.

The match was not a classic and the absence of Christy Ring was still being lamented by Cork followers. I have no great memories of performances that afternoon except that Noel Gallagher scored two of Cork's goals. Waterford, true to form, fought back from being well behind to almost level the scores with a late Phil Grimes free. Uncharacteristically, Phil failed to convert and the Leesiders drew a huge sigh of relief as the final whistle sounded. The score read Cork 4-10; Waterford 5-6. The Rebels, without being spectacular, had booked a place in the final against, guess who? – Tipperary of course. I was at home during the two weeks prior to the final.

The saga of Christy Ring was ongoing. Conflicting reports which had abounded for so long continued to do so. Some said that Ring let it be known that he no longer wished to be considered for a place on the county senior team, while others said that was not the case, and basically he had been dropped by the selectors. Ring, then 43 years of age, continued to play a major role in the fortunes of his club, Glen Rovers. He captained the team to county championship victory in 1964 and scored a personal tally of one goal and four points in the final.

Many astute followers of hurling in Cork, not all Glen Rover followers I must add, were in no doubt that the maestro was good enough to be on the county senior team. Indeed he was considered by many to be the best forward on view in Cork that summer. Like so many people I talked to at the time, including a Kerryman who knew Ring well, I cannot believe that he excluded himself from selection for the county. After all, he was a showman in the best sense of the word. He loved the big 'stage' and the bigger the occasion the better.

On the July Sunday so much looked forward to in Munster, Cork took on a Tipperary team which showed four or five changes from the All-Ireland winning side of 1962. Present were the Doyles, Maher, Carey, Burns, Wall, English, Nealon, McKenna, McLaughlin and Devaney, all stalwarts of other years. A Cork side striving to emerge from obscurity and unquestionably the shadow of Ring were given only a slim chance of victory over their illustrious opponents. Still, followers of the Rebel County flocked to Limerick, determined to do what they could to encourage 'the boys'. Being underdogs isn't always a bad thing but I must admit that in spite of a 44,240 attendance at Limerick that day, much of the customary pre-match excitement and tension was absent. Was it being taken for granted by both sets of supporters that Tipperary were going to win? I asked myself if my mind was too focused on the herculean deeds of the past masters who wore the red jerseys. Basically I believe that lack of real success over a long period takes the sharp edge off enthusiasm.

During the first ten minutes of the match there was nothing to suggest that the pundits who forecasted a Tipperary win would be proved wrong. The Premier County team was strong in all positions. It was a beautifully balanced and talented team. An uphill battle was a certainty for the Corkmen. Not even Sarsfields' man, Paddy Barry, who was recalled to strengthen the forwards, could make any impression. To the best of my knowledge Paddy, then a 36-year-old, had not played championship hurling for the county since 1961. The only glimmer of hope came when team captain John O'Halloran scored a goal after about fifteen minutes into the match. As on previous occasions Jimmy Doyle tormented the Cork defence and ended up with a personal tally of ten points on the day. John O'Halloran and Mick Archer tried hard in the Cork attack but a magnificent Tipperary defence, led by the immaculate Tony Wall, outplayed them. Paddy Barry, the goalie, and Denis Murphy did sterling work in defence for the Rebels. John Hayes at midfield also played well. The final score was Tipperary 3-13; Cork 1-5. It was a fair reflection of the match and really a humiliating defeat for the Leesiders.

THE DARK CONTINENT
The best efforts of all concerned with Cork hurling were undoubtedly channelled into bringing success to the county but obviously the task was proving difficult in the short term. While Una and I were busy preparing for our wedding and a cruise via the Canary Islands that would take us to West Africa and finally to Benin City, Nigeria, popular American country singer Jim Reeves died in a plane crash. Around the same time NASA landed a spacecraft fitted with cameras on the moon. It took that particular craft only 68 hours to complete its journey. The craft we sailed on

took thirteen days to reach its destination.

Nigeria had undergone various stages of political development in modern times before becoming a federal republic in 1963. Elections were being held as we arrived in the country but unfortunately the outcome was not to the liking of all Nigerians. In time that was to prove a source of major unrest and bitter conflict which led to civil war.

Our home for the foreseeable future was situated six degrees north of the equator. Slowly we adjusted to the hot, tropical, humid, climate with an annual average temperature of 32 degrees Celsius (90 degrees Fahrenheit). It was not an ideal setting for hurling matches but that did not stop some of the Irish lads from having the occasional 'puck' around. For the duration of our stay I was dependant on newspapers to keep in touch with developments in Ireland. In September I read of yet another All-Ireland victory for Tipperary.

The impressive 5-13 to 2-8 win over Kilkenny before an attendance of 71,282 at Croke Park on 6 September gave the Premier County the famous McCarthy Cup donated by Liam of the same surname, and a native of Shanagrague, Ballygarvan, County Cork. It was the third time of lifting the trophy by Tipperary team captains in the current decade. Michael Murphy was the recipient on that occasion.

My interest in Cork hurling remained as keen as ever. I longed for the day when I would read about a 'crop' of good young players coming up through the ranks. One thing was certain – I was not going to see any hurling matches in 1965. I knew there would be other years though when the men in the red jerseys of Cork would thrill their followers. And I would be there!

1965

PARTY TIME IN NIGERIA, PRESSURE ON MENTORS AND A
COSMONAUT WALKS

A new year with a difference! On day one of 1965 under a
sweltering African sun 42 Irish expatriates met at a Club
the location of which could best be described as being in
the middle of nowhere.

It was in fact near a village called, Ososo, about 80
miles from Benin city where we lived. Ososo was chosen
because it was reasonably central for all concerned, even
though some people travelled more than 150 miles of
awful roads to be there. The vast majority of the gathering
were, like myself, teachers employed by the SMA
Missionary Order. To the best of my knowledge nine of the
32 counties were represented. Sadly for me, one of them
was Tipperary.

Wisecracks regarding the high flying hurlers of that
county, with Cork at the butt of many jokes, was the order
of the day. Fortunately there were a number of Galway folk
present and their attention was firmly focused on that
county's fine football team, the current All-Ireland champions. They didn't know it then but that team was to add
two further All-Ireland titles in in 1965 and 1966 – a magic
three in a row.

During the course of the day a few hurleys and a sliotar appeared from somewhere. Interspersed between high
jinks in the swimming pool and consuming pint bottles of
a locally-produced beverage called 'Star' beer, perspiration
flowed freely as the men from Armagh, Cavan, Donegal,
Galway, Mayo, Kerry, Tipperary, Limerick and Cork took
turns at wielding the camans. It was a great day and only
God knows how some of us returned to our destinations in
one piece. That get together led to further meetings and
mini-parties at weekends which were greatly looked forward to. There was wonderful camaraderie amongst the

Irish community. The BBC radio world service was our main source of daily news. Not surprisingly there was no reference to Gaelic games on any of its programmes. I was dependent on newspapers from home and the occasional returning priest or teaching colleague for scraps of information on the fortunes or otherwise of Cork hurling. It was becoming clearer that years of defeat in crucial championship matches, sometimes at an early stage, was causing immense frustration for followers, players and mentors alike. The latter were coming under increasing pressure to produce a winning team.

'Cork expects' had almost become a war-cry. The Rebel County had not contested an All-Ireland final for nine years and it was eleven years since the McCarthy Cup was last paraded through the streets of Cork. A lame excuse might be that Tipperary and Waterford had produced great teams during that period. The ardent follower found it difficult to understand why Cork could not at least match those teams. Not since 1960 did the Leesiders put up any real challenge to their opponents. Those were difficult times and the longer this desperate situation continued the more nervous selectors became. There was no time to 'blood' young players and no time to establish a settled side. The pressure both on players and mentors was immense. The question now was how and when could we free ourselves from the shackles of further defeats?

Understandably the worldwide music scene was totally unaffected by the misfortunes of Cork hurling. Georgie Fame and the Blue Flames were first to show with a number one hit called 'Yeh Yeh'. In late January and early February it was 'Go Now' by the Moody Blues, 'You've Lost that Lovin' Feelin'' by the Righteous Brothers, the Kinks with 'Tired of Waiting for You' and, the Seekers 'I'll Never Find Another You', that made it to the top spot. In March the Tom Jones recording of the evergreen, 'It's not Unusual' was favourite.

However, in the same month the Soviets disagreed with that sentiment and did something that was unusual – cosmonaut Aleksei Leonov became the first man to walk in space. During his fifteen-minute adventure he shot some film. In April, while the Beatles record 'Ticket To Ride' remained at the pinnacle for three weeks, the United States continued with the space theme and launched the first commercial communications satellite called *Early Bird*.

THE SAME OLD STORY AT THE GAELIC GROUNDS
The arrival of May brought with it thoughts of yet another Munster hurling championship. It wouldn't be long until the resolve of the Corkmen would be tested again. What fate lay ahead for the troubled Rebels? The possibilities were often discussed late into the night when our Irish colleagues, otherwise known as 'the boys from the bush', arrived in town for the weekend. Just how sensible those discussions were as the night wore on was anyone's guess but as long as the beer lasted and the mosquito coil continued to spiral its repellent smoke upwards nobody cared too much. As Cork's hurlers prepared to take on Waterford in the Munster semi-final one of the most popular records being played was 'King of the Road' sung by Roger Millar.

At the same time satellite television was born – millions of viewers in nine countries could tune in to a common programme. On the day of the Cork/Waterford encounter, while I relaxed beside a swimming pool, my heart was very much in Thurles. I could visualise the whole day's happenings as they unfolded. Nostalgia ran high! The result somehow came through amazingly quickly. The following evening one of the mission priests called to tell me that the match ended in a draw. He had no further details. I was later to read of a Cork fight-back with important second-half goals scored by Eddie O'Brien and Colm Sheehan.

Reference was made to an exciting ending. The score was 2-6 to each side. The replay resulted in a Cork victory with Noel Gallagher, Eddie O'Brien and Charlie McCarthy contributing most to a hard-earned 1-11 to 2-5 win. The match was said to have been marred by unpleasantness between some players. The news I didn't really want to hear soon filtered through – Tipperary would once again be Cork's opponents in the Munster final. Surely it would not again be lambs to the slaughter in Limerick for the third time in five years!

Almost intolerable pressure must have been on Cork to somehow overturn the outcomes of the immediate past encounters. Once again the Gaelic Grounds would be packed! What could the mentors and players of Cork do to alleviate the humiliation and frustration experienced by their long suffering, faithful followers?

When the great day arrived 40,000 people turned up to witness the clash. Alas, the match report which I still have to hand once again made very sad reading. The Cork team fielded had fewer household names than usual and showed some changes from the side which beat Waterford. It is not clear to me whether Paddy Barry or Finbar O'Neill played in goal, but Donal Sheehan, Patsy Harte and a man called John Redmond, all absent in the previous round, were brought in. Excluded for whatever reason were Charlie McCarthy and Colm Sheehan. I believe Colm was sent off during the replay with Waterford. The overall tone of the report inferred that the Cork team were unable to cope with the vastly experienced and talented Tipperary side. Two first-half goals from far out the field by Theo English virtually killed off Cork's challenge. A third goal early in the second-half saw a disheartened team wilt under Tipperary's superiority. A hopelessly one-sided affair ensued. In the entire game the Leesiders scored a mere single point from play. The final score was Tipperary 4-11; Cork 0-5.

Things seemed to be going from bad to worse! One observer noted Cork followers leaving the Gaelic Grounds at half-time – a sad day indeed for Rebel County hurling. Many who over the years had predicted a Cork return to greatness were beginning to have their doubts. The ignominious defeat of 1965 was devastating. A further twist of the knife was inflicted by the Premier County in September when it went on to beat Wexford by a score of 2-16 to 0-10 in the All-Ireland final. For some that was the unkindest cut of all because John Doyle equalled Christy Ring's record of eight All-Ireland senior hurling medals. Perhaps Nigeria was a good place to be just then. The further one is removed from the scene of the anguish, the less painful it is.

WHITE EMULATES AND TWO FIRSTS BUT A CHILD IS BORN

While the names of Sandie Shaw, Elvis Presley, the Beatles and the Hollies vied for number one hits, an American astronaut, Edward White, emulated the feat of Aleksei Leonov by taking a twenty-minute walk in space. He remained attached to his *Gemini 4* spacecraft. Two firsts of 1965 were the introduction of starting gates for horse racing and the linking of France and Italy by road. The former took place at Newmarket (England) and the latter was achieved by building a tunnel road through the Alps. The tunnel, which is over seven miles long took six years to complete. It was in 1965 on 15 August, while a Beatle concert in New York was creating a new outdoor audience record by attracting 56,000 fans that 20,000 National Guards were called out to control race riots in Los Angeles.

The end of a first full year in Nigeria was filled with joy for at least two Irish expatriates because on 16 December our first child, a baby girl, saw the light of day in Benin City. While 1965 might be a year to forget in the annals of Cork hurling, we had good reason to remember it.

— 1966 —

Joan, John and Sophia Make News
but What about Christy?

Joan Baez, a female vocalist from the United States, had a series of hit singles in the charts during 1965 and 1966. In January 1966 'Farewell Angelina' was one such number. There was, however, another reason why the 25-year-old singer made news headlines as Joan was imprisoned. It was her obsession with anti-Vietnam war activities which led to the ten-day sentence. Hitting the headlines in early 1966 was a statement made by Beatle John Lennon. With reference to the Beatles he said, 'We're more popular than Jesus Christ right now'. While he didn't suffer the same fate as Joan Baez, the remark was regarded as outrageously inappropriate by many people. The number one hits of January and February had a distinctive athletic ring to them. Firstly it was the Spencer Davis Group with 'Keep on Running', followed by 'These Boots were made for Walking' sung by Nancy Sinatra.

With the tropical sun daily blasting the laterite surrounding our home in Benin city I could be excused for doubting the credibility of one particular hit called 'The Sun Ain't Gonna Shine Anymore' by the Walker Brothers. On 9 April, the marriage between Sophia Loren, one of the screen goddesses of the era, and film producer Carlo Ponti took place. The event received much publicity. With no publicity at all Mike Tyson, who was to become a world heavyweight boxing champion, was born on 30 June. In the interim the information I gleaned on the hurling scene from Ireland made for sad reading where Cork was concerned. It was the men who wore the black and amber jerseys of Kilkenny and those displaying the blue and gold of Tipperary who were again prominent. In the league semi-final Kilkenny easily beat Cork. The final score of 4-11 to 1-8 left the Rebel County followers still despairing. Even the most ardent follower found it unrealistic to confidently predict an upturn of fortune in the forthcoming championship. Once again it was the unenviable job of the selectors to look around for new talent. Was a bit of 'old' talent a possibility?

Amazingly 46-year-old Christy Ring was still playing well for the Glen Rovers club. Could it be that in spite of being out of the county team for two years we would see him don the red jersey again? Certainly there were many who thought it a real possibility.

While the pros and cons of Ring's return were debated, it seemed that a majority of the selectors were looking towards more youthful players to return Cork to its winning ways.

A JOYOUS HOMECOMING, NOSTALGIA AND RELIEF AT LIMERICK
Cork played a good Clare team in the first round of the Munster championship. The match took place in Limerick and ended in a draw. It took a last minute goal by Justin McCarthy to level the score.

The replay, again in Limerick, saw Cork emerge as easy winners. Seanie Barry accounted for 2-6 of Cork's total score of 5-11. Clare registered 1-7. So Cork had beaten Clare well but still no one was getting too excited. Just as significant was the fact that at the Athletic Grounds, Limerick eliminated the all-conquering Premier County men from the championship. Cork would now meet Limerick in the Munster semi-final at Killarney on 10 July.

Regardless of the thousands of miles separating me from the hurling scene, thoughts of that fixture excited me. Perhaps it was intensified by the fact that on 12 July I would be back in Ireland on holiday – a holiday that would last until 12 September. As we waited at Heathrow Airport for a connecting flight to Belfast, I read a match report on the 'Sunday game'. A glance at the first line gave me the news I most wanted to hear – Cork had won – they had beaten Limerick by eight points. The words, 'new, young team', were music to my ears. I remember noting the names of Mick Waters and John O'Halloran, my UCC contemporaries, and that the McCarthy surname was prominent. I was elated because now I would see Cork play on Munster final day. I couldn't believe my luck!

As chart toppers 'Strangers in the Night' sung by Frank Sinatra and, 'Sunny Afternoon' by the Kinks entertained the population at large that July, 34-year-old French film star and sex-symbol, Brigette Bardot, married millionaire playboy Gunter Sachs. It was good to be back in Ireland! The excursion to Limerick for the provincial decider between Cork and Waterford brought back memories of past visits to the Treaty city. There was a buzz about the place and a new-found hope was evident in the hearts of Rebel County followers. Their team had a refreshing look. Yes, there was 'something in the air' that day, yet history of the recent past had firmly ingrained an apprehension which would remain at least into the late afternoon when the final whistle sounded.

There were few, if any, in Limerick that day who gave a thought to England's football team who were on the verge of becoming world champions. Interest too would have been minimal on the securing of the number one spot in the hit parade by Chris Farlowe and the Thunderbirds with the tune 'Out Of Time'. As hurling followers trod the familiar route to the Gaelic Grounds maybe some with an interest in equestrian matters found time to discuss a development which was to bring about an element of equality in the world of racehorse training. A woman, Mrs Florence Nagle, was about to be granted a training licence in England. She was the first woman ever to be recognised as such by the Stewards of the Jockey Club.

All stray thoughts were obliterated from the mind by the cry of, 'programme of the match', coming from boys on the roadside. It took me a little time to familiarise myself with the Cork team line-out though I did recognise some names immediately. Stalwarts such as Paddy Fitzgerald, Peter Doolan, John Bennett, Gerry O'Sullivan, Denis O'Riordan and Paddy Barry had passed this way before. Still the presence of youth was evident with the emergence of three McCarthys – Gerald, Charlie and Justin, Seanie Barry, Tony Connolly, Mick Waters and to a certain extent John O'Halloran and Colm Sheehan. Could that team end Cork's ten-year Munster championship drought? Whenever I reflect on Munster final matches it is always those played against Tipperary which come to mind. The fierce intensity of those encounters left a lasting impression. The match against Waterford that day did little to erase that fixation.

In truth it was a poor, one-sided game. Cork played against a strong breeze in the first-half and led by a goal at half-time. A most inept performance by the Waterfordmen showed little spirit, determination or will to win. The sole exception was Larry Guinan. His brilliant second-half display was crowned by a wonderful goal at the end of a 100-yard solo run. It is always a great pleasure to recall such a marvellous individual feat. The name of Cork's veteran corner-forward John Bennett, then 33 years of age, was also on the lips of many because he scored two well-taken goals to ensure that his county did indeed end its sad chapter in championship hurling history. The final score was Cork 4-9; Waterford 2-9.

The men of the Rebel County were again Munster champions! Relief and a degree of elation summed up the mood of all associated with Cork hurling as they left the Gaelic Grounds after the match. Niggling questions still remained in the minds of many followers. Their team had not really been tested by Waterford; it had scraped past Clare on the first outing; so far luck had played some part. How would it fare against better opposition like the Kilkennys of this world?

THRILLED BEYOND BELIEF – A GREAT DAY

In keeping with the mood of the time the summer of 1966 was for the most part fine and sunny. There was an air of optimism all around.

For the first time multi-national companies began to open up factories in Ireland. All of a sudden money seemed to be more plentiful than ever before. In August, while the hurlers of Cork and Kilkenny booked their places in the All-Ireland final, the world of popular music was dominated by the hit tunes 'With a Girl Like You' by the Troggs, and a double dose by the Beatles in the form of 'Eleanor Rigby' and 'Yellow Submarine'.

To know that on Sunday 4 September I would take my place among the thousands of hurling followers in Croke Park thrilled me beyond belief. It didn't matter that Cork were rank outsiders. On that most wonderful of Sunday mornings Dublin's O'Connell Street was transformed. Cars with banner-waving passengers sped by as pedestrians bedecked with rosettes, denoting allegiance to one county or the other, crowded the footpaths. The Noresiders, displaying the black and amber, may have had more of a swagger about them but they were outnumbered by the Leesiders who flaunted the red and white. It may have been ten years since Cork last contested an All-Ireland final but the county had a proud and enviable record. Croke Park was resplendent. Its green carpet-like surface had been mowed to perfection. In the packed stands and terraces the sea of colour was magnificent. Followers, now a little excited laughed and joked nervously as they waited with patient expectation for the teams to emerge from the changing rooms. The eagerly awaited hurling contest between the esteemed rivals and renowned exponents of the game was foremost in the minds of the 68,000 attendance. The Cork team lined out with a single change from the side that won the Munster crown. Gerry O'Sullivan replaced the injured Denis O'Riordan at centre-half back. Paddy Barry was the goalkeeper. The full-back line read Peter Doolan, Tom O'Donoghue and Denis Murphy. At half-back were Tony Connolly, Gerry O'Sullivan and Paddy Fitzgerald. The midfield pair were Justin McCarthy and Mick Waters. Seanie Barry, John O'Halloran and team captain, Gerald McCarthy made a formidable half-forward line, while up front Charlie McCarthy, Colm Sheehan and John Bennett completed the starting line-out.

The weather on the day was not as kind as it might have been. A strong wind blew towards the Railway end and showers left the surface of the pitch a little slippery. As throw-in time approached tension increased and it was the Cork supporters who felt it most. The doubts returned: most of the Cork team had no Croke Park experience and certainly none on All-Ireland day; team captain Gerald McCarthy was still an under-21 player; they were really raw recruits up against a vastly-experienced Kilkenny side. Yet, when the teams ran on to the pitch it was the men in red who received the greatest ovation. Perhaps it was because visits to Croke Park had become second nature to Kilkenny folk. With the team photographs taken and the pre-match puck about over it was time for the parade. Behind the Artane Boys band, led by respective captains, came the 'novices' of Cork and the tough, talented and experienced men of Kilkenny. My heart pounded as the parade passed by and at that moment all the pride, passion and emotion which had ebbed away somewhat during the years of defeat flowed back like a swollen river – in torrents. Kilkenny's captain Jim Lynch won the toss and elected to play with the wind. The players took up their positions, faced the tricolour, and stood to attention as the strains of our national anthem filled the air – another poignant moment. By then every nerve in my body was tingling. I wasn't alone though. I could sense it all around me. With all eyes now focused on the referee and the four players in the middle of the park the match got underway. I was immediately impressed by the workman-like approach of Cork. They chased, pulled on the sliotar, blocked, closed down and competed in a way that I had not seen from the Rebels for a long time. Playing against the wind the Cork defence was doing a tremendous job in curtailing and frustrating the Kilkenny forwards. Paddy Barry, who was having an outstanding match, made two magnificent saves in the first-half. The first score, a point by Eddie Keher, went to Kilkenny. Cork continued to battle well but were not rewarded until well into the half when Seanie Barry scored a point from a free.

Kilkenny at that stage led by two points. By then every person in Croke Park was aware that this Cork team meant business and were not going to be beaten easily. Justin McCarthy and Mick Waters were winning the all important midfield battle with John Teehan and Paddy Moran. It was no less pleasing to see Seanie Barry, John O'Halloran and Gerald McCarthy denying the Kilkenny half-back line of Seamus Cleere, Ted Carroll and Martin Coogan the kind of possession they required to get their forwards moving. Then, in the twenty-first minute, the Rebel County followers went delirious when Colm Sheehan caught the sliotar as it rebounded off the crossbar and shot it to the net. A great goal! It further encouraged the Cork players who ended the first-half looking the better side. The score at the interval was Kilkenny 0-7; Cork 1-2. Charlie McCarthy was the scorer of Cork's second point, a ground shot that went over the bar.

The second-half began with the Rebels again showing a determination which was food and drink to their followers. Early scores from Gerald McCarthy and Seanie Barry left the score level. Then came a vital score. Again it was Colm Sheehan who supplied it. He took a pass from John Bennett and smashed the sliotar to the net for Cork's second goal. The followers of the men in red were ecstatic even before Seanie Barry further increased the lead. When a speculative puck towards the posts by John O'Halloran ended up in the net, apparently off the shoulder of Colm Sheehan, the place erupted as Cork supporters, starved of success, purged themselves of the misery that had bedevilled them for so long. Further points by Justin McCarthy and Seanie Barry made life even more difficult for the men in black and amber. A late Kilkenny goal by Tom Walsh did little to change the match or the mood of the Cork supporters and further points by Seanie Barry and John Bennett put the icing on the cake.

The final score was Cork 3-9; Kilkenny 1-10. It was indeed a remarkable victory which was received with all the pomp it deserved. It was a proud day for the supporters and men who represented their county so admirably. The team which many down by the Lee had reservations about, was given no chance of winning by punters outside of Cork. A great day indeed! The pertinent question being asked in the aftermath of the triumph was, 'Have Cork hurling at last emerged from the shadow of Ring'. Less than a week later Una, our baby daughter Carrie, and myself returned to Nigeria.

A WORLD OF SADNESS AND HISTORY MAKING

In October the world was shocked and saddened by a disaster which claimed the lives of 144 people. It happened in the small Welsh village of Aberfan. A huge coal tip slipped and engulfed part of the village, including a junior school. 116 children lost their lives! On 8 November Edward Brooke became the first black senator in the history of the United States, and at the comparatively young age of 65, Walt Disney died on 15 December.

Looking back on the number one hits of late 1966, 'Distant Drums' sung by Jim Reeves occupied the number one spot for five weeks during September and October. 'Reach Out I'll Be There' by the Four Tops had a three-week stint at the top in October and November, but it was the song that echoed the sentiments of all expatriates, 'Green Green Grass of Home', sung by Tom Jones, that remained number one for seven weeks throughout December and early January.

1967

THE DELTA, ROBERT DEPARTS, A SHOCK!, CELTIC GLORY, ALI AND ELVIS

The Niger delta region of Nigeria is not a particularly inviting place at any time of year. Yet it was there that the New Year of 1967 was welcomed in by some Irish folk. Those of us who made our way to the outpost of Osoro the previous day woke up the following morning to find the whole area enveloped by a fog, or mist, so thick that visibility was down to a matter of feet. Within one hour the fierce rays of the equatorial sun had forced their way through the stupor thereby causing a sharp temperature rise accompanied by a humidity level that made it almost impossible to breathe. Perspiration literally flowed through the body pores in streams. It was in this mosquito-ridden African outpost situated more than 30 miles from Warri that four Irish lads lived and worked. Perhaps they had invited us just to experience the conditions. However, all was not doom and gloom and once we had established defences to keep the mosquitoes at bay, party-time began. In spite of the difficult conditions the 'delta-lads', one of them Hugh McGonigle a Sligo county Gaelic footballer, did us proud. The party lasted two days. It was a long, long 170 miles back to Benin City on 3 January. Early 1967 was reasonably uneventful and only the death of physicist Robert Oppenheimer, who was in charge of the development of the atomic bomb, catches the eye.

Number one hits by the Monkees, 'I'm a Believer', and Petula Clark's 'This is my Song', preceded the very popular 'Release Me' by Engelbert Humperdinck. More than ever my thoughts were with the team which had made 1966 so special for all Corkonians with an interest in hurling. I was satisfied that the team could only get better and regretted that this year I would miss seeing them play. With those sentiments in mind I waited in patient expectation for a report on a first round Munster championship match.

The All-Ireland champions had been drawn against a

Waterford side which had faded out of prominence since 1963. The outcome was not in doubt – Cork would trash them. The newspaper bearing an account of the match duly arrived. As I hurriedly opened up the paper Una advised me to prepare myself for a shock. Waterford had beaten Cork! I couldn't believe what I was reading! As I scanned the passage I noted a final score of 3-10 to 1-8; Cork full-back, Tom O'Donoghue, dismissed; Cork fail to score in the second-half. How could what was widely believed to be an up and coming Cork team fall at the first hurdle to lowly Waterford? What had happened to the team which just nine months ago showed so much character, spirit, grit and determination in disposing of a strong, talented Kilkenny side in the All-Ireland final? Was the restoration of Cork hurling to the top flight to be short lived? Those and many similar questions were left unanswered in the wake of the fiasco which had occurred at Walsh Park.

While there may have been despondency in Cork, that was certainly not the case in Glasgow, or at least part of it. Celtic Football Club had just won the European Cup final! The Scottish champions conquered Inter Milan at the Stadium of Light, Portugal, thus becoming the first British club to win the trophy. The side was managed by Jock Stein, winger Jimmy 'Jinky' Johnstone was the star of the show and Steve Chalmers scored the winning goal six minutes from time. The final score was 2-1. Elsewhere engaging issues included Muhammad Ali, world heavyweight boxing champion, being stripped of his crown for refusing to be conscripted into the United States Army. But for millions of females worldwide the event which caused greatest anguish was the marriage of Elvis Presley to Priscilla Beaulieu, in Las Vegas, on 1 May. Frank Sinatra, who combined with daughter Nancy, pushed 'Something Stupid' all the way. Then along came Sandie Shaw who took off her shoes and, singing barefoot, made 'Puppet On A String' the favourite number.

FRANCIS TOPS, NIGERIA ADIEU, WARS LONG AND SHORT
An outstanding solo achievement of 1967 was the round-the-world voyage by 65-year-old yachtsman Francis Chichester. It took 119 days to complete the trip which ended in Plymouth on 28 May. Two days later, while Francis Chichester was being toasted by friends and the

yachting fraternity throughout the world, the political situation in Nigeria worsened. Cause for concern became a reality.

In a development which had filtered down from the overthrow of the civilian government and the murders of leading figures, including the prime minister, one of the four regions which made up the federation unilaterally seceded. The breakaway Eastern Region adopted a name which was later to become synonymous with famine and starvation – Biafra. The military-led Nigerian government was aggrieved by the Biafran breakaway and insisted that the federation must be preserved. Biafra refused to conform and civil war ensued.

Almost immediately the exodus of expatriates began with Americans leading the way. Initially the conflict was confined to the Eastern Region/Biafra, with actual fighting first reported on 8 July. The imposing River Niger separated the Mid-West Region where we lived from the Eastern Region. The only road crossing was 90 miles away at the newly-erected state-of-the-art bridge linking Asaba with the Eastern Region town of Onitcha. Against all predictions the war quickly spread into the Mid-West Region and at 9am on Wednesday 9 August Benin City was taken over by the Biafran Army.

Consternation followed – we were moved out of our house while frantic behind-the-scenes negotiations involving the British High Commission took place. The aim now was to secure safe passage out of the country for hundreds of expatriates including the Irish. An incident on the morning of the Biafran takeover stands out in my mind. Two federal army soldiers, on-the-run, came to our door and demanded civilian clothes. They had guns but seemed in no way threatening. Nevertheless, Una did not hesitate to grant their request. They quickly changed, discarded their uniforms and guns in our sitting room and ran out the backdoor. Before we were moved out of the house we put the soldiers belongings into a wardrobe. Later we learned that houses were being searched and a radio announcement stated that those found helping or harbouring members of the Nigerian federal army would be executed. The contents of our wardrobe had to be retrieved and dumped! The risky quarter-mile journey back to our house in the midst of gunshots coming from the nearby airport will long remain with Una and myself.

On a lighter note, in spite of the gravity of our plight in the days that followed, an Irish couple who had planned to marry a year later and honeymoon on the way home, decided to bring the wedding forward. So in the midst of a civil war, long after curfew, in a secluded church, by the light of flickering candles, our friends Tom and Maura became Mr and Mrs McMahon.

On Sunday 13 August a convoy of cars and buses packed with Irish and British nationals left Benin City for the port of Sapele. There we boarded a German cargo ship which landed us in Lagos the following day. From Lagos, British Airways flew us to London where we were given refugee status. Thus ended a three-year sojourn which for the most part was a thoroughly enjoyable experience and certainly a memorable period.

Nigeria was not the only troubled nation at the time. The Vietnam war continued to rage on and a short but significant war between Israel and its Arab neighbours lasted only six days. The outcome was a decisive victory for the Israelis with massive territorial gains. On 8 July cinema fans were saddened by the death of 53-year-old Vivien Leigh who starred in the film 'Gone With The Wind'. During the spring and early summer the number one hits to rule the roost were 'Silence is Golden' by the Tremeloes, 'Whiter Shade of Pale' by Procol Harum, and 'All You Need is Love' by the Beatles.

A Job, the Unexpected, a Trio Depart and Worldwide Attention

Within weeks of our return from Nigeria I took up a teaching post at Cross and Passion College, Ballycastle. On Sunday 3 September I was unexpectedly back in Croke Park for the All-Ireland hurling final. The teams competing for the ultimate trophy in hurling that day were Tipperary and Kilkenny. Would Kilkenny be denied by a Munster team for the second year running? Would the Noresiders in the black and amber overcome the stigma of not having beaten the Premier County in an All-Ireland final since 1922? The 64,241 attendance witnessed the answers unfold first hand. A majestic performance from Pat Henderson, backed up by Pa Dillon and team captain Jim Treacy sowed the seeds for a win which was more decisive than the four-point margin suggests. Ollie Walsh in the Kilkenny goal gave a brilliant display. The final score was Kilkenny 3-8; Tipperary 2-7.

There was a hint of finality about the titles of two chart toppers in the autumn of 1967 – the 'Last Waltz' by Engelbert Humperdinck and 'Let the Heartaches Begin' by Long John Baldry. There was a finality too in the lives of 33-year-old Brian Epstein, the man most responsible for the emergence of the Beatles, and of 70-year-old Sir John Cockroft, the nuclear physicist who, along with Irish physicist Ernest Walton, succeeded in splitting the nucleus of an atom for the first time. In October, the shooting dead of the 39-year-old charismatic revolutionary, Che Guevara, by Bolivian troops was received with mixed feelings. The man who had helped Fidel Castro win power in Cuba was admired and renowned for his guerrilla techniques. The year was drawing to a close when the Bee Gees sang their way to the top with 'Massachusetts' and the Beatles began a seven-week stay in pole position with 'Hello Goodbye'. Yet to come in 1967 was an accomplishment which was to command worldwide attention. On 3 December in a Cape Town hospital the extraordinary surgical skills of Dr Christian Barnard successfully performed a human heart transplant operation. It was the first human organ replacement of its kind. The achievement which gave 'new heart' to many sufferers was probably the most widely discussed topic of 1967.

1968

CONTRASTS

What a difference a year can make! The contrast experienced between the sweltering heat of the Niger delta in January 1967, and the icy-cold , biting, wind blowing on to the north coast of Ireland in January 1968 could scarcely have been greater. Perhaps the blood had thinned a little in the tropics. For whatever reason the winter weather of early 1968 seemed extremely cold. It was good to be back in Ireland and I looked forward to the milder days of spring and the renewed vigour it would bring with it.

TIPPERARY REINFORCES CLAIM

The Cork hurlers were somehow caught-on-the-hop by Waterford last year. Surely they would bounce back in the forthcoming championship! But was there any reason to suggest that would happen? The first real test of Rebel County resolve came when they met Tipperary in the National Hurling League semi-final. The hopes of Cork followers who believed that their county was now good enough to beat the men in blue and gold were shattered. The catalogue of defeats at the hands of Tipperary which had now spanned an unbelievable eleven years continued. A 1-15 to 2-7 score-line made sad reading for Leesiders. With the passing of each year the Premier County's claim to the title of undisputed kings of Munster hurling grew stronger. What could Cork do to challenge the claim? Whatever it was it lay with the mentors, selectors and players. One thing was certain – there would be no hiding place and the steadfastness of all concerned would be put to the test on the playing fields of Thurles or Limerick in early summer.

WINNERS AND LOSERS

Popular music boasted eight number one hits between January and April. It began with the 'Ballad of Bonnie and Clyde' by Georgie Fame, and ended with 'What A Wonderful World' by Louis Armstrong. Between times there was, 'Everlasting Love' by Love Affair, 'Mighty Quinn' by Manfred Mann, 'Cinderella Rockefella' by Ester and Abi Ofarim, 'The Legend Of Xanadu' by Dave Dee, Dozy, Becky, Mitch and Tich, 'Lady Madonna' by the Beatles, and 'Congratulations' by Cliff Richard.

The title of the latter hit could well have been directed towards renowned skier Jean-Claude Killy. In 1968 the Frenchman won all three men's gold medals at the Winter Olympics in Grenoble. He was only the second man to do so. Across the world though there was much grief and sadness. Leading civil rights leader Dr Martin Luther King, recipient of the Nobel Peace Prize in 1964, was shot dead. Sadness too accompanied the death of 32-year-old motor racing champion Jim Clark. He was killed when his Lotus went out of control while taking part in the Formula Two championship at Hockenhein. Tragedy struck our own country too when on a beautiful mid-summer Sunday afternoon, Aer Lingus Viscount Flight 712, inexplicably plunged 17,000 feet into the sea two miles south of the Tuscar Rock. Of the 57 passengers and four crew members who perished only fourteen bodies were recovered. It was the single biggest loss of life in Irish aviation history. In early June, five years after the assassination of President John F. Kennedy it was the death of John F.'s brother Robert which monopolised news bulletins worldwide. The 42-year-old Senator was shot in the head at a Los Angeles hotel.

THEY WILL IMPROVE
Back home the Munster hurling championship was underway. Cork played Limerick in the opening round at Thurles. A match report refers to a comfortable win for the Leesiders. The names of John O'Halloran at centre-forward, Mick Waters at midfield, and Tony Connolly at full-forward, received special mention. The final score was Cork 3-11; Limerick 2-9. Galway were Cork's opponents in the semi-final. The venue was the Gaelic Grounds, Limerick. Cork cruised to a 3-15 to 1-6 victory. So Cork had recorded two good wins – the five-point margin over Limerick being tripled in the disposing of Galway. Still few believed that the Rebels would topple their arch rivals. The Tipperarymen were strongly tipped to retain their crown. I travelled to the Minster final more in hope than

with any real conviction of a Cork victory. Before the match, in spite of the 43,238 attendance, the atmosphere was somewhat subdued. Tipperary followers had become saturated with success while Cork's faithful were punch drunk from repeated defeats at the hands of their neighbours. The clashes between the counties had now lost the keen edge which had been honed in the past by equally matched teams displaying a rivalry and competitiveness of mammoth proportions.

The match that day was indeed to prove a further disappointment. Cork struggled from the start. Tipperary played well within themselves and looked capable of upping the pace if required to do so. The scores were level early in the second-half, yet Cork's hold on the match was so tenuous that when a speculative shot by Tipperary's Michael 'Babs' Keating found its way to the net the match as a contest was over. A late scrambled goal by Tom Ryan for the Rebels did little to change the inevitable outcome. The final score was Cork 1-7; Tipperary 2-13.

It was well into the small hours of Monday morning when my fellow travellers and I arrived home. Discussions on the match, the teams, the personalities and the future took up much of the time during the long journey back to north Antrim. Around stalwarts like Burns, Nealon, Doyle (Jimmy), McKenna and Devaney, younger men slotted in very comfortably. The consensus of opinion was that the Tipperary team we saw that day may not yet be as formidable as of yore but it would only be a matter of time until they were. On the evidence to date the same could not be said of Cork. In fact it looked as though the 1966 All-Ireland victory had been a flash-in-the-pan. As Tipperary geared up for another Croke Park visit there was little to suggest that in the foreseeable future the Leesiders, or any other Munster county, would challenge its superiority.

AN AMAZING MATCH
On Sunday 1 September along with a few hurling-mad north Antrim men I took up a place on Hill 16. The teams to contest the All-Ireland final that year were Wexford and Tipperary. Soon after I got to know hurling enthusiasts in Antrim, I discovered that on All-Ireland day they tended to support the Leinster team – Kilkenny was probably the favourite. On this occasion I concurred by supporting the

underdogs, Wexford. I would have to admit that my motive was largely negative. I wanted Tipperary beaten!

As the first-half of the match unfolded my disappointment with Wexford was matched by admiration for Tipperary. The Premier County men were outstanding and gave what could justifiably be described as one of the great Croke Park performances. Team captain Mick Roche demonstrated vast skills with the greatest of ease. It was a sad Wexford team which left the field at half-time. A late goal by Jack Berry gave the score a respectability Wexford scarcely deserved. It read Tipperary 1-11; Wexford 1-3. The second-half began with Tipperary mounting attack after attack. Now the Wexford defence was showing more resolve and the scores did not come as easily as in the first-half. In fact it was Wexford who scored first, a point by Jack Berry. Midfield too was beginning to dominate through the efforts of Phil Wilson and Dave Bernie. Importantly, a half-time change in the Wexford team which brought Paul Lynch on to Mick Roche was paying enormous dividends. Was one of the greatest turnabouts ever seen in an All-Ireland final about to manifest itself? A typical goal by the powerful Tony Doran was to further encourage the Wexfordmen.

Tipperary, however, were in no mood to bow to the rejuvenated Slaneysiders, and a battle ensued with veteran Liam Devaney prominent. Wexford held their nerve and when midway through the half Paul Lynch scored a goal from a 21-yard free, the sides were level. In spite of the relentless efforts of Tipperary, further goals from Berry and Doran were to prove decisive. The final score was Wexford 5-8; Tipperary 3-12. The 63,461 attendance had witnessed an amazing match. So many of the ingredients which make hurling the great game it is were demonstrated by elite performers. Full marks to the great men who thrilled the Croke Park patrons and, to none more so than Wexford's team captain Dan Quigley. Dan, with an inspirational second-half to his credit, was a tower of strength at centre-back – a true captain indeed.

HITS, PRAGUE AND DERRY
As the seasons of 1968 progressed in natural order, pop musicians churned out number one hits with apparent ease. Groups or individuals to make it to the top included

Union Jack, Rolling Stones, Equals, Des O'Connor, Beach Boys, Beatles, Mary Hopkins, Bee Gees, Hugo Montenegro, Joe Cocker and Scaffold. It was Mary Hopkins singing 'Those Were the Days' who remained longest at the pinnacle. Other popular tunes were 'Lily the Pink' by Scaffold, 'Hey Jude' by the Beatles and,'The Good, the Bad and the Ugly' by Hugo Montenegro and his Orchestra and Chorus. The Beach Boys hit 'Do it Again' coincided with the Soviet invasion of Prague. It is unlikely that the Soviets took their cue from that tune title when in August they decided 'to save the Czech nation' from moves towards democracy introduced by Alexander Dubcek. The Soviet masters in Moscow decided to restore the established communist doctrines. Nearer home in October the title of Mary Hopkins hit might have been interpreted as a sign of things to come. It was on 5 October that a civil rights march in Derry was broken up by police using water cannons and batons. The actions in Derry that day may well have been the spark to finally ignite a smouldering, long felt dissatisfaction born out of perceived injustices.

As 1968 drew to a close a note of sadness accompanied the announcement that the world's largest passenger liner *Queen Elizabeth* had made her last transatlantic crossing. The ship that transported the rich and the famous in the lap of luxury, had finally been decommissioned - it was no longer economically viable. Though John Steinbeck died just before Christmas, thankfully his realist novels such as *The Grapes of Wrath, East of Eden* and *Of Mice and Men* will live on for ever.

1969

HISTORY AND SONG

The titles of both song and the group responsible for the number one hit on 1 January left one wondering what 1969 had in store. It was the catchy number 'Ob-La-Di-Ob-La-Da' by Marmalade. 'Lily the Pink' returned briefly but, it was 'Albatross' by Fleetwood Mac which reigned supreme at the end of the month. There was little interest in popular music in Czechoslovakia. In that country the Soviet invasion led to the crushing of recently-introduced economic, political and cultural reforms with awesome military might. On 19 January, Jan Palach, a young student, set fire to himself in Wenceslaus Square, Prague, in protest against the invasion.

Early February was marked by the emergence of long-time nationalist politician Yasser Arafat as leader of the Palestine Liberation Organisation. Worthy of note too was the death of actor Boris Karloff who specialised in horror films, including the monster in 'Frankenstein'. The Beatles were to cause widespread anguish among their fans in 1969 when they gave their last live performance in London on the roof of the Apple building. The world of pop music rolled on and groups, some of whom were inspired by the Beatles, continued to entertain with hits such as 'Blackberry Way' by Move and, the much loved 'Where do you go to my Lovely' by Peter Sarstedt.

During March and April Israel was brought to our attention by two entirely different happenings. In March 70-year-old Golda Meir made history by becoming Israel's first female Prime Minister. A month later a group called Desmond Dekker and the Aces had a number one hit with 'The Israelites'.

TALES OF THE SEA AS CORK SUCCEEDS

With spring in the air at least one young man's thoughts turned to love; Beatle John Lennon married Yoko Ono. Perhaps though it was the more adventurous achievements of spring and early summer which were most widely acclaimed. Robin-Knox Johnston became a household name within days of completing a solo, non-stop round-the-world trip in his yacht, *Suhaili*. The voyage took 312 days to complete. On a similar theme, Irishman Tom McLean became the first person to make a transatlantic crossing in a rowing boat. His voyage began at Newfoundland and ended at Blacksod Bay, County Mayo. Shortly after Tom's feat, again it was an Atlantic crossing which created interest. Thor Heyerdahl of Kon-Tiki fame along with seven crew members set sail from Morocco to conquer the ocean in a boat built from papyrus reeds.

June, as always, meant only one thing for hurling enthusiasts – the provincial championships. In Munster, Cork had already beaten Clare after a replay. The score was 3-8 to 1-4, with Charlie McCarthy scoring all three goals for the Leesiders. At Limerick, in the Munster semi-final, Galway met the Corkmen. The 3-15 to 1-10 score-line was reported as a fair reflection of the match. Galway, who were not to play in the Munster championship again, succumbed easily to Cork. The Leesiders, as often in the past, had brushed aside all comers only to meet stonewall-like Tipperary in the Munster final. Were we to be disappointed again on the big day?

Things were a little different than in previous years because the Rebel County men were current National League champions. In the semi-final of that competition on a date for Corkmen to remember, 13 April 1969, their team beat Tipperary for the first time since May 1957! By all accounts there was great jubilation in Thurles that afternoon. Cork went on to overcome the challenge of All-Ireland champions Wexford in the final and take the Royal Liver National Hurling League trophy back to Leeside after a sixteen-year interval. The pedigree of the Cork team to face Tipperary in the Munster final of 1969 was better than of late. Dare we raise our hopes for the clash scheduled to take place on 27 July?

There was certainly some optimism in the air and the apparent powerful magnetic force which had attracted me to Munster finals for so long was showing an upturn in strength that July. Among the 43,569 attendance at Limerick's Gaelic Grounds the red and white of Cork was much more prominent than the blue and gold of Tipperary. Were Tipperary followers waiting for the All-

Ireland final? The match was scarcely underway when Youghal man Willie Walsh received a pass from Tom Ryan and crashed the sliotar to the net. Points were exchanged before Willie again beat Tipperary goalkeeper John O'Donoghue.

Further points were exchanged before Charlie McCarthy added a third goal to Cork's tally. At half-time the score read Cork 3-4; Tipperary 0-4. We had to pinch ourselves to make sure it was not a dream. In addition to the aforementioned, Tom Ryan and Pat Hegarty had also contributed to Cork's score. Jimmy Doyle had accounted for three of Tipperary's points, with a single from P.J. Ryan.

Cork were playing well but the crowd somehow gave the impression that they were waiting for Tipperary to explode into action. It was far too tense to allow any thoughts of victory to enter one's head.

Cork played into the breeze after the re-start and ominously Tipperary scored five points without reply. But somehow Denis Coughlan, who was playing well at midfield, stepped in to stop the rot. By then it was well into the second period of play. It was a trying time for Cork with the defence being severely tested and goalkeeper, Paddy Barry, performing heroics. This time the Rebels withstood onslaughts that in the past would have sunk them. They were playing well as a unit, better than I had seen for a long, long, time and finally the belief that maybe our day had come slowly dawned. Party time began when Willie Walsh scored his third goal of the day. That along with a second Denis Coughlan point set Cork on their way to victory. Tipperary were not to score again! Cork finished convincing winners.

My eyes were fixed on the scoreboard. It read Cork 4-6; Tipperary 0-9. I believe that Cork followers were shocked by the score margin and, by the magnificent victory for which we had waited so long. How I wished I was heading back to Cork that evening. It was the following day before the real significance of the win sunk in. A mighty veil had been drawn over all the defeats of the past twelve years. The Tipperary spell had finally been broken! The men who did it were Paddy Barry, Tony Maher, Tom O'Donoghue, Denis Murphy (captain), Donal Clifford (who I believe was the first player to wear a helmet in inter-county hurling), Justin McCarthy, Gerald McCarthy, Denis Coughlan,

Roger Touhy, Tom Ryan, Willie Walsh, Pat Hegarty, Charlie McCarthy, Charlie Cullinane, and Eddie O'Brien. Ray Cummins came off the bench to make his Munster championship debut when he replaced the injured Charlie Cullinane.

MOON WALK, MARS AND END OF 'THE ROCK'.

Maybe it was the chart topper 'Something in the Air' by Thunderclap Newman which inspired the Corkmen that summer. Or could it have been 'Honky Tonk Women' by the Rolling Stones! What did take place was the birth of tennis star Steffi Graf and, the death at her London home of singer and actress Judy Garland. The summer headlines included a men's singles tennis match at Wimbledon between Pancho Gonzales and Charlie Paserell which lasted five hours twenty minutes – a record. A matter of days before hundreds of millions of television viewers witnessed the first Moon walk in history by United States astronaut Neil Armstrong, the political career of Senator Edward Kennedy took a major setback. The 37-year-old Senator's behaviour was brought into question when he was involved in a motor accident that resulted in the death of his passenger, Mary Jo Kopechne. Space exploration was to remain topical and generated excitement in August when an unmanned United States craft beamed back to Earth pictures of the planet Mars – another first.

As Cork prepared to take on Kilkenny in the All-Ireland final, troubles in the north of the country necessitated the introduction of British troops onto the streets of Belfast. In late August, many boxing fans were shocked by the death of 45-year-old Rocky Marciano, former undefeated heavyweight champion of the world. 'The Rock' who had won all of his 49 professional fights, 43 of them inside the distance, died in a plane crash.

A LEARNING PROCESS

The weather on Sunday 7 September was fine and mild. It was perfect for hurling. There was only one place to be and that was Croke Park. What a wonderful and colourful experience it always is. I had a seat in the Cusack Stand which had its advantages over Hill 16, where I stood the previous year. Still I missed the banter, the fun and the wit among the 'Hill folk' which was less prevalent in the stands.

It was the Kilkennymen wearing the black and amber vertical stripes who were about to face Cork in a contest that would determine the McCarthy Cup's resting place for another year. As the teams paraded before the match I felt all the old pride and passion return. It seemed as if Cork hurling was back in its rightful place. The fact that the team, led by captain Denis Murphy, had achieved the apparently unachievable by beating Tipperary made the occasion even more special. Closer inspection of the parade revealed that one of Cork's most influential and talented players was absent. A severe blow had been dealt to the Leesiders' chances of victory when Justin McCarthy, the tall, elegant centre-back from Passage West fractured his leg in a motor cycle accident days before the final. His replacement, though not directly in the team line-out, was the young, tall, slim, Blackrock man, Ray Cummins.

A glance at the Kilkenny team led by Eddie Keher sent a shiver down my spine. It was a powerful outfit brimming with household names. At that indescribable moment when the cheers following the National Anthem died down, the 66,844 attendance focused on the referee. Within seconds the throw-in of the sliotar set the 1969 All-Ireland hurling final in motion. With Ray Cummins at full-forward, Charlie Cullinane at centre-forward, and Munster final hero, Willie Walsh, filling the vacancy left by Justin McCarthy, Cork got off to a flying start – a goal by Charlie McCarthy in the second minute. A period of sparkling hurling followed during which six points were equally shared by the teams. Cork appeared to have the edge and when Eddie O'Brien smashed the sliotar to the net after a Pat Hearty pass it was looking very good for the Rebels. The six-point advantage was further increased when Eddie O'Brien pointed and Charlie McCarthy added a brace. The single reply for the Noresiders was a point by Eddie Keher. It was in the closing minutes of the first-half that the Kilkennymen were to show their mettle. Pat Lawler led the way with a point. Then came what many have since described as the turning point of the match. Cork's goal-keeper, Paddy Barry, somehow dropped his stick as he moved out to collect the incoming sliotar. His attempted catch failed and Kilkenny's Martin Brennan whipped the sliotar to the net. When the half-time whistle sounded Cork, in spite of dominating the match for most of the half, were only three points to the good. The score was 2-6 to 1-6. It was a disappointing margin.

At the interval it was the Kilkenny supporters who were the more jubilant. It has to be said that the one man who stood out in the first-half was Kilkenny's right-full back Ted Carroll. He gave a brilliant display of defensive hurling at its best and kept his county's hopes alive when the team struggled.

The second-half began with Kilkenny dominating play to the extent that Cork were limited to three points for the entire half. All three scores came from Charlie McCarthy, bringing his total on the day to 1-6. Kilkenny grew in stature. There was nothing more discouraging for the Corkmen than to see Kilkenny substitute, Paddy Moran, score a point from 80 yards. Eddie Keher moved to centre-forward when Pat Delaney went off injured and from then on there was no stopping them. At the final whistle the score read Kilkenny 2-15; Cork 2-9.

The disappointment among the Cork followers was not as great as one might have expected. The feeling was that we came, we saw, and while we didn't conquer, we did have a team with potential. Maybe it folded under the might of Kilkenny on the day but it was a learning process for the Corkmen.

The firm belief was that they would be back.

CONCORDE AND TWO LITTLE BOYS
On 1 October those even mildly interested in aviation had their attention drawn towards France. Concorde, an aircraft carefully designed to withstand severe buffeting at near sonic speeds, was tested and duly obliged by successfully breaking the sound barrier. Later that month singer Bobby Gentry was to see his recording 'I'll Never Fall in Love Again' go to number one in the charts. Before the year was out along came the Archies with 'Sugar Sugar', which was to endure at the top for eight weeks. Then came the voice of Rolf Harris with a song called 'Two Little Boys'. It was to touch the heartstrings of listeners over Christmas and long into the New Year.

1970

January 1970 heralded the beginning of the end of an episode in history which is close to my heart – the Nigerian civil war. 11 January saw General Ojukwu, the rebel Biafran leader, flee the country and the secessionist state surrender to Nigerian federal troops the following day. Thus ended the bitterly fought, ruinous, three-year civil war which left thousands of starving men, women and children in a devastated corner of Nigeria. It was on 12 January while television coverage brought horrific pictures from defunct Biafra that a Boeing 747 jet plane made its maiden transatlantic flight from New York to London. The Jumbo jet age had arrived!

THE SIGNS WERE GOOD

Interest in the fortunes of what was widely regarded as an up and coming Cork hurling team was as keen in early 1970 as it had been for a long time. Performances of individual players and the team as a whole were watched, analysed and discussed in detail. There was a belief among the faithful that the county which had produced so many giants of hurling in the past, was about to do so again. It was pleasing to see the Rebel County taking the National League competition seriously.

In New York the home side provided the Leesiders with stiff opposition. A two-point margin by virtue of the aggregate score of two matches was enough to put Cork into the semi-final where they met Tipperary. The Leesiders duly disposed of the Premier County and did likewise to Limerick in the final. The Rebel County thus became Royal Liver National Hurling League champions for the second year running – encouraging signs indeed for the championship.

EVEN THE SOCCER PLAYERS SANG

Lovers of popular music kept Rolf Harris' 'Two Little Boys' on top of the charts until 31 January. Then it was the turn of Eddison Lighthouse with 'Love Grows' who took over for five weeks, before Lee Marvin cut in with 'Wand'rin' Star'. Simon and Garfunkel were then to fill the gap with 'Bridge Over Troubled Water', until along came Derry lass, Dana, singing the Eurovision Song Contest winner 'All Kinds of Everything'. Dana's song remained on top for two weeks in April. Cork hurlers were vigorously preparing for the Munster hurling championship as the World Cup soccer competition kicked off in Mexico. England's football squad cut a disc called 'Back Home', which went to the top and remained there for three weeks.

JOY AND SORROW
Cork beat Limerick at Thurles in the opening round of the Munster Championship by a score of 4-13 to 3-6. A good win and Cork reportedly played well in spite of the absence of Willie Walsh and now regular half-back Con Roche. We were set for another showdown between the old adversaries, Cork and Tipperary.

Unfortunately all was not so well in the world at large. Coincidentally, on the very day a journalist won the Pulitzer Prize for his reporting of a massacre by American troops in the Vietnam village of My Lai, United States National Guardsmen shot dead six students who were taking part in anti-Vietnam war protests. The shootings took place at university campuses in Ohio and Mississippi.

On a celebratory note, legendary singer and songwriter Bob Dylan, was awarded an honorary degree at Princeton University. It was certainly celebration time all the way in Mexico when Brazil became World Cup soccer winners for the third time. The trio of wins meant that the Jules Remit Trophy would have a permanent home in Brazil. The summer of 1970 is also linked to the first 'open-air concert' in England. It was entirely appropriate that the Mungo Jerry number one hit from mid-June to early August should be called 'In the Summertime'.

VICTORY TINGED WITH SADNESS
Back in Ballycastle the school was closed for the summer holidays. I was a free agent for most of the summer. Still, my focus became most firmly fixed on the possible outcome of the contest which was to be sorted out at Limerick later in July. In spite of the comparatively small attendance

of 34,000, there was a good atmosphere in the Gaelic Grounds before the match. Both sets of supporters were a little apprehensive. Tipperary followers feared the balance of power might just be on the change, while Cork's faithful lived in hope that that was so.

The opening period of the match was not at all encouraging. The midfield battle was being decidedly won by the Tipperary pairing of Mick Roche and P.J. Ryan. Cork seemed to be in trouble. The defence was under severe pressure and had it not been for an excellent all round performance, Tipperary would have the match won at half-time. At the interval Cork followers were strongly of the opinion that changes in the team were necessary if we were to stand any chance.

When the teams took the field for the second-half the status quo had been maintained and no changes had been made. Yet Tipperary were not to be as dominant, and when Cork fought back from being eight points down to level the scores at 3-6 each, a great finale was in prospect. Cork's Gerald McCarthy, who I was later to learn carried an injury into the match, was replaced at midfield by Seamus Looney. Then an incident which resulted in the dismissal of Tipperary defender Liam King appeared to bring about the turning point. Cork became dominant and when the final whistle sounded the score was Cork 3-10; Tipperary 3-8.

The Leesiders had performed well and registered a splendid two-point victory. I went back to Antrim happy in the knowledge that bar the most unlikely outcome,when Cork played London in the semi-final, I would be in Croke Park on the first Sunday of September.

However, celebrations following the marvellous victory at Limerick on that July Sunday were marred by the tragic news that former Cork hurling star Pat Healy had died in a motor accident on his way home from the match. Followers of the county's hurling fortunes in the 1950s will remember that Pat played both minor and senior hurling on the same day at Limerick in the Munster semi-final of 1956. Having played brilliantly on the minor team, he was brought on to the senior team at half-time and contributed handsomely to a win over Tipperary.

STATISTICS
Cork beat London in the All-Ireland semi-final in a one-sided match played at Limerick which finished with the score Cork 4-20; London 2-9.

It was time to start looking for All-Ireland tickets or at least check out possible sources for when the time came. Meanwhile Mungo Jerry's 'In the Summertime' had been deposed and its place had been taken by the very popular Elvis Presley number, 'The Wonder of You'. As the build up to the All-Ireland final gained momentum I studied the form of Cork's opponents on the day. It was a Wexford team which had beaten Dublin and Kilkenny in Leinster, and Galway in the All-Ireland semi-final. In the campaign to date statistics showed that Wexford scored 11 goals and 50 points to Cork's 11 goals and 43 points; twelve players scored for Wexford, thirteen scored for Cork; Ned Buggy was Wexford's top scorer with 1-15, Charlie McCarthy led the way for Cork with 0-14. The form book indicated odds close to evens. Possibly Wexford had the edge, having played Galway in the semi-final, while Cork had the easier match against London.

THE MAGIC OF EDDIE MAKES CAPTAIN PADDY HAPPY
Sunday 6 September was the day earmarked for the decider. Where would the McCarthy Cup rest on the following Monday night?

Before a sliotar was struck the match was to go down in history. It was the first 80-minute final ever played. The Cork team selected to represent the county showed eight personnel and positional changes from the team which lost to Kilkenny in 1969. Gone from the full-back line were Tom O'Donoghue and Denis Murphy. They were respectively replaced at full-back and left corner-back by University College Corkman, Pat McDonnell, and a young, blond haired Blackrock player, John Horgan. The centre-back position was filled by last year's left-half forward Pat Hegarty. Gerald McCarthy moved from left-half back to centre-field. The position vacated by Gerald was taken by St Finbarrs' man, Con Roche. The second midfield player was UCC's Seamus Looney, who replaced Roger Toughy. Willie Walsh, last year's centre-back, moved to his more familiar position of centre-forward at the expense of Charlie Cullinane who moved to the left wing. The full-forward line remained unchanged. The players to occupy the same positions as in 1969 were goalkeeper and team captain Paddy Barry, Tony Maher, Donal Clifford, Tom Ryan, Charlie McCarthy, Ray Cummins and Eddie O'Brien. A feature of the Wexford team was the presence of four Quigley brothers Dan, Martin, John and Pat, all in the starting fifteen.

Once again it was great to be in Croke Park on All-Ireland day. The occasion and the setting never fails to impress. At 3.15 pm the 65,062 attendance saw the sliotar thrown between the midfield players by referee, Wicklow man, Jimmy Hatton. Cork started well against a Wexford team which seemed to be out of sorts. As the first-half progressed Cork were obviously enjoying the lion's share of the play without being stretched. An Eddie O'Brien goal for the Leesiders after eleven minutes paved the way for what proved to be a surprisingly one-sided game, with Cork always on top. Eddie was to score two further goals before halftime. At the interval Cork led by 3-12 to 3-2. More goals and points galore were to follow. By the end of the match a torrent of scores, 42 in all, had been amassed. Charlie McCarthy, Willie Walsh and Charlie Cullinane tacked on a further three goals for Cork. Wexford scored two in the second-half to bring their total to five – Tony Doran (2); Pat Quigley (2); Dan Quigley (1). Unfortunately the match lacked bite, was low key, and generated little excitement. Cork won even more easily than the 6-21 to 5-10 score-line suggests.

Regardless of the quality of the match it was another proud day for the Cork hurling fraternity and none more so than team captain Paddy Barry who proudly accepted the McCarthy Cup. Paddy walked in the tradition of the county's outstanding goalkeepers and Cork followers will never forget the immeasurable contribution he made in the marvellous All-Ireland victory over Kilkenny in 1966. Cork had notched up their twenty-first All-Ireland crown! Followers flowing through the various arteries leading from Croke Park to the city centre and elsewhere were aglow with pride. It was a great day for a Corkman to be alive!

TOUGH AT THE TOP BUT WHAT IS THE SDLP
The school would reopen tomorrow and it would be back to the classroom where the pupils would inform me that

'Tears of a Clown' by Smokey Robinson and the Miracles was the current number one hit. They would be correct, but one week later 'Band of Gold' by Freda Payne was to take over. The profusion of groups and individual performers insured that no one hit would remain at the top for long, so it was no surprise when Matthews' Southern Comfort came along with 'Woodstock'. In turn it was replaced by the Jimi Hendrix Experience with 'Voodoo Chile'. A late November date marked the Gay Liberation Front's first demonstration in London. It coincided with the arrival of a chart topper which was to reign supreme right through to January. It was called 'I Hear You Knockin'' by Dave Edmunds.

While there was plenty to remember 1970 by, perhaps one of the more significant developments in this country was the formation of a new nationalist political party in Northern Ireland. A little-known Derry school teacher, John Hume, and a high profile Belfast, Labour leader, Gerry Fitt, were among the founder members. The party was to be the nationalists non-violent mouthpiece for the furtherance of peace and justice. It was named the Social Democratic and Labour Party – SDLP.

1971

NEW YEAR JOY AND SORROW

The Scots certainly know how to party. New Year's Eve 1971 was no different from other years in cities, towns, villages and sea coast crofts of the country renowned for its whisky, Highland grandeur and mystic lakes. The following day was largely a day of rest, a time for a gentle return to normality. On 2 January supporters of Glasgow Celtic and Glasgow Rangers football clubs had a special treat to look forward to. In the afternoon the 'Old Firm' match between Celtic and Rangers was scheduled to take place at Ibrox Park stadium – Rangers grounds. In addition to the match being a local derby, a fierce rivalry tainted by a hint of tribalism existed between the supporters of the two clubs. It was the match most looked forward to in the Scottish football calender. By 3pm Ibrox Park was packed to the rafters. Both sets of supporters were carefully segregated in order to prevent trouble. The match was tense, Celtic had scored, and time was almost up. Some Rangers supporters, anxious to avoid the taunts of their Celtic counterparts, began to leave the grounds before the match was over. On the way out they heard cheers which informed them that Rangers had equalised. Apparently they turned and ran back, causing confusion inside the ground which led to metal barriers giving way and people being swept onto the terraces. By the time rescuers reached the trampled mass of bodies, 66 had died. A further 200 were injured. It was an appalling tragedy which echoed around the world.

A few days later further sadness was to invade the world of sport when Sonny Liston, a high-profile former world heavyweight champion boxer of the early Ali era, was found dead at his home in America.

GRANDAD TO THE RESCUE

Just when all seemed doom and gloom, along came Clive Dunn, alias Sergeant Jones of the TV comedy, 'Dad's Army', and cheered us with his rendering of the simple, child-like, 'Grandad'.'Grandad' remained at number one in the charts until 'My Sweet Lord' by George Harrison moved up three weeks later. Among the items making news abroad in the early days of January was the official opening of the Aswan High Dam on the river Nile by President Sedat of Egypt. Perhaps though it was the seizing of power in Uganda by Major General Idi Amin – Dada – that was to have the greatest humane ramifications. Amin led a coup which deposed President Dr Milton Obote. He then set about expelling 50,000 Asians while conducting a reign of terror over his own people. On 9 February, when the first British soldier was killed in the current Northern Ireland troubles, nobody foresaw the awful catalogue of atrocities which lay ahead.

RENEWED LIFE
Once Easter passes, the results of Sunday's hurling matches and comments on performances by teams or players begin to take on a significance which was absent for much of the winter. The end of the National Hurling League is in sight and participating teams in the final stages are known. Cork, Tipperary and an up-and-coming Limerick team were each doing well in the league. Cork played Tipperary in the semi-final at Limerick on 9 May. The Premier County won by two points. Michael 'Babs' Keating of Tipperary excelled on the day. The final score was Tipperary 2-12; Cork 2-10. A good Limerick team lined out against Tipperary in the final at Cork. A point from a free in the final seconds of the match was enough to give Limerick a great win and the Royal Liver National Hurling League trophy. The free was taken by that fine hurler Richie Bennis. The final score was Limerick 3-12; Tipperary 3-11.

Cork's hurlers' next date with destiny was to be a first-round Munster championship match against league winners Limerick at Thurles. It sounded a good one to me – the current All-Ireland champions, Cork, versus the current league winners, Limerick. Should I think about going? I would have to see the lads about it!

MONEY, CELEBRATION AND BLISS
There was a sporting contest about to take place in the United States on which all eyes were focused. The historic fifteen-round world heavyweight title fight between Joe

116

Frazier and Muhammad Ali was to be the most lucrative sports meeting ever. The contest realised an astonishing $20,000,000.

A totally different reason was responsible for celebration on the island of Haiti. Unusually, the extolment was caused by a death – that of hated leader, 63-year-old Francois Duvalier, known as 'Papa Doc'. The dictator was associated with violent suppression of the island's people by a private army of hoodlums known as Tonton Macoute. During his lifetime he survived six assassination attempts.

The names of Mick Jagger and Stevie Wonder were in the news in May. A much-published Roman Catholic ceremony at St Tropez was the setting for the marriage of Mick to beautiful Bianca Perez Morena de Macias; Stevie Wonder didn't get married but on his twenty-first birthday he did get one thirtieth of his $30,000,000 earnings to date.

THE MUSIC GOES ON AS LOUIS LAYS DOWN HIS TRUMPET
'Hot Love' by T.Rex, which had a six week run was followed by Dawn's 'Knock Three Times', and Middle of the Road's 'Chirpy Chirpy Cheep Cheep', each of which endured for five weeks. Shorter stays at the top were experienced by Mungo Jerry's 'Baby Jump', Dave and Ansil Collins' 'Double Barrel', and T.Rex's 'Get It On'. Sadness was to taint the world of music in July. A giant of the entertainment world, an all time great died. He was jazz legend, 71-year-old Louis Armstrong, affectionately known as 'Satchmo'. His virtuoso trumpet playing and gravelly voice will live on record when many others are long forgotten. In the midst of other happenings around the world India employed its army to prevent cholera-stricken refugees from Bangladesh entering the country, and three Russian astronauts were found dead in a spaceship. Lack of oxygen due to a malfunction in the final stage of the twenty-day trip was the cause of death.

A WELCOME LIMERICK BREAKTHROUGH AND RTE COLOUR
Championship hurling in Munster began and virtually ended on the same day where I was concerned. Cork were beaten in the first round. This time it was by the Limerick team which had been knocking on the door for some time. I did not travel to the match in Thurles because I couldn't muster up a 'crew' as keen as myself to make the journey.

The match was described as a classic in the press. It was a very sweet victory for the Shannonsiders who had not beaten the Rebel County in championship hurling for 33 years. On the day Cork were without Gerald McCarthy. A few new names appeared in the team line-out. Included were Paddy Crowley who played at full-back, Martin O'Doherty, a half-back, and Connie Kelly, a forward. While the press used the word classic in describing the match, Cork followers felt that their team did not play well. Two goals by Ray Cummins in the first-half kept the Leesiders' hopes alive but it was Limerick playing against the wind in the second-half who were to finish the stronger. The final score was Limerick 2-16; Cork 2-14. Few begrudged Limerick the breakthrough they had worked so hard for. It was a case of full marks to the men who persevered over the years in spite of many demoralising defeats.

Now that Cork were out of the championship I took an interest in the fortunes of the Limerickmen and would dearly have loved to see them win the All-Ireland championship. Their immediate opponents, Tipperary, were ready and waiting to take them on in the Munster final. The match was played in Killarney, an 80 minute decider in a torrential downpour. A huge Limerick following travelled to Fitzgerald Stadium. The neutrals, many of whom knew little of the illustrious and legendary Mick Mackey led Limerick teams of the 1930s and 1940s, were firmly behind the underdogs. The names of famous clubs which appeared on the match programme brought back memories of by-gone days. There was Claughaun, provider of goalkeeper Jim Hogan, centre-forward Mick Graham, and the brilliant Cregans, Mick and Eamonn. Patrickswell, with whom team captain Tony O'Brien, the great half-back Phil Bennis, midfield player Sean Foley, and half-forward Richie Bennis, played their hurling. South Liberties produced two of the very best in full-back Pat Hartigan and wing-forward Eamonn Grimes. Old Christians contributed with the powerful midfield player Bernie Hartigan, and half-back Christy Campbell. Doon, Bruree and Cappamore didn't let the side down. Respectively they supplied Jim O'Donnell at centre-back, Jim O'Brien at left-corner back, and Donal Flynn at right-full forward. The clubs of Croom and Garry Spillane too appeared on the substitute listing.

An eye-catching name at the foot of the programme

was that of Jackie Power – Coach and Selector. Jackie was a member of the Limerick teams of the 1930s and 1940s – a hurling career that spanned fifteen years. His exceptional talents and versatility in the game enabled him to play in several positions. For Munster at inter-provincial level, he played in five different positions in different years, including midfield, centre-forward and centre-back. Not known at the time was that his son Ger was to follow closely in his footsteps, albeit as a Kerry Gaelic footballer.

The pitch conditions at Fitzgerald Stadium, Killarney on match day did not suit the Limerick style of hurling. They liked to move the sliotar fast. Yet it was Limerick who took the initiative. It was a dispirited, downcast, Tipperary team which left the field at half-time. Limerick led by 2-10 to 1-7. But Tipperary were Tipperary and it only took their wise mentors to make a few changes, both positional and personnel, to produce a 'new look' team. The restart saw a new approach from the Premier County men which had Limerick under pressure from the word go. The Shannonsiders continued to battle on but they were knocked out of their stride again and again. The match was on a knife edge with the end of the long 40 minute, energy sapping, second-half in sight. The closing seconds were being played, the sides were level and then it happened! Tipperary's John Flanagan hit the sliotar over the bar to give the Premier County another Munster title. When referee Frank Murphy sounded the final whistle a devastated Limerick hurling fraternity could only look at the scoreboard in disbelief. It read Tipperary 4-16; Limerick 3-18. A statistic from the match is that Michael 'Babs' Keating scored a personal tally of 3-4 for the Premier County.

Tipperary, led by team captain Tadgh O'Connor, went on to beat Kilkenny in the All-Ireland final. The final score was 5-17 to 5-14. For the record it was the first decider to be screened on RTE in colour. Eddie Keher, the Kilkenny master craftsman, registered a stunning 2-11, but ended up on the loosing side. I am told that his tally is the 'official' record for an All-Ireland hurling final of modern times.

THE GOOD AND THE BAD
Eddie was not alone in the annals of sporting achievement that year. Round the world, lone yachtsman, Chay Blyth, in his all steel ketch *British Steel* completed a 30,000 mile

voyage in 292 days. In spite of sailing against the prevailing winds he beat the existing record by 21 days. The annals of history too will record that Nikita Khrushcev, one-time ultra powerful and abrasive premier of the Soviet Union, died in obscurity. In the sometimes strange world of the United Nations, Taiwan was expelled from the organisation in order to make way for the People's Republic of China. In the north of Ireland, internment without trial of the largest number of republicans since 1921 began in mid-summer. Halloween 1971 marked a fireworks display not appreciated by the people of London. The IRA exploded a bomb at the top of the Post Office Tower. Greatly appreciated in Ballycastle on 7 October was the birth of our son, John. He went on to win an under sixteen All-Ireland hurling championship medal with Antrim. I wonder where his interest in the game came from!

TAMS TELL DIANA

Sporting achievements or world affairs did not slow down the flow of music. When Diana Ross made it to the top with 'I'm Still Waiting', the Tams hit back in a matter of four weeks with 'Hey Girl Don't Bother Me'. Then it was the turn of Rod Stewart with 'Maggie May'. 'Coz I Luv You' by Slade proceeded the final number one hit single of 1971. It was the very popular 'Ernie (the Fastest Milkman in the West)', by Benny Hill.

VICTIMS

The year came to a close leaving news items with elements of satisfaction and deep sadness. Compensation, if that is the correct term, was paid by the British Government to thalidomide victims. In Belfast, shortly before Christmas, the IRA planted a bomb in a busy city centre bar. The bomb exploded on a Saturday afternoon when the premises was crowded. Fifteen innocent people died and many more were seriously injured. In Dacca, east Pakistan, 3,000 children died when an orphanage was erroneously bombed by Indian planes. On a less serious note a change took place during the year which was to add confusion and perhaps a little nostalgia to the lives of some older citizens – decimal currency came into use – gone for ever were half-crowns, florins, shillings, tanners and other familiar coins.

1972

The title of the New Seekers number one hit in January 1972, 'I'd Like to Teach the World To Sing' (in Perfect Harmony), sent out the perfect New Year message. The catchy song with its infectious rhythm remained at the top for four weeks. Unfortunately 'perfect harmony' did not prevail in the north of Ireland. On a bright, cool, January Sunday afternoon, thirteen civilians were shot dead by members of the British Army on a Derry street. For the second time in the present century the label 'Bloody Sunday' was assigned to atrocities carried out in Ireland by British soldiers. A few days later in an act of revenge, protesters burned down the British Embassy in Dublin. 22 January was a historic day in the history of the Irish Republic when along with the United Kingdom and Denmark it became a member of the EEC.

Major happenings elsewhere in the world were not at a premium in early 1972. A headline was made when fire destroyed the one-time luxury liner, *Queen Elizabeth*, in Hong Kong harbour. Since being decommissioned in 1968 the once grand lady of the high seas, and former pride of the Cunard fleet, had served as a floating university - –Seawise University.

Regardless of what went on at home and abroad the hunger for popular music continued. In a thriving business the groups T.Rex, Chicory Tip, and Nilsson, got the thumbs up during February and March. Respectively they were responsible for the number one hits 'Telegram Sam', 'Son of my Father', and 'Without You'.

Celebration by the Lee

Cork's performances in the National Hurling League through the winter and into spring had been patchy. It began to look as if they would not qualify for the final stages of the competition. It had reached a point where they had to win by a particular margin against Offaly in order to get through to the the semi-final. As it happened they went on a scoring spree and met the requirement with lots of goals and point to spare. The final score was Cork 6-6; Offaly 1-3. That victory set up a semi-final meeting with old rivals Tipperary. A typically tough, close encounter ended with a Cork victory by a score of 5-12 to 4-8. The neat, sharp, accurate striking of Charlie McCarthy accounted for 1-9 of Cork's total. Ray Cummins delighted followers; he was now clearly a handful for top defenders in the game. Cork's opponents in the final were Limerick.

Another close encounter was envisaged by all and sundry when the teams met in Thurles on 7 May. On that occasion 'all and sundry' were right. Limerick pushed Cork all the way to the final whistle.

Again the name Ray Cummins, along with that of Denis Coughlan and Con Roche, came to the fore. At the end of the day a 3-14 to 2-14 score line meant the Royal Liver National League trophy was on its way to Leeside. It would be assured of a warm welcome by the most loyal, good-natured, witty supporters in the land. Cork followers now felt that it was very much a case of, 'watch this space', for the Munster championship.

JOHN AND SYLVIA ROWED BUT STORMONT AND IGOR SUNK
From early 1972 onwards the changing political situation in Northern Ireland began to attract worldwide attention. The nationalist Social Democratic and Labour Party, formed in 1970, had worked hard in the interests of the people it represented. Some important reforms had been implemented but they were not enough.

Then, what would have been unthinkable a few years previously occurred. The British government suspended Stormont, the Northern Ireland Parliament, and imposed direct rule from Westminster. Protestant Unionists were appalled. They had dominated Catholic nationalists at all elections since the formation of the Parliament in 1921 on a four to one ratio. The bastion of Protestant Unionism in Ulster had been abolished.

Elsewhere the death of Russian born composer Igor Stravinsky closed a chapter on the works of an extraordinarily versatile and sometimes controversial writer of music. It is highly likely that both John Fairfax and Sylvia Cook were not immediately aware of Stravinsky's demise. That is because they were busy being the first people to row a boat across the Pacific. It is possible though that they were welcomed ashore in Australia by music of The Pipe and Drums and Military Band of the Royal Scots Dragoon Guards, current chart toppers with the melodic strains of 'Amazing Grace'. T.Rex, who had two long-stay number one hits in 1971, repeated the achievement in 1972. 'Metal Guru' replaced 'Amazing Grace' in late May but before that, 'Telegram Sam' had had its stint. Don McLean fans will be aware that his 1970s single, 'Vincent', was tops in mid-summer. At the half-year mark it was Slade with 'Take Me Back 'Ome' who made it to the top of the pile.

DRAW AND REPLAY
While I didn't quite get all the way 'Back 'Ome' I did get as far as Limerick on Sunday 9 July for the Munster hurling semi-final replay between Cork and Tipperary. In May Cork disposed of Waterford in the opening round of the championship by a score line of 3-16 to 4-6. On 25 June it was old rivals Tipperary who opposed the Rebels in the semi-final at Limerick. I remember listening to the match on the radio and can clearly recall that at half-time Tipperary led 3-7 to 2-1. In a similar situation for the greater part of the 1960s that would have meant certain defeat for Cork. Tipperary would have steamrollered on to another final. But now the Leesiders were made of sterner stuff. The attack, led by the superb Ray Cummins, included five other players, each of whom was capable of distinguishing himself at the highest level; the midfield pair of Justin McCarthy and Denis Coughlan were well capable of holding their own in any company; and the defence, sprinkled with high-calibre players had a 'solidness' about it. Tony Maher and Con Roche, for example, were usually masters of their particular domains. Standing alone between the post was the tried and tested custodian supreme, Paddy Barry. In the second-half Cork's mentors made a number of astute changes. The team seemed to move up a gear and were soon back in contention. An inspired spell of play by the Rebels followed and at the final whistle the score was Cork 3-8; Tipperary 3-8. Tipperary could no longer sweep Cork aside! I vowed I would be in Limerick for the replay.

On Sunday 9 July, along with my father-in-law, we took our places among the 38,126, spectators. In the curtain raiser, as we watched the minor hurlers of Cork and Tipperary do battle for Munster honours, we noticed and discussed one particular player. He was centre-forward on the Cork team. In contrast to the others he had short cropped hair. That made his considerable sideburns stand out more. Little did we know then the extent to which the slim, athletic, silken skilled, eighteen year old was to stand out from the crowd in the years to come. He was none other than the great Jimmy Barry Murphy. The Cork team for the senior match showed two changes from the drawn game. Gerald Mc Carthy and young Nemo Rangers player, Brian Murphy, replaced Donal Collins and Paddy Crowley. When the referee got the match underway at 3.30pm the atmosphere was lively but somewhat tense. Those present, who had previously experienced the cut-and-thrust of equally-matched Cork versus Tipperary teams, knew they were in for a thriller. It soon became evident that if Cork were to advance in the championship they would have to do it the hard way. Tipperary were playing so well that they opened up an eight point gap. Half-time was nigh when Mick Malone, who had moved to full-for-ward in a switch with Ray Cummins, scored a vital goal.

Resumption of the match saw a Tipperary five-point lead become six before things began to happen for the Corkmen. A Gerald McCarthy goal and a Ray Cummins point narrowed the gap to two points. It was still early in the second-half but I somehow knew that Cork had cracked it – the magic was there. Teddy O'Brien replaced Cork's centre-half back Seamus Looney, who went off injured. All was now well, and soon points apiece by the bearded, flying Mick Malone and fellow hurling genius Charlie McCarthy, levelled the scores. The Premier County men were not finished though, and it was the fine hurler from Borrisoleigh, Noel O'Dwyer, who restored a one point lead for Tipperary. Still it was only a dying kick. Ray Cummins, Mick Malone, Gerald McCarthy and Con Roche went on to total 1-3 without reply. It was an altogether magnificent outcome for the Leesiders. They had come out on top after an excruciatingly hard fought contest.

Tipperary had given them a close examination and they had passed with flying colours. The final score delightfully read, Cork 3-10; Tipperary 2-7. It was a momentous after-noon for Cork followers. We felt we were back where we belonged and the lads had certainly done us proud. The Munster final could now be looked forward to with confidence. Cork's opponents in the Munster hurling final were Clare. The decider was played in Thurles on 30 July. A 6-18 to 2-8 victory for the Rebels tells its own story. Barring an upset by London in the All-Ireland semi-final, Cork would be back in Croke Park on 3 September – All-Ireland final day!

MAYHEM AT MUNICH AS MARK STRIKES GOLD

In 1972 the summer Olympic Games were held in Munich. The most striking achievement by a participating individual was undoubtedly the winning of seven gold medals, all in record time, by United States' swimmer Mark Spitz. Unfortunately though, it is not only for the brilliance of the American that those Games will be remembered. Palestinian terrorists struck at the heart of the Olympic Village resulting in the deaths of two Israeli athletes. Eighteen others escaped and nine were taken hostage. The hostages were used by the terrorists in order to secure certain demands. Tragically, in an error of judgment, or a mix-up at Munich airport, all nine athletes died in a shoot out between German police and the terrorists. Four terrorists and a policeman also died.

CHECKMATE

The game of chess is not among the activities one might associate with concentrated worldwide media attention, yet that was very much the case for a sustained period in 1972 when American champion Bobby Fischer took on USSR champion Boris Spassky in Reykjavik, Iceland. The obvious hostility which existed between the two men was ever present and the unprovoked capricious fits of ill-temper displayed by the American kept television viewers glued to their sets. Twenty-nine-year-old Fischer, celebrated for his unorthodox psychological tactics, was dubbed the world's most unreasonable person. At the end of a two-month marathon session, he became the first American world chess champion.

Donny Osmond's 'Puppy Love' reached number one, as did Alice Cooper's, 'School's Out', 'You Wear it Well' by Rod Stewart, and 'Mama Weer All Crazee' by Slade. As David Cassidy made it to the top with 'How Can I Be Sure', All-Ireland hurling final fever was well on its way.

LEFT CONFUSED

Kilkenny qualified to meet Cork in the championship decider. A classic encounter was anticipated. The press extolled on the unique glamour of Cork and Kilkenny teams on All-Ireland day. The style and colours of jerseys were compared and contrasted. At least one scribe was certain that those factors had a direct bearing on the images projected by the teams on the field. The contrasting styles of hurling played by the counties were analysed. Conclusions were drawn from the urgent, sincere, razor-sharp, fiercely proud approach by the Leesiders, when compared with that of the contemplative, slower thinking, serene Noresiders. We were reminded of the extraordinary record of close scores between the counties, often just one point margins. The message going out to the nation was, followers of the game were seldom disappointed at the end of a Cork versus Kilkenny final and 1972 would be no different. Both teams had players with awesome reputations for all that is good in the game of hurling. One would be reluctant to single out individuals because on a particular day any one of the 30 starting players and many of the substitutes were capable of starring.

Sunday 3 September was a beautiful sunny day. Splendour reigned in Croke Park. The red and white of Cork, and the black and amber of Kilkenny casually cohabited among the 66,135 attendance. For convenience Hill 16 was mainly assigned to the lively Cork followers, while the Canal End was occupied by those of the black and amber persuasion. The stands housed followers from both counties with a blatant disregard for segregation. Trouble and other evils which bedevil some sporting occasions elsewhere were the last things on the minds of those who made up the largest crowd to witness an All-Ireland hurling final in the 1970s.

Referee Mick Spain of Offaly got the match under way. The first score of the match, a point, came from the stick of Kilkenny man Mick Crotty. Ray Cummins replied for Cork with a superbly executed goal. From virtually the first minute of action the assembled audience were enthralled. The next score, a point by Pat Henderson, came from a long free taken immaculately by the powerful Kilkenny centre-half back. Successive points by Liam O'Brien put the Noresiders ahead. Then it was free-taker supreme, Eddie

Keher who put them further ahead. The contest on the pitch was not for the faint hearted. Pat Henderson was stamping his not inconsiderable authority at every opportunity. At midfield for Cork, Denis Coughlan was supplying his attackers well and full-forward, Ray Cummins, was giving Kilkenny full-back Pa Dillon a torrid time. The match had developed into a marvellous spectacle.

The scoring continued. Charlie McCarthy tapped over two 21-yard frees with the combined neatness, control and self confidence which were the hallmarks of the compact St Finbarrs' man. Charlie was soon to notch up another point to cancel an earlier Keher effort. The scores were level. Kilkenny team captain and goalie Noel Skehan had by now made a number of spectacular saves. The play flowed and soon Ray Cummins put Cork ahead by a point. There was no let up and soon Liam O'Brien restored the status quo. Mick Malone not to be outdone, opened up the narrowest of score gaps again. It was added to by Con Roche, the 110 per cent player in the Cork defence. He drove a 65-yard free over the bar. The Noresiders kept the pressure up, and not for the first time it was the forever-running and foraging, Liam O'Brien, who was to add to their score. Then Mick Malone, himself always a busy player, beat Noel Skehan. But the resilience of Kilkenny would not go away. John Kinsella made that clear by scoring his first point of the day. There were three further points scored before the interval. Eddie Keher, who had been superbly marked by Tony Maher, registered from a free, Charlie McCarthy replied, and the man who had the first score of the day, Mick Crotty, was also to have the last of the first-half. Cork led 2-8 to 0-12. Paddy Barry in the Cork goal had given his usual accomplished display. Sadly, Frank Norberg had to retire late in the half because of injury. Frank, who had captained Cork and contributed so much throughout the championship from the right-half back position, was replaced by the experienced and dependable Teddy O'Brien. Surely there can't have been a spectator present who didn't regard what they had just seen as one of the most absorbing first-half performances of all time.

The second-half turned out to be both absorbing and intriguing. There were a total of 22 scores registered – six to Cork, three of which were goals, through Mick Malone, Ray Cummins and Seanie O'Leary respectively – sixteen to

Kilkenny, three of which were goals, two by Eddie Keher and one by Frank Cummins. The tenth score was a point which resulted from an 80 yard puck by Con Roche. At that stage there were thirteen minutes of playing time left and the score stood at Cork 5-11; Kilkenny 1-15. Only the most ardent Kilkenny supporter could have given their team any chance of victory. But Cork were not to score again while Kilkenny went on to add a further 2-9. The mother of all turnabouts had taken place! On a day in which several Cork players had distinguished themselves, the team totally lost its way in the final ten minutes. To look at it from another angle, there were no words to describe the magnificence of the Kilkenny team performance during that period. In spite of being held scoreless from play for the entire first-half and much of the second-half Eddie Keher ended up with a personal tally of 2-9.

I have never been able to come up with any logical explanation for what happened. Confusion still reigns in my mind when I recall the collapse by Cork on the finest of early autumn afternoons at Croke Park in September 1972. I believe that it is over simplistic to attribute the turnabout to an Eddie Keher switch. Once moved from the shackles of Tony Maher, Eddie did come into the game in a way that he had been unable hitherto, but could he have motivated a whole team in one fell swoop? Could it be that a coasting Cork team became complacent when Con Roche struck over the long range point? It was a score which had followers on Hill 16 prematurely celebrating a victory.

Perhaps it was a combination of many things. The certainty is that for whatever reason Cork were not able to counter a rampant Kilkenny team during that late period of the match. The final score was Cork 5-11; Kilkenny 3-24. As full-time approached my lasting memory is of sitting in the Hogan Stand mesmerised.

WHAT HAPPENED TO CORK YESTERDAY SIR?
In years when Cork failed to win the All-Ireland hurling final, it took to the end of September for the pupils to get fed up of annoying me about it. In 1972 I decided on a stratagem to divert their attention. I told them to go and find out what was happening elsewhere in the world, write it down and bring it to me but there was to be no mention of hurling. The reporting back varied from the death of 'Hop

Along Cassidy', alias actor William Boyd, to the mass expulsion of 80,000 Asians from Uganda by Idi Amin. He gave them all of 48 hours to leave the country. The highlight of the research was the admitted acts of cannibalism committed by survivors of an air-crash in which fifteen passengers died. The Uraguyan plane came to rest in the Andes mountains. Only a few pupils noted the death of Harry Truman, thirty-third president of the United States. In the music charts 'Mouldy Old Dough' by Lieutenant Pigeon, dominated for much of October and November. It took Gilbert O' Sullivan and his rendering of 'Clair' to depose it. Chuck Berry then had a very popular hit with 'My Ding-A-Ling' before 'Long Haired Lover From Liverpool' by Little Jimmy Osmond swept the boards over Christmas.

Christmas was not a happy time for all. Over a twelve-day period, a massive bombing of Hanoi, the capital of North Vietnam, by United States armed forces resulted in the deaths of 1,600 civilians. An estimated 36,000 tons of bombs were dropped. Hanoi was devastated. Terrorism at Munich, political unrest in the north of Ireland, and a year of hurling which left me elated and confused were my vivid memories of 1972 as yet another New Year beckoned.

——— 1973 ———

The New Year began as 1972 had ended with Little Jimmy Osmond trying to keep the world happy with 'Long Haired Lover From Liverpool'. He did not succeed in bringing happiness to all though! Elvis Presley was unhappy with his lot, or at least with his wife Priscilla. So much so that on 8 January, on his thirty-eighth birthday, he sued for divorce. Was it a coincidence that Elvis recorded 'Separate Ways' at the same time? As Sweet took over the number one spot with 'Blockbuster', President Nixon of the United States declared the Vietnam War over.

Only those with long memories, who were survivors from the black and white movie era, would have noted that actor Edward G. Robinson, famous for his legendary gangster roles, died in late January. In mid-February, the death of Irish novelist Elizabeth Bowen took place. She was responsible for the autobiographical *Bowen's Court*, a volume of short stories called *Encounters*, and the novels *The Death of the Heart, The Heat of the Day*, and *The Little Girls*. On the last day of February, Indian activists took over a village in South Dakota, called Wounded Knee, and then challenged the United States government to repeat the massacre of 80 years ago.

While the invitation from the captors of Wounded Knee was being considered, the women's movement became euphoric. A major victory led to much celebration as for the first time a woman stockbroker set foot on the floor of the London Stock Exchange.

A Pablo Legacy is not Just a Yellow Ribbon
It was only March, but to date 1973 had been full of surprises. Was it an omen? Were the Cork hurlers going to surprise us and sweep the board? I remembered that they had

130

developed the nasty habit of flattering only to deceive – great promise shown one year only to be knocked out in the first round of the championship the following year. Those negative thoughts must not be entertained in mid-March. By then Sweet had been replaced by Slade with 'Cum on Feel the Noize'. But the Osmond connection had not gone away. Donny popped up with 'Twelfth of Never' and made it all the way to the top. Pablo Picasso, who was responsible for 140,000 paintings and drawings, 100,000 engravings, 300 sculptures and thousands of other documents died at the age of 91 on 8 April. Gilbert O'Sullivan had a number one hit with 'Get Down' before my favourite song of 1973 and beyond moved in. It was 'Tie a Yellow Ribbon Round The Old Oak Tree' by Dawn featuring Tony Orlando. Maybe it was inspired by the ending of the Vietnam War.

WASHINGTON POST OPENS WATERGATE AS SKY AND DEV MAKE NEWS

Unknown to many, certainly in this part of the world, the newspaper *Washington Post* won a prize – the Pulitzer Prize for the investigative work of two reporters who exposed a United States political scandal – Watergate. The term, Watergate, and its associated activities were seldom to be out of the media over the following two years. It was eventually a trial bearing the same name which decided President Nixon's resignation from office rather than face possible impeachment. The world was enthralled by the televised United States' Senate hearings on the Watergate 'affair', when on 14 May, *Sky Lab 1* was launched.

Adapted from the upper stage of a *Saturn 5* rocket, it was to house successive three man crews for weeks at a time in space. Aviation was to make further news in June when a supersonic aircraft, said to be the Russian equivalent of Concorde, exploded at the Paris Air Show, killing six crew members and over twenty spectators. Watergate became a byword, aviation had its moments, and the President of the Irish Republic, Eamon De Valera, retired from office on his ninetieth year.

Unperturbed, the bands played on. 'See My Baby Jive' by Wizzard remained in pole position for four weeks in

May and June before Suzi Quatro caught the imagination with 'Can The Can'. A group with a name resembling a volumetric measurement, 10CC, and a song with a title better known on the streets of Derry and Belfast, 'Rubber Bullets', led the way briefly in late June. On the very last day of the month it was 'skweezed' out by Slades 'Skweeze me Pleeze me'.

STUNNED!
What of the hurling in 1973? Cork's involvement in the championship did not begin until July. It was a first round match. Tipperary were the opponents and the venue was Limerick. It was late on Sunday evening when I got the match result. I remember listening to the radio and my eyes became transfixed on the speaker as the impartial voice coldly quoted figures from a script. It was saying Cork 1-10; Tipperary 5-4. Stunned, I thought, no! It just could not have happened again! I quickly resorted to mental arithmetic, converted goals to points, subtracted one score from the other – Cork had indeed lost by six points. I made very poor company that Sunday night! On Monday morning I opened up the newspaper and there on the inside of the back page was a heading in large bold, black print – Flood Gates Open. The content of the report made sad reading for Leeside hurling followers as it spelled out the raw facts. Scanning the typescript I noted: Cork had led 1-7 to 1-3 at half-time; at the end of the match Cork had totalled 1-10; in spite of the abysmal scoring, Cork were incredible, leading Tipperary with eight minutes of playing time remaining; then the Leesider's defence collapsed and Tipperary scored four goals. From the team line-out as it appeared at the end of the report, I was able to work out that there were seven changes of personnel from the side defeated by Kilkenny in last year's All-Ireland final. In defence Tony Maher, Pat McDonnell, Frank Norberg and Seamus Looney were replaced by Martin O'Doherty, John Horgan, John Buckley and Teddy O'Brien; at midfield Donal Clifford partnered Denis Coughlan instead of Justin McCarthy; introduced to the attack were Willie Walsh and Pat Moylan for Pat Hegarty and Seanie O'Leary. Mick

Malone was the scorer of Cork's only goal. The Tipperary goals were scored inside the last eight minutes. John Flanagan, Francis Loughnane, Sean Hogan and Roger Ryan were the marksmen. Summing up, Cork had once again played poorly in a first-round championship match, and on that occasion allowed Roger Ryan and his fellow Tipperary forwards to run riot.

RICHIE WAS THE MAN AMONGST MEN IN THURLES

By virtue of defeating Clare, Limerick qualified to meet Tipperary in the Munster final. The venue was Semple Stadium and the match was played on Sunday 29 July. The day and the date will remain forever in the annals of Limerick hurling. Towards the end of a match already filled with incident and drama, the sliotar crossed the end-line near the Tipperary goal mouth. The umpire judged that it went off a defender and signalled a '70' for Limerick. As Richie Bennis crossed the pitch to take it, referee Mick Slattery indicated to him that he had to score directly as time was up. There was pregnant hush around the stadium as all present were aware of the significance of what was unfolding. If Richie scored, Limerick would be Munster champions for the first time in eighteen years! All eyes were now on the Patrickswell man. He stood over the sliotar and looked at the uprights before steadying himself, bending, lifting the sliotar on the tip of the hurley and striking it long and high. The sliotar soared towards the target, straight and true at first, then with a slight drift to one side. Eyes dropped to the man in the white coat beside the goal post. Before he raised the flag all present knew Limerick were Munster senior hurling champions for the first time since 1955. The final score was Limerick 6-7; Tipperary 2-18. Pandemonium is the only word to describe the scenes which followed as Limerick followers wept and danced with joy. For the record, Limerick lined-out as follows: Seamus Horgan, Willie Moore, Pat Hartigan, Jim O'Brien, Phil Bennis, Jim O'Donnell, Sean Foley, Richie Bennis, Eamonn Grimes (captain), Liam O'Donoghue, Mossie Dowling, Bernie Hartigan, Frankie Nolan, Ned Rea and Eamonn Cregan.

CLASSY EAMONN

On Sunday 2 September, before an attendance of 58,009, Limerick became All-Ireland champions for the first time since 1940! Richie Bennis' point in Thurles then took on an even greater significance. The final score was Limerick 1-21; Kilkenny 1-14. A feature of the match was that Eamonn Cregan lined-out at centre-half back in the absence of Jim O'Donnell. Eamonn scored two goals from the left-corner forward position against Tipperary at Thurles in the Munster final back in July. His prowess as a forward was well known but the brilliance of his defensive hurling on All-Ireland final day left many aghast, perhaps none more so than his opposite number, Pat Delaney of Johnstown.

DRUG NEWS AS ARCADE BURNS AND, BETTY, BRUCE AND PAUL SAY ADIOS

During July and August Peters and Lee had a number one hit with 'Welcome Home'. Gary Glitter had a similar experience with 'I'm the Leader of the Gang, and Donny Osmond returned to the top with a new record called 'Young Love'.

Many noted the death of one-time Hollywood mega star, Betty Grable, who at the height of her fame insured her legs for $200,000. The untimely death of actor Bruce Lee at the age of 32 shocked and saddened his huge following worldwide. Untimely too was the death of Paul Williams, an original member of The Temptations.

Thalidomide, a word with horrific overtones, was again in the news. Families of victims born with malformed limbs were awarded £20,000,000 in compensation. When an amusement centre on the Isle of Man was destroyed by fire the tragic aftermath left 50 people dead and 80 others injured. There were an estimated 7,000 people, mostly holiday makers, in the building at the beginning of the outbreak.

AN UNEXPECTED JULY BONUS

I had behaved ostrich-like for some time after Cork's hurlers exited the Munster hurling championship. Then something happened at the Athletic Grounds in Cork on 15

July! The Rebel County senior football team, captained by Billy Morgan, stunned the world of Kerry football by thrashing the mighty Kingdom in the Munster final. A final score which read, Cork 5-12; Kerry 1-15 was indeed a rare sight. In view of the hurlers demise I turned to following the fortunes of the football team. Reports on the Munster final described the performance of goalkeeper Billy Morgan as brilliant. The goal scorers were Jimmy Barrett, who accounted for two; Billy Field, Denis Long and a chap called Jimmy Barry-Murphy, added one apiece.

Now where had I seen the latter name before? I soon recalled he was the Cork minor hurler Archie and myself noticed at Limerick the previous year. Among the scorers too was Ray Cummins. A closer look at the team line-out revealed the familiar names of Denis Coughlan and Brian Murphy. Cork did always produce top class dual players - remember Jack Lynch in the 1940s.

TIME RIGHT FOR BREAKTHROUGH
Ulster champions, Tyrone, were to be Cork's opponents in the All-Ireland semi-final. Long since I had pencilled into my diary a Croke Park appointment for Sunday 19 August. The match programme contained a write-up under the heading, 'Time Ripe for Breakthrough' introducing the players and setting in context their football careers to date. The undoubted potential present in the squad was account-ed for by the fact that Cork had won four All-Ireland minor titles since 1967, and Under-21 championships in 1970 and 1971. The win over Kerry was taken as proof of the presence of team spirit, determination, skill and finishing power. Experience was present in the form of Billy Morgan, Frank Cogan, Brian Murphy and Denis Coughlan – all of whom were described as having links with the 1967 All-Ireland senior team which lost to Meath, and the 1971 team which lost to Offaly at the semi-final stage.

Even among the newer members of the panel, bright prospects like Jimmy Barry-Murphy and Robert Wilmot were present, both of whom played in the 1972 All-Ireland minor hurling and football finals. Humphrey Kelleher, Kevin Ger O'Sullivan, John Coleman, Ray Cummins,

Jimmy Barrett and Denis Long were obvious pillars of the team. There was a feeling that this time a talented Cork team would not be inhibited by the occasion.

The Sam Maguire Cup had not rested at Leeside since 1945. The current proud Corkmen were now ready to take a first step towards rectifying that. Naturally the Tyronemen saw the situation differently. At this penultimate stage, Cork were to be confronted by Ulster champions who recorded fourteen wins and two draws in sixteen outings. Included in that count were three Ulster championship wins. They had last been beaten thirteen months previously by Donegal. Tyrone, like Cork, had been doing well at minor level and, had won the last three Ulster championships. Tyrone's captain, Frank McGuigan, was a top performer – he had played county minor in 1971, played for Ulster in the Railway Cup in January, travelled to San Francisco with the Carrolls All Stars party, and had recently won his second Under-21 provincial medal.

An attendance of 28,997 saw referee Dr Mick Loftus get the match under way. At half-time, for those who were more frequent visitors to Croke Park on major hurling occasions, the score board had a strange look about it – Cork 1-4; Tyrone 0-1. Cork's early scores came through Declan Barron and Ned Kirby points. It took all of fifteen minutes before the next score – a point from a free by Declan Barron. Cork's goal was punched to the net by Ray Cummins, following a good approach work by Connie Hartnett and Jimmy Barrett.

A few minutes into the second-half Cork suffered a serious setback. Billy Field, their top scorer with 2-14 to his credit in the championship so far, suffered a broken leg. Teddy O'Brien replaced the unfortunate Billy. From the moment Declan Barron finished a clever Ray Cummins cross to the net, the match suddenly came to life with Cork rampant. An exchange of scores followed in which Jimmy Barry-Murphy helped himself to two goals, and Seamus Coughlan added a third. Tyrone did score two goals but the outcome seemed well beyond doubt at that stage. The final score was Cork 5-12, Tyrone 2-4. Cork were a step nearer to taking 'Sam' back home.

HEROES TO A MAN

The All-Ireland football final of 1973 was played in Croke Park on 23 September but I was not to be among the 73,000 attendance, as I was unwell. On the great day I had to settle for watching the match on television at a curate's house in Ballinlea, County Antrim – one of the few houses in the area that, 'could get RTE'. In Fr Parks front room I lay on the floor, front down, propped on cushions, and made the best of my lot. In contrast to the semi-final against Tyrone, both Cork and Galway settled quickly. Cork did well from the start in the all-important scoring sector; the forwards were getting the upper hand of a highly-rated Galway defence. Cork too seemed to be quicker and sharper, and as time went on, fitter and stronger. Midfield man, Denis Coughlan, a star and an untiring worker of so many wonderful Cork occasions both in football and hurling, was majestic. A newspaper match report the following day bore the heading, 'Cork Team Has Everything'. Once again Ray Cummins showed what a fine player he really was – sure, confident, clever, inspirational and a calming influence on his fellow forwards by having the ability to hold up play while they moved into the most advantageous positions.

Nineteen-year-old Jimmy Barry-Murphy also showed what a class act he was. When referee John Moloney sounded the final whistle the score was Cork 3-17; Galway 2-13. It had been a glorious day for Cork football and the names of Billy Morgan (captain), Frank Cogan, Humphrey Kelleher, Brian Murphy, Kevin Ger O'Sullivan, John Coleman, Connie Hartnett, Denis Long, Denis Coughlan, Ned Kirby, Declan Barron, Dave McCarthy, Jimmy Barry-Murphy, Ray Cummins and Jimmy Barrett were indelibly inscribed in the county's football annals. Neither will the considerable contribution of the unfortunate Billy Field go unnoticed. The inspirational and managerial figure behind Cork's success was the former dual St Nicholas and Glen Rovers star, Donie O'Donovan. A year which early on promised little on the Gaelic games scene where Cork was concerned was later to turn on its head as the Sam Maguire Cup nestled by the Lee and celebrations went on until Christmas.

OPEC JOLTS, THE PACT SWAYS, AND SLADE SINGS AS CHARLES CLOSES ATLAS

In October 1973 the whole of the Western Europe, including Ireland, had cause for concern. Arab oil-producing countries on whom the West relied for 80 per cent of its liquid fuel demanded a 70 per cent price increase. An accompanying announcement warned of cutbacks in production as well. The expected resultant consequence in this country and others was an inflation hike accompanied by petrol rationing. In December a pact between the United Kingdom and the Republic of Ireland governments, together with Northern Ireland politicians, drew up an agreement for a power sharing executive in Northern Ireland. It was called the Sunningdale Agreement. Alas, it was to be short lived. The year ended with Slade singing their way to the top with a hit which conveyed the traditional seasonal greeting to all – 'Merry Xmas Everybody'. Among the late December obituaries there was one readily-recognisable to many people. It was that of original strong man, Charles Atlas. He had died at the age of 71.

1974

SEXTUPLETS, SKYLAB, KIDNAPPED AND HIDING

January 1974 secured its place in history when in Capetown, South Africa surviving sextuplets were born. In America, a record was established when at Dallas, Texas the world's largest airport became operational. January was ending when Sam Goldwyn (real name Samuel Goldfish) died at the age of 92, leaving films like 'Wuthering Heights' and 'Guys and Dolls' as his legacy. The New Seekers were first on the popular music scene with the number one hit 'You won't Find Another Fool Like Me'. It was shortlived though because Mud's, 'Tiger Feet' ousted it. In early February a thirteen-year-old Swede scored all 272 points in a basketball match. The feat may not have received the publicity it deserved because on the day it was achieved, Patti Hearst, daughter of multi-millionaire and United States newspaper publisher, William Randolph Hearst, was kidnapped. Much publicity too was given to the successful *Skylab 1* mission. The astronauts returned safely to Earth after 85 days in space. Very few column inches were reserved for the story of a Japanese soldier found hiding in the Philippines 29 years after Second World War hostilities had ceased. He believed the War was still ongoing.

HISTORY REPEATS ITSELF

To prove that Cork's hurlers were not hiding, they won the Oireachtas Tournament for the first time in 1973 and went on to register an emphatic win over Limerick in the Royal Liver National League final at Limerick on 5 May. The score was Cork 6-15; Limerick 1-2. John D. Hickey of the *Irish Independent*, headed his match report on Monday 6 May, 'Super Cork Demolish Limerick – One-way traffic in NHL decider'. There was no cup for presentation after the match and joyous as the day was for Cork, the team were left a little frustrated and annoyed at having to go home without it. Team captain, John Horgan, was presented instead with the cup won in the curtain raiser by North Tipperary in the All-Ireland Vocational Schools Hurling Final. Alas, two weeks later in a championship first-round match against Waterford at Walsh Park the gods conspired and Cork went tumbling. As in 1967 at the same venue, the Rebels failed to master the Decies men. By 5pm on 19 May the Munster hurling championship of 1974 was an irrelevance to Corkmen. The final score was Waterford 4-9; Cork 3-8. The unexpected exit by Cork was probably linked to the sending off of goalkeeper Paddy Barry before half-time. Was it to be a summer of discontent, or could the footballers again come to the rescue?

WORKERS STRIKE AS NIXON MOVES OUT AND ISABEL MOVES IN
Popular tune titles, 'Devil Gate Drive' by Suzi Quatro, 'Jealous Mind' by Alvin Stardust, 'Billy Don't be a Hero' by Paper Lace, 'Seasons in the Sun' by Terry Jacks, 'Waterloo' by Abba, and 'Sugar Baby' by Rubettes each made it to number one in the charts before May was out. May, the month traditionally associated with greenery, brightness and optimism, was anything but in Northern Ireland. The Sunningdale agreement brokered in December 1973 was overwhelmingly rejected by the Protestants in the north . The short-lived executive lasted only five weeks. A general strike – the Ulster Worker's Strike – brought it down, and the province to a standstill. The way was again open for paramilitary organisations to reek vengeance. On political fronts elsewhere, Golda Meir, the 70-year-old grandmother who became prime minister of Israel in 1969, resigned. Isabel Peron, third wife of Juan Peron, succeeded him as president of Argentina. In the United States, Richard Nixon made history when he became the first president to resign while in office. The damaging findings of the Watergate Inquiry left him little choice. Within a day of Nixon's stand-down, history was again in the making. Gerald R. Ford, who succeeded Richard Nixon, was the first American president to take office without going through the election procedure.

A DATE TO PENCIL IN

On 9 July and 14 July, the Cork senior football team dealt competently with Tipperary and Kerry respectively. They dismissed Tipperary by a score of 3-14 to 2-2 and went on to eliminate Kerry in the Munster final. The score at Fitzgerald Stadium was Cork 1-11; Kerry 0-7. Cork had booked a place in the All-Ireland semi-final. I booked a day out by writing the words, Croke Park beside Sunday 11 August in my diary.

MUSIC GALORE BUT HOMEWORK SHOWS THE BRILLIANCE OF DENIS

Throughout the summer a plethora of harmonies invaded the charts but it was Charles Aznavour's 'She' which enthralled most. It remained at number one for four weeks. Only 'Rock Your Baby' by George McCrae, and 'When will I see you Again' by the Three Degrees mounted a late challenge. In the weeks leading up to the All-Ireland football semi-final I did my homework on the Cork team which was to meet Dublin, the Leinster champions. With a single exception the line-out was that of the team which triumphed over Galway in the previous year's All-Ireland final. Frank Cogan had stood down and Donal Hunt got the nod for the coveted place. Cork's total score for the two championship matches played in Munster was a very impressive 4-25. Against that Cork conceded 2-9. Those figures speak well for both attack and defence. Ray Cummins was top scorer with 1-8. It was satisfying to note that all six forwards and both midfield players had contributed handsomely. To date the team credentials were the most impressive ever paraded by a football squad from the county. St Nicholas' club man Denis Coughlan, who was then 28, captained the team. The tall, perfectly built athlete was easily recognisable. Over the years Denis gave tremendous top-class service to the county as a dual player. In 1967, from centre-half back, he captained the Cork senior football team which lost to Meath in the All-Ireland final. Subsequently he established himself as an outstanding midfield player and marksman.

141

HEFFO'S TALENTED BLUE ARMY

On the Sunday morning of the match we drove to Dublin in confident mood, as were all the Cork fans. I went Croke Park in time for the curtain raiser, an All-Ireland minor football semi-final between Cork and Wicklow. It kicked-off at 2pm. The Wicklow boys found the going tough against a good Cork side which went on to beat Mayo in the All-Ireland final. On the Cork minor panel that day were players who in later years were to distinguish themselves on many major occasions at Croke Park. Included were Tom Cashman, Johnny Crowley and Dermot McCurtain, each of whom became a household name for hurling prowess. Referee Patsy Devlin was the man who got the senior match underway at 3.30 pm. Dublin immediately launched into a fast, slick, passing game which left the Corkmen chasing shadows at times. A highly-rated and well proven Cork defence were finding it difficult to cope with the elusive Dublin forwards. The style of play was obviously bothering the Leesiders. A score of 2-11 to 1-8 in favour of the Liffeysiders sent Cork home empty handed. Little did we know that the seeds were sown for a purple patch in Dublin football – the county team was to appear in the All-Ireland finals of 1974, 1975, 1976, 1977, 1978 and 1979 – becoming champions in 1974, 1976 and 1977.

Heffo's army was the tag used by Dublin followers due to the major role played by coach Kevin Heffernan in bringing Dublin football to the fore in the 1970s. As a Dublin player of the 1950s, Kevin had outstanding football credentials. He captained the county to All-Ireland victory in 1958 and was named at left-corner on the football team of the century. Throughout Dublin's golden spell in the 1970s, the names of Jimmy Keavney, Donal Hickey, Anton O'Toole, Bobby Doyle, Brian Mullins, Tony Hanahoe (captain 1976, 1977, 1978, 1979), Paddy Cullen, Sean O'Doherty (captain 1974, 1975), Gay O'Driscoll, Robbie Kelleher, George Wilson, Aidan Larkin, Barry Brogan, Tommy Drumm, Kevin Moran, Pat O'Neill, John McCarthy, Mickey Kennedy, Mick Holden, Fran Ryder, and many other Dublin players earned the right to take their places amongst the elite of Gaelic football players.

ALI IS KING, NIXON IS PARDONED AND TELETEXT ARRIVES

In September, Gerald Ford, thirty-eighth president of the United States, must have been in a generous mood when he granted his predecessor, Richard Nixon, a full pardon for his part in the Watergate scandal. Could it be that he was spurred on by the Osmonds number one hit 'Love Me for a Reason'.

In more belligerent disposition, or so it seemed, Carl Douglas sang his way to the top with 'Kung Fu Fighting'. When Muhammad Ali and George Foreman travelled to Kinshasa, capital of Zaire, that autumn, it wasn't Kung Fu they had in mind. It was a world heavyweight championship boxing contest in which Ali knocked out Foreman in the eighth round. Thus he regained the title he was stripped of in 1967 when he refused to be drafted into the United States Army.

There was no hint of hostility associated with John Denver's, 'Annie's Song'. Nevertheless it knocked 'Kung Fu Fighting' off the top in mid-October. As songs like, 'Sad Sweet Dream' by Sweet Sensation, and 'Everything I Own' by Ken Booth queued up and moved to the top of the charts, an invention called 'teletext' came into being. Ceefax, a system developed by the BBC, was the world's first teletext.

Barry White's 'You're the First, the Last, my Everything' seemed a little confused and David Essex responded with 'Gonna Make You a Star'. Mud sang the Christmas number one hit, 'Lonely This Christmas'.

At the end of life's trek, an individual has come, seen, and along the way may have conquered or not. Among the conquerors to complete the trek in 1974 were: Duke Ellington, one of the great jazz musicians; Sir James Chadwick, the physicist who discovered the neutron; U Thant, former secretary general of the United Nations; Jack Benny, American comedian, whose radio programme made him a national institution in the United States. One birth in 1974 which was significant for me took place on Sunday 7 July during the World Cup final between Germany and Holland. It was the birth of our daughter, Yvonne!

1975

OPEC NOT CAMBODIA'S PROBLEM

As the mid-1970s loomed, talk of Vietnam was largely confined to the aftermath of a horrific and bloody war. Yet the
troubled region of south-east Asia was again to the fore. A
catalogue of atrocities, even on a greater scale than the
Vietnam fiasco, was to materialise. A communist rebel
movement known as the Khmer Rouge, backed by north
Vietnam and the Viet Cong, had been engaged in conflict
with the United States-backed government of Lon Nol for
more than a decade. By January 1975 the Khmer Rouge virtually controlled the whole country. The crises made news
headlines when the capital Phnom Penh came under direct
siege. The name of Pol Pot, Khmer Rouge leader, became
notorious as a policy of deportations and executions on a
massive scale came to light.

In Europe it was the restless Organisation of Petroleum
Exporting Countries (OPEC) who were causing concern. A
ten per cent increase in the price of crude oil was certain to
have a cost of living knock-on effect.

THE LADY WHO MADE HISTORY

Early February heralded the appointment of Margaret
Thatcher as leader of the Conservative party in Britain. The
appointment was historic in that she was the first female
party leader. She later proved to be a formidable prime
minister and fashioned a political ideology known as,
'Thatcherism', which is no longer confined to Britain.
Maybe there was some significance in the fact that Status
Quo had a number one hit with 'Down Down' about the
same time as Mrs Thatcher's appointment. The Tymes hit
which took over from 'Down, Down' was 'Ms Grace'. On 22
February, 'Make me Smile' by Steve Harley and Cockney
Rebel replaced 'Ms Grace'. By early March 'If', sung by
Telly Sevalas, moved to the top.

A GONG FOR CHARLIE AS JIMMY SHINES AND PORTUGAL LETS GO
A springtime call to Buckingham Palace for silent movie
star   Charlie Chaplin meant that Charlie became Sir
Charlie. The St Patrick's Day weekend, with its feast of
Gaelic games at Croke Park, was the catalyst required to
get followers back in the groove after the winter lay off.
The cream of the country's players would display their tal-
ents in the finals of the Railway Cup and All-Ireland Club
Championships – hurling and football. But one player
would steal the show. On St Patrick's Day Jimmy Barry-
Murphy lined out for St Finbarrs (Cork), in the All-Ireland
Club Championship hurling final, contributing 1-4 of the 3-
8 total scored against the Fenians Club (Kilkenny). St
Finbarrs won by 3-8 to 1-6. The following day he lined-out
for the Munster Railway Cup football team and scored a
magnificent four goals in the final against Ulster. He had
won two national winners medals on successive days. The
Gaelic sporting genius had previously won an All-Ireland
senior football medal (1973) and Bank of Ireland All-Stars
Awards (1973 and 1974).

The Bay City Rollers chart topper called 'Bye Bye Baby'
may well have hit the right note in Portugal because the
Iberia peninsula country waved goodbye to three overseas
colonies during 1975. Independence was granted to
Angola, Mozambique, and the Cape Verde Islands, thereby severing links established in the fifteenth century.
Interestingly, the first free elections for 50 years were held
in Portugal in April. Former exile Mario Soares, leader of
the Portuguese Socialist Party, won, and later became
prime minister.

SAIGON FALLS, TAMMY STANDS, CHAMPIONSHIP UP AND
RUNNING
On 30 April our attention was once again drawn to
Vietnam. The Americans said the War was over and in fair-
ness the South Vietnam government, on whose side the
United States forces had been fighting, did sign up to a
ceasefire. Nevertheless, they continued to fight the com-
munist north Vietnam forces. When on 30 April the North
Vietnamese took over Saigon, the capital of South Vietnam,

then the War was definitely over. Mud were at number one with 'Oh Boy' whilst shortly afterwards Tammy Wynette sang her way to the top with 'Stand By Your Man'.

In Munster, Cork played Waterford in the first round of the championship. The Leesiders made no mistake this time and soundly beat the Decies. The final score was Cork 4-15; Waterford 0-6. In the Munster semi-final they met Clare, and again Cork had a comfortable victory, winning by 3-14 to 1-9. By all accounts Cork were playing well, with Ray Cummins, Charlie McCarthy and Seanie O'Leary causing all sorts of problems for defences. It was to be a Cork versus Limerick decider. Even though Limerick had been Munster champions for the past two years and had beaten Tipperary in the current championship, old traditions die hard and the attraction of a Cork/Tipperary encounter was not there. It was the first 70-minute Munster final. Both teams had several players with pedigrees which placed them in the thoroughbred category. The likely outcome of the match was difficult to predict and accordingly the pundits were cautious. The first-half lived up to expectations, with both sides more or less cancelling each other out. Early on in the second-half the highly acclaimed Cork forwards began to get the better of their opponents. Gradually the Leesiders began to dominate and were eventually easy winners. The final score was Cork 3-14; Limerick 1-9. I decided there and then to be in Croke Park for the All-Ireland semi-final.

Again the names of Ray Cummins, Jimmy Barry-Murphy and Seanie O'Leary were prominent on match reports the following day.

TRIUMPH, FAILURE, DISCOVERY AND REVULSION
Throughout the summer, headlines were made by Junko Tabei of Japan, who became the first woman to reach the summit of Mount Everest, and by stuntman Evel Knievel who suffered severe injuries while attempting to jump over thirteen buses in his car. Arthur Ashe made history by becoming the first black men's Wimbledon singles champion. In the news too was the American singer and actress Cher who was granted a divorce from Sonny Bono.

before three days later marrying Gregory Le Noire Allman. On the tenth day of the union Cher again filed for a divorce!

Perhaps the most fascinating discovery of 1975 took place in China, when archaeologists unearthed a miniature army of 8,000 terracotta figures, sculpted and fired in the shapes of warriors, chariots and horses. The figures were created more than 2,000 years ago.

In days following 31 July, Ireland was shocked, horrified and bewildered at the murders of the Miami Showband members by Protestant gunmen. The atrocity occurred when a van in which they were travelling was ambushed near Newry, County Down.

HURRAY FOR THE TRIBESMEN

In August, on one of the finest Sunday's of 1975, Cork played Galway in the All-Ireland hurling semi-final at Croke Park. Traditionally, a semi-final against Galway had not been taken too seriously by the giants of Munster and Leinster hurling. Galway last won an All-Ireland semi-final in 1953 – the era of great players such as Joe Salmon, Josie Gallagher and Inky Flaherty. The talented Cork team was installed as firm favourite in advance.

However, the Galway team were current National League winners. In achieving that status they had played Cork in the quarter-final and won 4-9 to 4-6; Kilkenny in the semi-final and won 1-9 to 1-6; and Tipperary in the final to come out on top by a score of 2-7 to 2-4. In other words they had taken on and beaten, in the final stages of the National League, what many regarded as the cream of hurling counties at the time – Limerick of course were also up there.

I was among the 27,000 attendance at Croke Park on semi-final day. As I studied the line-out on the programme, the names of John Connolly, P.J. Molloy, Sean Silke, Iggy Clarke, Niall McInerney and P.J. Qualter all rang a bell but I had never seen them play. The Cork line-out had that now familiar look about it, with only the names of goalkeeper Martin Coleman and left-half forward Denis Allen giving the team a new look. Galway had very strong, enthusiastic support which led one to believe that expectations were high. As referee Mick Spain of Offaly got the match underway it was a case of into the unknown.

Galway settled very quickly and confidently. They looked sharp, competitive, hungry, and were in no way intimidated by the occasion or the reputation of Cork. It was obvious that here was a well-prepared team. Soon they were winning individual battles in several positions. Inky Flaherty, the Galway team trainer, with a wealth of personal experience, had indeed moulded a formidable side. Cork had been hit by a much better, more committed and talented team than expected. Galway scored 2-2 in the first eight minutes without reply. Frank Burke, a strong running centre-half forward, blasted home the first goal at the end of a twenty-yard run. Brilliant midfield player John Connolly, at the end of yet another run, hit the second. P.J. Qualter and P.J. Molloy supplied the points. It was agony for Cork followers to see their side struggling to come to terms with the speed, craft and commitment of their opponents. Jimmy Barry-Murphy was first to register a score for Cork and P.J. Qualter added another goal to the Galway total. Further evidence of Cork's jitters came in the form of a close in free hit wide of the upright by the usually reliable Charlie McCarthy. Striving to emerge from the setback they were experiencing, Cork, as many teams before them had done, resorted to going for goals when point scoring chances were the obvious options. It took a Jimmy Barry-Murphy goal midway through the half to bring a semblance of stability to the Cork team.

The match was hard fought all over the pitch. John Connolly and Gerald McCarthy were having a battle in the middle of the park. Sean Murphy, the other Galway midfield player, was getting the better of Pat Hegarty. Frank Burke was certainly troubling Cork's centre-half back Martin O'Doherty. The Galway half-back line of Joe McDonagh, Sean Silke and Iggy Clarke were turning the sliotar well, leaving the feared Cork inside forward trio with only minimal chances. Denis Allen and Willie Walsh points for Cork were cancelled out by efforts form Gerry Coone and P.J. Molloy. Likewise further points by Charlie McCarthy from a 21-yard free, and a Con Roche '70', were negated by P.J. Molloy and P.J. Qualter. The half-time score was Galway 3-7; Cork 1-6.

Teddy O'Brien was replaced by Denis Burns in an effort to curtail P.J. Molloy, who interestingly enough did not score in the second-half. The Cork mentors decided on a further measure to negate the Galway half-forward line, and Frank Burke in particular. John Horgan was introduced for Martin O'Doherty. John switched with left-corner back Brian Murphy who took over at centre-half back. Frank Burke did not score again in the match. Onto the Galway team came Michael Connolly for injured right-corner forward Marty Barrett.

Cork now looked a much better side and began the second-half by scoring two points per Seanie O'Leary and Gerald McCarthy. Newcomer Michael Connolly made his presence felt by adding a brace for Galway. Then Con Roche, one of the finest half-backs to grace any team, drove a '70' right between the uprights before a fluke goal by Galway came as a setback for the Leesiders just when they were beginning to make inroads.

They battled on – Seanie O'Leary and Ray Cummins added points apiece before Padraig Fahy, who was now getting the better of Cork's Tony Maher, scored twice. With Cork badly needing a goal, Con Roche dropped a '70' into the square. Backs and forwards jostled as the sliotar landed close to the goal-line. It went off the hurley of Galway goalkeeper, Michael Conneely, and into the net – a goal for Cork. With seven minutes to go Cork had reduced the score deficit to four points. Scores by Con Roche, Seanie O'Leary and Gerald McCarthy brought the difference to a single point. Was the marvellous fight-back by Cork going to deny the Tribesmen after all? Excitement was at fever pitch. With players now exhausted by the pace of the match Gerry Coone scored a very important point to widen the gap. Another Con Roche point from a '70' was to bring the score difference back to a single point. Time was running out when Galway were awarded a '70'. The pride of Galway hurling, John Connolly, was to have the last say and made no mistake by sending the long puck right between the posts.

The final score was Galway 4-15; Cork 2-19. A two-point victory for the gallant Tribesmen. Galway played superbly for 70 minutes and maintained shape and concentration in the vital closing stages when Cork were within a whisker of snatching victory. The Leesiders, who were slow to start, left themselves a mountain to climb. All interested in the furtherance of the game of hurling had to be delighted with the breakthrough by Galway.

DISAPPOINTMENT, A FIRST FOR AMERICA, RICHARD AND LIZ DO IT AGAIN

The Tribesmen were not to collect the coveted McCarthy Cup in 1975. Days before the first American saint, Elizabeth Ann Bayley was canonised, Kilkenny beat Galway by a score of 2-22 to 2-10.

In July the Bay City Rollers 'Give a Little Love' hit the number one spot but the title of tune and group were in harmony when 'Barbados' by Typically Tropical topped the charts for two weeks in August. 'Can't Give You Anything (But My Love)' by the Stylistics displaced it, and three weeks later Rod Stewart took over with the popular 'Sailing'. Four weeks later it was the turn of David Essex with 'Hold Me Close'. It could well be that the title of the next number one inspired the re-marriage of Richard Burton and Elizabeth Taylor, in Botswana. It was the very romantic, 'I Only Have Eyes for you' by Art Garfunkel. 'Space Oddity' by David Bowie took over from Art Garfunkel's hit after two weeks. Next came Billy Connolly's 'D.I.V.O.R.C.E.', but it was Queen and 'Bohemian Rhapsody' that was to outdo all other number one hits in 1975 by remaining at the top for nine weeks.

Those looking back over 1975 with an eye out for prominent people who passed away would have noted the following: P.G. Woodhouse, creator of Bertie Wooster and Jeeves; Susan Hayward, one of the finest actresses of her time; Aristotle Onassis, Greek shipping tycoon; Chiang Kaishek, Chinese Nationalist leader; Haile Selassie, deposed emperor of Ethiopia; Eamon de Valera, Irish Republic statesman, three times Taoiseach, and President (1959-73); and Generalissimo Francisco Franco, Fascist Spanish dictator.

1976

COMPUTERS, HOT PANTS AND FACIAL OUTGROWTHS

Now that the 1970s were well advanced it was time to take stock of the changes in everyday life which had or were taking place. Probably more than anything else microchip technology came to the fore. The use of computers for recording and storing information became common place. International Business Machines (I.B.M.), the largest manufacturer of computers in the world, produced a unit which could record and store data on a 'floppy disc' which was light and easy to transport. The development was a further advancement on the original 1950 magnetic disc recording concept. Beside the television set the video cassette recorder began to appear. In some homes and many offices, Apple 2, the first mass produced practical computer, became a familiar sight before the end of the decade. For the first time people on the streets and elsewhere listened to music on their personal stereo headphones, whilst carrying a portable listening device, a Walkman, which had been launched by Sony (Japan). Another technological development of the 'Seventies was that of the first automatic camera.

What of fashion changes? It was not only the women who were involved – the men also let their hair down. An attempt was made early on in the decade to move ladies away from the leggy-look mini skirt to the calf length midi skirt. That particular move, much to the cost of clothing manufacturers, was largely a flop. Most women, particularly the younger ones, did not approve. The next fashion move was to the hot-pants, which just about covered the behind.

As the decade progressed elegance in ladies fashion became less evident. The shape of the body disappeared under layers of floppy clothes. A drop in hemlines was now welcomed by many women. The importance of certain items of underwear too became less acute and the bra, for many, went out at the beginning of the decade. The return of wedge shoes, commonly called platforms, first worn by the more daring ladies of the 1940s, was a big departure from the pointy toe and stiletto heeled footwear of the 1960s.

The most dramatic changes of all though were reserved for the men. The 1970s certainly left its sartorial mark on the century. Bell-bottoms, platform shoes, wide collars, smocks, suede, the wrinkled look and flared trousers became the order of the day. The wider the flares the better. Then before the decade was out, skinny hipster trousers and turtle neck jumpers were to become fashionable.

Perhaps the biggest fashion change of all where men were concerned was the return to wearing full beards, such as had not been seen since the turn of the century. Hair fashions too sometimes made it difficult to distinguish between men and women. The word unisex came into everyday vocabulary.

While the 1970s did not have the swagger, or should I say swing, of the 1960s, nevertheless the underlying demise of lifestyle as experienced in the immediate post war years continued. The whole attitude and outlook certainly belonged to a new era of liberalism and confidence which many parents and the more conservative members of society found difficult to understand.

The title of Abba's January number one hit, 'Mama Mia', may well have reflected the thoughts of many who dwelt on the 1970s fashion and changes.

COUNTRY ROCKED, ISABEL FELL BUT SOWETA RIOTS
In February the world was knocked back on its heels by the magnitude of the death toll in Guatemala. Over 22,000 people were killed when a massive earthquake rocked the country. Slik had a chart topper with 'For Ever and Ever', and Four Seasons followed with 'December '63', before Tina Charles made it to the top with 'I Love to Love'. By then it was March and Isabel Peron, president of Argentina, was about to be deposed as the result of an army coup. She was replaced by president Videla. Two very different but

very popular songs topped the charts for ten weeks leading up to early June. They were, 'Save All Your Kisses for me' by Brotherhood of Man' and, 'Fernando' by Abba. In June while many people in this country were turning their attention to the hurling championship which began for Cork on 13 June, serious racial driven rioting broke out in South Africa – the Soweta Riots.

CORK ON TRAIL AND PÁIRC IS TOPS
At Limerick, Cork met old rivals Tipperary in the Munster semi-final. The usual tough, unyielding, intense confrontation took place between counties which expected no less of each other. There was nothing between the two sides but on that occasion it was Cork's turn to come away with a single point victory. Martin Coleman, who made two outstanding saves, had a fine game in goals. The final score was Cork 4-10; Tipperary 2-15. Cork played Limerick in the Munster final at the newly-opened GAA headquarters in Cork, Páirc Uí Chaoimh. The new stadium, situated on the site of the athletic grounds, has an accommodation capacity of 50,000. It also incorporates a range of facilities in keeping with modern expectations, including shops, a bar, a cafeteria, a first-aid station, a special broadcasting and journalists' complex and administration offices for the Cork County Board. Work commenced on the project in April '74 and was completed by early June 1976. It was dedicated to the memory of Pádraig O Caoimh, former secretary of the Cork County Board and secretary of the Grounds Committee.

The new stadium was indeed very impressive and comfortably accommodated the 46,800 attendance. The match was a little disappointing in that the cut and thrust one might expect was not present, though it was gratifying to see Cork playing so well, being easy winners. The final score was Cork 3-15; Limerick 4-5. In the two championship outings to date, Charlie McCarthy had scored 2-5, leaving him Cork's top scorer. The Leesiders would have to wait until 22 August to find out who their All-Ireland final opponents would be.

Galway and Wexford played a semi-final match at

153

Páirc Uí Caoimh on 15 August which ended in a draw. I had the privilege of seeing that great, hard fought match. I was not at the replay when Wexford edged out Galway. The final score was Wexford 3-14; Galway 2-14. Cork and Wexford were to be the All-Ireland hurling finalists.

LIVERPOOL AND YOUTH SHINE, NIKI ESCAPES BUT AFRICANS MISSED
Elsewhere in the world of sport, Liverpool Football Club became English champions for a record ninth time, and twenty-year-old Swedish tennis player, Bjorn Borg, became the youngest player for 45 years to win the men's singles championship at Wimbledon. At the Montreal Olympic Games fourteen-year-old Nadia Comaneci won the admiration of the world when she was awarded the perfect score, ten out of ten, for a gymnastics display. She was to be awarded five other perfect scores on her way to winning three gold medals. But all was not well at the Montreal Olympic Games. A boycott by 22 African nations in protest against New Zealand's sporting links with South Africa, eliminated many of the world's best athletes. The runners were sorely missed. In motor racing, champion Niki Lauda narrowly escaped death when his car spun out of control and exploded after hitting a safety barrier. In addition to severe facial burns he suffered near fatal injury to his lungs by inhaling raw petrol fumes. As the American spacecraft *Viking* sent out pictures from Mars, number one hits 'No Charge' by J.J. Berrie, 'Combine Harvester' by the Wurzels, 'You to me are Everything' by the Real Thing, 'The Roussos Phenomenon' by Demis Roussos, and 'Don't Go Breaking My Heart' by Elton John and Kiki Dee, all took turns at the top.

IT DOESN'T GET ANY BETTER
A sunny, warm, windless, autumn afternoon on Sunday 5 September was to be the Croke Park setting for the All-Ireland hurling final between Cork and Wexford. The supporters of both counties did justice to the occasion by splashing the stands and terraces of the sun drenched stadium with a sea of contrasting colours – the red and white

of Cork and the distinctive purple and gold of Wexford. Closer examination revealed small pockets of the black and amber of Kilkenny and the blue and gold of Tipperary displayed by supporters of the competing minor teams.

At 3.15 pm precisely referee Paddy Johnston of Kilkenny set the ball rolling. Wexford got off to a great start while Cork were once again found wanting in getting away quickly from the starting blocks. Wexford ran up a score of 2-2, without reply from the Leesiders! Tony Doran, the Model County's captain and full-forward, was causing all sorts of havoc in front of the Cork goal. Pat McDonnell, the Rebels full-back, was standing shoulder to shoulder with the strong, muscular Wexfordman, yet Doran managed to score or make scores for his forwards. With six minutes of play gone Cork followers were despondent to say the least. The team in red and white were in serious trouble at that stage.

Pat Moylan was the first player to register a score for Cork. It came from a 65-yard free. Tony Doran continued to dominate and won yet another free which Mick Butler converted. Mick Malone replied for the Corkmen. At last the Leesiders were showing signs of settling down. They adopted a first-time pulling policy which kept the ball moving and denied possession to their opponents, thereby curtailing the lift and strike game preferred by the Wexfordmen. Denis Coughlan was doing very well at left-half back and the supply of sliotar coming from him was helping to set up Cork attacks. The next score, a point, came from Charlie McCarthy after good work by Ray Cummins. Against Galway in last year's All-Ireland semi-final, Con Roche gave an exhibition of long-range free taking. Con called it a day where inter-county hurling was concerned after that match and now the free-taking responsibility was that of newcomer, Blackrock's Pat Moylan. Pat must have been watching Con, because his striking too was impeccable. Before the end of the match he was to score ten points, eight from frees and two from play. One score came from an 80-yard free. On the basis that scores win games, that particular match has been referred to as Pat Moylan's All-Ireland final. Like Tony

Doran, Ray Cummins, Cork's full-forward and captain was now beginning to trouble the Wexford full-back, fair-haired Willie Murphy. Ray began to win crucial frees from which Charlie McCarthy and Pat Moylan were unerring. The Cork midfield of Gerald McCarthy and Pat Moylan were getting the better of their counterparts, Ned Buggy and Billy Rowsome.

Importantly, John Crowley, at centre-half back for the Rebels, was doing very well against Martin Quigley. Likewise, Pat Barry at right-half back, was holding his own against John Quigley. Cork clawed their way back into the match and when Ray Cummins kicked the sliotar to the net, the scores were level – Cork 1-9; Wexford 2-6. A great comeback had been staged by the Leesiders. The hurling from both teams was now superb. Further scores were exchanged before half-time, and as the whistle sounded the sides were again level, Cork 1-11; Wexford 2-8.

Seanie O'Leary who had been limping for much of the first-half did not return for the second period. It was a second period which did not begin as Cork followers would have wished for because Tony Doran quickly added another goal to Wexford's total. Mick Malone was playing extremely well around the half-forward line. He was a strong runner who always troubled defenders. Shortly after Tony Doran's goal, Mick was awarded a free from which Pat Moylan notched up a point. Then we were to experience a typical Charlie McCarthy stoke on the half volley which sent the sliotar whistling into the Wexford net – a sweet goal for the Leesiders. Pat Moylan and Martin Quigley exchanged points before the Cork mentors put their heads together and replaced the tiring Pat Barry by John Horgan, the blond bombshell from Rochestown. John went centre-back with Johnny Crowley moving to the wing.

One of those mentors was none other than the greatest hurler of all time, Christy Ring. It was tremendous to see the maestro once again display his enormous enthusiasm and will to win, by running along the sideline urging players to give the last calorie of energy to the cause. The cause was a Cork win.

Wexford though were in no mood to capitulate. Ned

Buggy set up a chance which ended in the Cork net, courtesy of Mick Butler. Mick was having a great game, and his namesake, Mick Jacob at centre-half back, was majestic. Wexford again had gained the initiative as the Cork defence began to look shaky. In spite of attack after attack, through wastefulness the Model County men failed to score. Instead it was a Pat Moylan free which added a point to Cork's total. Cork's mentors again rearranged the defence by bringing Brian Murphy to full-back, left-corner back Martin O'Doherty to centre-half back, and John Horgan to left-half back. Pat McDonnell went to right-corner back. From that point on the defence looked more solid. A further Cork team change brought Jimmy Barry-Murphy to centre-forward in direct opposition to Mick Jacob. That too proved to be a good move, with Jimmy making his presence felt almost immediately. Following a Mick Malone point from a free, Jimmy Barry-Murphy added a brace to put Cork a point ahead. Again it was approach work by Jimmy Barry-Murphy that set Ray Cummins up for a point. There was only five minutes of play left, the warm day had taken its toll, and all of a sudden the Wexford team did not look as fit as the Corkmen. They seemed to have given their all. John Horgan was clearing the sliotar away down into the Wexford half every time it came near him. Jimmy Barry-Murphy, who had been fairly anonymous until his move to the half-forward line, now added another point, but fittingly it was Pat Moylan who had the last score of the match. The final score was Cork 2-21; Wexford 4-11. What a marvellous match it had been and what a comeback by Cork when it seemed they had lost their way.

As for Wexford, they had contributed to one of the best All-Ireland hurling finals seen in Croke Park for many a day. I'm sure that was little consolation to them. It was a pity that one side had to lose. The fact was, Cork had taken it's twenty-second All-Ireland hurling final. The Cork team was: Martin Coleman, Brian Murphy, Pat McDonnell, Martin O'Doherty, Pat Barry, John Crowley, Denis Coughlan, Gerald McCarthy, Pat Moylan, Mick Malone, Brendan Cummins, Jimmy Barry-Murphy, Charlie

157

McCarthy, Ray Cummins (captain) and Sean O'Leary. The
Wexford team was: John Nolan, Teddy O'Connor, Willie
Murphy, Jim Prendergast, Liam Bennett, Mick Jacob, Colm
Dornan, Ned Buggy, Billy Rowsome, Johnny Murphy,
Martin Quigley, John Quigley, Mick Butler, Tony Doran
(captain), and Christy Keogh.

JIMMY IN OFFICE, JOAN ADDS WEIGHT AND JOHNNY'S
CHRISTMAS MAGIC
While Cork folk celebrated, Abba entertained with their
new number one hit, 'Dancing Queen'. It remained
favourite for six weeks until 'Mississippi' by Pussycat
came along. When Democrat Jimmy Carter became thirty-
ninth president of the United States in November, it was 'If
you Leave me now' by Chicago which topped the charts. In
Northern Ireland the Women's Peace Movement, otherwise known as the Ulster Peace Movement, brought 30,000
marchers to the centre of London. Present were the movement's co-founders, Mairead Corrigan and Betty Williams.
The march was supported by a large contingent from
Europe and the United States, including famed folk singer
and anti-Vietnam war activist, Joan Baez.

Among the prominent people who died in 1976 were
Agatha Christie, crime fiction writer; Paul Robeson,
singer, actor and American civil rights campaigner; Jean
Paul Getty, oil billionaire; Busby Berkley, choreographer
and film director; and Mao Zedong, Chinese political
leader.

Showaddywaddy enjoyed top hit status for three
weeks with 'Under the Moon of Love' until most appropriately on 25 December, Johnny Mathis took over with the
beautiful, 'When A child Is Born'. With profound lyrics, it
was the perfect Christmas song.

A PROUD DAY
Before closing the chapter I must mention a Croke Park
visit on Sunday 26 September, All-Ireland football final
day. In the senior match were the exciting Kerry and
Dublin teams of the 1970s.

My interest was in the minor football final between

Cork and Galway, especially the Castlehaven player who lined-out at left-half back on the Cork team – James Nolan, my nephew. It was a great family occasion and I was very proud of the young man. Sadly for the Cork lads, Galway became All-Ireland champions but as the *Irish Press* reported, 'James Nolan had a fine game at left-half back'.

1977

BOEING WOE BUT RUMMY TOPS AS POLITICIANS MOVE

As the New Year settled in, 'Don't Give up on Us,' sung by David Soul remained in pole position for four weeks. 'Don't Cry for me Argentina' by Julie Covington was next to fill the top spot, but it lasted only a week before Leo Sayer with 'When I Need You' toppled it in mid-February. Manhattan Transfer, with their number one hit, '*Chanson D'Amour*' was at the height of its popularity when horrific news was reported from Tenerife. Two Boeing 747 Jumbo jets collided and burst into flames on the runway at Las Rodeos airport. One belonged to Pan Am and the other to KLM. All passengers and crew on the KLM plane, a total of 248 died. The 326 passengers all died on the Pan Am plane, making a total of 574. Of the Pan Am passengers, 70 escaped death but many of them suffered severe burns. The accident was caused by poor visibility due to fog.

On 2 April horse racing enthusiasts everywhere took off their hats to a twelve-year old gelding – Red Rum. 'Rummy', as he was affectionately known, won the Grand National for an unprecedented third time.

World political leaders were very much on the move during the first half of 1977. Indira Gandhi, prime minister of India, resigned after an election defeat; Menachem Begin became prime minister of Israel; and Leonid Ilyich Brezhnev became president of the USSR.

As the bands played on few were more popular than Abba. Their chart-topper 'Knowing me, Knowing you' filled the airwaves for five weeks in early summer. It was Deniece Williams with a song called 'Free' who took over from Abba, but only briefly, because 'I don't want to Talk About it' by Rod Stewart was soon to move in. Four weeks later Kenny Rogers very popular 'Lucille' deposed Rod.

DOUBLE AT THURLES

Cork took on Waterford in the Munster hurling championship semi-final at Thurles. The Leesiders came away with a five-point win over the Decies men. The final score was Cork 4-13; Waterford 3-11.

According to reports Cork played well with eight of the team contributing to the score total. Charlie McCarthy notched up a personal tally of 1-5. The two newcomers to the side, Tom Cashman and Tim Crowley, playing at midfield, each scored and acquitted themselves well in general play.

Clare beat Tipperary, and Limerick in order to qualify for the Munster final showdown with Cork. It was to be a clash between the current All-Ireland champions, Cork, and the current Royal Liver National Hurling League winners, Clare. A good Clare team had beaten Kilkenny in the League final by 2-8 to 0-9 at Thurles on 24 April. Several of the Banner County side including goalkeeper Seamus Durack, and out-field players, Jackie O'Gorman, Jim Power, Ger Loughnane, Gus Lohan, Sean Stack, Jimmy McNamara, John Callinan and Noel Casey were all known to be accomplished hurlers. Cork were aware that the Clare team had the potential to cause an upset.

On 10 July, Munster hurling final day, a car load of us headed off for Thurles. One of the passengers was fourteen-year-old John Cleary. John was later to distinguish himself as a talented Gaelic football player who gave great service to Castlehaven and Cork. Followers of Gaelic football will remember the two crucial goals he scored from penalties against Dublin in the All-Ireland senior semi-final of 1989.

The match was played in warm sunshine in front of an attendance of 44,586. Another wonderful day of excitement and thrills at Thurles lay in store. The waiting was over when at 3.30 pm referee Noel Dalton threw in the sliotar between the flailing camans of the midfield players. Clare started well. Cork took time to settle. They had, however, come to terms with the challenge before Clare's full-back Jim Power was sent off just before half-time. The dismissal of the Banner County player had a detrimental effect on the match. The Leesiders dominated the second-half and were not at all flattered by their winning margin of five points. The final score was Cork 4-15; Clare 4-10. The Cork scorers were: Jimmy Barry-Murphy 2-0; Charlie McCarthy 0-5; Tom Cashman 0-5; Tim Crowley 1-0; Ray Cummins 1-0; Mick Malone 0-2; Gerald McCarthy 0-1; Seanie O'Leary 0-1; and Pat McDonnell 0-1. No fewer than nine Cork players scored. Tom Cashman and Tim Crowley who lined-out at midfield showed what assets they were to the team. The neat, skilful Cashman contrasted with the strength, power and dogged determination of the talented Crowley. The Cork team was: Martin Coleman, Brian Murphy, Martin O'Doherty (captain), John Horgan, Dermot McCurtain, John Crowley, Denis Coughlan, Tom Cashman, Tim Crowley, Mick Malone, Gerald McCarthy, Jimmy Barry-Murphy, Charlie McCarthy, Ray Cummins and Seanie O'Leary. On 7 August at Croke Park, Cork met Galway in the All-Ireland hurling semi-final.

MUSIC ALL THE WAY AS CORK HURLERS SECURE A PLACE
'Show You The Way To Go' by the Jacksons preceded Hot Chocolate's 'So You Win Again' at number one. Donna Summer was next to take over top spot with 'I Feel Love'. Donna's hit remained at the top for four weeks until mid-August when the Brotherhood of Man took over with 'Angelo'.

The semi-final between Cork and Galway again showed what a good team Galway were. Captained by Iggy Clarke, they led by three points on four different occasions during the 70 minutes. Maybe they didn't have the killer instinct just yet. A Seanie O'Leary goal at a critical time sent the Leesiders on the road to victory.

The final score was Cork 3-14; Galway 1-15. Cork scorers were: Charlie McCarthy 1-2; Seanie O'Leary 1-2; Jimmy Barry-Murphy 1-0; Tim Crowley 0-3; Dermot McCurtain 0-2; Gerald McCarthy 0-2; John Horgan 0-1; Tom Cashman 0-1; Ray Cummins 0-1. Ten players got their names on the score sheet – a great sign.

NOT ONLY THE KING DEPARTED
The death of rock 'n' roll king Elvis Presley on 15 August

had fanatical fans openly grieving all over the world. The 42-year-old entertainer revolutionised popular music in the 1950s and the eruption of rock music in the 1960s owed a great deal to him. Perhaps there was some significance in the fact that shortly after his demise, one of his recordings, 'Way Down', became a number one hit.

The passing of several other show business personalities in 1977 was also mourned. Among then were: Joan Crawford, American film star; Groucho Marx, comic and, one of the famous Marx brothers; Maria Callas, whose glorious voice dominated opera in the 1950s and 1960s; Bing Crosby, screen actor and singer; Sir Charles Chaplin, film actor, director and comic genius; and Marc Bolan, lead singer of T-Rex, who died in a car crash.

TECHNOLOGY SHOWS CORK AND WEXFORD AROUND THE WORLD

Sunday 4 September was All-Ireland hurling final day. On that occasion it was wet and windy. Wexford were again Cork's opponents. Cork were favourites to win. The match was shown live in London, Bristol, Sydney and Melbourne. N.B.C. in North America showed it at a later date, and the New Zealand TV Service did likewise. Television viewers in Holland and northern Germany saw edited highlights, as did viewers in Britain.

The Wexford team of 1977 showed only a single change in personnel from the team which lost to Cork a year ago - Dave Bernie replaced Billy Rowsome at midfield. John Nolan was again custodian. The forwards were switched around with only Martin Quigley and Tony Doran retaining their respective centre-half forward and full-forward positions.

The Cork team showed four personnel changes from the 1976 starting line-out. John Horgan, Dermot McCurtain, Tom Cashman and Tim Crowley replaced Pat McDonnell, Pat Barry, Pat Moylan and Brendan Cummins. Analysis of Cork's performances in the Munster championship would suggest that the team of 1977 was better than that of 1976. The new players on the team had all shown a high level of accomplishment. They slotted in beside established and experienced stars such as Gerald McCarthy, Denis Coughlan, Ray Cummins, Charlie McCarthy, Mick Malone, Brian Murphy, Martin O'Doherty, Jimmy Barry-Murphy, Seanie O'Leary and Martin Coleman, to make formidable opponents for any team. As referee Sean O'Grady threw in the sliotar to start the match there wasn't a slouch among the 66,542 attendance. The Leesiders were well in charge throughout a rather disappointing match. Gerald McCarthy playing at centre-half forward, had a wonderful game as did did full-back and team captain, Martin O'Doherty. Brian Murphy and John Horgan were then probably the best corner backs in the game.

The team now had the hallmarks of a well-oiled machine firing on all cylinders. We had come along way from those dark times early in the 1960s when one wondered if Cork would ever rule the roost again. Already the question being asked was, 'Is this Cork team as good as the 1952-4 sides which won three All-Irelands in a row'? It was a difficult comparison, not least because the 1950s sides had Christy Ring who was a man apart and a menace to entire defences.

When the final whistle sounded on that damp September afternoon the score was Cork 1-17; Wexford 3-8. Cork's winning margin of three points in no way reflected their supremacy over the 70 minutes. Still three points were enough to bring the McCarthy Cup back to Leeside for another year.

IAN ACCEPTS AND BOAT PEOPLE FLEE AS JIMMY PARDONS

In November, just as number one hit 'Silver Lady' by David Soul was displaced by Baccara's 'Yes Sir, I Can Boogie', Ian Smith prime minister of Rhodesia finally but reluctantly accepted the principle of black majority rule. December brought with it a new expression – 'boat people'. It was used to describe illegal emigrants arriving by sea, mostly in ramshackle boats, from the war torn countries of Vietnam, Laos and Cambodia. Their intended destinations were usually Hong Kong, Thailand, Indonesia, the Philippines, or Malaysia. Many never reached their places of refuge due to drowning when boats sank or capsized. Attacks by pirates was a further hazard for the unsuspecting escapees. As time went by and numbers grew, overcrowding in the host countries became acute. Western nations were asked to help by taking in some refugees. Already the United States had taken 165,000 since 1975.

The year was well into its twilight stage when Abba had a second chart topper called 'Name of the Game'. But it was 'Mull Of Kintyre' by Wings which saw the year out. Before the New Year arrived it seemed that the United States' president Jimmy Carter wanted to draw a line beneath the Vietnam War controversy. He pardoned all citizens who dodged being drafted into the army during the south-east Asia conflict.

1978

OPTIMISM, CONCERN, SENTIMENT AND TRIUMPH

In the early days of 1978, Cork hurling followers wondered if the county senior team would complete a hat trick of All-Ireland championships. Yet they were not doing well in the National League. Other counties might well be encouraged by such poor results. Sleeping giants such as Tipperary, Limerick, Clare, Galway, Wexford and Kilkenny were always lurking in the background.

On the music scene, 'Mull Of Kintyre', which topped the charts in December 1977 remained at number one for the whole of January and into February – nine weeks in all. It was 'Up Town Top Ranking' by Althia and Donna which took over briefly, before 'Figero' by Brotherhood of Man replaced it. Abba were next to move into top spot with 'Take a Chance on Me'. The Swedish government was apparently in no mood for taking chances, because in 1977 it decided to ban the use of ozone-depleting aerosol sprays. Sweden had good reason for reacting to the impending dangers resulting from such sprays. The ozone layer over northern Europe was said to be disappearing at a rate of about five per cent every ten years.

Further south, off the coast of Brittany, there was a further problem. On St Patrick's Day the massive oil tanker, *Amoco Cadiz*, ran aground and split in two. Its cargo of crude oil began to leak into the sea causing enormous pollution problems, not least the devastation of marine life.

Undeterred by a depleting ozone layer and oil spillage, Kate Bush had four weeks at number one in the charts with 'Wuthering Heights'. In early April she lost out to 'Matchstalk Men and Matchstalk Cats And Dogs' by Brian and Michael. Meanwhile sentiment ran high when it was announced that Red Rum was to go into retirement. Grand National day would not be the same without him! 'Night Fever' by the Bee Gees, followed by Boney M's, 'Rivers of

Babylon' were chart toppers in May and June.

Again that time of year had come around when memories of winter were obliterated from the mind. Cork's senior hurlers were to meet Waterford at Thurles in the Munster semi-final on 25 June. Preparations were well underway in both camps when on 8 June, Naomi James became the first woman to sail solo round the world. The New Zealander, in her yacht *Express Crusader*, completed the trip in nine months. It was in June too that for the first time Argentina won the most prestigious competition in international soccer – the World Cup. The South American's beat Holland by two goals to nil after extra time in the final.

THE CHAMPIONSHIP IS ANOTHER STORY
So poorly did Cork hurlers fare in the 1977-8 Royal Liver National Hurling League that they were relegated to Division 1B. Cork's Munster championship semi-final against Waterford proved to be a rather one-sided contest. A very early goal by Ray Cummins put the Rebels on their merry way to a comfortable win resulting in a final score of 3-17 to 2-8. Cork scorers were: Jimmy Barry-Murphy 1-3; Tom Cashman 1-2; Ray Cummins 1-1; Seanie O'Leary and John Horgan 0-3 each; Charlie and Gerald McCarthy 0-2 each; and Tim Crowley 0-1. Clare had again qualified to meet Cork in the Munster final by beating Limerick 4-12 to 3-8.

All roads led to Thurles on 30 July for a repeat of last seasons final. As in 1977 Clare were Royal Liver National League winners and Cork were current All-Ireland champions. To prove that expectations of a classic encounter were high, the largest attendance at a Munster final since 1961 was registered. A crowd of 54,181 passed through the turnstiles.

Before a sliotar was struck Cork suffered a setback by having to line-out without the services of stalwart right corner-back, Brian Murphy and ace marksman, left corner-forward, Seanie O'Leary. Both players were out of the team through injury and their places were taken by Denis Burns and Mick Malone who was himself recovering from injury. Cork played with a strong breeze in the first-half.

As the match unfolded it became clear that the expected brilliance and sparkle was not to materialise. In the first-half Cork had the lion's share of the play but shot thirteen wide and managed to score only five points, none coming from the forwards. Clare had three scores on the board for the same period. The half-time score was: Cork 0-5; Clare 0-3. A two-point margin did not seem enough for the Corkmen, and few present believed that they would hold out against a wind-aided Clare in the second-half. However, the fear was unfounded and in the second-half we saw why Cork were All-Ireland champions.

Martin O'Doherty was superb at full-back, Denis Burns proved an excellent stand-in, and John Horgan, who accounted for four of the five first-half points, was simply a pleasure to watch as again and again he unerringly cleared the sliotar up-field. The half-back line of Dermot McCurtain, John Crowley and the elegant Denis Coughlan was a neat, classy, dependable unit. Tom Cashman was the midfield star. He displayed the skills of top class hurling at a level seldom seen. Once his partner Tim Crowley settled, he too was very effective. For once the forwards were poor by their own high standards. Maybe that was a tribute to the Clare defence. The introduction of Eamonn O'Donoghue for the unfit Mick Malone (recovering from injury) seemed to bring about an improvement. Pat Horgan was brought in for Pat Moylan without making a significant difference. In spite of excellent defending and more than adequate midfield advantage, at the final whistle only two points separated the sides: Cork 0-13; Clare 0-11. In fairness to the Clare defence, especially the full-back line, and right half-back Ger Loughnane, they acquitted themselves very well indeed. The Cork scorers were: Charlie McCarthy 0-5; John Horgan 0-4; Ray Cummins 0-2; Tim Crowley and Tom Cashman 0-1 each. It was interesting to note that in the championship so far, left-corner back John Horgan shared the top scoring place with Charlie McCarthy at seven points apiece. In the final analysis, Cork, the All-Ireland champions made their followers very happy indeed. After the interval they picked themselves up and dominated the match. They deservedly took the Munster senior title for the thirty seventh time in all, and the fourth in succession.

WE HAD WINNERS, HUMAN SCIENCE, AND DISCO BUT POPES DID THE TRIPLE

Cork were not the only achievers that summer. In July two German mountaineers reached the summit of Mount Everest without the use of oxygen, which had been essential to all previous expeditions. Martina Navratilova, the Czech tennis player, at the age of eighteen, won the Wimbledon ladies singles championship. Later in the year she defected to the West and asked the United States for political asylum. The Wimbledon men's singles tennis championship was won for the third successive time by Swedish tennis star Bjorn Borg.

The item of news which probably caused greatest sensation in 1978 was the announcement of the birth of the world's first test tube baby. It was delivered by Caesarean section at Oldham General Hospital. A number one hit by John Travolta and Olivia Newton-John called 'You're the One that I Want' from the hit film 'Grease' proved extremely popular, so much so that it remained at the top for nine weeks. John Travolta had a further claim to fame because the film 'Saturday Night Fever' in which he had also starred was largely responsible for the worldwide 'disco' fanaticism which began in 1978. 'Three Times A Lady' by the Commodores was the next number one.

The death of Pope Paul VI took place in August followed by the death of his successor, Pope John Paul I, 34 days after his appointment. And finally John Paul II was installed. Born in Poland and christened Korol Wojtyl, he was the first non-Italian pontiff for 456 years.

1969 AND 1972 WERE INDELIBLY STAMPED ON OUR MINDS

As September loomed there was only one thing on the minds of Cork and Kilkenny hurling followers – All-Ireland hurling final day. It was a clash between two very old adversaries, but Cork had good reason to heed the more recent All-Ireland finals of 1969 and 1972, when Kilkenny snatched victory from the jaws of certain defeat.

The day of reckoning finally arrived and 64,155 spectators poured into Croke Park expecting to see an exciting, closely contested 70 minutes of hurling. Magic was very much in the air as Laoisman, referee Jimmy Rankins, got the match underway. Within 30 seconds Jimmy Barry-Murphy scored a point for the Leesiders. As the teams settled, and thankfully Cork did so quickly, the Rebels looked the more cohesive side. Yet it was Kilkennyman Kevin Fennelly who was at hand to capitalise on a misunderstanding between two Cork defenders and drove the sliotar to the net. Pressure was being exerted by the Leesiders, but worryingly, scores were not coming. More anxiety was caused among the Cork followers when Tim Crowley had a penalty saved by Kilkenny's goal keeper, Noel Skehan. The usually ultra-dependable John Horgan was not finding the target with long distance frees either!

Still, Cork kept up the pressure and as a result scored three hard-earned points without reply. Then a spell followed where points were quickly exchanged. With about ten minutes left to half-time Cork's mentors switched Tim Crowley to midfield, with Tom Cashman moving to the half-forward line. Gerald McCarthy also switched with Jimmy Barry-Murphy. There were signs that Kilkenny were beginning to dominate but Charlie McCarthy scored a point from play to level the scores at the interval – Cork 0-7; Kilkenny 1-4. Charlie McCarthy was doing well against Dick O'Hara and continued to score very important points from frees. Cork pressed but Kilkenny held fast with Noel Skehan making some good saves. We now had an exciting match in progress. Stylish, top class, open hurling was absent, save for a few glimpses of individual brilliance.

Martin O'Doherty was majestic at full-back. He completely obliterated his opposite number, Brian Cody. The long clearances by himself and left-corner back John Horgan proved vital in the long run. It has to be remembered too that right-corner back Brian Murphy held Matt Ruth scoreless. The half-back line was copper fastened by the dominance of Johnny Crowley at centre-half back, the dependable Denis Coughlan, and the economical, neat play of Dermot McCurtain. Perhaps the Tim Crowley move to midfield earlier in the match was the most significant of all. He gradually wore down the dominance of Kilkenny's Frank Cummins. There was a particular moment when he broke away down the wing on a strong solo run and shot over a spectacular point. The Corkmen were spurred on by that positive piece of action. A decisive stage in the match had been reached.

Suddenly Cork were playing with more assurance. Soon Charlie and Gerald McCarthy scored points apiece. At that stage the Leesiders led by three points. John Allen had replaced Tom Cashman before Liam O'Brien reduced Cork's lead to two points. Minutes later a Jimmy Barry-Murphy shot from well out the field found its way to the Kilkenny net. The Noreside mentors, realising that the match was slipping away from them, decided to take off Liam O'Brien and introduce Pat Henderson at centre-half back, with his brother Ger moving to bolster up the midfield. For once the move did not pay off because Ger, who had been outstanding in defence did not perform nearly as well at midfield. Pat's performance too was well below par. The Cork half-forwards now came much more into the match. Mind you Billy Fitzpatrick scored a good goal for Kilkenny before Ray Cummins and Charlie McCarthy finished the scoring. When referee Jimmy Rankins put the whistle to his mouth for the last time that afternoon the scoreboard read Cork 1-15; Kilkenny 2-8. A four point victory for Cork in a tough, uncompromising match which the Kilkenny's full-back Phil 'Fan' Larkin did his damndest to win.

The Noresiders led on four occasions and the sides were level no less than eight times. There were tears of joy everywhere as team captain Charlie McCarthy held the McCarthy Cup high above his head. Charlie would now do what Ray Cummins did in 1976, and Martin O'Doherty did in 1977 – to take the coveted trophy back to Cork in 1978. A magnificent trio of successive All-Ireland wins for the Leesiders. The Rebels current captain, Charlie McCarthy, was one of Cork's greatest scoring forwards. In the 1978 final he had a fine game, was top scorer with seven points, five from frees, and fittingly enough hit the last score of the championship. The Cork team was: Martin Coleman, Brian Murphy, Martin O'Doherty, John Horgan, Dermot McCurtain, John Crowley, Denis Coughlan, Tom Cashman (0-1), Pat Moylan, Jimmy Barry-Murphy (1-1), Gerald

McCarthy (0-2), Tim Crowley (0-2), Charlie McCarthy (captain) (0-7), Ray Cummins (0-1), Sean O'Leary (0-1). Subs: John Allen for Tom Cashman; Eamonn O'Donoghue for Seanie O'Leary.

PUNK, HEAVY METAL, AND FITNESS RULE BUT TYRANTS KILL MANY

With the McCarthy Cup safely back home for another year it was time to take stock of what was happening elsewhere. In the midst of a new youth culture described as 'punk rock', and its associated heavy metal music, John Travolta and Olivia Newton-John sang another number one hit from 'Grease', the 1950s styled 'Summer Nights'. Somehow it didn't fit in with the Sex Pistols, Johnny Rotten, Sid Vicious, or other symbols of punk rock. However, 'Summer Nights' remained at the top for seven weeks, at which time 'Rat Trap' by Boomtown Rats took over. After a two weeks stay, Rod Stewart moved up with 'Da Ya Think I'm Sexy'.

One of the most striking phenomena of 1978 was the emergence of the move towards physical fitness. Fitness became fashionable for all ages. Over the next decade, jogging, weight lifting, aerobics and dieting spread throughout the western world like wildfire. There was a proliferation of fitness clubs and complexes.

Among those who died in 1978 were: Jomo Kenyatta, president of Kenya; Golda Meir, former prime minister of Israel; and Aldo Moro, Italian Christian Democrat politician and one-time prime minister, who was kidnapped in Rome and later shot by the Red Brigade. Five of his bodyguards were also shot dead.

It was in December 1978 that the world learned the full truth of recent horrors in Cambodia. The Khmer Rouge had waged a campaign of genocide during which thousands were murdered, and others died of starvation, overwork and disease, in what became known as the 'killing fields'. Number one at the close of the year was Boney M's charming 'Mary's Boy Child – Oh my Lord'.

1979

Could the Cork senior hurling team win a fourth All-Ireland title in a row? That was the question on the minds of many as the New Year began to unfold. At Ballycastle in early March there was a huge treat in store for Ulster hurling enthusiasts. The Blackrock Club from Cork (Munster Club Champions) and the local McQuillians Club (Ulster Club Champions) met in the All-Ireland Clubs' semi-final. Both teams were star studded. Virtually the entire Mc Quillians team had donned the saffron jersey of Antrim at some stage. The Blackrock line-out had a distinctive look of Cork county teams which had won All-Ireland championships in 1976, 1977 and 1978. There was one notable exception, that was none other than Frank Cummins, the mighty Kilkenny midfielder who played his club hurling with Blackrock. The team boasted an awesome array of hurling talent including Ray Cummins, Dermot McCurtain, Frank Norberg, Pat Moylan, Eamonn O'Donoghue, Francis Collins, Donal Collins, Brendan Cummins and current Bank of Ireland All-Stars, John Horgan and Tom Cashman.

Alas, the gala weekend which had been so looked forward to was marred by news of the death of Christy Ring, the greatest hurler I have ever seen. The winner of eighteen Railway Cup and eight All-Ireland medals, died suddenly on 2 March in Cork. He was aged 58. While the Antrim club ensured that the game was not all one way traffic, Blackrock always had the edge and won fairly comfortably. The death of a hurling legend in Ireland was unlikely to make headlines in Iran but 1979 was to prove a momentous year in the history of that country. The Shah's regime was tainted by corruption and brutality which eventually led to its downfall. In the face of mounting opposition masterminded by Aytollah Khomeini, the Shah was forced to flee the country. With the way opened, the Aytollah returned from exile and declared a provisional government. Later, almost in dictatorial style, he pronounced Iran an Islamic republic. He then set about getting rid, by fair means or foul, of those who had shown allegiance to the Shah.

Liberalisation and western ways introduced by the Shah were quickly reversed. The United States, which had supported the Shah in his dream of restoring Iran to the days of Persian grandeur, came in for special treatment from the Aytollah. That included taking 100 Embassy staff as hostages and holding some of them for 440 days. The Shah who suffered from ill health later died in Egypt.

On the music scene, for three weeks in January, the Village People's 'Y.M.C.A.' was a number one hit, until Ian Drury and the Blockheads replaced it with 'Hit me with your Rhythm Stick'. While Nottingham Forest football club was busy negotiating the first ever £1000,000 transfer of a football player, that of Trevor Francis from Birmingham City, Blondie was busy keeping number one hit, 'Heart of Glass', at the top for four weeks. Sid Vicious was destined to succeed no more, because sadly the former punk bass player with the Sex Pistols died of a heroin overdose at a party in New York. In the year on which Trivial Pursuit first came on the market, there was nothing trivial about the near catastrophic happening at Three Mile Island nuclear power station at Harrisburg, Pennsylvania. Thousands of residents fled the area when, through a series of human and mechanical errors, intensely radioactive fuel rods became partially exposed. Only at the end of a twelve-day ordeal did people return to their homes satisfied that the danger had been averted. During that time experts managed to prevent the release of deadly radioactive rays and explosive hydrogen gas into the atmosphere.

There were few who would believe that the title of the Bee Gees number one hit, 'Tragedy', was in any way applicable to the ousting of President Idi Amin from Uganda. The ruthless dictator who exercised a reign of terror over his people, fled to Libya when insurgent Ugandan and Tanzanian troops invaded the country in April 1979. Just before Margaret Thatcher replaced James Callaghan as prime minister of Britain, Gloria Gaynor appropriately topped the charts with 'I Will Survive'. Bishop Muzorewa became the first black prime minister of Rhodesia and on 1 June Rhodesia took the name Zimbabwe.

It was still early summer when Elton John became the first western rock star to play in Israel. Likewise, it was another first when later in May he played to full houses in Leningrad and Moscow. Meanwhile Art Garfunkel and Blondie had number one hits respectively with 'Bright Eyes' and 'Sunday Girl'. As the year reached the mid-way point, Pope John Paul II decided to go home for a visit. The pontiff returned to his native Poland where he made a 32-stop tour of the country. It was an extremely emotional occasion for many, especially the elderly. The latent messages to his fellow Poles were that the Church maintained its longstanding opposition to Communism, and its support for the confederation of independent trade unions, then in its infancy. The movement would later be known as Solidarity, under the leadership of Lech Walesa.

THOSE MAGNIFICENT MEN IN THE RED JERSEYS
In Ireland we would have a general election later in the year but in the meantime, Cork again set out on the trail of the Munster title with virtually the same team as last year's All-Ireland winning side, the exception being John Fenton. Royal Liver National League winners, Tipperary, were Cork's opponents in the Munster semi-final. It took a goal at a crucial stage by Jimmy Barry-Murphy to put Cork on their way to victory by the narrowest of margins – a single point.

Limerick, who had beaten Clare in the other semi-final, would take on Cork in the final. A fine display of hurling by the Corkmen disposed of Limerick at Thurles before an attendance of 47,849. The final score was Cork 2-14; Limerick 0-9. The Shannonsiders sorely missed the services of their great full-back, Pat Hartigan. Pat, recipient of Carrolls' All-Star awards on five successive years – 1971 to 1975, had picked up an eye injury in training. Cork, too, fielded without ace marksman, Seanie O'Leary, but with Jimmy Barry-Murphy slotting into the left-corner forward position, things were not too serious. John

Fenton, who had played well against Tipperary, partnered Pat Moylan at midfield, while Tom Cashman filled the vacancy left by Jimmy Barry-Murphy at left-half forward. It was a disappointing day for Limerick followers who believed that time was running out for men like Pat Hartigan, Eamonn Grimes, Sean Foley, Eamonn Cregan, Liam O'Donoghue and Joe McKenna. Those players were all part of the 1973 All-Ireland winning team. It was felt that 1979 might well be their swan song.

After the match in Thurles on that July afternoon there were few who would have bet against Cork going all the way to make it four All-Ireland crowns in a row. They had already amassed five successive Munster titles – 1975, 1976, 1977, 1978, 1979. The potential was still there for Cork to progress. Talent, laced with experience, now abounded. Close inspection of the team must have sent shivers down the spines of many an opponent. Martin Coleman, fronted by Brian Murphy, Martin O'Doherty, John Horgan, Dermot McCurtain, Johnny Crowley and Denis Coughlan made up a formidable defence. The midfield pair of John Fenton and Pat Moylan would give any opponents a torrid time. The attack, made up of Tim Crowley, Gerald McCarthy, Tom Cashman, Charlie McCarthy, Ray Cummins and Jimmy Barry-Murphy were tops when it came to creating and taking scores. Not since the early to mid-1950s had we seen such an elite body of players represent the county. The next hurling outing on the agenda would be at Croke Park on All-Ireland semi-final day, 6 August.

BRIGHTON GOES BARE AND BERRY IS SENTENCED AS SEAS CAUSE HAVOC
In the summer of 1979 a sign was placed at the perimeter of a beach at Brighton in the south of England which was the first of its kind to appear in Britain – 'Clothes Need Not Be Worn Beyond This Point'. While the local council had given its blessing to the naturalistic tendencies of some, not surprisingly many inhabitants of the seaside town were not amused.

Not amused either was American rock-and-roll singer,

songwriter and guitarist Chuck Berry, because he received a three month prison sentence in the United States for tax evasion.

Anita Ward, Tubeway Army and the Boomtown Rats respectively had number one hits with 'Ring My Bell', 'Are 'Friends' Electric' and 'I Don't Like Mondays'.

Life on the ocean wave was most unkind in August when fifteen yachtsmen lost their lives while taking part in the classic Fastnet Race. The unexpected force-ten gale and accompanying mountainous seas caused havoc. Of the 306 yachts which started the race only 177 completed the course; 23 sank or were abandoned and many others were disabled.

WHAT A GOOD INNINGS WE HAD

The All-Ireland hurling semi-final between Cork and Galway brought together virtually the same teams as in '75 and '77. Honours were equally shared at a win apiece. To my immense disappointed I did not get to Croke Park for the '79 match. Reports referred to a much improved and, naturally a much more experienced Galway team. The fit, talented side did not allow Cork to settle. Fighting their way to the top on three successive seasons was bound to have taken its toll. Joe McDonagh led the Tribesmen to a four-point victory. Now that we had become so accustomed to Cork winning, it came as a shock to the system when they lost. The first Sunday of September would not just be the same in 1979. The reality was that Cork hurling followers could not complain. We had had a marvellous innings. Sadly some of the squad would not appear in Croke Park again.

Galway and Kilkenny were 1979 All-Ireland hurling finalists. The match will for ever be remembered as the final Galway threw away. Two unfortunate goalkeeping errors were largely responsible for denying a fine Galway team the honour of taking the McCarthy Cup west of the Shannon for the first time since 1923. Instead it returned to familiar territory down by the River Nore for the twenty-first time.

A DASTARDLY ACT, A VISIT, A MOTHER HONOURED, AND
PETRA FORMS GREEN

Cliff Richard's recording of 'We Don't Talk Anymore' was
so popular in August that it remained a number one hit for
four weeks. Gary Numan's 'Cars' eventually replaced it,
but only briefly, because after one week it was 'Message in
a Bottle' by the Police which occupied the top spot.

Sadly there was cause for shame and revulsion among
the vast majority of people in this country when 79-year-
old Earl Mountbatten of Burma, his fourteen-year-old
grandson, and his grandson's seventeen-year-old friend,
died instantly as result of an explosion in a small pleasure
boat off Mullaghmore, County Sligo. The IRA claimed
responsibility for the dastardly act. On the same August
day eighteen British soldiers were killed by the IRA at
Warrenpoint, County Down. The highlight of the year for
hundreds of thousands of Irish people was the visit of
Pope John Paul II to their country. During his visit all
roads led to designated open-air venues where the Pontiff
addressed the assembled masses. Included were the
Phoenix Park, Dublin, a field near Drogheda, and the race
course at Galway. It seemed as if everything else came to
a standstill with people either going to or coming from
one of the venues.

In October I'm sure that Mother Teresa, recipient of the
1979 Nobel Peace Prize for her ceaseless efforts in helping
the destitute of Calcutta, would have approved of the message delivered by Lena Martell in her number hit, 'One
Day at a Time'. Dr Hook had a chart topper in November
called 'When You're in Love with a Beautiful Woman'.
Meanwhile, Petra Kelly founded the world's first political
Green Party and the Police's 'Walking on the Moon' was at
number one in early December.

Meanwhile, Charles Haughey had his feet firmly on the
ground and was elected Taoiseach of the Republic of
Ireland. The year was drawing to a close when on St
Stephen's Day the USSR invaded Afghanistan.

The final number one hit of 1979 was called 'Another
Brick in the Wall' by Pink Floyd. Names to be found in the
obituary columns of 1979 included those of: Mary Pickford,

Canadian actress; Gracie Fields, music hall entertainer, and actress; John Wayne, veteran Hollywood star; and Richard Rogers, one of the century's top composers of musicals. With the end of another decade nigh, memories of heady days at Munster and All-Ireland finals flooded back; the Paddy Barry-led Cork hurling team set the pace in 1970; while the '71 campaign faltered, back came the magic in 1972; a lull in 1973 and 1974 cleared the way for the brilliance that was to follow. Here's to the 1980s.

1980

The 1970s were now history, yet it was hard to obliterate the legacy of terror it left behind. January 1980 was a time to look forward and perhaps to dream of better times ahead.

Foremost in the minds of those dependent on fuel oil and petrol was the question, 'When are the rising price going to stop?' There had been steady increases since 1975 as a result of OPEC setting the price of crude oil spiralling upwards. Should we prepare ourselves for a decade of change? Well, on the face of it, all the old institutions appeared to be firmly in place. The 'iron curtain' seemed unshakeable as Soviet leader Leonid Brezhnev laid down the law. To the untrained eye, at least, there was not a sign of a single crack in any wall, never mind that of Berlin. Relations between the Americans and the USSR were not good but there was nothing strange about that. Prime Minister Pieter Botha seemed well in control in South Africa when he described Nelson Mandela as an 'arch-Marxist', and condemned him to an eighteen-year incarceration at Robben Island Prison, off Cape Town. Southeast Asia was to continue in a state of turmoil but world focus was no longer fixed on that area of the globe.

Overriding all else was the certainty that we were on our way to what might be called the Electronic Revolution. Yet there were few who had any concept of what was to come in terms of the scope and magnitude of that particular revolution. In a matter of years cars, washing machines, calculators, air conditioners, timepieces, telephones, televisions, radios, and a host of other machines too numerous to mention would all make use of the electronic wizardry. Development of the computer had come a long way from its humble beginnings when little beyond dealing with business accounts and scientific calculations were envisaged. As production techniques were perfected the cost of circuit components decreased, while the scope of those same components increased. The consumer benefited enormously from electronic development. The pace of change was indeed dazzling, and to date only the tip of the iceberg had been touched.

PAUL DETAINED AND A PLATFORM TOPPLES AS AMAZON AND SEVE SHINE

January saw the Pretenders' 'Brass In Pocket' at number one, followed by The Specials with 'The Special Aka Live!' in February and Kenny Rogers' 'Coward of the County'. Blondie, who had three number one hits in 1980, called her first hit of the year 'Atomic'. Japanese customs officials did not take kindly to finding marijuana in the luggage of ex-Beatle, Paul McCartney. After detaining him in prison for nine days, the authorities decided to deport him. A more dramatic report in March described how a storm was responsible for overturning an oil platform in the North Sea. Of the 200 men who were relaxing aboard, over 100 drowned. Not so widely published was a gold rush in the Amazon jungle following the discovery of the precious metal by a rancher. By the end of the year, in spite of shoot-outs and a merciless sun, some 25,000 prospectors had hacked out more than £25,000,000 worth of nuggets.

In April, it may well have seemed to Spanish golfer Severiano Ballesteros that he too had struck gold because he made sporting history on two counts. Not alone was he the youngest player ever to win the United States Masters but he was also the first European to do so.

HISTORY MADE AS CUBANS FLEE TO A LAND OF RUMBLINGS AND RIBBONS

Cork GAA experienced a red-letter day in its illustrious history on 18 May 1980. On the finest of early summer Sundays, the county crashed its way into sporting history at Páirc Uí Chaoimh when the county's hurlers emulated the feat of its footballers to chalk up the first ever National League double. A replay was necessary by the hurlers to overcome the challenge of a gallant Limerick team in the final.

The match, which attracted an attendance of 34,610 on a scorching hot day, ranked among the best League deciders ever played. Cork even threw in the now almost customary added ingredient of allowing opponents to run up a score without reply. On that occasion the score was 1-4 to 0-0 in favour of Limerick after thirteen minutes of play. The excitement was fed almost to bursting point by a brand of hurling which tends to make Munster matches special – matches where raw courage is allied to the great arts and crafts of arguably the world's greatest field game.

Two magnificently motivated and well matched sides gave their all in a glorious bid for victory. Cork's most avid followers, even myself, conceded that the winning margin of 4-15 to 4-6, did scant justice to the valiant Shannonsiders. In the closing six minutes of play the lads in the red jerseys notched up 1-5 without reply. It was those scores which decided the outcome. In the end, relief as much as exultation, showed on the faces of Cork players, selectors and followers. The standing ovation for the winners as they made their way to collect the trophy was well earned. For one player it was an extra special afternoon! Jimmy Barry-Murphy, who was no stranger to winning All-Ireland and League medals, became the first player in the history of the GAA to figure on National League winning teams in both hurling and football. Mind you, Jimmy was fortunate because a hamstring injury made him very doubtful for the hurling final, though he came on as a sub for Danny Buckley. The start of the Munster hurling championship was now less than a month away. Judging by what had been served up at Páirc Uí Chaoimh on 18 May, we could look forward with relish to the forthcoming matches.

Meanwhile, Johnny Logan's number one hit 'What's Another Year' was a big favourite in Ireland. In Cuba many citizens obviously believed another year was too long to spend under the rule of Premier Fidel Castro. No less than 125,000 of them joined a 'freedom flotilla' to Florida. The overseas migration, which went on for five months, brought conflicting reports of moral and political victory from both the United States and Cuba. However, it was a fact that Miami ended up with the largest Cuban population outside

Havana. The regime of Ayatollah Khomeini held 52 Americans hostage in Iran. The American people were left to show solidarity with their detained compatriots by decorating houses, trees and lapels with yellow ribbons. The troubled United States was further disturbed by a sleeping giant when after two months of rumblings Mount Saint Helens erupted on 18 May. Dormant since 1857, the Washington State Mount spewed a cloud of ashes 60,000 feet into the air. The eruption, which was the first on the United States mainland for more than half a century, claimed 60 lives and billions of dollars in property damage. The music played on with 'Theme From M*A*S*H' by Mash, 'Crying' by Don McLean, and 'Xanadu' by Olivia Newton-John and the Electric Light Orchestra, respectively reaching the top spot between late May and mid-July. 'Use it up and Wear it out' by Odyssey was a number one hit from late July to 9 August.

A J.R. POSER BUT WALESA AND BJORN SEEM TO HAVE THE ANSWER
During the summer of 1980, television viewers worldwide were united by a single question – 'Who shot J.R.?' J.R. Ewing (played by Larry Hagman), was a member of a fabulously wealthy Texas oil family in a television programme called, 'Dallas'. At the height of its popularity, 'Dallas', which uniquely had no squeaky clean characters, was broadcast in 91 countries and stayed on air for fourteen years.

Back in the real world a plain-spoken, bluntly charismatic, unpretentious leader, Lech Walesa, became an international symbol for the aspirations of Poland's embittered people. Poor working conditions, lingering shortages of fuel, food, and clothing, resulting from mismanagement by Communist Party Leader, Edward Gierek, led to mass venting of grievances by disillusioned workers. Walesa, himself a sacked shipyard electrician, became head of an inter-factory strike committee which in time became the kernel of a national union called Solidarity. By August, the Poles, through Walesa and Solidarity, had negotiated from Communist government representatives concessions beyond their wildest dreams. Meanwhile at Wimbledon the men's final brought together Bjorn Borg, going for a record fifth consecutive crown, and a young American, John McEnroe, who had just burst onto the tennis scene. The fourth set is remembered by tennis fans to this day. At six-all, the set moved into a tie-break and try as they might, neither player could open up the two-point lead required to secure the set until the score reached an incredible 18-16. McEnroe finally came out on top. However, Borg was not to be denied! He won the fifth and deciding set to claim the match and record.

BONE CRUSHING TACKLES AND TUSSLES WERE THE ORDER OF THE DAY

Back at home Cork hurlers were bracing themselves for another onslaught on the Munster championship. Seldom had their pedigree been so exalted. As they faced Tipperary in the semi-final, Cork, the recently-crowned Royal Liver National League champions had won twelve, drawn one and lost three of their last sixteen matches.

Indeed the Rebel County men were unbeaten in their last eight matches, since Limerick pipped them by a single point back in February. Good news for the Leesiders were the performances and immaculate accuracy of John Fenton. John was Cork's top scorer with 2-28, which included 2-24 in his last four outings. The magnificent Ray Cummins, and the now established Eamonn O'Donoghue, had each scored seven goals since October. It was a formidable Cork team that was seeking to qualify for a sixth Munster final. In contrast, since their 1968 final victory by 2-13 to 1-7, Tipperary had only beaten Cork on one of the six occasions the sides had been drawn together in the Munster championship, seven years ago when they won a semi-final clash by 5-4 to 1-10. Another statistic showed that Tipperary hadn't won a single championship match since losing the 1973 provincial decider to Limerick by 2-18 to 6-17.

Tipperary's fortunes were not to change in 1980 as Cork went to beat the Premier County. Limerick were Cork's Munster final opponents. No one doubted that a duel was on the cards. Munster final – Thurles, 20 July – the words were magic to my ears. The National League final matches, particularly the re-play, set the tone of expectation for the followers of both counties. There wasn't a hurling enthusiast in Cork or Limerick who wouldn't go through fire and water to be at Thurles. The pre-match atmosphere both in the town and at Semple Stadium was tremendous.

To all and sundry it was clear from early on that Limerick meant business. They had done their homework well. The curtailment of Cork's John Horgan was obviously a priority. It was believed in Limerick that in the recent League final encounters, Horgan's long clearances from behind his own half-back line gave the Limerick defenders little respite and thus reduced the opportunities of setting up attacks.

The resulting match could be described as blistering rather than brilliant. The Limerick full-back line of Donal Murray, Leonard Enright and Dom Punch did well in marking the experienced and arguably the most able full-forward line in the land. Swift, hard, low play both cross-field and into the forwards made defending much more difficult. The ultra-reliable Cork full-back line of Brian Murphy, Martin O'Doherty and John Horgan, was troubled by Limerick that day. One of the defining moments in the torrid match came in the second half when Cork's John Horgan and Martin O'Doherty collided in their urgency to deny the Limerick forwards possession. The outcome was that a free, unmarked corner-forward Ollie O'Connor was at hand to score the easiest of goals'. The urgency and tension on the pitch communicated itself to the 43,090 attendance. With time ticking away those of us wearing the red and white rosettes waited with pounding hearts for the last-minute Cork scores which would surely come. For once we were to be disappointed! The 'true-grit' and sustained pace of the Shannonsiders won the day. The final score was Cork 2-10; Limerick 2-14. Limerick had worked hard and on the day won deservedly. It had been their first win over Cork in a Munster final since another famous day at Thurles, 40 years ago, when Mick Mackey, the only Limerickman to be named on the team of the century, lifted the Munster Senior Hurling Trophy. In September of that year the famous Ahane man, rounded off an illustrious playing career by bringing the McCarthy Cup home.

OLYMPICS SUFFER AND A SAD DINGO STORY BUT JOY FOR REAGAN

While the hurling and football championship deciders were foremost in the minds of many in this country, Abba had a number one hit with 'The Winner Takes it All', and appropriately the Moscow Olympic Games were in progress. As in Montreal four years previously, again the Games were depleted because of a political boycott. This time it was the Soviet invasion of Afghanistan which prompted the leaders of more than 30 nations to withdraw their athletes. David Bowie had made it to the top with 'Ashes to Ashes' at about the same time as when, in the Ayers Rock region of Australia, a dingo snatched a nine-week-old baby and carried it off into the night. A subsequent search of deserted bushland for traces of the missing baby proved fruitless.

Sadly for Limerick hurling followers, long before Ronald Reagan was elected fortieth United States president on 4 November, the McCarthy Cup had travelled west across the Shannon to Galway. Galway had made a very strong case in recent years to recapture the trophy which had eluded them since 1923, but Limerick too had made great efforts to add to their 1973 victory, the only one since 1940. However, a final score of 2-15 to 3-9 in favour of the Tribesmen sent a jubilant Galway captain, Joe Connolly, to the post-match Hogan Stand presentation, while Limerick captain, Sean Foley, was left to wonder if his chance would come again.

One of the greatest achievements of 1980 was the eradication of small-pox. The virus, which annually killed almost 2,000,000 people right up to the 1960s was, according to the World Health Organisation, no longer a threat.

LENNON TARGETED, THE FAMOUS DIE AND ASIA'S I'S ENGAGE

While the Jam celebrated with a number one hit called, 'Start', following up to topple it was Kelly Marie who told the world, 'Feels Like I'm in Love'. The Police followed

The Cork team, 1952; back row, left to right: B. Murphy (selector), G. Murphy, J. Lyons, D. Creedon, L. Dowling, J. Twomey, P. Barry, M. Fouhy, J. Barry (trainer); front row, left to right: G. O'Riordan, W.J. Daly, C. Ring, A. O'Shaughnessy, W. Abernethy, W. Griffin, J. O'Brien, V. Twomey.

The Cork team, 1953; back row, left to right: A. Scannell (chairman), J. Barrett (selector), D. Hayes, J. Twomey, D. Creedon, L. Dowling, G. Murphy, J. Lyons, G. O'Riordan, Pat (Fox) Collins (selector), J. Barry (trainer); front row, left to right: P. Barry, A. O'Shaughnessy, W.J. Daly, J. Hartnett, C. Ring (captain), T. O'Sullivan, V. Twomey, M. Fouhy.

September 1956: Christy Ring kissing the ring of the Archbishop of Cashel, the Most Reverend Dr Kinane.

Jim Barry and Christy Ring with the McCarthy Cup in 1953.

The Cork team 1954; back row, left to right: J. Barrett (selector), A. Scannell (chairman), D. Creedon, G. O'Riordan, J. Lyons, D. Hayes, M. Tuohy, G. Murphy, Pat (Fox) Collins (selector), J. Barry (trainer); front row, left to right: E. Goulding, W.J. Galy, T. O'Shaughnessy, J. Clifford, J. Hartnett, C. Ring, P. Barry, V. Twomey, W. Moore.

The Cork team, 1966; back row, left to right: J. Barrett (selector), D. Murphy, T. O'Donoghue, J. O'Halloran, T. Connolly, P. Doolan, M. Waters, J. McCarthy, P. Fitzgerald, D, Sheehan, J. Bennett, J. Barry; front row, T. O'Sullivan, C. Sheehan, P. Barry, C. McCarthy, G. McCarty (captain), S. Barry, F. O'Neill, G. O' Leary.

6 September 1970: An Taoiseach Jack Lynch and wife Maírín attend the All-Ireland Hurling final, Cork versus Wexford.

The Cork team, 1970, led by Paddy Barry, captain on All-Ireland Final day, 6 September.

The Cork team 1976, All-Ireland champions; back row, left to right: J. Barry-Murphy, M. Malone, J. Crowley, P. Barry, M. O'Doherty, P. Moylan, B. Murphy, D. Coughlan, Fr B. Troy (coach); front row, from left to right: C. McCarthy, B. Cummins, G. McCarthy, R. Cummins, M. Coleman, P. McDonnell, S. O'Leary.

The Cork captain, Ray Cummins and Wexford full-back Willie Murphy struggle for the sliotar: Cork versus Wexford, 5 September 1976.

Wexford's Willie Murphy is sandwiched between brothers Ray and Brendan Cummins, watched by Jimmy Barry-Murphy: Cork versus Wexford, 5 September 1976.

The Cork captain, Martin O'Doherty, 4 September 1977.

Rival captains Ger Henderson, Kilkenny, and Charlie McCarthy, Cork, watched by referee Jimmy Rankins, 3 September 1978.

Jimmy Barry-Murphy is tackled by Kilkenny's Dick O'Hara, 3 September 1978.

Jimmy Barry-Murphy shoots a goal past Kilkenny's Richie Reid, 3 September 1978.

A determined Seán O'Leary with the ball gripped tightly in his left hand tries to get clear of Offaly corner-back, Liam Carroll, 2 September 1984.

Jubilant Jimmy Barry-Murphy, Cork versus Offaly centenary game at Thurles, 2 September 1984.

Jumping for joy! A Cork supporter 'over the moon' as the final whistle is blown, 2 September 1984.

The Cork team 1986; back row, left to right: J. Crowley, J. Barry-Murphy, R. Browne, G. Cunningham, T. Mulcahy, K. Hennessy, G. Fitzgerald, D. Mulcahy; front row, left to right: T. O'Sullivan, J. Cashman, T. McCarthy, T. Cashman (captain), D. Walsh, P. Hartnett, J. Fenton.

Steve Mahon (left) and Tony Keady (right) of Galway take on Cork's Jim Cashman in the Cork versus Galway Final of 1986.

The Cork team, All-Ireland Champions, 1990; back row, from left to right: T. McCarthy, J. Fitzgibbon, S. O'Gorman, J. Cashman, M. Foley, G. Cunningham, D. Walsh; front row, from left to right: T. O'Sullivan, B. O'Sullivan, K. McGuckin, T. Mulcahy (captain), K. Hennessy, S. McCarthy, G. Fitzgerald, J. Considine.

The Cork team, All-Ireland Champions, 1999; back row, left to right: D. O'Sullivan, B. Corcoran, J. Browne, F. McCormack, W. Sherlock, D. Óg Cusack, S. Óg Ó hAilpín; front row, from left to right: S. McGrath, M. O'Connor, M. Landers (captain), N. Ronan, F. Ryan, T. McCarthy, J. Deane.

with their chart topper, 'Don't Stand So Close To Me' before Barbara Streisand took over with 'Woman In Love'. Blondie's recording of 'The Tide is High' had a two week stay at the top whilst Abba's 'Super Trouper' had feet tapping as Christmas approached.

On 8 December the world of pop music was shocked by the murder of 40-year-old, ex-Beatle, John Lennon who was shot dead on a New York street by Mark Chapman. On 20 December, Lennon's recording, 'Starting Over', became a number one hit.

Among others who died in 1980 were: Jesse Owens, an American athlete and winner of four gold medals at the 1936 Munich Olympics – the man whose hand Hitler refused to shake because he was black; Alfred Hitchcock, the screen's master of suspense; Tito (Josip Broz), Yugoslavian president; Peter Sellers, British comedy actor; Steve McQueen, American film star; Mae West, American film star and the original screen sex symbol; and Jimmy Durante, American comedian.

While Iran and Iraq were firmly engaged in a particularly sanguineous war which would drag on for most of a decade, the year was pleasingly rounded off by St Winifred's School Choir singing their number one hit 'There's No One Quite Like Grandma'.

—— 1981 ——

ECHOES OF LENNON AND A BRIEF U.S. RELIEF
BUT TROUBLES AHEAD

Over a six-week period during January and February, two of John Lennon's recordings, 'Imagine' and 'Woman', were number one hits.

In January, the newly-inaugurated president of The United States, Ronald Reagan, was relieved at the release of the Iranian-held American hostages, after more than a year. Respite would be brief. Unrest and tension between American-backed Israel and its Arab neighbours was about to take on a new impetus. The Israeli authorities were concerned about the vulnerability of their country and reacted by bombing a partly completed Iraqi nuclear reactor. That incident did nothing to increase their popularity and when they followed up by bombing PLO headquarters in Beirut, relations all-round worsened. Egyptian leader, Anwar al-Sadat, aided and abetted by the Americans, had recently entered into an agreement with Israel. It was an agreement which did not meet with the approval of his own people, nor with most of the Middle-East nations which led to Sadat's unpopularity both at home and in neighbouring Arab countries. American diplomacy was sorely tried by unrepenting Israelis and determined Arabs.

A further thorn in the side of the Americans was Libyan leader, Muammar al-Qaddafi. In recent years the flamboyant demagogue had pursued an anti-American agenda and supported terrorist groups including the IRA and the PLO. Furthermore his ambitions caused concern to neighbouring countries. A concerted effort, partly warlike, by the Ronald Reagan-led United States administration eventually curtailed Qaddafi's antics. Unfortunately the hatred generated at the time left a legacy of destruction.

On 30 March, President Ronald Reagan was seriously

wounded in an assassination attempt. His assailant was John Hinckley, with no apparent motive. While President Reagan was recuperating at George Washington Hospital, Shakin' Stevens had the popular music world gyrating to the sounds of his number one hit, 'This Ole House'. He had moved to the number one spot at the expense of 'Jealous Guy' by Roxy Music. Before that 'Shaddap You Face' by Joe Dolce Music Theatre had a three week spell at the top.

A REAL CHAMPION AS CORK SETTLES FOR LEAGUE
In April, cancer sufferers and the population at large drew tremendous hope from the magnificent achievement of one-time sufferer, Bob Champion who rode 'Aldaniti' to victory in the Grand National. Before April was out, Bucks Fizz had a number one hit with 'Making Your Mind Up' but Adam and the Ants were more demanding when a few weeks later they hit the top spot with 'Stand And Deliver'.

On Sunday 4 May at Thurles the Rebels took on an up-and-coming Offaly team in the National League final. In total contrast to the scorching hot day at Páirc Uí Chaoimh a year ago, the weather was atrocious. A strong wind accompanied by occasional downpours made for a miserable afternoon. Spectators took what cover they could in the stands. On that afternoon of high wind and lashing rain Cork got off to a flying start and scored 2-3 without reply in the opening minutes. To the credit of the Faithful County men they matched the Leesiders for the greater part of the match. The deficit accrued early on was too much to claw back and eventually Cork won by 3-11 to 2-8. We didn't know it then but before the year was out we would hear much more about the Offaly team of 1981.

Cork returned home with the Royal Liver National League Hurling Trophy for the second year in succession. In the recent past, followers of Cork hurling had enjoyed a share of excitement, entertainment, passion and glory only dreamt about in most counties. Between 1975 and 1981, the Rebels competed in six Munster finals, winning five; were All-Ireland champions thrice; and won the National League twice. What more could one possibly ask for?

REFRESHING AND REUSABLE BUT APPETITE FOR STATUS AND IDEALS ONLY

Refreshingly for many hurling followers in Munster, it was the reigning champions Limerick, and near neighbours Clare, who contested the final. Limerick had six points to spare over the luckless Banner County. Joe McKenna, the big Limerick full-forward, had one of his many excellent games in the green and white jersey, breaking the hearts of Clare players and followers in the process.

Away from Munster, at the far side of the Atlantic, fever pitch excitement was being experienced at the Kennedy Space Centre. A revolutionary spacecraft, called *Columbia*, which was reusable, had been launched from a pad in the usual way. The difference was that with its mission complete, on re-entering the Earth's atmosphere, the craft landed on a runway just as a conventional aircraft does.

'The troubles' in Northern Ireland continued to be a nightmare for many, especially in parts of the cities and in border areas. There were times when heightened tension made us all conscious of divisions and unrest. One such period was when incarcerated IRA man, 27-year-old Bobby Sands decided on a hunger strike tactic, to win prisoner-of-war status for imprisoned IRA activists. This extreme measure made no immediate impression on the British government who refused all concessions requested. When Bobby Sands died on 5 May, after 65 days without food, Prime Minister Thatcher seemed unmoved and merely remarked, 'He chose to take his own life. It was a choice that his organisation did not allow any of their victims'.

Nevertheless he was seen as a martyr by many who previously had little sympathy with the IRA struggle. When nine other young men followed Bobby Sands to their deaths tension ran high. The strength of feeling among many nationalist communities was reflected when on the fortieth day of his hunger strike Bobby Sands was elected to the British parliament.

On 13 May world media attention was directed towards Rome, where Mehmet Ali Agca, who claimed he disapproved of American and Russian imperialism, shot the Pope in protest. Pope John Paul II was hit four times as he blessed crowds from his open-top jeep.

THE RIPPER, A HORSE APART, AND A WEDDING

Peter Sutcliffe, nicknamed the 'Yorkshire Ripper', was found guilty of murdering thirteen women and, for attempting to murder seven others the accused also received a guilty verdict.

On the equestrian calendar early June shines out like a great light. It denotes a meeting at Epsom, Surrey – the Derby – blue riband of the English horse-racing season. It was won in 1981 by 'Shergar', a horse owned by the Aga Khan, trained in Ireland and ridden by Irishman, Walter Swinburne.

By midsummer the voice of Smokey Robinson was good enough to take his recording 'Being With You' to number one in the charts. Two weeks later Michael Jackson's 'One Day In Your Life' laid claim to the top spot. That was followed in July by the Specials, 'Ghost Town'.

And on 29 July, 750,000,000 viewers watched the marriage ceremony of Prince Charles and Lady Diana Spencer on television.

JOY AND SORROW AT CROKE, THE BLADE GOES, AND WHAT A REUNION

In between Shakin' Stevens' number one hit 'Green Door' and Sebastian Coe proving he was the number one middle distance runner in the world, Limerick hurlers again suffered a disappointment in the All-Ireland hurling semi-final, at Croke Park, on 2 August.

Last year's All-Ireland champions, Galway, who beat Limerick in the final, again opposed the Munstermen in this year's semi-final. It was a tension-filled encounter which had players on edge.

Eight minutes into the match, Limerick's Sean Foley, the 1980 captain, was dismissed by the referee for what was judged as dangerous play. In an unfortunate incident during play, Galway's P.J. Molloy, received a nasty facial injury. Limerick, reduced to fourteen players, showed their true grit and character by holding a good Galway team to a draw.

The replay was an enthralling contest on 16 August, and the weather was fine in Croke Park. Limerick were without the services of key players, Dom Punch, Pat Herbert and Sean Foley. During the course of a match in which no quarter was given or expected, the Shannonsiders were further handicapped when their sterling full-back Leonard Enright had to go off injured. John Connolly was a man apart and his presence alone gave the Tribesmen an extra dimension. The Limerick side, which refused to bow to pressure or handicaps, gave a blistering display. Unfortunately from their point of view, at full-time the score read Galway 4-14; Limerick 2-17.

In September, Aneka had a number one hit with 'Japanese Boy' and, Soft Cell followed with 'Tainted Love'. Just as Adam and the Ants took over with 'Prince Charming', President Mitterand of France abolished the guillotine. Not many were aware that the threat of having one's head chopped off by a sharp blade was still a possibility. After eleven years, Simon and Garfunkel played to an audience of 400,000 in New York's Central Park. Perhaps the reunion influenced the title of the Dave Stewart with Barbara Gaskin hit, 'It's My Party'.

SADAT PAYS PRICE AS POLES ARE CHECKED BUT FONDA FITNESS IS IN
On 6 October Arab world displeasure long focused on Egypt's President Anwar-al Sadat, finally reached a climax when he was assassinated as he watched a military parade in Cairo.

In November, the Police were first in with a number one hit called 'Every Little Thing She Does is Magic', but it was a Queen and David Bowie number one, 'Under Pressure', which best described the fortunes of the Solidarity movement in Poland. On the night of 12 December, seventeen months of liberty suddenly came to a halt when the Communist rulers decided that things had gone too far. Solidarity leader, Lech Walesa, was arrested, and troops were brought on to the streets to enforce the will of the Communist government. Martial law was not lifted until 1983, and Lech Walesa remained in jail for more than a year.

In December, the recordings of Julio Inglesias, 'Begin The Beguin' and, Human League's 'Don't You Want Me' were number one hits. Worthy of note too is that Jane Fonda's exercise video became the top-selling tape of all time. The Academy Award actress and political activist also published a best seller called *Fonda's Workout Book*. It was the centrepiece of a growing health industry she was nurturing along.

In 1981 the deaths took place of such famous personalities as: Bill Haley, the man who will always be associated with the swinging number, 'Rock Around The Clock'; Joe Louis, nicknamed 'the Brown Bomber', who was world boxing heavyweight champion between 1937 and 1949 and made a record 25 successful defences of the title; Bob Marley, a 36-year-old who brought reggae and his religion to the attention of the world, became a victim of cancer; Christy Brown, the severely handicapped Dublin author of *Down All Our Days*; William Holden, actor; and Natalie Wood, actress.

1982

FROM TURMOIL, AIDS, AND UNREST TO THE JOY OF
LIPOSUCTION AND E.T.

It was Bucks Fizz with their January 1982 number one hit 'Land of Make Believe', who endeavoured to cheer us up for the year ahead. Shakin' Stevens kept the tempo up when on 31 January he took over with his recording 'Oh Julie'. Yet, there were troubles looming at home and abroad. The Middle-East turmoil was destined to continue with accusations and counter accusations certain to result in death and bloodshed. The incidence of a new and deadly illness which first came to light in 1981 was doubling every six months. Acquired immuno deficiency syndrome (AIDS) had claimed the lives of nearly half the victims diagnosed since the disease was first discovered. The number of cases reported worldwide by the end of 1982 would reach almost 1,600.

Political unrest in Northern Ireland continued to bring heartache and grief to families who lost loved ones. 1982 will be remembered as the year liposuction became a reality. Somehow though, I feel that the arrival on the scene of Madonna, and the continuing success of Michael Jackson, might just have made a greater impression. Madonna Louise Ciccone was on her way to pop-culture goddess status from the time in 1982 when her first single, 'Everybody', became a hit in United States disco clubs and, on radio. Likewise the release of the Michael Jackson L.P. 'Thriller' in the same year, made him a pop mega star.

On the cinema screens in 1982 a film directed by Steven Spielberg, called 'E.T.', broke box-office records. The film, which presented aliens as gentle beings with child-like innocence charmed millions.

Argentina Underestimates, Diego Moves, and Sophia is Forgetful

It was during February that Kraftwerk and the Jam, respectively weighed in with number one hits 'The Model/Computer Love' and 'A Town Called Malice/Precious'. In early March, Tight Fit led the way with the popular, 'The Lion Sleeps Tonight', but it was 'Seven Tears' by Goombay Dance Band which entertained at number one when Argentina invaded the Falkland Islands. World media focused on the plight of the South Atlantic Islands as a result of an apparent attempt by junta boss, General Galtieri, to divert attention away from an ailing Argentinian economy. The Islands, though close to the Argentine coastline, had been controlled by Britain since 1833. With the Islanders apparently happy that the status quo should remain, the General underestimated the resolve of the British. A strong task force was sent to the Islands. After a short but ugly engagement the Argentine forces surrendered. Unfortunately, it was not until 967 lives had been lost and hundreds of others seriously injured.

One Argentinian who didn't wait around to pick up the pieces was football player, Diego Maradona. On 28 May, Barcelona football club paid Argentinos Juniors a record fee for the young man who would be voted best player of the 1980s by the world's press.

On 19 May, Italian screen goddess, Sophia Loren, was sent to jail for tax evasion. She was sentenced to a month in a women's prison near Naples.

The late spring and early summer were filled with the sounds of catchy and appealing number one hits including 'My Camera Never Lies' by Bucks Fizz; 'Ebony and Ivory' by Paul McCartney with Stevie Wonder; 'A Little Peace' by Nicole; 'House of Fun' by Madness; 'Goody Two Shoes' by Adam Ant; 'I've Never Been to Me' by Charlene.

Championship Joy Again! Were they Tested though?

Cork's opponents in the first round of the championship were Tipperary. With good reason Cork folk were sceptical about how their team would perform. Gerald McCarthy, now retired from playing, was coach. It was his second year dealing with a blend of players, some of whom he had played with in the three in-a-row All-Ireland winning sides of 1976-8.

As the team prepared for the meeting with Tipperary at Páirc Uí Chaoimh on 30 May, the word coming from the camp was that the players were happy about their preparation, the attitude was good, and a backbone of experienced campaigners and relative newcomers were jelling well. It all augured well for the task ahead. On the day the Premier County succumbed rather easily and Cork won by 1-19 to 2-8.

Expectations of the followers rose immediately. Cork's next match was against Clare in the Munster semi-final at Thurles on 20 June. On that occasion Clare were completely dominated by the Leesiders who won by 3-19 to 2-6.

The Munster final at Thurles on 18 July saw the Rebel County pitted against the men from the Decies. Waterford had qualified by beating Limerick by 2-14 to 2-13.

Cautious forecasting coming from Cork before the Waterford match put the odds at 50-50. The match was seen by some as a contest between two teams trying to assert themselves. Waterford's captain Pat McGrath said, 'The present team is the best I have ever played on. I believe that Cork will be under more pressure than us because of being favourites. I think we are going to win. We don't mind what the papers say.' Cork's captain, Jimmy Barry-Murphy said, 'The attitude this year is very different. You couldn't compare the preparation with the championship game against Clare last year. I honestly feel that we have not proved anything yet. We have to produce our best form over 70 minutes if we are to win. Our greatest test lies ahead.'

The Cork team lined-out as follows: Ger Cunningham, Brian Murphy, Martin O'Doherty, John Blake, John Buckley, Johnny Crowley, Dermot McCurtain, Tom Cashman, Tim Crowley, Tony O'Sullivan, Pat Horgan, Jimmy Barry-Murphy (captain), Seanie O'Leary, Ray Cummins, and Kevin Hennessy. Among the subs were a few familiar names, but perhaps none more so than that of John Fenton. A question being asked a thousand times was, Why is John Fenton not playing?

The match turned out to be a disappointment. The Decies men did not do themselves justice at all. On the day, they came up against a Cork team firing on all cylinders. Ger Cunningham, then Cork's established senior hurling goalkeeper showed his class; defenders Martin O'Doherty and Brian Murphy were straight out of the top drawer; John Blake and John Buckley, newcomers to the side, were not found wanting; stalwarts, Johnny Crowley and Dermot McCurtain excelled; midfield was dominated by Tom Cashman and Tim Crowley; a nineteen-year-old bright young star, Tony O'Sullivan, displayed the wonderful hurling talents we later came to expect from the classy Na Piarsaigh clubman; Pat Horgan, who had previously shone in the heat of battle, did so again. Jimmy Barry-Murphy, Seanie O'Leary and Ray Cummins, as always, were highly impressive and for the first time I witnessed the opportunism and drive of the tall, thin, red-headed youth, Kevin Hennessy. The match turned out to be a personal triumph for Seanie O'Leary. He scored four goals as Cork powered to a 5-31 to 3-6 victory.

As in the two previous championship matches of 1982, Cork looked very good, but a question mark remained as to just how good they were. On the way to adding another Munster championship to the 40 they had already won, unusually, Cork had not been tested.

MOON DID NOT BLIND THE CATS
An unusual wedding took place in New York's Madison Square Garden where the Reverend Sun Myung Moon officiated at a ceremony in which 2,075 couples were simultaneously married. The brides all wore identical traditional white wedding dresses, and the grooms wore identical blue suits. During the ceremony the couples were also ordained missionaries of Moon's Unification Church.

Captain Sensible recorded a new version of the 'South Pacific' song, 'Happy Talk' which went to number one. Irene Cara also had a number one hit with 'Fame'. Dexys

197

Midnight Runners, with 'Come on Eileen' reigned supreme when Kilkenny dismissed Galway from the championship. A comfortable 2-20 to 2-10 win over the Tribesmen was a good result. Cork and Kilkenny who last met in the All-Ireland final of 1978, when the Leesiders completed their three in-a-row successes, would do so again in 1982

FATHER AND SON DID NOT SEE BEST OF REDS AS SUPER CATS CRUSH

Sunday 5 September was a much looked forward to day in our home! After Cork's 1978 victory I promised my then six year old son I would take him to Croke Park to see the next All-Ireland final the Rebels played in. The time had come. He was eleven. The boy, though born in Antrim, could not possibly have grown up without having a strong leaning towards the county where he spent long summer holidays.

The Cork versus Kilkenny meeting of 1982 seemed as if it were hand picked for introducing a boy with Cork blood in his veins to the splendour of Croke Park on All-Ireland final day. Cork, having beaten Tipperary, Clare and Waterford with such ease, were firm favourites.

We were seated in the lower deck of the Hogan stand, towards the Nally Stand end – roughly level with the 21-yard line. A check on the Cork team line-out showed a single change from the Munster final winning side. Eamonn O'Donoghue replaced Kevin Hennessy at left-corner forward. The tag of underdog may well have spurred on Kilkenny. For whatever reason they played like men inspired from the word go. Cork were obviously knocked sideways by the sheer ferocity, determination and robustness of the play. Looking at it from a Kilkenny perspective, the performance of the men in the black and amber jerseys could well be seen as magnificent. Just before half-time, Kilkenny's full-forward Christy Heffernan scored two goals within a minute. The goals, coming through a man who had previously made only two senior championship appearances, destroyed Cork. At the interval the score was Kilkenny 2-11; Cork 0-7.

Cork's second-half efforts to save the day were admirable but futile. Noel Skehan was virtually unbeatable in the Kilkenny goal. The final score of Kilkenny 3-18; Cork 1-13 was a fair reflection of how the match went. What had previously been regarded as no more than a moderately-good Kilkenny team certainly spoiled the day not only for those who travelled from Cork but for at least two people who had made their way from the northern extremity. The Kilkenny heroes, who had to be admired for the way they went about their business, were: Noel Skehan, John Henderson, Brian Cody (captain), Dick O'Hara, Nickey Brennan, Ger Henderson, Paddy Prendergast, Joe Hennessy, Frank Cummins, Richie Power, Ger Fennelly, Kieran Brennan, Billy Fitzpatrick, Christy Heffernan, and Liam Fennelly.

The match programme of the day gave the line-outs of the Tipperary and Galway, All-Ireland minor hurling final teams. It is interesting to note the names of players who in later years blossomed to rank amongst the top exponents of the game. The positions of left-corner back, midfield, and the left-half forward on the Tipperary team were respectively occupied by, Cormac Bonnar, John Kennedy (captain) and Noel Sheehy. At number nineteen among the subs was Aidan Ryan. On the Galway team, names of those who would do their county proud at the highest level were, Peter Finnerty, at full-back, Gerry McInerney, at left-half back and Anthony Cunningham at left-corner forward. Tucked away at number 20 on the list of subs is another name which became synonymous with the game of hurling – Joe Cooney.

A CRY FOR HELP, PLASTIC HEART HELPS BUT POLLUTION WORRIES
As Cork supporters slowly recovered from the early September disappointment at Croke Park, Survivor had a number one hit with 'Eye of the Tiger'. It remained at the top for four weeks until 'Pass the Dutchie' by Musical Youth took over. Culture Club followed with 'Do You Really Want To Hurt Me'.

The problems caused by acid-rain, first suspected by

the Scandinavians in the 1950s, and further vented by the West Germans in the 1970s, was finally taken seriously in 1982. It was the Canadian authorities who highlighted the problem when they claimed that air pollution blowing in from some neighbouring American states had dissolved in the waters and killed fish in hundreds of lakes. On 2 December 1982, the retired dentist, Barney Clark, had the first permanent artificial heart implanted into his body. The operation took place at the University of Utah Medical Centre in Salt Lake City.

Among those who died in 1982 were: Ingrid Bergman, actress; John Belushi, comedian; Henry Fonda, actor, Princess Grace of Monaco, formerly the actress, Grace Kelly; and the uncompromising Communist Party Leader, Leonid Brezhnev.

In late November and early December, Eddy Grant and the Jam respectively had number one hits with 'I Don't Wanna Dance' and 'Beat Surrender'. Christmas-time saw 'Save Your Love' by Renee and Renato at number one. A good note on which to end the year!

— 1983 —

TV Breakfast, a Searching Mouse,
and a Snatch which is No 'Crack'

Renee and Renato's 'Save Your Love' not only saw the old year out but also the New Year in. In mid-January Phil Collins took over with a song called, 'You Can't Hurry Love'. At the same time a new phenomenon invaded our homes at breakfast time; the BBC introduced an early morning television programme. The compact disk had also arrived, along with the cordless telephone, the camcorder, and the computer with a mouse.

Men At Work soared to number one position with 'Down Under'. In February, Kajagoogoo overcame the title of their song, 'Too Shy', and took over the top spot and then it was the turn of Michael Jackson's 'Billie Jean' in early March. Bonnie Tyler with 'Total Eclipse of the Heart', ensured that 'Billie Jean' had only a one week stay. Duran Duran's number one hit, 'Is There Something I Should Know' could well have been the echo of a question asked by detectives as they searched in vain for traces of the whereabouts of the kidnapped Shergar. Arguably the world's finest racehorse, it was stolen from a stable in Co Kildare on 8 February. The thieves demanded a £2,000,000 ransom for the priceless animal. Even though suspicion was rife as to the identity of the culprits and the organisation responsible, no one was charged. In April all seemed well as David Bowie issued an invitation in the form of a chart topper called 'Let's Dance'.

Yet, as always, problems did exist, and a particularly worrying one was drug misuse. In 1983 addiction due to 'crack', a smoke-able form of cocaine, was rife in America. It was only a matter of time before it would become a worldwide problem. The word, ecstasy, when used in the context of drug misuse, took on a meaning well removed from its general interpretation. Some takers of the so called designer drug would bring little of the alleged delight to themselves or their loved ones.

A CORK JULY CRUISE

One hoped that the form shown by Cork's hurlers in the National League was not a pointer for the championship. They had won three, lost three and drawn one of the seven matches played. Two of the teams they lost to, Kilkenny and Wexford, qualified for the semi-finals of the competition. Kilkenny beat Limerick in the final. The score was Kilkenny 2-14; Limerick 2-12. Cork opened their championship campaign with a visit to Limerick on 12 June, where they played the home county at the Gaelic Grounds. The match ended in a draw with a scoreline of Cork 3-11; Limerick 2-14. The replay at Páirc Uí Chaoimh on 26 June resulted in a two point win for Cork. The final score was Cork 1-14; Limerick 1-12.

I didn't see either match. The reports were not exactly glowing and, gave the impression that maybe the Rebels were not the force they had been. The team line-out had begun to take on a new look. It takes time to come to terms with the exit of a star player, or players who have been at the heart of a team for some years. In 1983, for example, the absence of Ray Cummins and Martin O'Doherty was seen as a major body-blow. The initial reaction was, those men are irreplaceable. The situation would take time to resolve itself. Hopefully it wouldn't take too long.

In 1983, Donal O'Grady took over at full-back, Dermot McCurtain moved to the full-back line, Pat Horgan moved to right-half back, Tom Cashman appeared at left-half back, John Fenton returned to the team and partnered last year's half-back, John Buckley, at midfield. A half-forward line of Bertie Óg Murphy, Kevin Hennessy, and Tim Crowley had an unfamiliar look about it. The inside trio was made up of new-comer Tomás Mulcahy, more established half-forward Jimmy Barry-Murphy, and Eamonn O'Donoghue. Eamonn, along with Ger Cunningham, Brian Murphy and Johnny Crowley were in their accustomed positions. For the second year running Waterford were

Cork's opponents in the Munster final. Could it be that Waterford, who failed so miserably against the Rebels in the 1982 final, would muster up the spirit and determination to gain revenge.

The outcome at Limerick on 10 July 1983 was, from Waterford's point of view, only marginally better than a year ago. The final score was Cork 3-22; Waterford 0-12. I thought the Leesiders gave a good account of themselves. Regardless of another below par Waterford performance, the 'new-look' Cork seemed to have jelled well and looked confident. I might have been part of a small minority because the main consensus of opinion was that the Leesiders were again going into the All-Ireland series untested. One way or another, in the semi-final at Croke Park on 7 August, they would meet the winners of the match between the Connaught champions, Galway, and the Ulster champions, Antrim. A 1983 Munster championship statistic of interest is that Tipperary's victory over Clare was the Premier County's first win in nine years.

BORG SAYS GOODBYE, SALLY FLIES HIGH AND CORK DOES IT IN STYLE

During late spring and early summer pop groups Spandau Ballet, New Edition, and Police, respectively had number one hits with 'True', 'Candy Girl', and 'Every Breath You Take'. In July, the number one spot was shared between Rod Stewart's 'Baby Jane', and Paul Young's 'Wherever I Lay My Hat (That's My Home).

The Swedish tennis star, Bjorn Borg, announced his retirement from the professional game at the age of 26. He made his debut at fourteen, and went on to create an all-time record by winning six French Open titles, and five consecutive Wimbledon championships. Another former professional tennis player who became famous in June was Sally Ride who was the first woman to journey into space. Along with four male astronauts, she made up the crew of the shuttle, *Challenger*, on a six-day mission to deploy satellites.

Well removed from outer space at Mullingar on 24 July, Galway's hurlers defeated their Antrim counterparts as comfortably as the 3-22 to 2-5 scoreline suggests. That set up a Cork versus Galway All-Ireland semi-final. Prior to 1975, stretching right back to 1901, Galway had not registered a single championship win over Cork. The meetings of 1975, 1977 and 1979 resulted in two wins for the Tribesmen and one for the Rebels. The clear message was that Galway had become a hurling force to be taken seriously.

When the teams met some observers were surprised by the relative ease with which Cork won. The scoreline of 5-14 to 1-16 suggested there was not too much wrong with the Leesiders. Regardless of doubts coming from some quarters they had qualified for yet another All-Ireland final in fine style.

STRESS AND STRAIN YET JOHN BUCKLEY WAS SO NEARLY A HERO
Awaiting Cork at Croke Park on Sunday 14 September were their old adversaries, Kilkenny. Could Cork gain revenge for last year's humiliating defeat? There was certainly more than a suggestion abroad that Kilkenny simply played Cork's stars out of last year's final.

With my son beside me I kept my fingers crossed that Cork's performance would measure up to the picture I had painted of them over the years. We checked on both team line-outs. From the Cork team perhaps the most striking absentee was Ray Cummins. The tall, distinctive full-forward had been ever present to great effect, superb at times, since 1969. Seanie O'Leary was another notable absentee, although he was listed among the subs, and did in fact come on during the match. Martin O'Doherty, who had established himself as the prince of full-backs and who had graced Croke Park on many occasions with much panache would not do so that day. Disappointingly, John Blake and Tony O'Sullivan, two of last years debutantes, were not among the starting fifteen. Tony came on during the game, as did Francis Collins, a Blackrock player with strong Castlehaven links. Indeed Francis made a similar appearance the previous year.

The Kilkenny team showed some positional changes, but ominously, fourteen of last year's starting fifteen would again line-out. Nickey Brennan was the only absentee. Harry Ryan replaced him. During the pre-match activities it was obvious that some Cork followers were edgy. The atmosphere was tense and the normally buoyant Leesiders were a little subdued. Unsurprisingly, the sensation of carnival I had come to associate with All-Ireland day was not strikingly evident. The tension was certainly not eased when after just twelve minutes of play, the score was Cork 0-1; Kilkenny 0-5. At the interval the Noresiders led by six points.

Cork followers were plunged to deeper depths of despair within seconds of the restart. A Kilkenny goal had further extended the lead! Surely that was the final nail in the coffin! For some unknown reason, as often happens during the course of a match in any sport, a point is reached when the pattern of play changes. That day in Croke Park we experienced a welcome change. The Cork players to their credit knuckled down to the task and with a renewed determination turned the match around. The Kilkenny team, which seemed to be coasting to victory, were stopped in their tracks, so much so that they failed to score after the fifty-first minute – nineteen minutes of normal play plus time added on for stoppages without a score. Meanwhile Cork slowly cut back the deficit. Time was against them though. If only they had held a firmer grip on the match in the first-half! With the seconds ticking away, the now-brilliant Leesiders had got themselves into a position where at least a draw was on the cards. In the dying moments the dream became a reality but John Buckley's superb goal attempt just cleared the top of the crossbar. The final score was Cork 2-12; Kilkenny 2-14. So near but yet so far. I left Croke Park feeling that the Cork players had vindicated themselves! They lost the match, but their second-half performance showed they were capable of competing with the best.

AUSSIE JOY, BEIRUT MISERY AND DEPARTED GREATS
In September, while Cork folk bemoaned consecutive defeats by the hurlers of Kilkenny, it was celebration time in Australia. After 132 years of American dominance, the

vessel *Australia II,* brought home the world's top yachting championship, the Americas Cup. So significant was the victory that as Prime Minister, Bob Hawke got the party underway and was quoted as saying, 'Any boss who sacks anyone for not showing up today, is a bum'.

'Give It Up' by KC and the Sunshine Band went to number one, as did UB 40's 'Red Red Wine' in September. Culture Club's, 'Karma Chameleon' was the most popular number one hit of 1983 and held top spot for six weeks.

The complex and apparently unsolvable Middle-East strife continued unabated. Lebanon had become the centre of much unrest between Israel, Syria, the PLO, Palestine guerrillas, and the Islamic Jihad organisation. In February, a bomb killed 40 people including seventeen Americans at the United States embassy in Beirut. In October, Muslim fundamentalist car-bombers were responsible for the deaths of 58 French nationalists when they struck at a French barracks.

Simultaneously 241 Americans were killed when the same organisation bombed the United States' headquarters. It was hard to see where and when it would all end! During 1983 the natural order of things saw to the departure from this life people who had made-their-mark as they passed by. Included were: George Cukor, film director; Karen Carpenter, singer; Tennessee Williams, dramatist; Jack Dempsey, former world heavyweight boxing champion; and David Niven, actor.

As the year drew to a close, Billy Joel's, 'Uptown Girl' and 'Only You' by the Flying Pickets became number one hits, with 'Only You' remaining at the top throughout the festive season.

1984

SELF APPOINTMENTS COINCIDING WITH A LONG PIPELINE
AND A CENTENARY

On 1 January, reputedly world's richest man, the Sultan of Brunei, appointed himself prime minister, finance minister, and home affairs minister, as well as presiding over a cabinet of six, three of whom were his close relations. The leader of the newly formed independent state also purchased a Boeing 747 jet aircraft to carry himself and his horses to compete at international meetings. Paul McCartney didn't go into competition with the Sultan but he did start off the 1984 number one hit parade with 'Pipes of Peace'.

The world's longest pipeline, 2,800 miles long, stretched from Siberia's gas fields to the Czechoslovak border. In January 1984, the pipeline, a highly-acclaimed feat of engineering, was joined up to the French gas supply grid.

In Ireland, 1984 had a special significance for followers of Gaelic games. It was 100 years ago at Hayes Hotel in Thurles, County Tipperary, that the Gaelic Athletic Association came into existence. The founder members were Michael Cusack, Maurice Davin, and the Archbishop of Cashel, Dr Croke. The growth and stature of the association must have outstripped even the wildest dreams of the great men who met in Thurles all those years ago.

During February, Frankie Goes To Hollywood had a number one hit called 'Relax' whilst during March Nena took over at the top with '99 Red Balloons'.

FRAILTY, THOUGH NOT IN THE CASES OF JIM, ZOLA, OR MICHAEL

A glance at world affairs in early 1984 alerted one to the frailty of the modern Soviet leaders. Following the death of Leonid Brezhnev in 1982, 68-year-old Yuri Andropov was elected. He died fifteen months later on 9 February 1984.

His successor was the terminally ill, 72-year-old Konstantin Chernenko.

The endurance of Julio Iglesias was not in question! By 1984, the 40-year-old Spaniard had sold 100,000,000 records in six different languages. *The Guinness Book of World Records* described him as the bestselling musical artist in the history of recording.

A young lady who had her sights set on achievement of a different kind was South African runner Zola Budd. The British government had no problem with granting the seventeen-year-old citizenship just thirteen days after submitting her application form. There was just one factor that might have speeded up the normally lengthy process – she had agreed to run for Britain in the Los Angles Olympic Games later in the year. Unfortunately controversy surrounded her participation following an incident when Mary Decker, the golden girl of United States' athletics, tripped and fell during a race. Budd, who ran barefoot, was deemed responsible by the referee, and suffered instant disqualification.

An eight-man jury later ruled that the she was not at fault. By then it was too late and the disharmony surrounding the incident did not subside readily.

Zola Budd was not the only link between the Los Angeles Olympic Games and South Africa. For the third time in succession a political ban denied some of the world's top athletes the opportunity of competing. In 1984 it was the South African athletes who lost out because of the racial politics practised by their government.

FORD CAPTURED AND A FINAL PLACE IS SECURED
As spring gave way to summer, Lionel Richie, Duran Duran and Wham, each had number one hits, first with 'Hello', then came 'The Reflex', which in turn was followed by 'Wake Me Up Before You Go Go'.

Even those with no more than a passive interest in Gaelic games had to be aware that 1984 marked the Centenary of Gaelic Athletic Association's foundation. It was a very special year in the history of Gaelic games. Cork's hurlers showed plenty of enthusiasm for the celebration. Before the championship got underway they reached the National League semi-finals, and won the Ford Centenary competition. In the final of the latter at Croke Park on 20 May, the true potential of the 1984 Cork team began to manifest itself when they defeated Laois by 2-21 to 1-9. The Rebels first championship outing was a Munster semi-final fixture when they played Limerick, at Limerick. They had a useful 3-15 to 2-13 win over the Shannonsiders and again showed the mettle evident in the Centenary competition final by staging a strong second-half come-back. The scorers were: John Fenton (1-7); Jimmy Barry-Murphy (1-2); Seanie O'Leary (1-1); Pat Hartnett (0-2); Tim Crowley, Denis Walsh, and Kevin Hennessy (0-1 each). Cork's next date with destiny was on 15 July at Thurles. Thurles in July meant one thing – the Munster final. It had the makings of a great match because the Premier County were back in the contest after so long. There was little to suggest that Tipperary had the capability of beating Cork. Yet it had to be noted that their will to win would be pushed to the limit and of course anything can happen on the day. It was not a match to be missed and I for one would gladly travel from Antrim to see it.

A MEMORABLE ENCOUNTER AND A SEPTEMBER VISIT TO THURLES

On the July Sunday, Semple Stadium was vibrant. Tipperary followers cheered on their team with a passion. The magic generated by Cork versus Tipperary championship encounters which had been absent for long had returned. The prize at the end of the match was to be crowned champions of Munster, and Tipperary were desperate to once again become hurling kings of the province.

The match got underway with Cork playing into a slight breeze in the first-half. Tipperary were back at their best and went about winning the match like men inspired. Thankfully Cork matched them all the way. It was electric. Early on Cork looked more composed, and were possibly more effective than Tipperary. Yet Tipperary continued to play with a determination not experienced by Cork in the

1982 or 1983 Munster finals. In a few key positions the Premier County men were giving the Leesiders cause for concern. At the interval Cork led by two points, 2-10 to 3-5.

Tipperary restarted with even greater resolve than hitherto and it took all the guile and experience of the Corkmen to contain them. Tipperary slowly but surely chipped away at the Rebel's lead. Then the scores were level! With players being switched from one position to another, Cork continued to battle against a now dominant Tipperary. In spite of their best efforts, the Rebels were four points in arrears with about six minutes of play left. My mind shot back over the years to the 1960s when Tipperary broke my heart.

The supporters of the men in blue and gold were ecstatic and the red and white flags had been lowered. The end was in sight. Yet with time ticking away, Cork seemed the more focused side. But from the jaws of defeat Cork snatched a victory which minutes before seemed well out of their grasp.

Tipperary led by four points with six minutes remaining. When the final whistle sounded the same margin separated the teams but then it was in Cork's favour. Tipperary players and supporters were dazed and shocked by what had happened. The scenes of emotion which followed were unbelievable – tears of sadness and joy, people sitting on their seats stunned whilst others jumped for joy.

The final score was Cork 4-15; Tipperary 3-14. The Cork team was: Ger Cunningham, Denis Mulcahy, Donal O'Grady, John Hodgins, Tom Cashman, Johnny Crowley, Dermot McCurtain, John Fenton (captain 0-7), Pat Hartnett (0-1), Pat Horgan (0-3), Tim Crowley, Kevin Hennessy (0-3), Thomas Mulcahy, Jimmy Barry-Murphy (2-0), Seanie O'Leary (1-1). Replacements were, John Blake for Donal O'Grady and Tony O'Sullivan (1-0) for Tim Crowley. The Tipperary team was: John Sheedy, Jack Bergin, Jim Keogh, Denis Cahill, Pat Fitzelle, Jim McIntyre, Bobby Ryan (captain), Ralph Callaghan, Philip Kennedy (0-2), Nicky English (1-0), Donie O'Connell (1-2), Liam Maher (0-1), Michael Doyle, Seamus Power (1-6), Noel O'Dwyer (0-2). Replacements were, Brian Heffernan for Pat Frizelle, John

Doyle for Denis Cahill, Paul Dooley (0-1) for Bobby Ryan. Referee John Moore in charge of his first senior championship match had an outstanding 70 minutes.

On 5 August at Croke Park, Cork had a comfortable win in their All-Ireland semi-final match with Antrim. The men in saffron made a valiant effort to compete with the Munster champions but Cork's captain, John Fenton, with a personal tally of 0-12, inspired his men to victory. The final score was Cork 3-26; Antrim 2-5.

On the same day at Thurles, Offaly in the other semi-final also had a comfortable 4-15 to 1-10 win over Galway. On 5 September 1937 the All-Ireland final between Tipperary and Kilkenny was played in Killarney. Ever since the major decider had always taken place at Croke Park. But 1984 was special – it was centenary year, and to mark the occasion it was fitting that the final should be played at Thurles, the birthplace of the Association. Tens of thousands of Gaels flocked to the cathedral town on 2 September, the main attraction being the 1984 decider between Cork and Offaly.

CARNAGE IN CALIFORNIA AND BEIRUT, CARNIVAL TIME AT THURLES

Those who were not totally absorbed in GAA centenary celebrations may have noticed that Frankie Goes To Hollywood's 'Two Tribes', remained at number one for nine weeks during the summer of 1984. On 18 August, 'Careless Whisper' by George Michael finally replaced it at the top.

On 1 July Argentinian footballer, Diego Maradona, was transferred from Barcelona to Naples for a fee of £1,000,000 – £4,000,000 less than Barcelona had paid for him only two years previously!

On 19 July a McDonald's restaurant in California was the unlikely scene of carnage when a security guard ran amok. He shot dead twenty customers and injured sixteen others. The word carnage best describes the actions of a suicide bomber who drove a lorry loaded with explosives into the United States Embassy compound in Beirut. When detonated the explosives killed 40 people.

There was only one place to be on 2 September 1984. That was the Tipperary town of Thurles. It was there that at precisely 3pm, referee Pascal Long would set the Centenary All-Ireland Hurling Final in motion. When we arrived at Thurles at about 8pm on the Saturday, the town was heaving. It had all the appearance of carnival time. The weather was beautiful and the atmosphere in Liberty Square was akin to that of a continental resort. Hundreds of people sat outside or just stood on the pavement, with drinks in their hands, where they joked, laughed and some even sang. We joined in the craic and had a memorable evening which led to a memorable night. The following morning heads were a little sore.

The men who met in the billiard room of Hayes Hotel 100 years ago would have been mightily impressed by scenes in Thurles that morning. You could almost make yourself believe there was a smile on Dr Croke's face as he surveyed all from his memorial pedestal.

It was a surprise victory over Wexford in the Leinster championship semi-final of 1969 which brought Offaly hurling to the attention of the public at large. In spite of the emergence of fine, younger hurlers and the durability of stars such as Johnny Flaherty, Damien Martin and Pádraig Horan, Leinster championships of the 1970s were exclusively won by Kilkenny or Wexford. It had been difficult to see how Offaly were going to make a breakthrough in the face of ingrained tradition and the established power houses of hurling in the form of Kilkenny and Wexford. To their credit those involved with Offaly hurling never gave up the battle. Men like Pat Delaney, dual star Liam Currams, Pat Carroll, Brendan Bermingham, Pat Fleury, Ger Coughlan, Eugene Coughlan and Aidan Fogarty had quickly established themselves. In 1981 their day came when a team captained by Padraig Horan brought the McCarthy Cup to Offaly for the first time – a historic day for the county. I'm sure that even their opponents on the day, the gallant Tribesmen, did not begrudge the worthy Faithful County the recognition it so richly deserved. Here Offaly were in 1984, back at the pinnacle of hurling. The younger crop of players who lined-out that afternoon included Liam Carroll, Tom Conneely, Mark Corrigan, Declan Fogarty, and the baby of the team, a twenty-year-old, one Joe Dooley.

There was one change in the Cork line-out from the starting fifteen in the Munster final – Tony O'Sullivan was replaced by Pat Horgan. Midst a frenzy of excitement the match got underway. For most of the first-half it was evenly balanced, yet the battle-hardened Cork team hurled with more confidence

From the moment Seanie O'Leary scored the first of his two goals after 27 minutes of play, the tide swung Cork's way. Offaly trailed by a point at the interval. At half-time on that particular day even though the minimum gap separated the teams, I felt that Cork had a much better grip on the game and were going to win. Right enough, after the re-start Offaly were almost immediately under pressure. Cork had stepped up a gear which I felt had been in reserve throughout the match. Disarray in the Offaly team gradually heightened as Cork began to dominate in more and more positions. After seventeen minutes of play the Rebels led by twelve points. Offaly failed to score during that period. Further goals from Kevin Hennessy and Seanie O'Leary, copper fastened Cork's superiority. The Leesiders' half-back line of Tom Cashman, Johnny Crowley and Dermot McCurtain were magnificent. Ger Cunningham too gave an outstanding display, and Seanie O'Leary, who had long since established himself as a top class corner-forward, again showed enthusiasm, determination, courage, skill and speed, to a level which belied his 32 years. He had earned himself the reputation of being one of the best match-winners in the game. John Fenton's leadership and point scoring talents were a feature of the match. John's outstanding midfield partner was the powerful Pat Hartnett. The performances of the duo in that key sector ensured that Cork dominated throughout. Indeed it was a day when all of Cork's players excelled. Offaly, on the other hand, did not do themselves justice. The final score was Cork 3-16; Offaly 1-12. There were no Cork followers in Thurles

213

on that historic late afternoon less than seven feet tall! What a difference a year makes.

BRIGHTON, BHOPAL AND NEW DELHI SADNESS, BOB'S BAND AID JOY

A few days after the All-Ireland hurling final, Stevie Wonder had a number one hit with the catchy 'I Just Called to Say I Love You'. On 20 October Wham took over at the top with 'Freedom' and next it was the turn of Chaka Khan who had a three-week stay in pole position with 'I Feel For You'. That was followed by two recordings, each of which were chart toppers for one week. They were 'I Should Have Known Better' by Jim Diamond and 'The Power of Love' by Frankie Goes To Hollywood. On 12 October, the action of IRA members who exploded a bomb at the Grand Hotel in Brighton, showed little in the way of regard for life. Several floors of the hotel where the British Conservative Party Conference was being held collapsed, killing four people and injuring 30 others.

On an early December night the population of Bhopal, India, experienced a major disaster. From a nearby chemical plant a toxic gas escaped into the air through a faulty valve. As a result 2,000 people died within days. A further 2,000 subsequently died, and up to 250,000 suffered severe lung, kidney, liver and eye disorders. On a global scale the death which caused the greatest shock was that of India's prime minister, Mrs Indira Ghandhi. While walking in the garden of her home she was shot dead by an assassin. Death too came to such distinguished individuals as: Count Basie, jazz pianist and band leader; Richard Burton, actor; J.B. Priestley, novelist and dramatist; two-week-old 'Baby Fae', a baboon heart replacement patient of fifteen days; James Mason, actor; and Liam O'Flaherty, Irish writer.

Among the most magnanimous humanitarian acts of 1984 had to be the Bob Geldof-inspired Band Aid effort. In order to help victims of famine-ridden Ethiopia, he and Midge Ure wrote a song and invited a host of rock stars to sing it. Those who responded to his call free of charge included Phil Collins, Sting, George Michael, Bono and

Boy George. The record, 'Do They Know It's Christmas', was released on 7 December and became a number one hit on 15 December. All proceeds went towards famine relief. What a wonderful gesture and what a wonderful way for a caring man and his friends to see 1984 out.

1985

It's a Hole, a First for Ireland, but Glasnost Rules
It was in 1985 that Nintendo video games came on the market and that for the first time, the expression, 'a hole in the ozone layer', began to reach us through the media. Scientists first suspected the problem in 1977 but delayed an announcement until they had fully satisfied themselves that the 'hole' did exist.

It was 19 January before Band Aid's, 'Do They Know Its Christmas' was overtaken at number one spot by Foreigner with 'I Want to Know What Love is'. It remained for three weeks at the top until 'I Know Him so Well' by Elaine Paige and Barbara Dixon took over. Four weeks later, on 9 March it made way for 'You Spin Me Round (Like A Record)' by Dead or Alive.

Meanwhile on 21 February, contraceptives went on sale for the first time in the Republic of Ireland. In early March, the USSR mourned the death of leader number three in as many years. Within days, 54-year-old Mikhail Gorbachev was elevated to the Soviet's Unions highest post. He was the youngest leader in the history of Soviet Communism. A reform programme initiated by the progressive Gorbachev quickly gathered an almost uncontrollable momentum which eventually led to the collapse of the Union. Associated with his plans for a revitalised USSR were two Russian words which resounded worldwide; *perestroika* (restructuring) and *glasnost* (openness). Gorbachev was well received by leaders of Western nations.

Could it be that Phyllis Nelson was smitten when she issued a very cosy invitation in the form of her number one hit, 'Move Closer'. Immediately preceding this was 'Easy Lover' by Philip Bailey and Phil Collins, and 'We Are the World', by USA For Africa at the pole position.

THE UPS AND DOWNS OF SPORT

May and June of 1985 proved the be low points in the history of English soccer clubs. On 11 May an outbreak of fire in the main stand at Bradford City Football ground resulted in the deaths of 40 people. Up to 180 others were injured. Later in the same month at the Heysel Stadium in Belgium, before the start of a European Cup final between Liverpool and Juventus, 41 fans died and 350 were injured when rioting broke out. On 2 June because of recurring hooliganism at Continental venues, English clubs were banned indefinitely from playing in European competitions.

In Ireland, as the provincial championship matches got underway, thankfully, hooliganism was not a problem. In the early rounds I listened to the radio broadcasts and most of what I heard pleased me well. The results coming through indicated a Cork versus Tipperary Munster final. Confirmation of that had me punching the air as I sat alone in my car at the sea-front in Ballycastle. At that stage I took it for granted that the match would be played at Limerick, but as it turned out Tipperary elected to travel to Cork which coincided with our family holiday in west Cork.

The contest on Sunday 7 July at Páirc Uí Chaoimh between old rivals Cork and Tipperary never reached the dizzy heights experienced when the counties met at the same stage a year ago. That is not to say that the 48,912 attendance didn't get value for money. It was a match which Tipperary could have won, but didn't, because they failed to convert chances into scores. Donie O'Connell ran right through the Cork defence on a couple of occasions but failed to capitalise. Such opportunities cannot be spurned. Cork on the other hand showed their prowess at score taking.

It was a day when Jimmy Barry-Murphy, playing at full-forward, once again showed his hurling genius to best advantage. He caused havoc in and around the opponents square. Another player to impress was Tipperary's Nicky English. Tipperary did play with fire and determination, yet the Corkmen always had their noses ahead and when it really counted they stepped up a gear which left Tipperary in their wake. The final score was Cork 4-17;

217

Tipperary 4-11. It was a convincing win by any standards.

Cork were Munster champions for the fourth time in the 1980s, missing out only in 1980 and 1981. An All-Ireland semi-final at Croke Park in August beckoned.

BOEING BLASTED, BORIS IS TOPS, A RAINBOW SUNK BUT LUCK AT SEA

It was Paul Hardcastle's number one hit, '19', denoting the average age of U.S. soldiers in Vietnam, which had the longest run at the top in the summer of 1985. After a five-week stay at the top, '19' was replaced by Crowd with 'You'll Never Walk Alone'. Two weeks later on 27 June, Sister Sledge with 'Frankie' was tops. It remained at number one for four weeks until the Eurythmics' 'There Must be an Angel (Playing With My Heart)' topped it.

It was high summer on 23 June when an Air India Boeing 747 flying off the south-west coast of Cork exploded. All 329 people on board died instantly. It is believed that Sikh extremists planted the bomb on the plane before it left Montreal en route to Bombay.

Away from the numerous acts of terrorism which raged throughout 1985, a young man was making a name for himself at Wimbledon. Seventeen-year-old Boris Becker became the youngest ever men's singles tennis champion. Championing the environmental cause took Greenpeace activists to New Zealand in July. They were en route to Muroroa Atoll in the Pacific Ocean where France was carrying out nuclear tests. In Auckland their protest ship, *Rainbow Warrior*, was sunk. Agents of the French government were responsible. A nautical venture with a happier ending was that of treasure hunter, Mel Fisher. After a twenty-year search for the wreck of a Spanish galleon which sunk off Key West, Florida, he literally struck gold. Indeed it was not only gold, there was also silver and jewels – in all about £100,000,000 worth. Still at sea, a little later in the year, a research submarine discovered the wreck of the *Titanic*, the luxury liner which sank with 1,500 people on board in April 1912 on its maiden voyage.

A Wet and Windy Day but the Tribesmen were not Deterred

Madonna's number one hit 'Into The Groove' may well have been an invitation to those looking forward to the All-Ireland hurling semi-final at Croke Park between Cork and Galway. Madonna took over the top spot on 3 August. The Rebels and the Tribesmen did battle on 4 Sunday. I had been looking forward to the match. The attendance scarcely reached the 8,000 mark. Those of us present were treated to a high-scoring and often exciting match. It was the first time I had seen several of the younger Galwaymen in action. The half-back line of Finnerty, Keady and Kilkenny was magnificent. Cork played into the wind and rain in the first-half and seemed well set-up at half-time when they trailed by a single point – Cork 2-3; Galway 1-7.

After the restart Galway showed their mettle. In spite of the adverse conditions, their grit and determination kept them well in touch with their opponents. Neither were they lacking in skill. Goals by Joe Cooney and Brendan Lynskey gave the Tribesmen the edge in spite of a Kevin Hennessy major for Cork. As the half progressed, the Rebels began to look ragged. John Fenton was playing his heart out but the support he needed was not forthcoming. Reluctantly I have to admit that generally the Cork players appeared to lack real enthusiasm. As the All-Ireland crown slipped away from the Leesiders it was John Fenton who made a last do-or-die effort. He scored two goals and a point in a six minute spell at the closing stages of the match. Indeed he notched up a personal tally of three goals and two points. He was undisputedly man of the match, though Steve Mahon also had a fine game. At the end of the day Galway held on and were good value for their win. The final score was Galway 4-12; Cork 5-5.

Galway showed they had top-class hurlers, many of them young, which augured well for the future. The Cork team was: Ger Cunningham, Denis Mulcahy, Johnny Crowley, John Blake, Tom Cashman, Pat Horgan, Dermot McCurtain; John Fenton, Pat Hartnett, Denis Walsh, Tim Crowley, Tony O'Sullivan, Tomás Mulcahy, Kieran

Kingston and Kevin Hennessy. Jimmy Barry-Murphy, who was absent through injury did come on late in the match. The Galway team was: Peter Murphy, Seamus Coen, Conor Hayes, Sylvie Linnane, Peter Finnerty, Tony Keady, Tony Kilkenny, Michael Connolly, Steve Mahon, P.J. Molloy, Brendan Lynskey, Joe Cooney, Bernie Ford, Noel Lane and Anthony Cunningham.

ITS OFFALY, ROCK FALLS, EARTH MOVES, LESTER QUITS BUT AID IS LIVE
The All-Ireland hurling final was played in Croke Park on 1 September. The attendance was 61,814. Offaly, conquerers of Antrim in the semi-final, were Galway's opponents. The Faithful County came out on top with a scoreline of 2-11 to 1-12. Offaly made amends for the poor showing against Cork at the same stage of the championship in 1984.

Back in the ups and downs of everyday life. On 13 September the World Health Organisation announced that AIDS was a worldwide epidemic. No effective treatment had been discovered. A matter of weeks later news was flashed around the world that 1950s Hollywood heart-throb, actor Rock Hudson, had died from the disease.

In the latter months of 1985, two major earthquakes, one in Mexico, the other in Columbia caused widespread dev-astation. Tens of thousands of people lost their lives and many who survived were left homeless and bewildered.

On 29 October many horse-racing enthusiasts were filled with nostalgia. It was the day Lester Piggot, the most recognisable name in the business, ended his career at Nottingham. The legendary horseman, who preferred a unique high riding style was regarded as a brilliant tacti-cian. He had been champion jockey eleven times between 1960 and 1982, and had won the Derby a record nine times. During the autumn months of 1985 the buying power of popular music fans moved 'I Got You Babe' by UB40 and Chrissie Hynde to number one. It was followed by 'Dancing in the Street', a David Bowie and Mick Jagger recording. Midge Ure's, 'If I Was', next took over the top spot. Then on 12 October it was Jennifer Rush with 'The Power of Love' who soared to pole position.

Power of another kind was also in the air in 1985. The fourteen nations of the European Community drew up detailed procedures for full economic integration. The idea was to establish the world's largest trading bloc, thereby putting Western Europe in a position where it could compete with the United States and Japan. Such an undertaking between countries, some of which were tearing each other apart not too long ago, was admirable. It was almost incredible in some ways because inherent in the plan was the free movement of goods, services, capital and people across sovereign borders.

Lives lost in 1985 included actors Orson Wells, Yul Brenner and Phil Silvers. Others who departed this life were, Laura Ashley, fashion designer; Ladislo Biro, inventor; and Anne Baxter, actress.

If indeed music be the food of love, then the likelihood of love dying was extremely remote. On 16 November, 'A Good Heart' by Feargal Sharkey reached number one. Soon Wham breezed in with 'I'm Your Man'. Whitney Houston's number one hit, 'Saving All My Love For You' remained at the top over Christmas, yet it was Shakin' Stevens 'Merry Christmas Everyone' which stole in just as the year ended.

In the minds of many the outstanding event of 1985 was Live Aid. Following the 1984 fund raising success of Bob Geldof inspired Band Aid, USA for Africa was equally successful with a star-studded recording of a Michael Jackson/Lionel Richie composition, 'We Are The World'. On 3 July, satellite technology linked up Band Aid and USA for Africa in an intercontinental extravaganza of popular music – Live Aid. It was watched by almost 2,000,000,000 people and raised $50 million.

Magnificent though those fund raising efforts were, more than 2,000,000 Africans, mostly Ethiopians, had already died from starvation. Many more died in subsequent years because of drought and world indifference.

End of year reviews would, among other things, remind us that in 1985, Barry McGuigan became featherweight boxing champion of the world when he defeated Pedrosa for the title; Ireland won rugby's Triple Crown;

Denis Taylor became snooker champion of the world; the Anglo-Irish agreement came into being; and Knock Airport opened. On the last day of December 1985 the world of rock music was shocked and saddened, by news of Rick Nelson's death. Along with his fiancee and four band members, all six died in a plane crash while travelling between concerts in the United States.

— 1986 —

CHALLENGER AND CHERNOBYL GRIEF BUT RACE BRINGS AID
AND BOB IS MADE SIR

Christina McAuliffe, a high school teacher in America, was
the envy of millions in January 1986. She had won her
place on a space flight in the shuttle, *Challenger*. It was to be
the spacecraft's tenth mission. The launch did not go as
scheduled and was in fact postponed five times. When it
did go ahead it was after ice had been chipped from the
outside of the shuttle. Millions of viewers watched the televised launch turn to a tragedy as Challenger's fuel tanks
exploded shortly after takeoff. Christina, along with six
others aboard, were killed instantly. On an April morning
in 1986, scientists at a Swedish nuclear power station
detected unusually high levels of radiation in the surrounding air. Later in the same day similar findings were
reported from Denmark, Norway and Finland. Later still,
Soviet television, in a rather low-key announcement,
admitted an 'accident' had taken place at Chernobyl
Nuclear Power Plant, north of Kiev in the Ukraine. No
details of the 'accident' were given, and it took some time
before it emerged that human error and poor design had
conspired to cause an explosion which blew one of four
reactors apart, allowing 100,000,000 curies of radiation into
the atmosphere – the dreaded possibility of a meltdown
had become a reality. The consequential suffering inflicted
on the population of the immediate area and beyond
would amount to a human catastrophy of unthinkable proportions – experts estimated in the region of 40,000 cancer
cases and up to 7,000 deaths. Clearly the full extent of the
disaster would not be known for at least a generation.

In those early months of 1986, popular music fans continued to be catered for in the manner to which they had
become accustomed. Number one hits included 'West End

Girls' by the Pet Shop Boys, 'The Sun Always Shines on TV' by A-ha, 'When the Going Gets Tough the Tough Get Going' by Billy Ocean, 'Chain Reaction' by Diana Ross, 'Living Doll' by Cliff Richard and the Young Ones, and 'A Different Corner' by George Michael.

Throughout the 1980s, following the Bob Geldof initiative, the plight of starving people in Africa continued to inspire fund-raising activities. Perhaps the single outstanding fund-raiser of 1986 was the Sport Aid, 'Race Against Time'. Worldwide, 30,000,000 people ran. In June, Bob Geldof was given an honorary knighthood by Queen Elizabeth II.

SUMMERTIME AND THE HURLING IS GOOD

With the sun high in the sky, championship hurling was high on the agenda of many people in Ireland. Cork having been defeated in the league semi-final by Kilkenny in Thurles on 27 April, defended their Munster crown against the challenge of Waterford at Páirc Uí Chaoimh on 8 June. A spiritless Waterford side offered little resistance and allowed Cork to amass a score of 6-13. In reply the Decies men chalked up 0-9. Cork's opponents in the Munster final would be Clare. On their way the Banner County defeated Limerick 2-14 to 0-14, and Tipperary 2-10 to 1-11. Both matches were played at Cusack Park, Ennis but even taking home advantage into account, Clare looked very good. The attendance of 16,085, and 21,665 at respective matches contrasted sharply with the 9,000 present at Páirc Uí Chaoimh for Cork's semi-final encounter with Waterford. The Munster hurling final was played at the famed and resplendent Fitzgerald Stadium, Killarney, on Sunday 20 July. Cork to some extent were an unknown quantity. They had not been tested by Waterford and the manner of the previous year's All-Ireland semi-final defeat by Galway had not yet been eroded from the memories of many. The winning of a fifth successive Munster championship by the Leesiders was not a foregone conclusion. The build-up to the match ensured that followers from Cork and Clare would flock to Killarney in their thousands.

So they did – 39,975 was the official attendance on the

day. Clare followers were confident that their team could topple Cork, and indeed their optimism did much to enhance the magnificent atmosphere which prevailed in Killarney.

One was never sure about Cork teams – they could play brilliantly, yet there were times when they just didn't click. There were occasions too when what appeared to be an over-relaxed and self-confident approach worried their followers.

At 3.30pm referee Terence Murray set in motion the process of unfolding the afternoon's fortunes. Soon it became obvious that the hype and attention which the clash had received had been fully justified. There was nothing between the teams! The standard of play and all-round commitment had spectators on their toes or on edges of seats. Clare's full-forward, Tommy Guilfoyle, was a real thorn in Cork's side – he had a superb game. Thankfully Cork were not over-relaxed and in fact showed that bit more grit than their opponents when it mattered. Evidence of that was seen in the closing stages when the Clare defence allowed Kevin Hennessy to run too far before making a telling pass from which Jimmy Barry-Murphy scored a goal. The final score was Cork 2-18; Clare 3-12.

Cork scorers were: John Fenton 0-8; John Fitzgibbon and Jimmy Barry-Murphy 1-1 each; Tony O'Sullivan 0-4; Kevin Hennessy 0-2; Pat Hartnett and Jim Cashman 0-1 each. Notable newcomers to Munster final hurling and the Cork team were Jim Cashman and John Fitzgibbon. Teddy McCarthy was listed among the subs. Cork would play Antrim in the All-Ireland semi-final at Croke Park, on 10 August. Meanwhile the Rebel County could bask in the glory of yet another remarkable achievement, that of winning five Munster championships in a row.

Throughout the summer number, one hits on the popular music scene came and went with great regularity. Gracing the top spot at different times were 'Rock Me Amadeus' by Falco, 'The Chicken Song' by Spitting Image, 'Spirit in the Sky' by Doctor and the Medics, 'The Edge of Heaven' by Wham, 'Papa Don't Preach' by Madonna, and 'The Lady in Red', by Chris De Burgh.

DIEGO AND RICHARD TRIUMPH

It was still summertime when footballer, Diego Maradona, led Argentina to World Cup victory. His inspirational skills throughout the competition and his wonderful performance when man-marked by West Germany's Matthaus in the final, made him the undisputed star of the 1986 football extravaganza. Another man in pursuit of glory was millionaire Richard Branson. Along with the crew of his speedboat, Virgin Atlantic Challenger II, he beat the Atlantic crossing record which had stood since 1952 by two hours nine minutes.

A BALMY DAY AT HEADQUARTERS

On 10 August at Croke Park, Cork's All-Ireland hurling semi-final with Antrim took place. It was remarkable only for high scoring. The final score was Cork 7-11; Antrim 1-24. Some observers described Cork's performance as laboured and sluggish. In spite of a good performance against Clare in the Munster final, again a suspicion that maybe the team was not firing on all cylinders crept in. In the other semi-final Galway demolished Kilkenny at Thurles.

A rare scoreline in championship hurling of Galway 4-21; Kilkenny 0-13 appeared in much larger print on the newspapers the following day than the scores of Cork and Antrim. The match has gone down in history as the day Galway elected to play with only two men in the full-forward line, allowing the third man to supplement the half-forwards or at midfield. The tactic seemed to confuse Kilkenny. Because Galway had beaten Cork a year before in the All-Ireland semi-final, and because of their recent performance in beating Kilkenny, the pundits and the media placed the Tribesmen as firm favourites to win the All-Ireland. Cork were installed as rank outsiders.

The men of Galway in their distinctive maroon jerseys and those of Cork in their equally distinctive attire met at Croke Park on Sunday 7 September. Cork relished the tag of underdogs and unconsciously or otherwise it helped to fire-up the team. Instrumental too were the hundreds of ardent supporters who gave their men a standing ovation as they came off Páirc Uí Chaoimh after a final training session on the previous Wednesday. A strong message of belief and encouragement was thus communicated. Then there was the man in charge, the coach, Johnny Clifford, who had convinced his charges that there was no way they were going to lose.

As 3.15pm approached the 63,451 attendance at sun-drenched Croke Park waited with bated breath for the moment when referee John Bailey would get the match underway. When the time came all eyes turned towards the area of pitch just below Hill 16. It was there that Galway's right-corner forward, Anthony Cunningham and Cork's left-corner back, Johnny Crowley, would normally have taken up position. On that occasion Johnny Crowley was all alone. Galway had again adopted the two-man full-forward line ploy which had worked so well against Kilkenny in the All-Ireland semi-final.

The opening minutes of the match belonged very much to Cork. The Rebels, playing into the breeze settled quick-ly while Galway seemed to be at sixes and sevens. No joy was coming to the Tribesmen from using a corner-forward further out the field. Indeed the opposite was the case, giv-ing Cork both territorial and psychological advantages. Johnny Crowley, who stayed put in his left-corner back position, made great use of the space and freedom at his disposal. Joe Cooney and Kevin Hennessy exchanged early points before Galway were rocked back on their heels by a John Fenton bullet-like 21-yard free which went straight to the net. A Cork goal, and joy for the Rebels followers! Teddy McCarthy, playing in his first senior hurling cham-pionship match ever, was now prominent and exerted much pressure on the Galway defence. The Tribesmen looked nervous and struggled throughout the first twenty minutes. During that period Kevin Hennessy scored Cork's second goal. After twelve minutes of play the score was Cork 2-3; Galway 0-3. The first sign of a Galway revival came from their half-back line when Peter Finnerty began to make an impression. Yet, with real cohesion lack-ing, confusion continued to reign. Galway had by now reverted to the orthodox team line-out. But had too much damage been done?

Maybe not, because after about twenty minutes they began to claw their way back into the match. Six points came through Steve Mahon, Martin Naughton and Tony Keady, without reply from the Corkmen. With five minutes of the first-half left it took a Tom Cashman clearance to prevent a goal being scored when Ger Cunningham was beaten. At that stage a single point separated the teams. Just before the whistle, a now-badly hobbling John Fenton (ankle injury), who had moved into corner-forward, added a point to Cork's tally, making the score at half-time Cork 2-5; Galway 0-10. Tony Keady's long range free taking had been a feature of the half.

The second-half proved to be a real duel. Followers, whether sporting the red and white of Cork or the maroon of Galway were totally absorbed by the titanic struggle taking place before them. Then in the fifteenth minute of the second half, Tomás Mulcahy, who had played well throughout, sent Cork supporters wild. He ran through the Galway defence, leaving Tony Keady and Conor Hayes in his wake, and smashed the sliotar to the net from a tight angle on the Nally Stand side of the goal posts.

Suddenly things seemed to go Cork's way and possibly the defining moment came when, with ten minutes to go, Kevin Hennessy picked up the sliotar, ran towards goal and unleashed a shot from about twenty yards out which hit the back of the net. Brilliant! John Commins, the Galway goalkeeper, brought his team and the hopes of their supporters back to life with a goal from a penalty. By then though, the whole Cork team were playing like men inspired. A further Galway goal by P.J. Molloy came too late to make any difference. Fittingly the last score of the day, a point, came from the hurley of one of Cork's all-time greats, Jimmy Barry-Murphy. Tom Cashman did what the great Ray Cummins did exactly a decade before; he had led Cork to All-Ireland victory.

Whenever Tom's name comes up in conversation I recall a remark made by the late Micheál O'Hehir. He was summing up individual performances after a match and when he came to Tom he said simply, in his own distinctive way, 'Well, Tom Cashman, was Tom Cashman'.

What a marvellous way to describe the many wonderful displays of hurling given for club and county by the sweet-striking Blackrock player. The Cork team was: Ger Cunningham, Denis Mulcahy, Richard Browne, Johnny Crowley, Pat Hartnett, Tom Cashman (captain), Denis Walsh, John Fenton, Jim Cashman, Teddy McCarthy, Tomás Mulcahy, Tony O'Sullivan, Ger Fitzgerald, Jimmy Barry-Murphy and Kevin Hennessy. Kieran Kingston came on for the injured John Fenton. Dermot McCurtain missed out through injury. The Galway team was: John Commins, Sylvie Linnane, Conor Hayes, Ollie Kilkenny, Peter Finnerty, Tony Keady, Gerry McInerney, Steve Mahon, Tony Kilkenny, Pierce Pigott, Brendan Lynskey, Martin Naughton, Anthony Cunningham, Joe Cooney, and Noel Lane. Peter Murphy and P.J. Molloy came on as subs.

A YOUNG PATIENT, RONALD, TYSON, E.C. NEW BOYS, AND POISONED RHINE

As summer faded into autumn, Boris Gardiner had a number one hit with 'I Want to Wake up with You'. By mid-September it was the turn of Communards with 'Don't Leave Me this Way'. After four weeks Madonna's 'True Blue' moved to the top, only to be overtaken a week later by Nick Berry's 'Every Loser Wins'.

Meanwhile, at Harefield Hospital, Middlesex, England, a two-and-half month old baby underwent a heart and lung transplant operation and was the youngest patient ever to do so.

The winter of 1986 had the media feasting on the Iran-Contra scandal. Did President Ronald Reagan approve arms sales to Iran or not? The President's reply was, 'The simple truth is, I don't remember'. Public confidence in the hitherto extremely popular Reagan and his administration was seriously shaken.

Not in the least shaken was Mike Tyson, when at the age of twenty, in Las Vegas on 22 November, his awesome punching power made him the youngest ever heavyweight boxing champion of the world. He defeated the current holder Trevor Berbick in under two rounds. In Europe, Spain and Portugal became members of the European Community, while further north, the river Rhine suffered an environmental catastrophe. A cocktail of up to 30 tons of agricultural chemicals were hosed into the river when fire broke out at a chemical plant near Basel in Switzerland.

As always, 1986 claimed its share of lives. Among those listed were: Phil Lynott, rock star; Ray Milland, actor; James Cagney, actor; Cary Grant, actor; Desi Arnaz, actor and television executive; Broderick Crawford, actor; Benny Goodman, musician; Harold Macmillan, British prime minister; and Vincente Minnelli, film maker. The number one hits which saw 1986 out were 'Take my Breath Away' by Berlin, 'The Final Countdown' by Europe, 'Caravan of Love' by Housemartins, and reaching out into the new year was 'Reet Petite' by Jackie Wilson.

In many ways 1986 was a momentous year in Ireland. Among the memorable occurrences were: the appointment of Jack Charlton as manager of the national soccer team; the closing of the Irish Sweepstake after 56 years; the successful defence, and subsequent loss, by Barry McGuigan of the world featherweight boxing championship; Tyrone first playing in an All-Ireland senior football final; Ryanair launched a new air-flight service; voters rejected proposals for the the introduction of divorce by almost 2:1; the cargo ship, *Kowloon Bridge*, ran aground off the County Cork coast; the Army were called out to clean up the streets of Dublin when Corporation Workers went on strike; Brian Keenan was kidnapped in Beirut, and 30,000 people emigrated in search of employment.

Personally, the outstanding memory of 1986 had to be that wonderful balmy afternoon at Croke Park when John Fenton, Kevin Hennessy and Tomás Mulcahy goals had us all jumping for joy, and of course the moment Tom Cashman lifted the McCarthy Cup high above his head.

1987

HOSTAGE COLLECTING AND A CUP GOES HOME

On 24 January, a Church of England envoy, Terry Waite, was kidnapped in Beirut by Iranian-backed Hizbollah guerrillas. The incident brought media focus more sharply than before on a foreign hostage-collecting practice which had gone on in the Lebanon for the previous five years.

The media did occasionally present some less intense topics. Among them was coverage of the world's premier yachting challenge – the Americas Cup. It had been four long years since Australia wrenched the famous trophy from the New York Yacht Club and on 4 February America regained the Cup.

TRAGEDY AT ZEEBRUGGE, STERN MEN NOT AMUSED, A DINGO DID IT

On 6 March, a British-owned cross-channel ferry packed with passengers and vehicles overturned outside the port of Zeebrugge, Belgium. More than 200 people were feared drowned. In May, a nineteen-year-old West German caused some hilarity when he evaded the entire Soviet air defences and landed his light aircraft in Moscow's Red Square. Early June saw claims by an Australian mother that her baby was killed and carried off by a dingo, finally vindicated. She received an official pardon from an earlier murder conviction.

A series of number one hits began on 24 January with 'Jack Your Body' by Steve 'Silk' Hurley. That was followed by 'I Knew You Were Waiting' by Aretha Franklin and George Michael. February saw 'Stand By Me' by Ben E. King installed. It was ousted in mid-March by Boy George's 'Everything I Own'. One further number one, 'Respectable' by Mel and Kim was registered before March ended.

DRAWS GALORE AS THE FULL SPECTRUM OF EMOTION IS GIVEN AN OUTING

The Munster hurling championship of 1987 was remarkable not only for the skills, artistry, athleticism and sportsmanship of players, but also for the unusual number of drawn matches. At the semi-final stage, the matches between Tipperary and Clare, and Cork and Limerick, both went to replays which resulted in wins for Cork and Tipperary. As we were to discover later there was still more drawn match drama in store. Cork, the current McCarthy Cup holders, entered the Munster championship at the semi-final stage.

Displaying a relaxed, self-confident attitude, the Rebels were lucky to snatch a draw with a Limerick team that beforehand was given little hope. An injury-time score was the saviour. In the replay, a sharper and more determined Cork team had an easy win over the Shannonsiders. Team captain Kevin Hennessy, and John Fitzgibbon each scored early goals. Later John Fenton added a third, the goal which has been acclaimed as one of the greatest ever scored at Semple Stadium. It was a day when the defence showed real solidness, with Pat Hartnett and Ger Cunningham excelling. The final score was Cork 3-14; Limerick 0-10.

On 12 July, a day on which many people in Northern Ireland have other matters on their minds, at 6am, my son and I left Ballycastle for Thurles. We arrived at our destination at 12.30pm. It was thronged and alive with excitement. The occasion was, of course the Munster hurling final – another Cork versus Tipperary showdown.

There were 56,005 paying patrons, and an estimated further 3,000 who forced an entry to Semple Stadium by breaking down two gates. Cork fielded a team which at a glance bore a striking resemblance to the 1986 All-Ireland winning side. Closer inspection revealed a few notable absentees. Gone was Jimmy Barry-Murphy. He had retired! Alas, we would not again see the particular brand of magic he had displayed in the red and white jersey of Cork for so many years. What great service he had given to his county and what joy he brought to Cork followers.

Not gone as such were, Tom Cashman (injured) and Ger Fitzgerald, both of whom were listed among the substitutes. Back from injury and into the starting fifteen came Dermot McCurtain, as did John Fitzgibbon and Kieran Kingston. The afternoon was humid, the atmosphere was charged, and Cork played into a slight breeze in the first-half. It was one of those matches when it was clear from the outset that nothing on the pitch was going to be easy. It was as if Tipperary were determined to wipe out all the years of disappointment. Playing like men inspired, they bottled up the Cork attack at one end of the pitch and kept the defenders under pressure at the other. Cork were taken aback by the determination of their opponents and looked shaky at times. Again and again the Rebels were forced into errors and were fortunate that Pat Hartnett at centre-half back, Denis Mulcahy at right-corner back, and Ger Cunningham in goal were playing particularly well. They were fortunate too to have a free-taker of John Fenton's calibre. Only four points separated the teams at half-time. The score was Tipperary 0-11; Cork 0-7.

In the second-half, Cork, aided by the breeze came more into the game and the forwards began to make an impression, but the superb goalkeeping of Tipperary's Ken Hogan was a major obstacle. As the half progressed it seemed as if anxious mentors had switched practically every player on the pitch from one position to another. Substitutes too began to appear with regularity as some players tired and others were finding it difficult to get into the action. In the forty-ninth minute Nicholas English showed some classy footwork which culminated in a Tipperary goal. The Premier County led by seven points at that stage. Followers of the men in blue and gold were going wild with delight. It seemed as if their team was about to take Tipperary hurling out of the wilderness. But the match was far from over. When it really mattered Cork rallied and showed the resolve, spirit, skill and craft, to register five points without reply.

Tipperary showed that they were made of sterner stuff and soon it looked as if it was going to be their day. Pat Fox, who had been the outstanding forward of the day, stopped the rot with a point from a sixty-fifth minute free. The mixture of anguish and joy experienced by the spectators was to continue, leaving many delirious. With four minutes of normal time left, Cork's John Fenton, who had already scored ten points, reduced his side's deficit to two points. It was the signal for an all-out assault by the Leesiders.

A passage of play involving Teddy McCarthy, Jim Cashman, Kevin Hennessy and Michael Mullins (sub for Tomás Mulcahy), ended with the sliotar running through the Tipperary defence to where Kieran Kingston was perfectly placed to strike a powerful ground shot to the Tipperary net. The team, which had trailed for 67 minutes of the match, were now one point ahead. It was agony time for the Premier County followers who, a brief few minutes earlier, were ready to cheer their victorious heroes off the pitch. Their Cork counterparts were drained but ecstatic. On the pitch, every single movement of the sliotar, one way or the other, took on an importance of enormous proportions. But it was Cork, again through John Fenton, who were to go further ahead through a delightful long range point from play. Tipperary teams of the recent past would certainly have buckled at that stage. They had done everything right and were the better team for the greater part of the match. Yet here they were with only a few minutes of play left, trailing by two points. When the odds were heavily stacked against them, back they came and won a free. As he had done all afternoon, Pat Fox narrowed the score gap to a single point. The emotions of the followers were again tugged at the roots. Play continued, the tension soared, referee Terence Murray had to sound the final whistle at any moment! Then, Nicholas English was fouled!

Pat Fox must have felt as if he was carrying the whole of Tipperary on his shoulders as he came across the pitch to take the free. It had to be one of the last, if not the last, stroke of the match!

With nerves of steel, or so it seemed, he guided the sliotar between the posts – the scores were level! As Ger Cunningham returned the sliotar into play the long whistle sounded. We had witnessed an altogether extraordinary game of hurling. It was a day to remember. The final score was Cork 1-18; Tipperary 1-18.

The Cork team was: Ger Cunningham, Denis Mulcahy, Richard Browne, John Crowley, Dermot McCurtain, Pat Hartnett, Denis Walsh, John Fenton (0-12), Jim Cashman, Teddy McCarthy (0-1), Tomás Mulcahy, Tony O'Sullivan (0-4), John Fitzgibbon, Kevin Hennessy (captain, 0-1), and Kieran Kingston (1-0). The Tipperary team was: Ken Hogan, John Heffernan, Conor Donovan, Sheamus Gibson, Richard Stakelum (captain, 0-1), John Kennedy, Paul Delaney, Joe Hayes, Colm Bonnar, John McGrath (0-1), Donie O'Connell (0-4), Aidan Ryan (0-2), Pat Fox (0-9), Bobby Ryan, and Nicholas English (1-1). The replay took place in Killarney one week later. We spent the week in Union Hall, and on Sunday 19 July took our places among the 45,000 all-ticket spectators at Fitzgerald Stadium.

Both teams showed changes, positional and personnel, from the drawn match line-outs. On the Cork team, Dermot McCurtain made way for the return of Tom Cashman, and Michael Mullins replaced John Fitzgibbon. Tipperary brought in Pat Fitzelle for the injured Joe Hayes, and Gerry Williams replaced John McGrath. Long before the match started there was a buzz of expectation all around the stadium but the tension born in Thurles the previous Sunday was also much in evidence. Referee Terence Murray was again in charge and at 3.30pm, to the delight of the packed stadium, a sharp shrill on his whistle was the signal for battle to recommence. Unlike the drawn match, Cork were first to settle. Playing into the breeze, John Fenton scored inside the first minute. A second point quickly followed from Tomás Mulcahy. Three further points by the Rebels were registered without reply. The score of 0-5 to 0-0, did not reflect what was happening on the pitch, because Tipperary were challenging, chasing, contesting and doing everything in their power to get into the game. Momentarily they were not able to convert their efforts into scores and missed chances by Pat Fox and Richard Stakelum didn't help matters. It took all of eleven minutes before they managed to put a score on the board – a point by Pat Fox.

For the first twenty minutes the whole Cork team played magnificently. Tipperary were fortunate to have a goalkeeper of the calibre of Ken Hogan at that stage. Again and again he denied the very active Cork forwards. Just when the Rebels seemed to have things reasonably well under control, a flash of hurling genius by Nicholas English beat Ger Cunningahm in the Cork goal. However, that Tipperary goal was quickly cancelled out when from the narrowest of angles Tomás Mulcahy shot to the net for Cork. The half-time score was Cork 1-10; Tipperary 1-5.

The restart was heralded by a spate of positional switches. Many were instigated by the Tipperary mentors in an attempt to break the stranglehold the excellent Cork defence had on them. Still, the Leesiders continued to have the edge and increased their lead to six points. Slowly Tipperary began to come more into the game. With about twenty minutes of normal time left, Tipperary had reduced Cork's lead to three points. Their supporters began to sense that maybe the men in blue and gold had ridden the storm. In the twenty-third minute Tipperary equalised. It was from then on that we saw the best of the Premier County's forwards – Donie O'Connell, who had troubled Cork's Pat Hartnett a little throughout, Nicholas English and Pat Fox became very prominent. At midfield where John Fenton and Tom Cashman had held sway for so long, the Tipperary pairing of Pat Fitzelle and Colm Bonnar began to break even. Cork badly needed a score! When a Tony O'Sullivan shot beat Ken Hogan it seemed as if our prayers had been answered; alas, the goal was disallowed.

A sad sight for Cork supporters was the great-hearted Tom Cashman having to leave the pitch because of a leg injury. As full-time approached I glanced at a little rectangle located between the titles, Corcaigh and Tiobraid Árann, on the match programme. Printed in it was the message, 'GAME IS 70 MINUTES (Extra-time if necessary)'. Unbelievably, at full-time the score read Cork 1-17; Tipperary 1-17; extra-time had become a reality! It was about the only thing that seemed real. As the early evening sun lit up the packed stadium, a scene of unprecedented euphoria rarely experienced at sporting venues was much in evidence.

My most vivid memories are of some players hobbling around unable to run because of cramp, others receiving treatment on the sideline, umpteen substitutions taking place, and generally an unreal state of confusion all-round. I remember that at the end of the first period of extra-time the score was, Cork 1-21; Tipperary 1-20. In the second period at last the more youthful Tipperary team really began to dominate their more experienced campaigners, and scored three goals to which Cork could only muster a single point in reply. The final score was Cork 1-22; Tipperary 4-22.

It had been a great day for sportsmanship and hurling,. It had been a particularly sweet day for Tipperary who richly deserved the victory, and in a way Cork celebrated with them. It took two fine teams to produce the extraordinary contests we had witnessed in over three hours of hurling. Tipperary captain Richard Stakelum, who led his team so magnificently, received the Munster Senior Hurling

Trophy with all the exuberance one might expect. Yet in the true spirit of Cork/Tipperary encounters, he did not forget to pay generous tribute to the Cork team. Tipperary lost to Galway in the All-Ireland semi-final with a score of 2-17 to 3-20. Many observers, including some mentors, believed that the two matches with Cork left the Premier County men mentally and physically exhausted. A superb Galway team went on to win the All-Ireland hurling championship of 1987. The final score was Galway 1-12; Kilkenny 0-9.

Spandau Minus Hess, a Massacre, a Pig's Life but not Legless

Among those to reach number one in the charts were 'Let it be' by Ferry Aid; 'La Isla Bonita' by Madonna; 'Nothing's Going to Stop us now' by Starship; 'I Wanna Dance with Somebody' by Whitney Houston; 'Star Trekkin' by the Firm; and 'It's a Sin' by the Pet Shop Boys. Later in the summer, Madonna returned to number one with 'Who's that Girl'. Later still it was Los Lobos with 'La Bamba' who proved the most popular. In mid-August it was the Michael Jackson/Siedah Garrett combination with 'I Just Can't Stop Loving You' which claimed the coveted spot and a variation on that title, 'Never Gonna Give You Up' by Rick Astley reigned throughout September.

News reports on 17 August recalled Adolf Hitler's first admirer and closest friend; the occasion was the death of 93-year-old Rudolph Hess. Having spent 46 years in custody, 21 of which he spent as a lone prisoner at Spandau jail in Berlin, he strangled himself with an electric cord. He had been convicted of war crimes at the Nuremberg trials. Two days later, on 19 August, world attention focused on the small town of Hungerford, England, where a lone gunman ran amok leaving fourteen dead, and a further fourteen injured. In late August, snippets told of a young Chinese girl who survived living with a family of pigs, and after three years of special training returned to normal life. She fared much better than the twelve-year-old wife of a Nigerian who reportedly had her legs cut off by a husband determined to stop her running away.

CD-VIDEO AND RECORDS BUT PIGGOTT NOT FREE FOR WEAPONS DEAL

Newsworthy in September was the launch by electrical goods manufacturers, Phillips, of the CD-video. The achieving of a record is usually a headline maker, and when the longest running comedy in the world, No Sex Please – We're British, closed at a London theatre after 6,671 performances, it entered the famous book. It was not alone in the record stakes that September, because race-horse trainer Henry Cecil joined the chosen few when jockey Steve Cauthen won the St Ledger on a horse called 'Reference Point'. The significant victory made it a previously unachieved 147 wins in a season for any trainer. In October, still on an equestrian theme, the rider of more than 4,000 winners, and eleven times champion jockey, Lester Piggott, was sent to prison for three years after pleading guilty to charges of tax evasion.

The title of the next number one hit by the Bee Gees was 'You Win Again'. The arrival of 8 December marked a red-letter date for those who campaigned so long and so vigorously to have nuclear weapons banned. A major step in the right direction was taken when the superpowers agreed to dismantle thousands of medium and short range missiles based in Europe.

EXPENSIVE ITEMS AT CHRISTMAS AS HUMAN FRAILTY PERSISTS

On 11 December, Christies auction establishment in London became the centre of attraction for collectors when the cane, bowler hat and boots of Charlie Chaplin came under the hammer. So keen was the interest that the cane and bowler fetched in excess of £82,000, while the boots were sold for over £38,000.

Midst the hustle and bustle of 1987, sombre moments continued to remind us of the frailty of life. Among the once famous who departed from this world were, Liberace, pianist and entertainer; Rita Hayworth, actress; Lee Marvin, actor; Fred Astaire, dancer and actor; Henry Ford II, industrialist; and John Huston, filmmaker.

On 14 November, T'pau's song, 'China in Your Hand', was declared a number one hit, but to see the old year out and the New Year in, it was Pet Shop Boys with 'Always on my Mind' which held the top spot.

In Irish politics, the Fine Gael/Labour coalition

government ended and a subsequent general election resulted in a return to power of Fianna Fáil. In the United Kingdom, Margaret Thatcher was re-elected as prime minister for a record-breaking third successive time. It was the year too in which Johnny Logan became the first person to win the Eurovision Song Contest for a second time. On the sporting front there was good reason for euphoria in Ireland.

Firstly it was because the Republic's soccer team broke new ground by qualifying for the European Championships, and secondly because cyclist Stephen Roche won, not only the Giro d'Italia and the World Championship, but he also became the first Irish winner of the Tour De France. Perhaps in the context of those achievements the launch of the Irish National Lottery was just another one of those things.

Hurling followers including myself will look back on July days in Thurles and Killarney, and recall with enormous pleasure the drama that unfolded as two superb teams locked in battle. Unfortunately though, a black day in November will be recalled with sadness and disgust by the vast majority of Irish people. It was a Sunday morning and people were gathering for a Remembrance Day ceremony in Enniskillen, County Fermanagh when a huge IRA bomb went off. Eleven innocent people, including three married couples, died instantly, and 63 were injured, some critically. Such were the contrasting experiences of 1987.

1988

REFLECTIONS AND IMAGES

Perhaps the most striking trait to emerge during the 1980s was a fiercely puritanical religious fundamentalism. As was seen by the reaction to Salman Rushdie's book, *The Satanic Verses*, Islamic fundamentalists demonstrated extreme and militant objection to what they regarded as an undermining of basic principles. Many countries including England, India, Pakistan, and particularly Iran witnessed violent protests. Iranian leader, Ayatollah Khomeini, condemned Salman Rushdie to death. The manner of his death was unimportant and anyone who died while attempting to eliminate the author was promised heaven.

The symbol of the late 1980s was surely the fax machine. To the amazement of those not technologically-minded, photographs, printed matter or drawings, when placed on the machine, were scanned by a transmitting device and converted into coded signals which travelled by way of telephone lines to a receiving fax machine where an image of the original document or photograph was created - facsimile transmission.

The first number one hit of 1988, Belinda Carlisle's 'Heaven is a Place on Earth'. Two week later, Tiffany made it to the top with 'I Think We're Alone Now', before Kylie Minogue followed up with a song which was to stay at number one for five weeks called 'I Should Be So Lucky'.

A LAST WALK IN GIB AND A SUMMIT FIRST

A leisurely walk on a Gibraltar street on a Sunday afternoon seemed like an attractive proposition for many on 6 March 1988. Among those who strolled along were three unarmed IRA members and a number of armed British soldiers. Without warning the serenity was shattered by a burst of gunfire. When it stopped two men and a woman lay dead on the street. The IRA members had been shot at close range by the soldiers!

In early May, well removed from the hazards of shootings, a Japanese television crew broadcast the very first transmission from the summit of Mount Everest.

A number one hit of the time by Fairground Attraction called 'Perfect', preceded 'Don't Turn Around' by Aswad, 'Heart' by the Pet Shop Boys, and 'Theme From S Express' by S Express.

SLEEP WALKING NOT FOR KAY AS RIG BLOWS
It was in late May we read of what was probably the most bizarre happening of the month. The story went that in Canada a man drove fourteen miles to the home of his mother, hit her with an iron bar and stabbed her. He was later acquitted of her murder on the grounds that he was sleep walking at the time. One who had neither the time nor the place for sleep walking was a lady called Kay Cottee. She did, however, sail into Sydney harbour on 5 June, having completed a solo round the world non-stop voyage, in time to enjoy the number one hits, 'Doctorin' The Tardis' by Timelords, and 'I Owe You Nothing' by Bros. Sadly on 6 June an explosion on a North Sea oil rig took 166 lives.

DRAMA BRIDLED AS PAUL CUTS ACCURATELY
The heady July days at Thurles and Killarney a year ago when the senior hurlers of Cork and Tipperary elevated passion, pride, skill, determination and drama to a hitherto unknown level, were unlikely to be repeated in the 1988 championship. Cork had had an indifferent league campaign and while Clare fell to the Rebels in the championship, the Leesiders had not impressed. It is fair to say that the Banner County men did not really test them. It was with such a pedigree that the current Cork team travelled to Limerick on Sunday 15 July. The occasion was the Munster final, and a very competitive, highly acclaimed Tipperary team provided the opposition. The mentors of the Premier County did not, of course, make the mistake of underestimating their southern neighbours.

Walking out the Ennis Road to the Gaelic Grounds brought back memories of bygone days, and especially of those who had accompanied me on the same trek over the years. Some had passed on, others had settled in various parts of the world – few from the early 1950s were now to be found in west Cork.

The Tipperary followers in Limerick that day had seen it all before and preferred to err on the side of caution. The match programme showed the Cork team included twelve of the starting fifteen from Killarney a year ago, while Tipperary had just one less. Cork though had lost vastly experienced and influential players in the form of John Fenton and Johnny Crowley. Kieran Kingston, a more recent acquisition, was the third. Tipperary were minus the services of John Heffernan, Richard Stakelum, Pat Fitzelle and Gerry Williams.

The Cork team was: Ger Cunningham, Denis Mulcahy, Richard Browne, Denis Walsh, Pat Hartnett, Tom Cashman, Jim Cashman, Teddy McCarthy, Paul O'Connor, Pat Horgan, Kevin Hennessy, Michael Mullins, Tomás Mulcahy, Ger Fitzgerald, and Tony O'Sullivan. The Tipperary team was: Ken Hogan, Noel Sheehy, Conor Donovan, Sheamus Gibson, Bobby Ryan, John Kennedy, Paul Delaney, Joe Hayes, Colm Bonnar, Declan Ryan, Donie O'Connell, Aidan Ryan, Pat Fox, Nicholas English and Pa O'Neill.

For the first fifteen minutes there was little between the teams with Tipperary possibly having the edge over the Leesiders. Then slowly but surely the Premier County began to dominate, not just in one or two positions, but in several. As a result, in a ten-minute spell, the Tipperarymen registered six points without reply. Cork's half-backs, midfield, and half-forwards were finding it difficult to really come to grips with the game. Then just before the interval came a devastating body blow to the Rebels. At the end of good approach work by Nicholas English, Declan Ryan blasted the sliotar past Ger Cunningham into the Cork net. At half-time the score stood at Tipperary 1-13; Cork 0-5. It was difficult to see how the Leesiders could make a comeback!

Their followers refused to be silenced as they continued to encourage their team. The restart was scarcely underway when Nicholas English extended Tipperary's lead. It was then that one of those inexplicable things which often happens during a match, took place; Pat

Horgan pointed a Cork free and all of a sudden his team came to life. The score seemed to be the catalyst which ignited the flame. Teddy McCarthy shot over a long range point, and a similar score from Tony O'Sullivan soon followed. The Rebels had raised themselves just when it seemed that the match as a spectacle was all over. Teddy was now prominent in setting up Cork attacks which eventually began to pressurise the Tipperary defence. Soon a weak clearance led to a sideline cut for Cork. Teddy McCarthy's midfield partner, Paul O'Connor, stepped up and with the greatest of ease sent the sliotar sailing over the crossbar. Just to show it was no fluke he repeated the feat with equal panache shortly afterwards.

The score was then Tipperary 1-14; Cork 0-10. The match had been turned on its head and followers of the Premier County were again haunted by days in the past when their countymen failed to hold a lead no matter how substantial. Cork's pressure continued to payoff. At the end of a typical run by Tomás Mulcahy the sliotar broke for Ger Fitzgerald who shot it over for a point. It got even better for the Corkmen when, from a Tom Cashman free, the sliotar went off the fingers of Tipperary's corner-back, Noel Sheehy, and found its way past Ken Hogan into the net – a goal! Our team had indeed come back from the proverbial dead.

With Tipperary's confidence shattered, their mentors had to act if the day was to be saved. They did, and they did so brilliantly. John Leahy who had come on at half-time for Pa O'Neill, moved to midfield instead of the injured Joe Hayes; the bearded Cormac Bonnar, who had been absent from the team for some considerable time, took over at full-forward, with Nicholas English moving to the corner. The influential Bonnar had an immediate affect on team morale. Still Cork, through a fine, long range point by Tony O'Sullivan, narrowed the gap to two points. Just when it seemed that the mighty men of Cork had taken control of the match, a hotly disputed free taken by Paul Delaney for Tipperary was flicked one-handed by Cormac Bonnar to the Cork net. It spelled the beginning of the end for the Cork team which had fought back so magnificently, but once again found themselves five points in arrears.

Against Tipperary's new-found confidence, Cork could not again raise themselves. There was still ten minutes of play left but they had given their all! The Premier County were not to relinquish its hold. The final score read Tipperary 2-19; Cork 1-13.

Cork's second-half performance made amends for an unimpressive opening period. I felt proud of the men who wore the red jerseys. They showed that they could hurl with the best and importantly, refused to roll over when the odds were stacked against them. Full credit too to Tipperary, they were deserving winners on the day.

STEFFI AND BEN

During the summer months of July and August 1988, two number one hits dominated the scene. First it was 'Nothing's Gonna Change My Love For You' by Glen Medeiros. Then came Yazz and the Plastic Population with 'The Only Way Is Up'. On the very day Phil Collins claimed the top spot with 'A Groovy Kind of Love', German tennis star, nineteen-year old Steffi Graf, showed that she was very much in the groove by winning the ladies tennis Grand Slam – the United States, Australian, French, and Wimbledon open singles in the one year. Sporting acclaim was not to be the lot of Canadian sprinter Ben Johnson. The Seoul Olympic Games of 1988 were the first to go ahead without involving a boycott since 1976. Consequently, contests between the world's top athletes created a renewed verve and interest which was reflected by the millions of television viewers the games attracted. It was no different on 24 September when an awesome performance by arrogant Ben Johnson won him the 100m race in record time. Alas, within days tests proved the flying Canadian had taken anabolic steroids to enhance his strength. Ben would be stripped of his gold medal and returned to Canada in disgrace. The medal went to his arch rival, second placed American, Carl Lewis, the fastest drug-free man in the world.

FAKE, MARRIAGE, AND NATURAL AND MAN-MADE DISASTERS

On 13 October, a discovery which those who venerated the Turin Shroud didn't want to hear, was published. Scientists at three different laboratories, in three different countries concurred, that on the basis of carbon-14 testing, the linen cloth dated from between 1260 and 1390 A.D. For centuries the shroud was purported as being the burial cloth of Jesus Christ. The Bishop of Turin accepted the findings and declared the cloth a fake.

The Hollies went to number one with 'He Ain't Heavy He's My Brother' in September. U2 briefly butted in with 'Desire', before Whitney Houston had a two-week spell in pole position with 'One Moment in Time'. It was Enya with 'Orinoco Flow' who was firmly installed, when on 30 October the head of the Unification Church, Reverend Sun Myung Moon, presided over the marriage of 6,516 couples in South Korea. Before being allowed to consummate their vows the couples were obliged to spend a 40-day introductory period.

The arrival of December was accompanied by natural disasters of enormous proportions. People were shocked by a cyclone devastation in Bangladesh which killed thousands and left millions homeless. Two days later more than 100,000 people died in an earthquake which rocked the north of Armenia – two cities near the Turkish border took the brunt of the eruption. On the evening of 21 December, as Pan Am Flight 103 departed London for New York, it was just another number in an extremely busy pre-Christmas schedule of departures and arrivals. Before the night was out, it was to occupy prime position on news bulletins and national newspapers, worldwide. All 248 people aboard died when the Pan Am Boeing 747 exploded over the village of Lockerbie in southern Scotland. Fragmented pieces of aircraft hurled to the ground claiming the lives of a further eleven people. Investigators pinpointed the cause of the disaster to a type of plastic explosive. The outrage had been perpetrated by terrorists. Families of innocent passengers, crew members, and natives of Lockerbie were left to mourn their nearest and dearest because of what was widely regarded as a wanton, senseless act by ruthless fanatics.

In spite of a grief-filled December, life went on. Time refused to stand still and as always a slow healing process began. Reviews of 1988 reminded us that among the millions who departed this life were personalities such as, the Bee Gees', Andy Gibb; Roy Orbison, rock n' roll singer and writer; and Enzo Ferrari, Italian motor manufacturer. Reviews further reminded us that during the year: controversial peace talks involving SDLP's John Hume and Sinn Féin took place; an Irish government initiated income tax amnesty was availed of by 170,000 citizens who left the State £500,000,000 better off; Jack Charlton's Republic Of Ireland soccer team performed brilliantly in the European Championships; Ireland's golfers won the Dunhill Cup; and Celine Dion, won the Eurovision Song Contest for Switzerland. To cheer us up as the year finally came to a close, initially it was Robin Beck with 'First Time' who had a number one hit, but it was Cliff Richard who held sway over the Festive Season with 'Mistletoe and Wine'.

1989

The closing year of the 1980s decade was marked by political upheavals which changed the face of Europe, the stance of South Africa's government on apartheid, and caused unrest in China. In the early days of 1989 few could have predicted the swiftness and completeness with which USSR disintegration would take place. Fired-up by the reforms of leader, Mikhail Gorbachev, calls for pluralist democracy and self determination were coming from all corners of the already-shaky Communist dictatorships throughout Eastern and Central Europe. By December the imperial power of Moscow had all but lost its administrative grip on Hungry, Poland, Romania, East Germany, Bulgaria, and Czechoslovakia. The most highly-publicised breakaway was that of East Germany. Television pictures first showed thousands of East Germans making their way via the recently liberated Hungry, to West Germany, or seeking asylum elsewhere. Later attention focused on the Brandenburg Gate and the infamous Berlin Wall. It provided an unexpected exit for the masses as guards stood aside or joined in as hordes began to disassemble the abhorred structure. With the exception of Romania, where up to 7,000 people died in the struggle, the transition to democracy in all other countries was bloodless. Nicolae Ceausecu's reign as leader and oppressor of Romania culminated in his execution.

It was in 1989 too that South Africa's ruling Nationalist Party began to disintegrate. Failure of President Botha's repressive policy prompted some within the party to look elsewhere for a solution to the apartheid problem. F.W. de Klerk replaced the ailing Botha, and slowly but surely reforms, which would have been unheard of in the recent past, became a reality. An early announcement to the effect that, 'all members of the public', were in future allowed on all beaches, may have seemed insignificant, but it did in fact represent an opening of the floodgates. The foundations of apartheid had begun to creak!

While pro-democracy movements on the continents of Europe and Africa were rewarded by success, there was to be no such outcome in Asia. The old-style Maoist hardliners were in no mood to yield when pressed by a wide spectrum of the workforce to bring about reforms in China. The revolt ended in disaster when a massive demonstration by students in Beijing's, Tiananmen Square was fiercely crushed by a show of government force. As armoured vehicles crashed through barricades, soldiers opened fire killing over 2,000, and injuring up to 10,000 demonstrators. Deng Xiaoping, leader of China, made it clear that Soviet bloc style unrest would not prevail in his country.

DISASTERS, THE BIZARRE AND KURT RUSSELL

While major political upheavals remained centre-stage, taking place too were more ordinary happenings, which may not affect the public at large, but nevertheless were of major significance to those directly involved.

On 8 January, whilst on flight to Ireland a plane crashed onto a motorway in England. Of the 125 passengers aboard, 50 died. In Kenya, it was the death of a sixteen-foot python which caused millions of tribesmen to mourn. They believed the snake had magical powers. In March, there could not have been many who did not hear the words, *Exxon Valdez,* coming over the airwaves. The words denoted the name of a supertanker which became holed when it hit a reef in Prince William Sound, Alaska. The consequences were dire – 11,000,000 gallons of crude oil leaked into the sea. It was the biggest spill in United States' history and, it killed an estimated 600,000 birds and 6000 otters.

Film star Kurt Russell proposed marriage to an apparently unsuspecting Goldie Hawn in front of a television audience of 1.5 billion. Among the weird and wonderful happenings of '89, sardines falling as 'rain' on a seaside town close to Brisbane must have figured prominently. There is an explanation for the phenomenon but it's best ignored because it spoils the story.

There was, however, another Australian phenomenon which could not be ignored. It was the Kylie Minogue/Jason Donovan contribution to the popular music scene. The combination first weighed in with number one hit 'Especially For You'. During a four-week spell, spanning parts of January and February, it was the Marc Almond with Gene Pitney recording, 'Something's Gotten Hold Of My Heart', which filled the top spot. Then before a solo Jason Donovan crept back to number one with 'Too Many Broken Hearts', it was Simple Minds with 'Belfast Child' which most punters favoured. Following up in a matter of weeks came Madonna with 'Like a Prayer'. Before Kylie Minogue was to reclaim pole position with 'Hand on your Heart', the Bangles record, 'Eternal Flame', had four weeks at the top.

HILLSBOROUGH NIGHTMARE FOLLOWED BY A NEW LEASE OF LIFE

On Saturday 15 April supporters of Liverpool and Nottingham Forest Football Clubs converged on the city of Sheffield. The occasion was an F.A. Cup semi-final and the venue was Hillsborough stadium. It was a day filled with anticipation as two of the finest teams in the land were expected to produce a classic encounter. Instead, a nightmare ensued; thousands of Liverpool fans arrived later than usual at the venue because of traffic holdups. In order to ease crowd congestion outside the grounds a gate was opened which allowed the late-comers to spill into an already packed spectator area. Those standing at the front were crushed against a high wire-mesh fence. In the midst of confusion, bewilderment and disbelief, 95 people died. It was English sport's worst disaster. Away from Sheffield and football, at the Brook Hospital in London one month later, hope and guarded optimism was to be the lot of a 66-year-old lady who became the first adult to undergo a successful hole-in-the-heart operation.

RARE EXPERIENCES FOR CORK FOOTBALL

Cork's hurlers tamely exited from the Munster championship at the first hurdle. It was bound to happen sooner or later, so I will leave it at that and concentrate instead on the fortunes of the Rebel County's football team. My interest was largely due to the presence of seven players from Castlehaven GAA club. The west Cork club had produced a great midfielder who I saw play the might of Kerry in the Munster senior finals of 1980 and 1981 called Christy Collins, one of seven footballing brothers, all of whom possessed natural talent in abundance. Indeed two of the family, Donal and Francis, also played hurling with distinction up to and including inter-county level. Had Christy played for a more fashionable club team in his heyday, instead of then virtually unknown Castlehaven, he would undoubtedly have had a much longer career at senior county level. In 1987, the Rebels had a long-absent belief in their own ability restored. I believe the commitment, skill, and on-field presence of Larry Tompkins and, the driving ambition of team manager and coach, Billy Morgan, were largely responsible for motivating a fine squad of players.

Victories over Kerry after a replay in the Munster final, and over Galway in the All-Ireland semi-final, again after a replay, during which Larry chalked-up some crucial scores laid the foundation for what was to follow. In the All-Ireland final a strong Meath team overcame the Corkmen, but the consensus was that the Leesiders would be back. The predictions proved correct in 1988 Cork did retain the Munster championship at the expense of old rivals Kerry at Páirc Uí Chaoimh. The final score was Cork 1-14; Kerry 0-16. On 14 August at Croke Park, Cork booked their place in the All-Ireland final by defeating Ulster champions, Monaghan. For the second year running Meath provided the opposition. In a hard fought, bruising battle the match ended in a draw on 18 September at Croke Park. The replay on 9 October proved to be an even more physical encounter. Meath were again victorious. It was a disappointing time for those associated with the Cork team. In 1989, Cork's senior football prowess went into the history books. The county completed a first-ever sequence of three Munster championship wins in succession. On 23 July, a day to remember at Fitzgerald Stadium, Killarney, the defending champions defeated Kerry by 1-12 to 1-9. Cork took on Dublin (the team they had defeated in the National League final), in the All-Ireland semi-final at Croke Park on 20 August. Larry Tompkins had emulated his feats of 1987 and 1988, by setting the pace in the scoring table; fourteen points in the two championship matches to date. Cork got off to a poor start! Dublin scored 1-4 without reply in the opening fourteen minutes. Then Larry opened the Leesiders account with a point. Soon afterwards Cork's John O'Driscoll shot the ball to the Dublin net. The 'goal' was disallowed for an infringement. Instead a penalty was awarded.

I was perfectly positioned on the lower deck of the Hogan Stand, as John Cleary stepped up and drove the spot kick past Dublin's goalkeeper, John O'Leary. Cork were back in the match! Soon afterwards a second penalty was awarded. John again took on the responsibility and to the enormous relief and elation of Cork's followers he made no mistake. Suddenly from what had been a dire position for the Rebels, John's perfectly-executed penalty shots had levelled the scores at Cork 2-1; Dublin 1-4. It was the tonic the Cork team needed to kick-start them. From there on they competed for every ball in a match where no quarter was given or asked. At half-time the score was Cork 2-2; Dublin 1-4. An incident before the interval caused the dismissal of Dublin's Keith Barr. The sun shone during a second-half. A fine performance by the entire team culminated in a final score of Cork 2-10; Dublin 1-9. Cork's scorers were: John Cleary 2-0; Larry Tompkins 0-3; Dave Barry 0-2; Denis Allen 0-2; Teddy McCarthy 0-1; John O'Driscoll 0-1; Paul McGrath 0-1.

A Cork senior football team graced Croke Park on All-Ireland day for the third year in a row. Mayo were the opponents on that occasion. The opening quarter of the match saw the Castlehaven duo of Tompkins and Cleary score four points before the Connaught champions replied. It was the brilliant Willie Joe Padden, wearing the number eleven jersey, who opened the scoring for Mayo with a fine point. That was the cue for the Westerners to come more into the match as a fine, sporting, competitive contest

251

developed. At the end of a very good first-half a scoreline of Cork 0-10; Mayo 0-8, just about reflected the balance of play. Soon after the restart a well executed Anthony Finnerty goal put Mayo ahead for the first time. Five minutes later points by Dave Barry and John Cleary had Cork back in front – 0-12 to 1-8. But Mayo would make Cork fight every step of the way. As time wore on though, Teddy McCarthy became very influential for the Leesiders in the role of a midfield, attacking player. Cork was fortunate to have players of the calibre of Mick McCarthy to call on as a substitute. He came in to the match with ten minutes of playing time left and added two vital points to his county's tally – vital in the sense that the sides were level when he was introduced and Cork had only a three point advantage at the final whistle. The final score was Cork 0-17; Mayo 1-11. The disappointments of '87 and '88 were erased as team captain Denis Allen collected the Sam Maguire Cup on behalf of the Leesiders. It had been all of sixteen years since the current team manager and coach, Billy Morgan, did likewise. It was a great day for a squad of players and their mentors who had persevered and worked so hard to make it all possible in spite of the setbacks of previous years. It is worth sparing a thought too for the pivotal role played by John Cleary.

Had the Castlehaven genius not converted the two penalties in the semi-final it is hugely debatable whether or not Cork would have recovered from a 1-4 to 0-1 deficit at a time when Dublin were dominating the match. The victorious Cork team lined-out as follows: John Kerins, Niall Cahalane, Stephen O'Brien, Jimmy Kerrigan, Michael Slocum, Conor Counihan, Tony Davis, Teddy McCarthy, Shay Fahy, Dave Barry, Larry Tompkins, Barry Coffey, Paul McGrath, Denis Allen (captain), John Cleary. The substitutes were: Michael Maguire, Tony Nation, Denis Walsh, Danny Culloty, Mick McCarthy, John O'Driscoll, Michael Burns, Colm O'Neill, and Owen O'Mahony.

By Boat, Rangers First, Cities Link, Mini Birthday, Computers Err

News snippets during the summer of 1989 told of various happenings around the world. First it was a further wave of refugee boats arriving in Hong Kong from Vietnam, swelling the numbers in camps to over 45,000. Then we learned that Glasgow Rangers Football Club had broken with tradition by signing a Roman Catholic player, the first in its 100-year history. By mid-August it was news of the first commercial airliner to fly between London and Sydney which caught the eye. Sentiment was generated in many quarters when on 26 August the arrival of the distinctive Mini car on the market celebrated its thirtieth birthday. September was the month in which two separate computer errors, one in Paris, the other in London, were respectively responsible for issuing 41,000 murder charges instead of traffic offences, and for giving a bank's customers £2 billion in half-an-hour. There were no errors as number one hits continued to light up the lives of popular music lovers. The combined talents of the Christians, Holly Johnson, Paul McCartney, Gerry Marsden, and Stock Aitken Waterman, took 'Ferry Across the Mersey' to the top. Three weeks later, Jason Donovan made a re-entry with 'Sealed with a Kiss'. Next came Soul II Soul featuring Carol Wheeler with 'Back To Life'. In July, Sonia seemed in confident mood as she sang her way to the number one spot with 'You'll Never Stop Me Loving You'. Jive Bunny and the Mastermixers entered the scene in August with the first of their three 1989 number one hits – 'Swing The Mood', 'That's What I Like', and 'Let's Party'. Interspersed were chart-toppers, 'Ride on Time' by Black Box,' All Around The World' by Lisa Stansfield, and 'You Got It' by New Kids on the Block.

Echoes of Paris, 'Frisco, Hong Kong, Beirut and Malta

October in Paris was party-time as the Moulin Rouge celebrated its centenary. In the same month there were no celebrations in San Francisco when an earthquake measuring 7.1 on the Richter scale rocked the city. Traffic accidents resulting from collapsing bridges and flyovers claimed up to 100 lives. Fortunately new buildings designed to withstand such tremors proved a success.

On 25 November when the Hong Kong authorities announced their intention to repatriate Vietnamese boat-people, riots broke out in the detention camps. A welcome development came to fruition in early December. On a ship off the coast of Malta an end to the 52-year-old Cold War was agreed by Soviet leader, Mikhail Gorbachev and United States president, George Bush. It ended the superpower rivalry which on several occasions over the years, looked ominous. Unfortunately there was no such deal between the warring Middle East factions. Violence, which was mainly centred in and around Beirut, was part and parcel of a fourteen-year-old civil war. It reached an all-time high in 1989.

THE END BUT WHAT WAS NEW

The end of an eventful year was nigh but there were some remaining headline makers worth recording; a general election in the Republic of Ireland resulted in Charles Haughey leading Fianna Fáil into a coalition with the Progressive Democrats, thereby forming Dáil number 26; the Republic had its first Lotto millionaire; proposals to mine for gold in County Mayo's holiest mountain, Croagh Patrick, were strongly opposed; Soviet leader Mikhail Gorbachev and his wife Raisa charmed crowds during a stop-over at Shannon Airport; George Bush became president of the United States; Teenage Mutant Ninja Turtles arrived on the market; a worldwide ban on ivory trading was announced; satellite Sky TV was launched; the Republic of Ireland soccer team qualified for the 1990 World Cup finals in Italy; and Christy O'Connor Jr. clinched Ryder Cup victory for Europe.

We were of course reminded of those who made their mark in life, but who had become past tense over the previous twelve months. Included were: Salvador Dali, surrealist Spanish artist; Sugar Ray Robinson, welterweight and middleweight boxing champion of the world; Daphne du Maurier, author; Georges Simenon, novelist and creator of the fictional detective Maigret; Samuel Beckett, Irish dramatist; Lucille Ball, actress; Irving Berlin, composer; Bette Davis, actress; Hirohito, Japanese emperor; Ayatollah Ruhollah Khomeini, Iran's ruler and religious leader; Ferdinand Marcos, president of the Philippines; and Sir Laurence Olivier, actor. It was Band Aid II, with their number one hit, 'Do they Know it's Christmas', which cheered up parties over the festive season and took us into the New Year.

1990

SWINGS AND ROUNDABOUTS

Coinciding with the arrival of the 1990s was a time of renewed freedom and self determination for millions around the world. The Cold War which had threatened to erupt on so many occasions over the past 45 years, virtually disappeared overnight. There was now only a single superpower! In that climate and with the breaking up of the USSR, cries for democracy sprung up in nations previously unheard of by many. However, it was not to be a bed of roses all the way and in some countries economic anarchy, crime and civil war became rife.

Suddenly nationalistic, tribal and religious fervours which had been held down by uncompromising Kremlin rule for so long were unleashed with horrific consequences. We were taking the first tentative steps into a decade where armed conflict forced refugees in their millions to be on the move.

Reports of people dying of starvation made headlines daily, and the scourges of cancer and AIDS continued unabated in spite of the best efforts of medical research. Perhaps the jewel in the crown was the removal of the cornerstone which had kept apartheid alive in South Africa.

PISA LEANS, GURU LOVES, NELSON FREE, BUT FERRY BURNS

In the context of major happenings around the world not many regarded too seriously a January press release to the effect that the Leaning Tower of Pisa was closed to the public. The explanation for the closure was that the leaning tendency had accelerated. Of no greater consequence to most was the death of a 58-year-old free love Indian guru. He had been banned from several countries on account of his teachings which included the doctrine that celibacy was a crime, yet he must have been doing something right because among his extensive range of possessions were almost 100 Rolls-Royce cars.

On 11 February, a red letter day in the history of South Africa, the de Klerk government released Nelson Mandela from jail. He had been incarcerated because of his opposition to the apartheid system of government. The early morning news bulletins of 7 April brought reports of a ferry boat tragedy in which 150 lost their lives. It happened when fire broke out while the vessel was on a night-time trip from Oslo in Norway to Frederikshavn in Denmark.

Popular music was not forgotten about in 1990. It all began with a New Kids on the Block record called, 'Hangin' Tough'. Kylie Minogue soon followed up with 'Tears on my Pillow'. Then it was Sinead O'Connor who held sway for virtually the whole of February with 'Nothing Compares 2 U'. It took the best efforts of Beats International featuring Lindy Layton to dislodge Sinead, with 'Dub be Good to Me'. In late March, it was Snap with 'The Power' which occupied the number one spot. However, Madonna was lurking, and two weeks later she took over with 'Vogue'. As the year approached the halfway mark it was Adamski with 'Killer' who ruled the roost.

A CASE OF MORALITY, A MISTAKE, BUT TRACY, MARTINA AND GERMANS WIN

In early May a court case with a difference was brought to our attention. A news item told of a retired lady brothel keeper who lost a fifteen-year legal battle with the Inland Revenue. Her defence for not paying income tax was that the government was breaking the law by living off immoral earnings. On a more serious note, it was in May that two Australians visitors to Holland died. In a case of mistaken identity they were shot dead by IRA gunmen.

Southampton sea front was a scene of much excitement and jubilation on 28 May when the yacht, *Maiden*, skippered by Tracy Edwards, sailed into the harbour. The occasions marked the completion of the Whitbread Round the World Race by the first yacht to do so with an all-women crew. Maybe it was a case of dirty work at the crossroads, but for whatever reason, in June the authorities in Florence, Italy brought smiles to many faces when they decreed that horses should be equipped with underwear to prevent fouling of public thoroughfares.

On successive days in early July, Martina Navratilova and West Germany were in the news. First it was Martina who went into the record book by winning a ninth Wimbledon ladies singles title. Then it was the Germans who defeated Argentina in the World Cup Final.

THE STUFF THAT DREAMS ARE MADE OF

Cork's senior hurling team made an early start in the 1990 championship. On Sunday 20 May they travelled to Tralee and played Kerry in the opening round. A final score of Cork 3-16; Kerry 3-7 seemed like a comfortable win for Cork, and so it was. Yet some doubts were expressed as to whether or not the Leesiders were a complete team. Two weeks later at Thurles, Cork's conquerers of the previous year, Waterford, took on the Rebels in the Munster semi-final. This time Cork made light of the opposition and finished easy winners. The final score was Cork 4-15; Waterford 1-8.

Mention of Tipperary, the current All-Ireland champions, as Munster final opponents immediately raised the interest of all Rebel County hurling fans. It had been four years since Cork took the coveted Munster crown back to Leeside. Could experienced campaigners of the Kevin Hennessy era, and exciting newcomers such as Kieran McGuckin, blend to bring the trophy home? We could be assured that Fr Michael O'Brien (coach) and Gerald McCarthy (trainer) would leave no stone unturned in their quest to bring the glory days back to Cork hurling. All would be revealed at Semple Stadium on 15 July!

As we took up our seats the adrenalin was already flowing. Injury had ruled out the selection of quality players Tomás Mulcahy and Teddy McCarthy for the Rebels. That factor added to the already strong case for the installation of Tipperary as favourites to take the title.

From the throw-in of the sliotar Cork made their intentions clear; they would not be easily brushed aside. A fine

team performance enhanced by top-class individual displays did indeed win the day for the Leesiders.
Outstanding were: Ger Cunningham, the ever reliable goalkeeper; Denis Walsh, dual star player; John Considine, the
tenacious right full-back; Kieran McGuckin team captain;
Jim Cashman, the accomplished centre-half back; Tony
O'Sullivan, the sweetest of players and scorer of splendid
points; Kevin Hennessy, the experienced player and scorer
of umpteen wonder goals; Ger Fitzgerald, the opportunist
supreme; and Mark Foley who literally played the game of
his life. The tall Timoleague man, playing in his first
Munster final, took on the Tipperary defence in cool clinical
fashion and notched up a magnificent individual score of 2-
7. The final score was Cork 4-16; Tipperary 2-14.

Another afternoon of riveting hurling had been witnessed by those fortunate enough to have been present at
Semple Stadium. Had it not been for the enormous contribution of Mark Foley, Tipperary might well have won the
day. It had been a special day for Denis Walsh, Cork's great
servant in both hurling and football. Playing at full-back he
had been majestic but that was nothing new for the St
Catherine's clubman. What made the day so special for
him was the winning of a Munster senior hurling medal to
go along with the Munster senior football medal he had
won earlier in the month. By doing so a 47-year gap was
bridged as it was in 1943 that Jack Lynch and Paddy
O'Donovan achieved the elusive 'double'.

All-Ireland hurling semi-final day at Croke Park was 5
August. In a high-scoring match Cork defeated Antrim.
The final score was Cork 2-20; Antrim 1-13. As in 1986,
Galway were Cork's opponents in the All-Ireland hurling
final. The match was played at Croke Park on Sunday 2
September. By then Cork's senior football team had quali-
fied for the All-Ireland football final – a possible double of
All-Ireland victories was on the cards. Later that day, as we
made our way to Croke Park, all the trappings of another
fabulous occasion were in place.

Galway had a hugely experienced team. As impressive
All-Ireland champions of 1987 and 1988 they had accounted for Kilkenny and Tipperary in respective finals. An

added incentive was to avenge the All-Ireland final defeat of 1986 at the hands of the Rebels. The bookies and pundits made them firm favourites to do so! By the time referee John Moore got the match underway, 63,954 had packed the terraces and stands of the stadium of dreams. All around the sense of occasion was in evidence. Play had scarcely begun when Kevin Hennessy had Cork's followers on their feet; in less than a minute the sliotar had found its way to the Galway net. Soon afterwards, Galway's captain, Joe Cooney, scored the first point of what would be an impressive 1-7 before the end of the match. During the opening fifteen minutes the Leesiders had the better of things. Kevin Hennessy added three points to his earlier goal, while Teddy McCarthy, John Fitzgibbon and Ger Fitzgerald chalked up points apiece. The outstanding Joe Cooney, a real thorn in the Cork defence, replied with two points.

Tony Keady and Noel Lane each added a point. Slowly but surely the Galway team, now inspired by centre-half back Tony Keady, began to dominate, and in the final fifteen minutes of the first-half scored 1-7 to a mere 0-2 by the Rebels. The half-time score was Galway 1-13; Cork 1-8. Kevin Hennessy at full-forward, Teddy McCarthy at midfield and Seán O'Gorman at left-full back had been prominent for the Leesiders. Cork would be wind assisted in the second-half and the general feeling was that in other circumstances a five-point gap could easily be closed. That day there was concern because of the increasing dominance of the Tribesmen before the interval. The opening minutes of the second period did nothing to relieve Corkonian concern. The early scores came from the sticks of Galwaymen, Michael McGrath and Anthony Cunningham. Shortly afterwards a significant positional switch which brought Cork's team captain Tomás Mulcahy to the half-forward line soon paid dividends. His strong running at the Galway defence accompanied by bursts of speed, made an immediate impact. Still, points by Tomás and Kevin Hennessy were matched by similar scores from Galway's excellent midfield player Michael Coleman, and the very lively left-half forward, Martin Naughton. It was then that Cork's tremendous and long-serving goalkeeper Ger Cunningham again displayed his prowess by making a brilliant if unorthodox save.

Important though that stop was, soon it would be over-shadowed by the contribution his lengthy puck-outs made to the outcome of the match. Such was the distance the slio-tar travelled high in the air that when it dropped it landed well behind the opponents half-back line.

The Cork forwards fed off that supply and soon bene-fited through Tomás Mulcahy (1-0), Tony O'Sullivan (0-1), and Mark Foley (0-1). Cork began to play better all over the field. It was noticeable that Galway's first-half star, Joe Cooney, was now being well marshalled by Jim Cashman. The introduction of David Quirke and Cathal Casey for the tiring Kieran McGuckin and Brendan O'Sullivan added further to Cork's resurgence. Teddy McCarthy continued to impress with his robust, bustling style of play. The scores were level as play entered the final seven minutes. Cork pressed on and it was John Fitzgibbon who set the red and white flags into wildly gyrating mode with not one, but two well-taken goals.

Brendan Lynskey, who had come on as a Galway sub-stitute, added a goal to their tally before Tomás Mulcahy and Tony O'Sullivan exchanged points with Martin Naughton and Joe Cooney. At the final whistle the score was Cork 5-15; Galway 2-21. Fair play to a Cork team which at one time seemed in trouble but survived to make an extraordinary comeback in the final quarter.

Worthy team captain Tomás Mulcahy, an inspirational player and a man for the big occasion was the toast of Cork as he raised the McCarthy Cup aloft on that glorious September, Sunday afternoon.

Post-match discussions served to highlight just how difficult it was to pick out a Cork player who did not play well at some stage. The full-back line of John Considine, Denis Walsh and Seán O'Gorman, did extremely well, with the latter excelling when it was most needed. Seán McCarthy, Jim Cashman and Kieran McGuckin each had their moments in a formidable half-back line. The mid-field pair of Teddy McCarthy and Brendan O'Sullivan complimented each other. Teddy was strong, physical, full of vigour, and scorer of three vital points. Brendan's turn of speed, his ground hurling, and his all-round workman-like performance enhanced the supply of sliotar to his for-wards. The half-forward line of Ger Fitzgerald, Mark Foley, and the delightful hurler Tony O'Sullivan, worked hard throughout and reaped their rewards in the latter stages of the match. The inside trio of Tomás Mulcahy (far more effective when moved to the half-forward line), Kevin Hennessy and John Fitzgibbon were outstanding. The experienced Kevin who over the years had been a jewel in Cork's scoring department, was once again a real headache for the Galway defence. Half the double had been achieved!

On 16 September the red and white trappings so long synonymous with Cork GAA were given a further airing at Croke Park. The occasion was the All-Ireland senior foot-ball final, and for the third time in four years Meath were the opponents. Cork had earlier swept Kerry aside in the Munster final, and in doing so had claimed the provincial crown for the fourth time in as many years. The Leesiders All-Ireland semi-final match with Roscommon proved to be a much tougher proposition. In a close, hard fought encounter the tide did not significantly go Cork's way until the introduction of Skibbereen's O'Donovan Rossa club-man Mick McCarthy midway through the second-half. At the long whistle the Rebels had seven points to spare.

All-Ireland day, the second in 1990 for many Cork fol-lowers, was not blessed with brilliant sunshine but there was no shortage of heat surrounding the occasion. Referee Paddy Russell of Tipperary, in charge of his first All-Ireland senior football final, got the match underway at 3.30pm. The rivalry generated due to the keenly contested recent meetings of Cork and Meath was much in evidence from an early stage in the match. It was perceivable from the attitude and remarks of respective followers and from the on-pitch action. The match did live-up to the huge media hype it had received in as far as that it was tough and physical. We experienced a tremendous level of pas-sion and commitment from the players, but style suffered as a result. In truth it has to be said it was a foul-ridden encounter. In the opening half, Cork slightly edged the robust exchanges. At the interval the score was 0-6 to 0-5 in favour of the Rebels. During a second-half which continued to be rugged, rough and tough, Cork had to cope without the services of full-forward Colm O'Neill who had been dismissed before the interval. In the midst of the fray there were some fine individual displays, and for Cork none more so than those given by Shay Fahy, Barry Coffey, Michael Slocum, Larry Tompkins, Niall Cahalane, Danny Culloty, Conor Counihan, Mick McCarthy and Paul McGrath. John Kerins, who made one exceptional save and distributed the ball so well with his long rangy kick-outs, had a fine game in the Cork goal. For Meath it was Martin O'Connell who stood out, with Kevin Foley and Brian Stafford also prominent. As the afternoon dulled further, it looked as if it was going to be brightness and light all the way for Cork.

Could it be that the 100 year gap since the county last won the double of All-Ireland hurling and football crowns was about to be bridged? Indeed it was, the final score read Cork 0-11; Meath 0-9.

A sweet victory for Cork, and a particularly joyous occasion for the dual players, Teddy McCarthy and Denis Walsh. Teddy was to have the unique distinction of being the only player ever to have won All-Ireland medals in both hurling and football in the same year as a member of the starting fifteen on each team. Denis, who was listed as a substitute on the football squad, was of course very much an integral part of the winning hurling team. What an honour it was for Cork's captain Larry Tompkins and how fitting it was that the man who had done so much in recent years to ensure Cork's football place at the highest level should be the recipient of the Sam Maguire Cup on such an auspicious occasion.

All present at Croke Park on those famous September Sundays of 1990, and indeed those followers whether at home or abroad who associated themselves with the mighty men of Cork's GAA games, will for ever look back with justifiable pride and satisfaction on a brilliant achievement.

The Cork team was: John Kerins, Tony Nation, Niall Cahalane, Stephen O'Brien, Michael Slocum, Conor Counihan, Barry Coffey, Shay Fahy, Danny Culloty, Dave Barry, Larry Tompkins, Teddy McCarthy, Paul McGrath, Colm O'Neill, and Michael McCarthy. The subs were Michael Maguire, Coleman Corrigan, Tony Davis, Paddy Hayes, John O'Driscoll, John Cleary, Jimmy Kerrigan, Denis Walsh, and Mark O'Connor.

SADDAM, KEENAN, THATCHER, AND MCDONALDS HEADLINES
On the pop music scene, Englandnewworder's 'World In Motion' was followed at number one by Elton John with 'Sacrifice/Healing Hands' which remained at the top for five weeks, only to be overtaken by Partners in Kryme with 'Turtle Power'. In late August, 'Itsy Bitsy Teeny Yellow Polka Dot Bikini' by Bombalurina took over. By mid-September it was 'The Joker' by the Steve Miller Band which became favourite. Before the month was out Maria McKee hit number one with 'Show Me Heaven'.

As autumn began to establish itself, Saddam Hussein, Iraq's leader, wearied of what he saw as an overproduction of oil by Kuwait, thus depressing prices, and consequently damaging the economy of Iraq. His solution, which was condemned by world leaders, was to invade Kuwait. At the same time in Beirut, another Middle East trouble spot, plans were afoot to release Irish hostage, Brian Keenan. November proved to be a momentous month in British politics: the Iron Lady's eleven year tenure as prime minister ended; her popularity plummeted after the government introduced a 'poll tax' in March; she attempted unsuccessfully to block the EC's plan for a common currency; rivals in government called for her resignation; John Major replaced her as prime minister.

December was equally momentous in Poland when Lech Walesa, the man jailed by Communist rulers for nine months in 1980, was elected president of his country. The world of commerce didn't stand still in 1990 either. It could be said that Capitalism took a definite step forwards when McDonalds opened a fast-food outlet in Moscow. A new phenomena to make a breakthrough was the sale of licensed merchandise goods such as T-shirts, sportswear, mugs, caps, etc. The names and logos of firms and personalities began to appear on all sorts of products. As the year drew to a close, the obligatory reviews reminded us of those who would no longer be concerned by happenings of this life. Among the departed were: Jimmy van Heusen, songwriter; Greta Garbo, actress; Sammy Davis Jr., actor and entertainer; Rex Harrison, actor; Leonard Bernstein, composer and conductor; Roald Dahl, writer; Ava Gardner, actress; and Jill Ireland, actress. In the last days of 1990, Cliff Richard with 'Saviour's Day' occupied top spot in the charts. It was preceded by The Beautiful South's, 'A Little Time', the Righteous Brothers, 'Unchained Melody', and 'Ice Ice Baby' by Vanilla Ice.

Had the GAA presented an inter-county achievement award for 1990 there was only one possible destination for it – where the McCarthy and Sam Maguire Cups sat side by side. Whatever 1991 held in store it was hard to see it surpassing the joy which 1990 had brought to Leeside followers of hurling and football.

1991

Like 1990, 1991 was again to be a year of major European political upheaval. The process which had begun to gain momentum a year ago continued to roll. Those of us who grew up with maps of Europe showing Yugoslavia firmly situated across the Adriatic Sea from Italy had no reason to believe it was not going to remain there for evermore. That was not to be the case. By the end of 1991 the country which had been held together for 45 years by the Communists began to collapse. A fragmented Yugoslavia formed no less that six 'new' republics – Slovenia, Croatia, Bosnia-Herzegovina, Serbia (part of which was Kosovo), Montenegro, and Macedonia. The sad aftermath of ethnic conflict associated with the reformed Balkan region is all too well known. In northern Europe, the Baltic states too were demanding independence from the USSR. At first the Lithuanian call was resisted by what was to be the last gasp of the once mighty Soviet empire. The intense desire for self determination could not be stopped. By September Latvia and Estonia joined Lithuania as the world's newest independent nations.

In the Middle East where conflict was never far away, the Gulf War broke out on 16 January. Saddam Hussein's refusal to withdraw from Kuwait prompted the Allies to bomb targets in Iraq, including the capital, Baghdad. In Russia, while Boris Yeltsin was calling on Soviet president, Mikhail Gorbachev to resign, Iraq's troops were preparing to withdraw from Kuwait. The Gulf War ended on 27 February.

UPS AND DOWNS

In late March it was announced that Diego Maradona, star of Napoli's team, was banned from all sporting activity in

Italy after failing a dope test.

In early April it was all good news for pop singer and actress, Madonna. Reportedly she was being snowed under by awards for just about everything imaginable in the world of popular music. She wasn't doing badly in the charts either. Her sales of 80,000,000 albums worldwide were surpassed only by Elvis Presley and the Beatles. There were nineteen number one hits in 1991. Iron Maiden led the way with 'Bring Your Daughter ... To The Slaughter'. That was followed by two one-week-stay hits of Enigma and Queen. They were respectively, 'Sadness Part 1' and 'Innuendo'. Early February marked the entry of '3 Am Eternal KLF' featuring Children of the Revolution. Simpsons, 'Do The Bartman', came next, and it was followed by the Clash recording, 'Should I Stay or Should I Go'. With six number one hits already accounted for, on 23 March 'The Stonk', by Hale and Pace made it seven. One week later, 'The One and Only' by Chesney Hawkes began a five-week tenure, which was then matched by Cher with 'Shoop Shoop Song'.

While the music played on an outbreak of cholera in South America was deemed to be the worst this century. Over 1,000 people died as a result of the disease and thousands more were registered as suffering from it. On the Asian continent a cyclone devastated Bangladesh, claiming 250,000 lives, and leaving millions of others marooned in the midst of floods. Still on the Asian continent, it was on 21 May that Rajiv Gandhi, former prime minister of India, suffered the same fate as his late mother, Indira Ghandi in 1984. The 46-year-old was assassinated by a woman terrorist suicide bomber who approached him during an election rally.

A PREMIER AFFAIR
The excitement generated by the 1990 hurling and football championships was still fresh in the minds of Cork's followers as the current season began. Leeside hurlers entered the fray on 2 June at Thurles. The occasion was a semi-final and Waterford provided the opposition. As in all but one of the recent encounters between the counties, Cork made no mistake. Yet, the Rebels who had been

expected to win easily, welcomed a John Fitzgibbon late goal to seal victory. Before an attendance of a mere 10,000, the final score was Cork 2-10; Waterford 0-13. Tipperary overcame the best efforts of Limerick in the other semi-final. The old rivals were again to face each other in the Munster final at Páirc Uí Chaoimh on 7 July. Champions Cork would have home venue advantage, and star forward, Tony O'Sullivan, the All-Star of 1982, 1986, 1989 and 1990, was the current captain. Not surprisingly, after the achievements of 1990, the team he led had an unimpressive League campaign. On a day when the Artane Boys Band entertained at Páirc Uí Chaoimh, a capacity crowd turned out to witness the latest saga in Cork/Tipperary dramatic meetings. The age-old rivalry between the teams ensured a tremendous atmosphere around the grounds. An added incentive for Tipperary to do well was the unexpected defeat by Cork the year before.

The match that afternoon may not rank with the classics of 1987 or 1990, yet it was a marvellous drawn final. Tipperary forward Pat Fox was surely the star performer. He scored a vital goal when Cork were six points clear, and later scored their equalising point. Pat came to the rescue of the Premier County on a day when Nicholas English uncharacteristically squandered several scoring chances. Six goals were scored and four of them belonged to Cork. The Cork team was: Ger Cunningham, John Considine, Richard Browne, Séan O'Gorman, Séan McCarthy, Jim Cashman, Cathal Casey, Brendan O'Sullivan, Pat Hartnett, Tomás Mulcahy, Mark Foley, Tony O'Sullivan (captain), Ger Fitzgerald, Kevin Hennessy, and John Fitzgibbon. The replay at Thurles was memorable for the way Tipperary fought back to win by four points after Cork opened up a nine-point lead early in the second-half. Remember, Cork too surrendered a six point lead in the drawn match! Veteran observers of Cork/Tipperary championship meetings were not altogether surprised by the outcome in 1991. I suppose it was Tipperary's turn to show the hurling world just how good they could be. The Tipperary team was: Ken Hogan, Paul Delaney, Conor Donovan, Noel Sheehy, John Madden, Bobby Ryan, John Kennedy, Declan

Carr (captain), Joe Hayes, Michael Cleary, Declan Ryan, John Leahy, Pat Fox, Cormac Bonnar, and Nicholas English. It was to be Tipperary's year! In September they became All-Ireland hurling champions at the expense of Kilkenny.

SNIPPETS FROM 1991

It is interesting to reflect on news items which made headlines in the autumn and early winter of 1991, and to note that so many are now virtually forgotten – almost as if they never happened. Remember the following!

The highly-published hostage ordeals of John McCarthy, Terry Waite and Thomas Sutherland came to an end when they were released by a terrorist group in the Lebanon. Worsening economic conditions in Albania led to tens of thousands of refugees crossing the Adriatic Sea to Italy in grossly overcrowded ships. The welcome they received was far from warm. The 22 English League clubs which made up the First Division resigned; their intention was to form a breakaway super-league under the auspices of the Football Association.

An attempted coup by Russian hardliners to depose President Mikhail Gorbachev failed, although his power base was greatly weakened and he resigned before the end of the year. The Soviet state ceased to exist on 5 September when the Congress of Peoples Deputies of the Soviet Union, under pressure from Mikhail Gorbachev, annulled the Union and handed power to the republics. An interesting statistic from the World Bank showed that the interest and capital repayments by Third World countries over the previous year were $1.56 billion more than the bank paid in new loans and assistance.

Perhaps the news item which has endured more than most is the mystery surrounding the death of colourful and controversial press magnate, Robert Maxwell. He drowned after falling from his luxury cruiser off the Canary Islands. Vic Reeves and the Wonder Stuff's 'Dizzy' made it to number one, preceded by 'I Wanna Sex You Up' by Color Me Badd, 'Any Dream Will Do' by Jason Donovan, 'I Do it for You' by Bryan Adams, and 'The Fly' by U2. The Bryan

Adams hit remained at the top for sixteen weeks. In late November, Michael Jackson returned with 'Black Or White'. With the advent of Christmas came George Michael and Elton John with 'Don't Let the Sun go Down On Me'. The sun was certainly not going down on Martina Navratilova's tennis acumen and to prove it, in November she equalled Chris Evert's record of 157 titles.

On 9 December the name of Robert Maxwell was again to hit the headlines. The question being asked was not how he met his death, but rather where are the missing £420 million? The money had been paid into a pension fund controlled by Maxwell. When unexpectedly his empire began to collapse, the chances of his former employees receiving an occupational pension spiralled to zero.

Among the personalities who died during 1991 were the following: Frank Capra, filmmaker; Margot Fonteyn, ballet dancer; Graham Greene, writer; Soichiro Honda, car manufacturer; Michael Landon, actor; and Fred McMurray, actor.

The final number one hit of 1991, 'Bohemian Rhapsody/These are the Days of our Lives' by Queen was re-released to mark the passing of Queen's flamboyant but brilliant lead singer, Freddie Mercury. At 45 years of age the man so adored by his fans died of AIDS on 24 November. He will long be revered by his admirers.

1992

Throughout 1992 civil conflict raged in many countries, including parts of Ireland. Indeed it was rampant in some recently-independent nations, especially those established as a result of the Soviet Union breakup. The situation in the former Yugoslavia went from bad to worse as fierce ethnic hatred between Moslems and Serbs ran amok. In spite of United Nations peacekeeping initiatives, reports of bombings, killings, destruction of property, rape and torture made daily headlines. Indeed it was described as the bloodiest unrest in Europe since the Second World War. A new term, ethnic cleansing, associated with the conflict, became part of everyday language. It was a euphemism for the attempted extermination of Croats and Bosnian Moslems by Serbs.

In another region of the defunct Soviet Union, again it was ethnic rivalries which spurred on brutal civil wars in Moldova, Georgia, Armenia, Azerbaijan, and Tiajikistan.

The African continent too was having its problems. On the east coast, in Somalia, civil war and famine attracted worldwide attention. Still on the east coast, further north in the Sudan, a decade-old civil war accompanied by famine, intensified. More than 1.5 million people were in danger of dying from starvation. On the west coast, in Liberia, violence re-emerged after a seventeen month ceasefire. Additionally, the dark continent was dotted with potential flash-points.

In Asia, there was Afghanistan, where, after Soviet withdrawal, a period of dictatorship, and later a coalition government failed to stabilise the war-torn country.

In Ireland, where sectarian strife continued, the shocking statistic of 3,000 dead as a result of the 'troubles' became a reality. England too was touched by Ireland's unrest with three IRA bombs exploding in London between February and October. Some optimism did emerge when Northern Irish Unionists and the Republic of Ireland government agreed to meet in talks. It was the first such meeting in 70 years.

In the midst of worldwide trouble and strife there were individuals and, day to day events, which made headlines. For example, Charles Haughey, Taoiseach, resigned in late January, and was replaced by Albert Reynolds, in February.

Mike Tyson, undisputed world heavyweight boxing champion from August 1987 to February 1990, was convicted of raping an eighteen-year-old Miss Black America contestant. He received a six-year prison sentence. At the Earth Summit in Rio de Janeiro, world leaders agreed that steps should be taken to protect the planet. Even though the conference did set an agenda for international efforts to be made, there was uncertainty about how to actually achieve them, and how the cost should be shared out. A major sporting headline in June came from Sweden, when Denmark surprisingly won the European Football Championship. Against the odds they defeated Germany 2-0 in the final. The name of Gianluigi Lentini came to the fore in July, when the Italian football player transferred from Turino to A.C. Milan for a record £13 million fee.

Number one hits in 1992 totalled twelve, a figure well below the annual norm which tended to be in the high teens. Presumably the conclusion to be drawn from that is, those who made it to the top stayed there longer. First it was 'Goodnight Girl' by Wet Wet Wet. Then along came Shakespears Sister with 'Stay' which stayed at number one for eight weeks until 'Deeply Dippy' by Right Said Fred replaced it. In May the punters saw 'Please Don't Go/Game Boy KWS' move to the premier spot. At the end of five weeks it gave way to 'Abba-Esque' by Erasure. By then it was Munster championship time, and at the top was Jimmy Nail with 'Ain't No Doubt'.

CHAMPIONSHIP FARE
My interest in the Munster hurling championship of 1992

began on 24 May when Cork and Kerry met at Páirc Uí Chaoimh. At the same venue on the same day, the same counties also played championship football. The hurling Rebels overcame the challenge of the Kingdom, albeit in mediocre fashion. There was little observable improvement on their earlier abysmal performance against Limerick in the League semi-final. Cork scored 0-22 to Kerry's 0-8. Ger Fitzgerald, the man who made his county senior championship debut in 1986, was captain in 1992. The tall Midleton clubman was holder of an impressive array of senior hurling medals, which included two All-Ireland inter-county, one All-Ireland club, three Munster club, and four county championship. It was Ger's honour to lead out Cork at Páirc Uí Chaoimh on 7 June on the occasion of the Munster semi-final match against the Premier County. Tipperary, the reigning All-Ireland champions were hot favourites. Yet the unpredictability factor which had crept into the outcome of confrontations between the counties since the 1987 marathon led to guarded forecasting.

In the presence of 42,416 spectators, referee Kevin Walsh got the match underway at 4pm. Soon all doubts about whether Cork's team had the ability, the spirit, and the all-round craft to deal with the highly-acclaimed Tipperary fifteen evaporated. It was the day on which Brian Corcoran, the newest member of the team, and the only one in a red jersey wearing a face guard, was the star performer. It was a day of triumph too for the experienced Tony O'Sullivan, who scored seven points, just two less than against Kerry in the previous round. Cork gradually gained the upper hand, but then having gained the initiative, seemed to relinquish it, making the closing stages extremely tense for followers of both counties. It was an energy-sapping experience for the partisans present.

On a day when goals were at a premium, the efforts of John Fitzgibbon and Tomás Mulcahy were like manna from heaven where Corkonians were concerned. When Kevin Walsh sounded the final whistle the score was Cork 2-12; Tipperary 1-12. Just a stroke of the sliotar separated the teams. Nevertheless, on that occasion it was the Rebels who stole a march on their arch rivals, and a very sweet victory it was. Cork's scorers were: Tony O'Sullivan (0-7), John Fitzgibbon (1-1), Tomás Mulcahy (1-0), Brian Corcoran (0-2), Ger Fitzgerald (0-1), and Kevin Hennessy (0-1). Cork and Limerick met in the Munster final at Páirc Uí Chaoimh on 5 July. By standards of recent past finals the 1992 match proved a disappointment.

Having been so excited by the victory over Tipperary, I couldn't possibly miss the final. The match generated little in the way of excitement, just an element of tension in the closing stages. Mind you I wasn't complaining as I happily joined the 48,036 attendance. Cork led by 1-12 to 0-5 at half-time, and as a result much of what happened in the second-half was inconsequential. In the opening period Cork settled quickly and by mid-way through the first-half were dominant. Limerick struggled, and at a time when their undoubtedly talented, well-established players couldn't get into the game, problems were compounded by a Tomás Mulcahy goal which should not have been allowed.

In Cork's defence, Jim Cashman, always a superb reader of the game, Cathal Casey, full of confidence, and Brian Corcoran, giving another brilliant exhibition of hurling, starved Limerick's forwards of possession. In the Cork attack Tony O'Sullivan and Barry Egan were well on top. The course of the match did however change but it was too late to make a significant difference to the outcome. In the second-half, Limerick's mentors made several positional changes, but none more telling than the switch of Ciarán Carey from centre-half back to centre-half forward. Fortunately, Denis Walsh who had a quiet first-half by his standards, raised his game, and the full-back line of Brian Corcoran, Denis Mulcahy and Séan O'Gorman did very well under pressure. Although Tony O'Sullivan and Barry Egan worked very hard, suddenly Cork's half-forward line began to struggle. Ger Manley who came on for the injured John Fitzgibbon, became very influential in the full-forward line at a time when Cork needed a boost. With time running out the Rebels led by three points. Limerick looked capable of equalising. It was then that Ger Manley brought an enormous sigh of relief from the Cork following as he pointed to give his side the insurance they needed. Referee Willie Barrett's final whistle did not sound a second too soon for the relieved Corkmen. The final score was Cork 1-22; Limerick 3-11.

The Cork team and scorers were: Ger Cunningham, Brian Corcoran, Denis Mulcahy, Seán O'Gorman, Cathal Casey (0-3, two from sideline cuts), Jim Cashman, Denis Walsh, Pat Buckley, Séan McCarthy (0-3), Ger Fitzgerald (captain), Tony O'Sullivan (0-7, 0-5 frees), Tomás Mulcahy (1-0), Barry Egan (0-4), Kevin Hennessy (0-2), and John Fitzgibbon. Subs: Ger Manley (0-3) for John Fitzgibbon, Teddy McCarthy for Cahal Casey. The Limerick team and scorers were: Tommy Quaid, Brian Flynn, Pa Carey, Anthony O'Riordan, Mike Houlihan, Ciarán Carey (0-1), Andy Garvey, Ger Hegarty, Mike Reale (1-0), Gary Kirby (1-8, 1-6 frees), Anthony Carmody, Declan Nash, Mike Galligan, Joe O'Connor (captain), Shane Fitzgibbon. Subs: Ray Sampson (0-1) for Andy Garvey, Don Flynn (1-0) for Anthony Carmody, Pat Davoren (0-1) for Mike Galligan. An All-Ireland hurling semi-final involving Cork and Down was played at Croke Park on Sunday 9 August. Down were Ulster Champions for the first time since 1941. Under the guidance of former Antrim manager Séan McGuinness, they had defeated Antrim in the final. The score was Down 2-6; Antrim 0-11. Team captain, Noel Sands, a deadly forward, was one of two Down players (the other was Michael Blaney), who led the field for individual scoring feats in the 1992 senior hurling championship. A spirited and entertaining performance by Down was not enough to unduly trouble the Leesiders who won by 2-17 to 1-11. Fine individual performances by Noel Sands, Noel Keith (a superb goalkeeper), Gerard McGrattan, Danny Hughes, and the Coulters, among several others, ensured that Down's senior hurling team had a very creditable first visit to the GAA headquarters. Cork's followers were again back at Croke Park on Sunday 6 September. It was, of course, All-Ireland hurling final day.

It was the day on which the seasoned campaigners, Ger Cunningham, Tony O'Sullivan, Tomás Mulcahy, and Kevin Hennessy were looking for a first victory over

Kilkenny in an All-Ireland final. The quintet who had won so many honours between them, had come away empty-handed from the 1982 and 1983 clashes with the Noresiders. They would have dearly loved to reverse that trend in 1992! Kilkenny had beaten Galway in the semi-final, though not impressively enough to install them as All-Ireland title favourites. Those who had experienced Cork versus Kilkenny championship hurling in the past knew what to expect. The tag of favourite, or not favourite, would mean absolutely nothing once combat began. Dickie Murphy was the man with the whistle, and possibly the only one on the playing surface with a coin in his pocket. As the captains of the opposing teams watched, Dickie flipped the coin, heads leaned forward, the Kilkennyman spoke – he had won the toss. He had no hesitation in informing the referee that they would play with the wind for the first half.

Cork followers were well pleased at the start made by their team. It was so good that they led by five points without reply. Soon a penalty awarded to Kilkenny changed that. D.J. Carey made no mistake as he drove the sliotar to the Cork net.

At the interval Cork led by two points. The thinking on the stands and terraces must have been fairly unanimous – Kilkenny in the second half would be very difficult to beat. Soon after the restart it became apparent that Cork were losing their grip on the match. They were at least temporarily floundering and it was hard to see how they could regain the initiative.

Changes made by Kilkenny's mentors, which included bringing Christy Heffernan onto the team and the switching of Michael Phelan from midfield to full-forward, made sure that Cork were not going to make an easy comeback. The Rebels battled on manfully and a Ger Manley goal brought with it renewed hope. Alas, again as in 1982 and 1983, it was to be Kilkenny's day. At the final whistle the Noresiders had four points to spare. The final score was Kilkenny 3-10; Cork 1-12.

Disappointment was not confined to the quintet already mentioned. It was in fact widespread among Cork followers who felt that defeat at the hands of Kilkenny in three successive All-Ireland finals somehow took away from the victories over Offaly in 1984, and Galway in 1986 and 1990. The September Sunday in 1992 belonged to Kilkenny, and to team captain Liam Fennelly who received the new McCarthy Cup for the first time. The Cork team was: Ger Cunningham, Brian Corcoran, Denis Mulcahy, Séan O'Gorman, Cathal Casey, Jim Cashman, Denis Walsh, Pat Buckley, Sean McCarthy, Teddy McCarthy, Tomás Mulcahy, Tony O'Sullivan, Ger Fitzgerald (captain), Kevin Hennessy, and John Fitzgibbon. The Kilkenny team was: Michael Walsh, Eddie O'Connor, Pat Dwyer, Liam Simpson, Liam Walsh, Pat O'Neill, Willie O'Connor, Michael Phelan, Bill Hennessy, Liam McCarthy, John Power, D.J. Carey, Eamonn Morrissey, Liam Fennelly (captain), and Jamsie Brennan.

OLYMPIC OPTIMISM, A PREMIER LEAGUE, AND CLINTON IS INSTALLED

The spectacular summer Olympic Games held in Barcelona were undoubtedly the the world's number one sporting event of 1992. There were no boycotts and South Africa returned to the fold after a 32-year ban. The recently-independent Baltic countries competed under their own flags, and a new rule which allowed professionals to compete opened the way for a team which was probably the best in any sport ever assembled. It was the United States basketball team – the Dream Team – led by the extraordinarily talented Michael Jordan. The Games shone brightly in the midst of the awful internal strife which plagued so many nations. The Barcelona extravaganza injected a badly-needed boost into a world where generally optimism was low.

Away from Barcelona on 15 August, a new Premier League of elite Soccer Clubs was launched in England. Back in the world of political intrigue, instead of the incumbent George Bush, the American people chose the young, dynamic and articulate Bill Clinton as their president. It marked the end of a twelve-year Republican hold on the White House, and consequently the end of the Reagan era of American politics which George Bush had so valiantly carried on.

'End Of The Road' by Boyz II Men was at number one in November. That recording, which had a three-week stay at the top, was preceded by 'Rhythm is a Dancer' by Snap, 'Ebeneezer' by Shamen, and 'Sleeping Satellite' by Tasmin Archer. 'Would I Lie To You?' by Charles and Eddie followed 'End Of The Road' to the top where it remained for two weeks until 4 December.

AS THE YEAR CLOSES

A year which had been lit up by the Summer Olympic Games, definitely its brightest star, was gradually coming to a close. It was, however, a year which had been somewhat dulled by memories of devastating civil wars, earthquakes and floods. Earthquakes in Turkey, Egypt and Indonesia claimed up to 2,500 lives, while in Pakistan, thousands died and millions were left homeless as a result of flooding. An interesting snippet from Sydney, Australia, tells of the world's first damages award made for illness brought on by passive smoking.

The names of those appearing in obituary columns of 1992 included: Menachem Begin, Israeli prime minister; Marlene Dietrich, actress; Alexander Dubcek, Czech political leader; Jose Ferrer, actor and director; Benny Hill, comedian; Perta Kelly, political leader; and Anthony Perkins, actor. The high flying number one hit during Christmas and well into the New Year was a song which brought much joy. It was called 'I Will Always Love You', beautifully sung by Whitney Houston. A fitting sentiment indeed on which to end the year.

1993

IT WASN'T ALL BLOODLESS
BUT AINTREE BROUGHT A CHUCKLE

While Whitney Houston's massive number one hit 'I Will Always Love You' held sway throughout January, Czechoslovakia formally split into the newly-independent republics of Czech and Slovak. Four years earlier not a drop of blood was shed when Czechoslovakia parted company with communism. In 1993, the equally amicable parting ended a 74-year union, during which only the occasional rumblings of disgruntled Slovaks caused ripples. It was all very civilised when taken in the context of what was happening in the Balkans.

Elsewhere, in Kinshasa, the capital of Zaire, all was not well when in late January more than 1,000 people, including the French ambassador, died during rioting.

As the first fortnight of February became history, Whitney Houston continued to reign supreme at the top of the hit parade. Then just days before the untimely death of Bobby Moore, captain of England's 1966 World Cup winning side, it was 2 Unlimited with 'No Limits' which took over the number one spot.

Terrorist bombs made news headlines in February, March and April. In February, it was a massive Moslem fundamentalist perpetrated explosion at New York's World Trade Centre which killed five people, injured hundreds and trapped thousands in the 110-story twin tower building. The bombs of March and April occurred in England when IRA devices exploded in Warrington and London. The Warrington horror, in a crowded shopping precinct, killed two children. It was still April when the world of sport was shocked and saddened by the news that most of Zambia's football team were killed in an aircrash while on transit to a World Cup qualifying match. A less serious incident with sporting connotations resulted in the

279

one-hundred-and-fiftieth Grand National being abandoned. Two false starts due to a malfunctioning starting tape was the culprit. The fiasco at the Aintree course which caused the race to be re-run at a later date was seen as 'not cricket' in some quarters.

REBEL FOOTBALL TO THE RESCUE BUT IT'S DERRY'S YEAR

The St Patrick's Day celebrations had just abated when 'Oh Carolina' by Shaggy made it to the top. It was soon replaced by the Bluebells number 'Young at Heart'. Four weeks later, in early May, it was 'Five Live EP' by George Michael and Queen with Lisa Stansfield which reached the pinnacle. Not to be outdone, on 22 May, Ace of Base weighed in with 'All That She Wants'. It had a three-week stay before being toppled by UB40 with '(I can't help) Falling in Love with You'. As dreams of what might have been faded for many hurling followers, Gabrielle experienced no such despondency as her song, 'Dreams', soared to pole position. Followers of Cork hurling had every reason to be optimistic as their team prepared for the Munster semi-final championship clash with Clare at Limerick on 13 June. The Rebels seemed to have bounced back well after the 1992 All-Ireland final defeat at the hands of Kilkenny. A slightly wayward League campaign was brought back on track, and in a three-way play-off the Rebels beat Clare, Waterford and Down to secure a semi-final place against Tipperary. Nobody expected anything but a tough, uncompromising contest when the teams met, and that's exactly what we got! Cork finished the match with fourteen players but thanks to the combined efforts of Kevin Hennessy and Tomás Mulcahy, a late goal saved the day for the Leesiders. The final against Wexford took no less than three attempts to sort out the eventual winner of the 1992/93 National League trophy. The first meeting resulted in a 2-11 to 2-11 draw. A replay which included extra-time produced a scoreline of Cork 0-18; Wexford 3-9 – a draw. A second replay finally saw Cork come out on top and the final score was Cork 3-11; Wexford 1-12.

The Cork team which lined-out at the Gaelic Grounds, Limerick on 13 June to take on Clare in the championship showed four changes in personnel from the side fielded in the previous year's All-Ireland final. Absent were Denis Mulcahy, Teddy McCarthy, Ger Fitzgerald (1992 captain), and Tomás Mulcahy. Into the side came John Considine, Timmy Kelleher, Ger Manley and Barry Egan. In Limerick that morning the consensus was that Cork had the experience and the talent to beat Clare. Later, on the pitch where conditions were not ideal for top class hurling, it was Clare who settled best. When referee Pat Delaney of Laois blew the whistle for half-time the sides were level; Cork 0-6; Clare 1-3.

As the second-half progressed Cork struggled to produce the fluent, crisp ground hurling which is their trademark. Clare, on the other hand, mastered the conditions better, and in the final analysis were deserving winners. The score was Clare 2-7; Cork 0-10.

So ended the Leesiders interest in the 1993 hurling championship. The Cork team was: Ger Cunningham, John Considine, Séan O'Gorman, Timmy Kelleher, Brian Corcoran, Jim Cashman, Denis Walsh, Cathal Casey, Séan McCarthy, John Fitzgibbon, Pat Buckley, Tony O'Sullivan, Ger Manley, Kevin Hennessy, Barry Egan. Subs: Paul O'Callaghan for Timmy Kelleher, Mark Mullins for Kevin Hennessy, Ger Fitzpatrick for Ger Manley. The Clare team was: David Fitzgerald, Brian Lohan, Anthony Daly, John Moroney, Pat Markham, John Russell, John Chaplin, John O'Connell, Declan Tobin, Eoin Cleary, Stephen Sheedy, James O'Connor, Jim McInerney, Cyril Lyons, Ger O'Loughlin Subs: P.J. O'Connell for Eoin Cleary, Fergus Touhy for Declan Tobin.

Clare lost heavily to Tipperary in the Munster final; 2-12 to 3-27. As on a previous occasion, again Cork's senior football team came to the rescue of Leeside followers who always relish a September visit to Croke Park. Victories over Clare, Kerry and Tipperary in the Munster championship, ensured an All-Ireland semi-final meeting with Mayo. On the day a below par performance by the Connaught champions facilitated an easy passage to the final where Ulster champions Derry provided the opposition. It was a match which Cork started well, then lost their way a little, and were unfortunate when before the interval, left-half back

Tony Davis was erroneously dismissed by referee Tommy Howard. To their credit Derry made exceptionally good use of the 'extra man'. The final score was Derry 1-14; Cork 2-8.

The result was of course a disappointment for the Cork team and its followers, but what joy and elation it brought to the mighty contingent from the Oak Leaf County. It was the very first All-Ireland senior football championship won by a Derry team. Derry had followed in the footsteps of near neighbours Donegal who in 1992 brought the Sam Maguire Cup to the shores of Bloody Foreland for the first time; heady days indeed for the north-western counties. The Cork team was: John Kerins, Brian Corcoran, Mark O'Connor, Niall Cahalane, Ciarán O'Sullivan, Stephen O'Brien, Tony Davis, Shay Fahy, Teddy McCarthy, Don Davis, Joe Kavanagh, Barry Coffey, Colin Corkery, John O'Driscoll, and Mick McCarthy (captain). Subs: Kevin O'Dwyer, Mark Farr, Conor Counihan, Danny Culloty, Liam Honohan, John Cleary, Paul Coleman, Pat Hegarty, and Brian Murphy. The Derry team was: Damien McCusker, Kieran McKeever, Tony Scullion, Fergal McCusker, John McGurk, Henry Downey (captain), Gary Coleman, Anthony Tohill, Brian McGilligan, Dermot Heaney, Damien Barton, Damien Cassidy, Joe Brolly, Séamus Downey, and Enda Gormley. Subs: Don Kelly, Danny Quinn, Dermot McNicholl, Karl Diamond, Eamonn Burns, Declan Bateson, Brian McCormick, Richard Ferris, and Stephen Mulvenna.

A PASSING COMMENT, A HANDSHAKE, TOWARDS DEMOCRACY, AND EC IS EU

Nepal, a landlocked country in the Himalayan mountain range of Central Asia, is remote by any standards. In that country during July 1993 1,750 lost their lives in monsoon rain floods. Because the catastrophe occurred thousands of miles away in an antipodean region, its magnitude failed to make any real impression on the world at large. Apart from lives lost, 250,000 people were left homeless.

High on the register of 1993 major political developments was the heralding of a new peace accord between Israel and the Palestinians. The agreement prompted the most publicised handshake of the year between old foes and once-sworn enemies, PLO chairman Yasser Arafat and Israeli prime minister Yitzhak Rabin. The greeting, which took place in Washington's White House lawn, in the presence of Bill Clinton, symbolised the desire to end hostilities and to bring an end to a long and sorry chronicle of bloodshed and tears.

A further political development of worldwide significance was the ratification by President de Klerk and Nelson Mandela of South Africa's first democratic constitution. The lifting of trade sanctions by the United States and Commonwealth countries gave ultimate recognition to the changing face of South Africa.

In Europe, the Maastricht Treaty on European union came into effect after months of wrangling. The newly designated European Union (EU) was adopted instead of the former identification of European Community (EC). The way was opened for the expansion of trade, reduction of competition, the abolishment of restrictive trading practices, the encouragement of free movement of labour and capital, and the setting up of a closer union among the people of the Community.

Could it be that the popular music group Take That were inviting us to pray for success in the good things happening around the world. For whatever reason their recording 'Pray' became a number one hit. Four weeks later it was Freddie Mercury's 'Living on my Own' which replaced it. Within two weeks 'Mr Vain' by Culture Beat took over. It was in late September that 'Boom! Shake The Room' by Jazzy Jeff and the Fresh Prince, made it to the top. Then came Take That featuring Lulu with 'Relight My Fire'. Before long, Meatloaf's 'I'd Do Anything for Love' won its way to the top where it remained for seven weeks.

HIGHS AND LOWS END ON OPTIMISTIC NOTE
The government of the Irish Republic, led by Albert Reynolds, and the British government led by John Major, co-operated closely while trying to find a way to bring peace and stability to our troubled land. In the midst of moves which led to the banning of Sinn Féin's leader Gerry Adams from mainland Britain, and the admission by the United Kingdom government of clandestine contact with

283

the IRA, John Major and Albert Reynolds formulated and announced the Downing Street Declaration on the future of Northern Ireland.

Other headline makers in 1993 included the murder of a two-year-old Liverpool child by two eleven-year-old boys; legalisation of euthanasia in the Netherlands; the retirement of Michael Jordan, arguably the greatest basketball player ever; and the introduction of a new speedy system which transformed the Internet, metaphorically speaking, from a country lane to a motorway. As a result a worldwide web of computer networks became accessible to anyone with a personal computer. Of all the publications by scientists in 1993, possibly the finding least well received was the one which declared the famous photograph of the Lough Ness monster to be a fake.

Mr Blobby had no problem about being well received, and to prove it a recording of the same name became a number one hit, not once but twice, during December. Squeezed in between for just a single week was 'Babe' by Take That. As a year filled with its share of solace and affliction slipped away to its inevitable ending, many looked back to April and reflected on the self-inflicted waste of life in Waco, Texas, when 85 people, including seventeen children, died. It was the final chapter in the lives of Davidian cult members who apparently set the compound in which they lived on fire. The extreme action ended a tense 51 day stand-off between federal agents and the religious cult.

Among those who would not have the opportunity of experiencing life in 1994 were, the late Arthur Ashe, tennis player and political activist; Raymond Burr (Ironside), actor; Dizzy Gillespie, musician; Audrey Hepburn, actress; Rudolf Nureyev, ballet dancer; Vincent Price, actor; and Frank Zappa, musician. As 1994 approached there was an optimism abroad that the future for at least some parts of the world looked more hopeful. The seemingly impossible had been achieved in South Africa – apartheid had ended. In recognition of that achievement, Nelson Mandela and F.W.de Klerk were recipients of the Nobel Peace Prize.

1994

BOSNIAN CONFLICT, A CITY TREMORS,
AND NANCY IS CLUBBED AS BAN GOES

As 1993 ended , so 1994 began with number one popular music hit 'Mr Blobby' still in place. There it remained until 8 January when 'Twist and Shout' by Chaka Demus and Pliers with Jack Radics and Taxi Gang became the first group in 1994 to occupy the top spot. Before the month ended it was D:Ream's, 'Things Can Only Get Better' which became the most in-favour number.

Things did not get better in Bosnia where in spite of an agreed ceasefire between warring Serbs and Moslems, Bosnian Serbs continued to pound Sarajevo and other Bosnian cities with mortar bombs. Widespread carnage resulted. The objective was to bring Bosnia under Serb rule. Both Bosnian and Serb armies were guilty of atrocities but mainly it was the Serbs who carried out a reign of terror which manifested itself in torture, murder and rape on a massive scale. By the spring of 1994, 200,000 people had been killed, and up to 4,000,000 driven from their homes. NATO, itself divided as to who exactly was at fault and on how to tackle the problem, was largely ineffective in bringing a solution to what appeared to be an almost insoluble situation.

In other parts of the world, bush fires raged and threatened the city of Sydney, and an earthquake rocked Los Angeles, killing 57 people and, causing $15 billion in damages to houses, businesses, churches, schools and motorways.

An attack by associates of United States ice skater, Tonya Hardy, took place on fellow skater, Nancy Kerrigan. Apparently the reason for the assault, which included knee clubbing, was to diminish the competition in the forthcoming Winter Olympics in Lillehammer, Norway.

Nearer home the Irish government decided it was time

to lift its longstanding ban on Sinn Féin.

PERSONALITIES, DEATHS, AIRPORTS AND A TUNNEL

It was still January when the Duchess of Kent converted to Roman Catholicism. Days later thousands of personalities and followers from the world of football went to Old Trafford to mourn the death of former Manchester United manager, Sir Matt Busby. On a day in early spring London's Heathrow Airport shut down for two hours after a third IRA mortar attack in five days. Gatwick Airport also closed because of bomb threats. Memories of Richard Milhous Nixon were evoked when he died in April. The former United States president was certainly amongst the most controversial of American's modern-era politicians. It was in April too that Robin-Knox Johnston and his crew on board the catamaran ENZA New Zealand, broke the round the world record. Speaking of records, many will remember a number one hit by Mariah Carey. It was called 'Without You'. Around mid-March it was 'Doop' by Doop, which led the pack. It was followed by the very popular 'Everything Changes' by Take That.

How true that title was in the context of South Africa; Nelson Mandela, the man who spent 27 years in jail as a prisoner of the apartheid regime, became the Republic's first black president. His position was assured following a landslide victory by the African National Party (ANC), led by the man himself, in the first multi-racial elections held in the country. The white national party led by F.W. de Klerk which had ruled the country since 1948 gained only twenty per cent of the vote. The song, 'The Most Beautiful Girl in the World' by Prince, led the way at number one in April and early May, until it was replaced by Tony Di Bart with 'The Real Thing'.

It was back in 1802 that a French mining engineer mooted the idea of tunnelling under the English Channel in order to provide a link between England and France. Well, the idea became a reality in 1994.

The world of sport was enormously saddened in May by the death of Brazilian Formula One driver Ayrton Senna. While negotiating a curve during the San Marino

Grand Prix at Imola, his car crashed into a concrete wall. The driver, who was idolised by his fans, was 34 years of age. It was yet another tragedy which made headlines in early June when a helicopter transporting 25 British leading counter terrorist experts crashed on the Mull of Kintyre.

'CORKIES NEY WIN THE GAME'
Mention of the Mull of Kintyre brings to mind other memories from 1994. On the weekend Cork's senior hurlers played the first round of the Munster championship against Limerick, I was island-hopping on the west coast of Scotland.

I was not able to receive RTE radio, but to my amazement, after the game, just as skipper Bill Marsh turned the yacht southwards, I heard a thick Scottish accent saying the words, 'Corkies ney win the game'. It was one of our friends on a fishing boat. I have no idea where he got the information from, or for that matter how he had become aware of my interest. Cork had indeed lost to Limerick in the first round of the 1994 Munster championship. A note in my diary made later that evening reads, 'My July trip to Cork is now up the creek'. A scan of a newspaper report the following day told me all I wanted to know. I read of a good match in inclement weather conditions. The final score was Limerick 4-14; Cork 4-11.

Limerick went on to beat Waterford in the Munster semi-final. The final score was Limerick 2-14; Waterford 2-12. In the Munster final the Shannonsiders took on and beat Clare by 0-25 to 2-10. An All-Ireland semi-final meeting with Antrim resulted in a 2-23 to 0-11 win for Limerick. In the All-Ireland final, Offaly emerged victorious in a match which Limerick seemed to have won until a late Johnny Dooley goal opened the floodgates for a scoring blitz by the Leinster Champions. At the final whistle a 3-16 to 2-13 scoreline left Limerick shocked, disappointed and bewildered. My lasting memory of the 1994 hurling championship will always be linked to a Scottish accent coming over the airwaves, off the island made famous by the exploits of St Columcille. Before or since I can't recall being astounded and disappointed in such an unexpected manner.

SIR BOBBY, TONY, AND A CEASEFIRE, BUT AIDS SOAR AS STAR IS SHOT

Occupying the number one spot over the duration were 'Inside' by Stiltskin, 'Come on You Reds' by Manchester United Football Squad, and the wedding day favourite, 'Love is All Around Us' by Wet Wet Wet. It held the number one spot for fifteen weeks. Along the way soccer star Bobby Charlton, became a Sir and the World Health Organisation in Geneva announced that the number of AIDS cases worldwide had increased from 2,500,000 to 4,000,000 over the past year. Newsworthy too was the election of Tony Blair as leader of the British Labour Party and, Brazil's victory over Italy in football's World Cup final. A disappointing 0-0 draw led to a penalty shoot out. A grave World Cup sequel emerged when it was reported that Anders Escobar, a Colombian football star, whose own goal eliminated his country from the Cup, was shot dead on his return to Medellin in Colombia. The highlight of August in Ireland was an announcement by the IRA of a complete cessation of military operations. The proclamation raised hopes for an end to 25 years of conflict in which 3,170 had died. It came eight months after the Downing Street declaration offering Sinn Féin a role in talks on the future of Northern Ireland, on condition that the IRA declared a ceasefire.

AUTUMN AND WINTER TALES

In most African national conflicts, tribalism and the relics of colonialism figure somewhere in the equation. Rwanda was no different when the Hutu and Tutsi tribes who had long peacefully coexisted before colonisation first by Germany, and later by Belgium. On independence the Hutu who had massacred 20,000 Tutsi's in 1959, were left in charge. It was a recipe for disaster. A particularly bitter conflict resulted in the most appalling suffering by civilians of all ages and sexes. It ended in 1994 with the Tutsi's in charge of a situation which looked fragile in the extreme.

Of particular significance musically in September was

'Saturday Night' by Whigfield; it was a number one hit which remained so for four weeks, until Take That came along with 'Sure', and toppled it.

It was in September too that Taoiseach Albert Reynolds had waited patiently on the tarmac at Shannon Airport to greet Russian president, Boris Yeltsin. The plane carrying the distinguished visitor came and went and Mr Reynolds was left to walk away without as much as a hand shake. In fact the Russian supremo failed to alight. Later he explained that he was having a nap during the stop over and his aides failed to wake him. I wonder if any of them ended up in the Siberian salt mines?

Tragedy in the Baltic when a roll-on, roll-off ferry sank with the loss of 912 lives made sad reading that autumn. Another mishap at sea was recalled when a court ordered EXXON to pay $5 billion to victims of the *Exxon Valdez* oil spillage on the Alaskan coastline in 1989.

The year had yet another uplift in store for the long-suffering people of Northern Ireland when seven weeks into the IRA ceasefire, the three main Loyalist terror groups also called a halt to activities. As the countdown to Christmas got underway, two personalities attracted media attention – 'Red Rum' and Taoiseach Albert Reynolds! They also had something in common - stepping down. Red Rum, the only horse to win the Grand National three times, retired from public life at the age of 29. Albert Reynolds resigned as Taoiseach saying, 'It was for the good of the nation'. The withdrawal of the Labour Party from the ruling coalition in protest against an appointment, left the Taoiseach with little option. A general election was called.

Pat Banton and Baby D respectively had number one hits with 'Baby Come Back' and 'Let Me Be Your Fantasy'. It is likely that heavyweight boxer George Foreman, at the age of 45, believed that he was living in fantasy world when he regained the world title 20 years after losing it to Muhammad Ali.

The inevitable end which comes eventually to all made its customary inroads in 1994. Among those who succumbed were: Telly Savalas (Kojak), actor; Melina

Mecouri, actress and politician; Mai Zetterling, actress and director; Henry Mancini, composer and band leader; Terry Scott, comedian; Ann Shelton, singer; Peter Cushing, actor; and Roy Castle, comedian and television presenter.

East 17 were riding high at number one spot with 'Stay Another Day', as the year ended. Then just before the curtain came down on 1994, John Bruton was elected Taoiseach, and British officials met representatives of Sinn Féin in Belfast for their first formal talks in 22 years.

1995

UPBEAT MIDST THE FORTUNES OF FRED,
ERIC AND GUY, BUT KOBE QUAKES

'Cotton Eye Joe' from the Rednex, became the first number one hit of 1995. Before the year was out fifteen other musical gems would occupy the coveted spot. It was in February that Celine Dion sang her way to the top with 'Think Twice'.

In January, when British troops ended daytime patrols on the streets of Northern Ireland, the move was seen as heralding a further milestone on the road to peace. The situation became even more upbeat when in Belfast, Prime Minister John Major and Taoiseach, John Bruton, presented their framework document for the future of Northern Ireland. Its provisions included the establishment of a legislative assembly and a termination of the Republic's constitutional claims to the six counties.

Frederick West had long been a household name when in January 1995 he was found hanged in a prison cell. An accused serial killer, he had been awaiting trial for the murder of twelve young women.

It was also in January that Manchester United football player, Eric Cantona, attracted unwanted media attention when he was banned for the remainder of the season. The notoriety arose from an incident when the player attacked a fan who insulted him.

In Japan tragedy struck the city of Kobe when 4,000 people died as result of an earthquake. A notable February anecdote was the achievement of Frenchman, Guy Delage, who arrived in Barbados having swum, and drifted on a raft across the Atlantic.

SPORTSMEN, AN OUTSIDER, A DNA FIRST, AND THE NORTH IS TOPS

In March the world of sport was stunned when football

291

stars, Bruce Grobbelaar, Hans Segars and John Fashanu were arrested during an inquiry into alleged match fixing. Still on a sporting theme, former favourite and world heavyweight boxing champion Mike Tyson was freed from prison after serving three years for a rape offence.

The Grand National was run at Aintree Racecourse, Liverpool in April. Those who backed the winner cost the bookies dearly, because 40/1 outsider, 'Royal Athlete' was the winner. It was in April too that history was made in Birmingham when the first National Computer Database of DNA records in the world was set up.

Meanwhile, Cher, Chrissie Hynde and Neneh Cherry with Eric Clapton had a number one hit with 'Love Can Build a Bridge'. After just a week, 'Don't Stop (Wiggle Wiggle)' by Outhere Brothers moved up but again only for a week. Then came the Take That recording 'Back For Good' which enjoyed a four-week stay. During May there were no less than three different number one hits; first was 'Some Might Say' by Oasis which was followed by Livin' Joy's, 'Dreamer' and finally the very popular 'Unchained Melody/(There'll Be Blue Birds Over) The White Cliffs Of Dover' from Robson Green and Jerome Flynn.

By early summer the notion that peace reigned in Northern Ireland for the first time in 25 years established itself in the minds of people far and wide. Further encouraged by what was the finest summer weather in years, tourist flocked from across the border and from overseas. It certainly was boom time and everyone loved it, visitors and locals alike. Van Morrison's song, 'My Momma Told Me there'd be Days Like This', epitomised the fabulous feel-good factor which prevailed. It was easy to identify with the Outhere Brothers number one hit, 'Boom Boom Boom', which monopolised the pop music scene during July and into August.

WINNERS AND FIRSTS BUT NOT DIVINE IN KOREA

News reports throughout the so longed-for period of elation in Northern Ireland informed us of happenings at home and abroad: in Belfast, the British government held ministerial talks with Sinn Féin, the first in 23 years; Alison

Hargreaves became the first woman to reach the summit of Mount Everest alone and without the aid of oxygen; in San Diego, the New Zealand yacht, *Black Magic 1*, scored a 5-0 victory over the United States, Young America, to win the Americas Cup; and Prince Charles became the first member of the Royal Family to make an official visit to Ireland since 1911. June in Los Angeles was a time when the name of prostitute Divine Brown along with Hugh Grant were blazed around the world when the actor was arrested after being caught in her company!

Before the year reached its halfway mark a freak accident in Korea caused by the collapse of a shopping centre roof which in turn claimed the lives of 640 people. All eyes were still focused on the 'new' South Africa when in the summer of 1995 it hosted the Rugby Union World Cup. The honour did not stop there when the famous Springboks, so long excluded because of apartheid sanctions, went on to win the prestigious trophy.

A KINGDOM EXPERIENCE, BANNER GLORY, AND A REBEL RECORD

On Saturday 20 May when Cork's senior hurling team travelled to Austin Stack Park, Tralee, it was generally taken for granted that the Rebels would emerge winners over the Kingdom in the opening round of the championship.

In 1994 I decided that enough was enough and opted for early retirement. Consequently my visits to west Cork were no longer limited to school holidays. Because of that I happened to be on one of my sojourns during May, and as I had never seen a Kerry hurling team play, I decided to do so on that occasion. I sat beside a fellow Cork follower in the stand. He pointed out that Kerry hurling was in the ascendancy and, despite dismissal of the Kingdom's chances by many pundits, the outcome was not a foregone conclusion.

In the early stages Kerry gave as good as they got. It was indeed a brave display by the men from the Kingdom, and the most outstanding player on view was Kerry's Pa O'Rourke. His midfield performance was the

293

most distinguished action of a first-half which ended with Kerry four points in arrears.

The second-half began with the Kingdom's team captain Mike Hennessy doing all in his power to inspire his men to even greater heights. Deep down I believed that Cork had the experience to turn on the style if and when it was required. Kerry hung on valiantly, and it wasn't until the last quarter that they began to wilt under sheer pressure from Cork's forwards. A final score of Cork 1-22; Kerry 0-12, seemed to flatter the Leesiders. However, it's only natural in those circumstances to feel that somehow the character and battling qualities of the underdogs had not been adequately rewarded. Really what happens is that the more skilful, measured, and subtle approach of the masters is less obvious. The latter invariable come away with the spoils. The Kerry team was: John Healy, John Foley, Mike Casey, Séamus McIntire, Christy Ross, Mike Hennessy, Tom Maunsell, Pa O'Rourke, Dinny McCarthy, Brendan O'Mahony, Pat O'Connell, Christy Walsh, Jerry O'Sullivan, Liam O'Connor, Brendan O'Sullivan.

By Sunday 11 June I had returned to Ballycastle. It was in such a setting that the distinctive voice and imaginative commentary of Micheál Ó Muircheartaigh brought me the story of the Cork versus Clare senior hurling championship match from the Gaelic Grounds, Limerick. At half-time all was going very much to plan. Cork had played against the breeze and led by three points. The restart saw the hopes of Cork followers further raised when within four minutes, the Rebels had increased their lead to five points. It appeared as if Cork were on their way to a semi-final victory. Crucially the Leesiders failed to put the match out of Clare's reach by spurning several scoring chances from frees. Opportunities missed by a team apparently well on top often serve to spur on opponents. So it was with Clare. By the twentieth minute, with centre-half back Séan McMahon outstanding, they had fought back to level the score. Points then came thick and fast but it was the Banner county men who led with five minutes of normal time remaining. With the final whistle due at any moment, Kevin Murray scored what had to be a decisive goal which gave Cork a two point lead. But the final whistle had not gone, and we should know that a match is never over until the proverbial fat lady sings. The extraordinary grit and determination shown by Clare that day did not desert them in the dying moments and their reward came when a late sideline cut by Fergus Touhy was deflected to the net by Ollie Baker – a goal for Clare; a one point lead. When referee Pat O'Connor sounded the long whistle a matter of seconds later it was indeed a stunned Cork contingent who tried to come to terms with what had happened. For the third year in succession the Leesiders left the Gaelic Grounds, Limerick on the losing end of championship matches. The final score was Cork 3-9; Clare 2-13.

The Cork team was: Ger Cunningham, Jim Cashman, John O'Driscoll, Pat Kenneally, Peter Smith, Brian Corcoran, Timmy Kelleher, Cathal Casey, Barry Egan, Darren O'Donoghue, Ger Manley, Mark Mullins, Kevin Murray, Alan Browne and Kieran Morrison. The subs were: Fergal Ryan for Cathal Casey; Séan McCarthy for Kieran Morrison; and Darren Ronan form Darren O'Donoghue.

The Banner county went on to beat Limerick (1-17 to 0-11) in the Munster final, and Galway (3-12 to 1-13) in the All-Ireland semi-final. Did Clare do in 1995 what they had failed to do since 1914? Yes, they became All-Ireland champions! What's more they took on and beat reigning All-Ireland champions Offaly. Sunday 3 September 1995 will forever be revered in the annals of Clare hurling.

The county always had marvellous exponents of the game among its ranks but somehow until now failed to make any real impression on the big-time. The final score was Clare 1-13; Offaly 2-8. The Clare team was: David Fitzgerald, Michael O'Halloran, Brian Lohan, Frank Lohan, Liam Doyle, Séan McMahon, Anthony Daly (captain), James O'Connor, Ollie Baker, Fergus Tuohy, P.J. O'Connell, Fergal Hegarty, Stephen McNamara, Conor Clancy and Ger O'Loughlin. The subs were: Stephen O'Hara, Cyril Lyons, Jim McInerney, Alan Neville, Ken Morrissey, Ger Moroney, John Chaplin, Christy Chaplin, and Brian Quinn. The victory was the culmination of great work done by many dedicated people over many, many years, and especially in the recent past by Fr Harry Bohan and their current outstandingly able manager, Ger Loughnane.

Strangely, at a time when Cork's senior hurlers weren't doing so well, the county's football team created a record. Almost unnoticed they had taken away the mantle of kings of Munster football from Kerry. The seventh Munster title win by the Rebels in a nine-year spell was indeed a record for the county. For the second year running, the Munster champions, captained by Niall Cahalane on this occasion, failed at All-Ireland semi-final stage. Against Dublin, they started well and appeared to be in control but did not convert superiority into scores. As Cork lost their way a little, the Dublin midfield began to dominate. Then, as a result of a slip by Cork's full-back, Mark O'Connor, Jason Sherlock scored a simple but costly goal. All in all the Rebels did not do themselves justice on the day! The final score was Cork 0-12; Dublin 1-12.

The Cork team was: Kevin O'Dwyer, Mark Farr, Mark O'Connor, Niall Cahalane (captain), Ciarán O'Sullivan, Stephen O'Brien, Brian Corcoran, Liam Honohan, Danny Culloty, Don Davis, Larry Tomkins, Pádraig O'Mahony, Stephen Calnan, Joe Kavanagh and Colin Corkery.

TESTS AND DISHES, OASIS AND A BRA, BUT NO METRIC FOR RUMMIE

While before and after discussions surrounding championship matches raged in pubs, clubs, or wherever two or more with an interest in Gaelic sport met, it was the music of Take That, Blur, and Michael Jackson which filled the number one hit spot. Respectively they succeeded with 'Never Forget', 'Country', and 'You are not Alone'.

Accompanying the arrival of autumn came unwelcome news to many, not least those who inhabited the region adjacent to the tiny Pacific atoll of Mururoa. It was there that France exploded a ten-kiloton nuclear weapon as part of tests being carried out on new defensive deterrents.

While the Pacific seabed trembled, the Iranian government saw fit to ban satellite dishes and in Sweden customs officials detained a lady who was trying to smuggle 65 baby snakes in her bra.

During October the second album from Oasis, '(What's The Story) Morning Glory' was anticipated with such fervour that when release day came, record shops throughout the United Kingdom opened at midnight to sell the first copies. The number one hit singles of September and October were 'Boombastic' by Shaggy, and 'Fairground' by Simply Red. With winter just around the corner and Metrication Day (all pre-packed food to be sold in metric units) at hand, the announcement of 'Red Rum's death just a year after retiring from public life brought a wave of nostalgia to his many fans.

INCIDENT PACKED NOVEMBER GIVES WAY TO CALMER YEAR ENDING

November was a month packed full of incident and intrigue. First it was the assassination of Israel's Prime Minister, Yitzhak Rabin, famous among other things for that handshake with Yasser Arafat which attracted worldwide attention in 1994. He was shot dead after speaking at a rally intended to counter opposition to the Israeli/ Palestinian peace deal.

A few weeks later at peak viewing time, millions stayed glued to television screens while Diana Princess of Wales divulged intriguing facets of her private life on a BBC Panorama programme. Two days later what was possibly the greatest human interest case of 1995 came to a conclusion when Rosemary West (wife of Frederick found hanged in a prison cell earlier in the year) was found guilty on ten counts of murder. She was given a life sentence. Even though the murders took place in the West's terraced house dwelling, neighbours perceived the couple as, just ordinary people.

During the final days of November media coverage was firmly focused on Northern Ireland. On 28 November all-party talks got the go ahead. The month ended on a real high note when President Clinton and the First Lady of the United States visited Ireland. The dignitaries received a rapturous welcome in Northern Ireland.

The music of Coolio featuring LV with 'Gangsta's Paradise' was a number one hit in October. Before the year ended two more recordings were destined to make it to the top 'I Believe/Up on the Roof' by Robson and Jerome, and 'Earth Song' by Michael Jackson. Eventful indeed 1995 was, but as the months passed so with them went a host of household names – personalities such as: Larry Grayson, comedian; Fred Perry, tennis player; James Herriot, author and vet; Harold Wilson, prime minister; Kenny Everett, comedian and disc jockey; Ginger Rogers, actress and dancer; Kingsley Amis, author; Lana Turner, actress, and Rose Kennedy, matriarch of the Kennedy clan.

Were the lean years of Cork championship hurling coming to an end? We could only hope, wait, and see. There was no need to wait until 1996 to find out the title of the new single currency. EU leaders agreed in December to call it the Euro.

1996

ENDINGS OUTNUMBER BEGINNINGS

Michael Jackson, who had two number one hits in 1995, carried on into 1996 with 'Earth Song'. However, all was not plain sailing for Michael because in mid-January his wife of fifteen months, former Lisa Marie Presley, filed for divorce. A high profile news item which had rumbled on since the death of publishing mogul Robert Maxwell in 1991, culminated in 1996 when his sons were cleared of a conspiracy charge. The £420 million Mirror Group pension fund deficit, like the circumstances surrounding Robert Maxwell's death, was to remain a mystery. The anti-climax which inevitably follows Christmas and the New Year was just on the wane when the euphoria generated by a seventeen-month IRA ceasefire came crashing down.

Yes, it was on 12 February that an IRA bomb devastated part of London's Dockland. Bad faith on the part of the British government was the explanation given by the IRA for the sudden and violent end to a ceasefire which had brought hope to so many. Two days later, in response to the return to violence, thousands gathered outside Belfast's City Hall to express their deep desire for peace.

It was in February too that Mick McCarthy took over as manager of the Republic of Ireland football team. Within days of that appointment Bob Paisley, former manager of Liverpool Football Club, died. He was the most successful manager ever in English football, winning a total of nineteen trophies in nine seasons and was in charge when the Merseyside club won the European Cup in 1977, 1978 and 1981.

A SUPERFLUITY

The spring and early summer of 1996 seem to rain a superfluity of news items, among which were: the production of identical sheep by human ingenuity – cloning;

the transmission of a trillion bits of information per second through an optical fibre – the equivalent of 12,000,000 simultaneous phone calls; the multiple murder of sixteen schoolchildren and a teacher at a primary school in Dunblane, Scotland; the alarming possibility of BSE (*bovine spongiform encephalopathy*), commonly known as Mad Cow Disease, being transmitted via the food chain to humans, resulting in a new strain of an incurable disease called CJD (Creutzfeldt-Jakob disease); the beginning of historical all-party talks on the future of Northern Ireland from which Sinn Féin were excluded because of continuing IRA terrorism; the IRA bombs which blasted Manchester city centre injuring 200 people; and the sale of a rocking chair used by former United States president, John F. Kennedy, which realised 300 times more than previously estimated.

What of the 1996 popular music scene? Well, in February one of the most successful groups of the decade, Take That, announced they were splitting up. George Michael with 'Jesus To A Child' began a deluge which continued to flow with 'Spaceman' by Babylon Zoo, 'Don't Look Back in Anger' by Oasis, 'How Deep Is Your Love' by Take That, and 'Firestarter' by Prodigy. By then March had come and gone. In April there was no sign of the flood abating as Mark Morrison made it to the top with 'Return of the Mack'. George Michael returned with 'Fastlove'. Next came Gina G with 'OOH AAH ... Just A Little Bit'. On 1 June, 'Three Lions' by Baddiel and Skinner and the Lightning Seeds began what was to be the first of two spells at the top. A similar situation arose when 'Killing Me Softly' by Fugees became a number one hit in June and again in July.

A MAY STUNNER AT THE 'PARK

One beautiful morning in May I set out on the 350-mile journey from Ballycastle, County Antrim to Union Hall, County Cork on holidays. I would be in the 'deep south' for the meeting of Cork and Limerick in the first round of the hurling championship at Páirc Uí Chaoimh on Sunday 26 May. The anticipation of an excitement-filled day ahead thrilled me to the bone. The journey northwards through the familiar and historic west Cork countryside was short-ened by the inevitable craic. The banter on the way to the match reached pantomime proportions. Why not? Sure Cork had an easy home match against Limerick! If added insurance was required, the Rebels had not lost a champi-onship match in Cork for 75 years. Belief in automatic suc-cess was further guaranteed by the fact that a past wizard of the caman, the still very youthful Jimmy Barry-Murphy, had taken over as team manager from his close friend, the great Johnny Clifford. If even the slightest doubt had been harboured as to the management capabilities of the star who had five senior All-Ireland medals, and twice that number of Munster championships to his credit, then we had only to look at his right-hand men, icons of Cork hurl-ing, the duo of Tom Cashman and Tony O'Sullivan. Inside Páirc Uí Chaoimh the air of invincibility continued to be generated by the fortress-like aura which the packed stadi-um itself exuded. That the Rebels had registered only one victory in the previous three championships seemed not to matter at all. We were swept forwards by glories which arched back well over the recent past.

Alas, the optimism, the belief, and I suppose the cocki-ness so firmly established in the minds of Cork followers proved to be unfounded. Expectations based on history which took none of Cork's recent hurling plight into account, left disillusioned followers along with bewildered players and mentors to ponder on what went wrong. Early on in the match it became clear that Cork were struggling against a well-prepared and talented Limerick team. Favoured by a strong breeze in the first-half the Leesiders were finding it difficult to match a free flowing, accom-plished and confident performance by the Shannonsiders. When compared to the Limerick side demolished at the same venue by Cork in the 1992 Munster final, a complete metamorphosis had taken place. Here we had a Limerick hurling team which was focused, hungry and determined. As for Cork, there were times when it looked as if some players wished they were 1000 miles away from the scene of the action. As the first-half progressed the Shannonsiders edged ahead and led by 0-7 to 0-3 with ten minutes to go. Then came the only period throughout the match when the Rebel County supporters dared to hope a little. A point by Jim Cashman was added to by Alan Browne who tacked on a goal and a point. The score at the interval was Cork 1-5; Limerick 0-7. Yet it was evident that nothing short of a collapse by Limerick, or a transformation in the home side, would save the day for Cork. Neither of the above happened!

Limerick, now wind assisted, led by 0-11 to 1-6 within minutes of the restart. Worse was to come when Limerick's full-forward, Pádraig Tobin, had the sliotar in the Cork net twice in quick succession. From then on a deflated Cork team wilted to a degree that I had seldom if ever seen previously. Not surprisingly, Limerick grew in stature.

A final score of Limerick 3-18; Cork 1-8 tells it own story. It was a day to remember for the followers of Limerick hurling who undoubtedly and justifiably believed that their day had been long overdue. Cork followers who should have known better were emphatically reminded that where hurling matches and the outcome thereof is concerned, nothing is carved in stone.

Following the morning and early afternoon euphoria, thoughts now turned to the magnitude of the task Jimmy Barry-Murphy had undertaken. We wondered too if we had seen the last of men like Jim Cashman, Teddy McCarthy and Ger Cunningham, who by then had long and illustrious careers in the Cork jersey. Perhaps though we were being previous!

The Cork team was: Ger Cunningham, Timmy Kelleher, John O'Driscoll, Fergal Ryan, Fergal McCormack, Jim Cashman, Kieran McGuckin, Brian Corcoran, Séan McCarthy, Barry Egan, Teddy McCarthy, Mark Mullins, Kevin Murray, Alan Browne, and Joe Deane. The substitutes were: Darren O'Donoghue for Teddy McCarthy, Séan Óg ÓhAilpín for Mark Mullins; and David Quirk for Alan Browne. The Limerick team was: Joe Quaid, Stephen McDonagh, Mike Nash, Declan Nash, Dave Clarke, Ciaran Carey, Mark Foley, Mike Houlihan, Séan O'Neill, Shane O'Neill, Gary Kirby, Mike Galligan, Owen O'Neill, Pádraig Tobin, and Damien Quigley. The substitutes were: T.J.

Ryan for Damien Quigley; Frankie Carroll for Shane
O'Neill; and Brian Tobin for Sean O'Neill.

Limerick went on to contest the All-Ireland final which
they lost to Wexford by 0-14 to 1-13. On the way the
Shannonsiders beat first Clare and then Tipperary after a
replay to become Munster champions. Antrim provided
the All-Ireland semi-final opposition.

A COCKTAIL OF VIOLENCE, SPORT, DEATH, LEVITY, CONCERN
AND FRANKIE

During the summer of 1996 the hurling problems of Cork
came as a very poor second in the eyes of many when compared to the turmoil on the streets of Northern Ireland. For
the first time, the words, 'Drumcree' and 'Gervaghy Road'
were flashed around the world by the media. In a situation
which severely damaged the Peace Process, Protestant
Orangemen reacted violently right across the province
when the RUC attempted to prevent them from walking
through a Catholic area, the Gervaghy Road in Portadown.
Unsurprisingly, when the RUC later decided to let the
march go ahead, the U-turn led to widespread rioting by
Nationalists.

A month earlier in the Republic a heinous crime was
committed on a Limerick street when 52-year-old, father of
five, Detective Garda Jerry McCabe, was shot in the back as
he was escorting Post Office cash deliveries in the company of another detective.

Across the Atlantic on 19 July, a Boeing 747 Jumbo Jet
exploded shortly after taking off from John F. Kennedy
Airport, New York. The Paris-bound flight had 228 people
aboard. A terrorist bomb was deemed the likely cause of
the explosion. In another part of the United States prepara-
tions were ongoing for the opening of the Centennial
Olympic Games, at Atlanta Georgia. Irish swimmer
Michelle Smith subsequently won three gold medals at the
Games. Towards the end of July, football player Alan
Shearer moved from Blackburn Rovers to Newcastle
United for a record transfer fee of £15 million - two million
more than the previous world record. Flash floods in
August devastated a campsite in northern Spain, killing

100 holiday makers and injuring 200 others.

The Spice Girls' 'Wannabe' was preceded at number one by Gary Barlow's 'Forever Love', and held top spot from the end of July to mid-September when 'Flava', by Peter Andre took over. A week later the Fugees returned to number one for the third time in 1996. On that occasion it was not 'Killing Me Softly', but with a new recording called 'Ready or Not'.

At Ascot, 28 September became a day to remember for Frankie Dettori. He became the first jockey ever to ride seven winners on the same day. As a result bookmakers were thought to have lost in the region of £10 million.

British Prime Minister John Major reacted angrily to a double car bomb in Northern Ireland which he described as, 'Wicked beyond belief'. The atrocity took place in early October inside the Northern Ireland Headquarters of the British Army at Lisburn, County Antrim. One person died and 34 were injured.

The weeks of October were shared out between four number one hits. It began with 'Breakfast at Tiffanys' from Deep Blue Something. Following on were 'Setting Sun' from Chemical Brothers, 'Words' from Boyzone, and 'Say You'll be There' from the Spice Girls. November was the month when 'What Becomes of the Broken Hearted/Up on the Roof/You'll Never Walk Alone' by Robson and Jerome and, 'Breathe' by Prodigy, respectively occupied the top spot.

SNIPPETS, A LANDSLIDE, A MARRIAGE, SPICY TORIES, BUT NO FUSS

Sport-related snippets from the autumn of 1996 referred to: 78 people being crushed to death at a World Cup qualifying match in Guatemala city; England soccer player Paul Gascoigne allegedly battering his wife of fourteen weeks; Peter Shilton, former England goalkeeper, who had made 1,000 football league appearances, a feat unprecedented in soccer history; and an eighteen-year-old Australian, David Dicks, who became the youngest yachtsman to complete a non-stop circumnavigation of the world.

As widely forecasted, the United States presidential

election, held in November, produced a landslide victory for Bill Clinton. He became the first Democrat since Franklin D. Roosevelt (1933-45) to win a second term in the White House.

Michael Jackson too began a second term, in his case a second term of matrimony. Following divorce proceedings which resulted in the termination of his marriage to Lisa Marie Presley, in November he wed Debbie Rowe, a 37-year-old nurse. A story with a difference emerged in late 1996 which told of a 98-year-old widow who wrote anonymously to the *Hull Daily Mail*. She informed the newspaper that she had a winning National Lottery ticket worth over £2 million but did not want to collect the money because, as she put it, 'The fuss would kill me off'. An unlikely release by the Spice Girls made headlines in December. According to an interview in a magazine, the all-female pop group which was currently topping the singles charts in 28 countries, was offering support to the British Tory Party Eurosceptics. The interview went on to say that the group rejected Labour Party tax policies, were opposed to a single currency, and declared themselves to be true Thatcherites. Geri Halliwell suggested that former prime minister, Mrs Thatcher, was the first 'spice girl'; according to 25-year-old Geri, Mrs Thatcher pioneered the Spice Girl ideology. The Spice Girls remained centre stage right up to the end of the year when in late December, '2 Become 1' became the last number one hit of 1996. It was preceded by 'I Feel You' from Peter Andre; 'A Different Beat' by Boyzone; and 'Knockin' On Heaven's Door – Throw these Guns Away' by Dunblane.

Knocking on heaven's door too were those who had passed on during 1996. Among them were: Micheál O'Hehir, sports commentator; Danny McNaughton, Cushendall, Antrim and Ulster Hurler; Ella Fitzgerald, jazz singer; Gene Kelly, actor and dancer; Michael Bentine, comedian; Beryl Reid, actress; and Leslie Crowther, TV personality.

1997

IT ALL SEEMED TO BE HAPPENING IN JANUARY

From early in the New Year of 1997, once darkness fell, people were found looking skywards. The source of the night sky attraction was the very visible, Hale-Bop comet. One man who missed out on seeing the phenomenon for at least five days was British yachtsman, Tony Bullimore. Whilst competing in the Vendee Globe round the world race his vessel capsized in the South Pacific Ocean. After five days sheltering in an air-pocket inside the upturned hull, he was rescued from his cramped accommodation by the Australian Navy. The survival feat of Tony Bullimore was perhaps matched by Norwegian explorer, Boerge Oouland, who completed the first solo unsupported crossing of Antarctica.

It seemed to be all happening in January 1997: President Clinton was sworn in for a second term of office; nine women were ordained as the first women priests in the Anglican Church; Peter Graf, the father of tennis star, Steffi Graf, was sentenced to imprisonment for evasion of more than £5 million tax on his daughter's earnings; and Martina Hingis became the youngest tennis player to win a singles grand-slam title this century. As '2 Become 1' by the Spice Girls remained at number one, serious social unrest erupted in Albania when pyramid finance schemes collapsed. In what was known as Europe's poorest country, people had sold houses, land and livestock to invest in the schemes. In this country, the lucrative live meat export trade with Egypt was suspended following an Egyptian newspaper claim that 'mad cows' were being imported from Ireland. Meanwhile the security situation north of the border continued to deteriorate with horrific consequences.

306

Divorce! O.J. Ordered, Champ Retires, Excellence Except for Aintree

With little sign of spring yet in the air, February 1997 will be remembered as the month divorce became legal in the Republic of Ireland. It was the month too in which No Mercy topped the hit singles chart with 'Where Do You Go'.

O.J. Simpson, the former American all-star who had earlier been acquitted of murdering his wife and her friend in 1994, was now ordered to pay a total of £17.7 million in compensation and punitive damages to their relatives. No such demands were made on former champion jockey Willie Carson who announced his retirement from racing, nor indeed on Martina Hingis, who added to her previous achievement by becoming the youngest ever world number one tennis player at the age of sixteen. In the limelight too was 21-year-old golfer, Tiger Woods who won the US Masters in a style hitherto unknown. Not only was he the youngest winner ever, he also scored the lowest ever stroke total and won by the biggest ever margin. A week later in the World Snooker Championship at Sheffield, Ronnie O'Sullivan made sporting headlines when he scored the fastest ever maximum break of 147; he cleared the table in five minutes twenty seconds.

Those who made their way to Liverpool's Aintree Racecourse to watch the Grand National on Saturday 5 April were to be disappointed. The prestigious race was postponed because of IRA bomb threats. Instead it took place on the following Monday.

Chaos, Arson, Election Fever and June, as Ken and Man. U. Shine

IRA activity in England was responsible for repeated disruptions to transport systems on mainland Britain. A series of small bombs combined with numerous bomb hoaxes provoked road and rail chaos. A measure of the violence which existed in Northern Ireland can be gauged from statistics which listed arson attacks at 48 places of worship, 71 schools and 44 halls throughout the six counties. All took place during the sixteen months leading up to April 1997.

South of the border, much attention was focused on the proceedings at Dublin Castle. It was the venue of a tribunal inquiry into payments allegedly made to politicians and political parties between 1986 and 1996.

With the arrival of May and the first signs of summer came general election fever both in Ireland and in the United Kingdom. Taoiseach John Bruton called for a day of reckoning on 6 June, while in Britain, following election success, Prime Minister Tony Blair formed a Labour government for the first time in eighteen years.

Regardless of other developments, sport continued to throw up interesting outcomes. Among them was the achievement of young Dubliner, Ken Doherty, who became snooker champion of the world, thus ending Stephen Hendry's five-year reign. In the world of soccer, Manchester United Football Club won the premiership for the fourth time in five years.

Throughout the spring and early summer of 1997 the popular music scene continued to boom with more records entering the UK top 10 in their first week than ever before. Number one hits were secured by, No Doubt with 'Don't Speak'; R. Kelly with 'I Believe I can Fly'; Cardigans with 'Lovefool'; and Hanson with 'Mmmbop'. 'Mmmbop' also topped the charts in the United States and Australia. In the UK it sold more than 500,000 copies in four weeks. In June 1997, as the Jimmy Barry-Murphy managed Cork team prepared to take on a proven Clare team in the Munster hurling championship semi-final, followers of the game down by the Lee simply did not know what to expect. Fresh in their minds was the ignominious defeat at the hands of Limerick in Páirc Uí Chaoimh a year ago.

A NARROW CLARE WIN WOULD BE A MORAL VICTORY FOR CORK! SURELY NOT!!
The Banner County win at the expense of Cork at the Gaelic Grounds, Limerick on 13 June 1993, marked the occasion of Clares' second championship win over Cork since 1955. Nobody in Limerick that day foresaw the meteoric rise to hurling fame which was waiting around the corner for the Claremen. In sharp contrast, Cork followers

saw their county spiral downwards at an alarming rate and indeed reach what must be regarded as rock bottom at Páirc Uí Chaoimh the previous May. The advent of the 1997 Guinness Munster hurling championship brought with it much speculation as to how Cork would fare against Clare at Limerick on 8 June. Jimmy Barry-Murphy and his selectors had tried out various combinations of players during the National League campaign and in a series of challenge matches. At the end of the day they opted for skill, youth and commitment. Indeed the team chosen to play Clare had five Under-21 members in its ranks, three of whom were making their championship debut. It was a courageous selection when one considered the current awesome standing of Clare hurling, and the likelihood that a heavy defeat in successive years would have been disastrous for all concerned with Cork hurling.

At 3.45 pm, referee Pat O'Connor threw in the sliotar. The 23,000 people present expected nothing short of another top class performance by the Claremen. Nobody knew how the young Cork team would respond to the occasion, and to the might of the Banner County. The opening minutes of play seemed to confirm that popular opinion had been correct. Clare made all the running with the midfield sector being dominated by Colin Lynch, and Timmy Kelleher being troubled by Fergus Tuohy. It took twenty minutes for Cork to come to terms with the superbly accomplished Clare team. The first signs that the match was not going to be all one-way traffic came when Brian Corcoran, Séan Óg Ó hAilpín and Seanie McGrath became prominent. Soon Cork began to compete well in most positions. It was good to see team captain Fergal McCormack not only holding his own with Ollie Baker but at times getting the better of him. Wind-assisted Clare were five points to the good after twenty minutes – 0-8 to 0-3. It was then that the Rebels rallied.

Good early ball to Seanie McGrath and Joe Deane began to have a telling effect. Barry Egan and Ger Manley too became influential. Brian Corcoran was outstanding. Superlatives to describe Ger Cunningham's display between the posts had all been used up over his long and illustrious career, which entered its seventeenth inter-county championship campaign that very afternoon. During the course of the match not only did he excel in all aspects of goalkeeping but he plucked the sliotar out of the air on two occasions when it was on its way over the cross-bar. At half-time the score stood at Clare 0-9; Cork 0-8. The Clare players went in at half-time the less happier of the two teams.

All the astuteness of Banner County manager Ger Loughnane was called upon to address the worrying turn of events. Typically he responded boldly and decisively by moving Ger O'Loughlin to full-forward, and by the dual substitution of Stephen McNamara and David Forde, for Niall Gilligan and Conor Clancy respectively. The changes were to reap rich benefits. Cork, with wind advantage in the second-half, levelled the score after six minutes. But Clare dug deep and while the Rebels continued to play well they were being stretched to breaking point. The now-rampant Banner County centre-half back Seanie McMahon, who incidentally scored three crucial points, simply could not be curbed. Yet Cork's defence held firm with Fergal Ryan and Diarmuid O'Sullivan doing particu-larly well in the full-back line. The half-backs maintained the high standard set in the first-half with Timmy Kelleher now imposing himself more and more. Perhaps it was a tribute to Seán Óg Ó hAilpín that Jamsie O'Connor scored just a single point from play. After twenty minutes of tough, entertaining hurling only a point separated the sides.

Battle continued and while it looked as if the experi-enced Claremen were getting the upper hand, yet they had only a two point margin entering the final minutes of the match. It was then that the goal, which throughout the sec-ond-half looked as if it might give victory to either side, came – Clare got it! It was scored by Stephen McNamara. Cork fought to the bitter end and it took a fine save from Clare goalkeeper David Fitzgerald to deny Seanie McGrath in the dying seconds. The final score was Clare 1-19; Cork 0-18. It had been a fabulous exhibition of hurling which received the admiration of partisan and neutral alike. From a Cork point of view one could only be proud of the magnificent display served up by a young, underrated team. Clare's mentors and players graciously acknowledged that it had taken a supreme effort to overcome the Leesiders. Ger Loughnane was quoted as saying, 'Cork were back at their brilliant best and they really put it up to us'.

The Cork team was: Ger Cunningham, Fergal Ryan, John O'Driscoll, Diarmuid O'Sullivan, Séan Óg Ó hAilpín, Brian Corcoran, Timmy Kelleher, Fergal McCormack (captain), Alan Cummins, Ger Manley, Kevin Murray, Barry Egan, Seanie McGrath, Alan Browne and Joe Deane. The subs were: M. Daly for K. Murray and D. Ronan for A. Cummins. The Clare team was: David Fitzgerald, Michael O'Halloran, Brian Lohan, Frank Lohan, Liam Doyle, Seanie McMahon, Anthony Daly (captain) Ollie Baker, Colin Lynch, Fergus Touhy, P.J. O'Connell, Jamsie O'Connor, Niall Gilligan, Conor Clancy and Ger O'Loughlin. The subs were: S. McNamara for N. Gilligan; D. Forde for C. Clancy; A. Whelan for G. O'Loughlin.

Clare went on to narrowly defeat Tipperary in the Munster final (1-18 to 0-18). Tipperary and Kilkenny entered the All-Ireland series through the 'back door' and were respectively successful in the quarter-finals, beating Down and Galway. The semi-final pairings were Clare versus Kilkenny, and Tipperary versus the Leinster champions, Wexford. While not universally popular, the Munster counties emerged as All-Ireland finalists. They had their big day out at Croke Park on 14 September, a day on which the repeat of the Munster final clash ended in an even narrower margin than the previous occasion but again the Banner County came out on top. The score was Clare 0-20; Tipperary 2-13. A fine Clare team thus captured its second All-Ireland hurling championship in two years.

BELIEF, SADNESS AND JUSTICE AS MIKE BITES AND POLITICIANS TRY

So Cork were out of the hurling championship for another year! The inevitable doubts began to surface in some quarters. A theory put forward was that the traditional commitment to Gaelic games in Cork was being seriously eroded by other codes. So seriously in fact that the future of our national games was in jeopardy. A few barren years in a county where expectations are always high never fails to germinate adverse comment. The fact that Cork hurling had lean spells in the past but duly recovered to shower itself in renewed glory seemed to be unknown or forgotten by some scribes.

In 1997 those close to the hurling scene in Cork could not fail to be impressed; firstly by the calibre and achievements of the minor and Under-21 teams, and secondly by the resolve of the vastly-experienced team of coach/manager, Jimmy Barry-Murphy, and his household name selectors. It was only a matter of time before the men in the red jerseys made good.

On the evening of 15 June, GAA followers along with people nationwide, were shocked when it became known that Tyrone player, eighteen-year-old Paul McGirr, had died as result of an accidental collision with another player during an Ulster minor football championship match. A sad and salutary day indeed! While we reflected on that unfortunate loss of a young life the longest trial in English legal history ended. On 19 June, after 313 days, the fast food chain, McDonalds, was awarded £60,000 libel damages against two campaigners who claimed that the company caused starvation in the third world and destroyed rain forests.

Starvation was unlikely to be an issue in a world title boxing contest between former heavyweight champion Mike Tyson and Evander Holyfield. Nevertheless, Tyson was disqualified after biting off part of his opponents ear. Yet another milestone in Irish politics was marked on 26 June when Bertie Ahern, leader of the Fianna Fáil party, took over the office of Taoiseach. There were two notable features associated with the newly formed coalition government. Bertie Ahern was the youngest Taoiseach to hold office, and his deputy, Mary Harney of the Progressive Democratic Party, was the first female to fill that position. On the same day, in an attempt to bring peace to Northern Ireland, British Prime Minister, Tony Blair, announced plans to begin talks with the various political parties. In an apparently significant step towards resolving the conflict he announced that any agreement reached at the talks would subsequently be placed before the people of Northern Ireland. He set May 1998 as a completion date. The initiative, later known as the 'peace process' had no immediate effect and two weeks later renewed violence during the climax of the 'marching season' led to an extra infantry battalion being brought from England to Northern Ireland to deal with rioting. Some crumbs of comfort resulted when the IRA announced an unequivocal restoration of its 1994 ceasefire.

THE LAW IN ACTION, UNTIMELY DEATHS, POLITICAL MOVES, SUPREME CLARE
It was in July that finally justice was done in the case of Fr Brendan Smyth. He was sentenced to twelve years imprisonment after being convicted on 74 instances of sexually abusing twenty individuals over a period of 36 years. Meanwhile, across the Atlantic, at his mansion in Miami, Florida, fashion designer Gianni Versace was shot dead.

The demand for popular music continued to flourish. The number one hit single to dominate the chart in July and August was the Puff Daddy and Faith Evans number, 'I'll Be Missing You'. It reflected perfectly the sentiment expressed worldwide at the untimely death of Diana Princess of Wales. Making headlines too in August was the second trial of football personalities Bruce Grobbelaar, Hans Segars and John Fashanu. It cleared them of conspiracy to throw football matches for money. By then the people of Ireland had become immune to the shady 'goings-on' in high places and nobody was surprised when a tribunal of inquiry into payments to politicians by Ben Dunne recommended that former Taoiseach, Charles Haughey should be prosecuted.

During September, traditionally the month of the All-Ireland hurling and football finals, it was the term, Mitchell Principles, associated with the 'peace process' in Northern Ireland, which flowed out from the media. Meanwhile, bombings and killings continued unabated. Mary Robinson, President of Ireland, chose early autumn to step down from office. Weeks later she was replaced by Mary McAleese. It was late October when Prime Minister Tony Blair and Sinn Féin leader Gerry Adams met at Stormont Castle. The occasion brought back memories of the last such meeting in 1921 when the then prime minister, Lloyd George, and Sinn Féin's Michael Collins signed the Anglo-Irish Treaty which formally partitioned Ireland.

Further afield, natural disasters didn't fail to take their usual toll of human life. Flooding and torrential rain claimed the lives of at least 15,000 people in Somalia during the autumn of 1997. In Mexico more than 400 people died when a hurricane hit its Pacific coastline. In Vietnam a typhoon hit the south coast with such ferocity that hundreds of people were killed and thousands went missing. In November, off the Shetland Islands in a 70 mile an hour gale, a helicopter winchman who had just rescued ten crew members from a wrecked ship in atrocious weather conditions, was himself drowned.

There was some good news in November, and perhaps none more so than the delivery of the first septuplets to be born alive. It took place in Iowa, USA. 'Men In Black' by Will Smith made it to number one in the singles charts in September, but it was Elton John's tribute to Diana Princess of Wales, 'Candle in the Wind', which was to achieve the status of bestselling single of all time. Within three months of its release it topped charts all over the globe, and a massive 33,000,000 copies were produced to satisfy demands. By the end of the year it had earned £20,000,000. Yet, in November it was Aqua with 'Barbie Girl' who took over at the top.

As the year petered out political observers in Ireland noted the resignation of Dick Spring as leader of the Labour Party, but for the troubled people of Northern Ireland it was the shooting dead of LVF leader Billy Wright in the Maze Prison by INLA inmates which generated a renewed fear in the nationalist community; reprisals were a certainty, where, when and how were the unknown factors!

Violence played no part in the deaths of the following

high profile individuals during 1997: Paul McGirr, Gaelic football player; Shirley Crabtree (Big Daddy), wrestler; Ben Hogan, golfer; Mother Teresa, Missions of Charity Founder and ceaseless worker for the poor; Jacques-Yves Cousteau, oceanographer; Dorothy Lamour, actress; James Stewart, actor; Robert Mitchum, actor; Red Skelton, comic actor; Stephane Grappelli, jazz violinist; Deng Xiaoping, Chinese political leader; Sese Seko Mobutu, President of Zaire.

The title of December's number one hit was 'Perfect Day', a fitting description for the day on which a superb Banner County team became All-Ireland champions for the second time in the 1990s. My end of year thought was that surely the present millennium will see Cork win another All-Ireland hurling championship! Maybe it was time for a wee prayer!

1998

THE GOOD, THE BAD AND THE UGLY

Whilst 'Perfect Day', a charity song recorded by various artists, was at number one, allegations of sexual harassment by one Paula Jones and an investigation into an alleged affair with White House assistant Monica Lewinsky made life uncomfortable for Bill Clinton, president of the United States. A later January number one hit by All Saints was called 'Never Ever'. Bill Clinton opted for the somewhat less definitive wording when he explained, 'I did not have sexual relations with that woman, Miss Lewinsky'. The fact that the president was accused of persuading Miss Lewinsky to lie under oath added greatly to his plight. There was more trouble in store for the president when a White House volunteer claimed he groped her.

There were troubled times in Ireland too as talks on the future of the North continued against a background of sectarian violence. In January at least eight people were killed in tit-for-tat shootings. As the United Kingdom and Irish governments published their blueprint for the way ahead, Mo Mowlan, Secretary of State for Northern Ireland, made an unprecedented visit to the Maze prison.

The purpose of the visit was to appeal personally to Loyalist prisoners to support the peace talks, yet the killings continued! Somehow, in the face of the most shocking outrages, which included massive bombs in the towns of Moira, County Down and, Portadown, County Armagh, the political nerve held firm. The situation was not helped when the IRA was accused of breaking the ceasefire, and as a result Sinn Féin were suspended from the talks for two weeks.

Snippets of news from elsewhere told of a twelve-year-old boy who had become Britain's youngest father; Liverpool dockers who reached a settlement with their employers in a dispute which had gone on since September 1995; an earthquake in north-east Afghanistan which caused the deaths of 4,000 people; devastation resulting from floods in Peru; and Michael Owen, an eighteen-year-old who had become the youngest footballer to play for England since the 1880s. In March at the Academy Awards in Los Angeles, the film 'Titanic' won eleven Oscars including Best Picture and Best Director. There were no Oscars being awarded in the province of Kosovo when news of demonstrations by ethnic Albanians first made headlines. Instead it was the deaths of the same Albanians resulting from clashes with Serb forces which caught the attention of the world.

Meanwhile, 'All Around The World' by Oasis, 'You Make Me Wanna' by Usher, 'Doctor Jones' by Aqua, 'Brimful of Asha' by Cornershop, and 'Frozen' by Madonna, all had spells at number one in the charts.

At a time when bombings and killings had become so commonplace in Northern Ireland as to virtually go unnoticed, there was widespread sympathy expressed when Dáil Éireann T.D. Hugh Coveney was found dead in the sea off Cork. Away from the political side of life, emergency and ground staff at Dublin Airport went on strike in support of colleagues. The move brought the airport to all but a standstill. Government intervention led to a swift return to work.

SEANIE, JOHNNY AND TED, JOIN JIMMY, TOM AND FRED
Statistics showed that Cork's senior hurlers had partaken in two competitions – the Oireachtas and the Waterford Glass sponsored South-Eastern league. They had fared well in both competitions. In the Oireachtas competition the Leesiders were victorious over Limerick and Waterford, and even though they lost to Wexford, they qualified to meet Galway in the final. The Tribesmen emerged as winners by a score of 0-14 to 0-8. In the South-Eastern league the Rebels were again finalists. On that occasion it was Waterford who collected the trophy. On 8 March the opening matches of the Church & General National Hurling League were played. By then Cork's team seemed to be well settled. Valuable assessment of talent and commitment of players had taken place during the

previous competitions by a now very-experienced management team. Over the winter Jimmy Barry-Murphy, Tom Cashman and Fred Sheedy had been joined by former county stars Seanie O'Leary and Johnny Crowley. Also to help-out came physical trainer Ted Owens.

Cork opened the league campaign in great style with a home win over Kilkenny and an away victory at the expense of Waterford. There were signs that maybe the men in red were back on track; it was early days, but the current combination of youth, experience, talent, and eagerness augured well. It was a case of watch this space!

A GOOD FRIDAY, A GAME SUMMIT, MICHELLE DENIES AND NO JOY FOR PAULA

While we kept a close eye on the progress of Cork's hurlers, Celine Dion's 'My Heart Will Go On', from the movie 'Titantic' went to number one in the charts, first in February and again in mid-March. On Good Friday, 10 April, against the odds, the British and Irish governments, along with Northern Ireland politicians involved in cross-party talks, signed an agreement on achieving a political settlement in Northern Ireland. It took place against the background of the seizure of a car bomb being driven onto a Holyhead bound ferry at Dun Laoghaire, and continuing terrorist activity. Within days of the historic signing, in a confidence-boosting gesture, the Irish government released nine IRA prisoners from Port Laoise prison. Yet it was the IRA who placed the first stumbling block in the way of the agreement when they refused to decommission any weapons.

Other developments at the time included a declaration of an unqualified ceasefire by the UVF, and U2 performing in Belfast in support of the Good Friday Agreement. On 22 May a referendum on the Agreement resulted in overwhelming backing in the Republic, and while the yes vote was not so decisive in the North, a majority did give it their blessing. Peace, it seemed, was finally on the cards for all the people of our troubled country. Perhaps we were some way down the line towards achieving what Boyzone

318

number one hit single suggested, 'All That I Need'.

Back in April, 'Earth Summit', winner of the English Grand National, had the unique distinction of being the first horse to win the corresponding races in Scotland and Wales. It was in April too that Irish Olympic swimming champion, Michelle de Bruin, denied having taken performance-enhancing drugs. The denial came in the wake of a finding by the Sports International Governing Body which stated that a urine sample taken in January showed signs of adulteration. In a counter statement Ms de Bruin accused FINA of conspiring to destroy her career. In August FINA imposed a four-year ban on the swimmer.

In the United States, just before the onset of summer, Paula Jones, was to learn that the harassment case she brought against President Clinton had been dismissed.

During the months of May and June the top spot in the charts was successively occupied by 'Under the Bridge/Lady Marmalade' by All Saints, 'Feel It' by Tamperer featuring Maya, 'C'est La Vie' by B*Witched, and '3 Lions '98' by Baddiel and Skinner and the Lightning Seeds.

KOSOVO WOE, BUT IT'S DELIGHT FOR THE LEESIDERS
As May progressed, apart from the Good Friday Agreement and the hopes it raised for an end to hostilities in our country, it was the turmoil in Kosovo, and especially the plight of ethnic Albanians which media attention focused on. Reports of widespread and co-ordinated Serb military action against largely defenceless people were becoming increasingly common.

It had now been almost two months since the Church & General National Hurling League began. Cork made a bright start back in March but did they continue? The short answer is an emphatic, yes! In fact the team secured a semi-final place by virtue of an unbeaten campaign; only Wexford held them to a draw. The home win over Laois in the concluding round was academic to Cork's progress. It was looking good for the Leesiders! The Rebels could not have met more formidable semi-final opponents on 3 May at Thurles than All-Ireland champions Clare. The first-half

319

performance by the Banner County was well below par and riddled with missed scoring chances. Cork led at the interval by 1-10 to 0-2. Seanie McGrath was the goal scorer. The consensus of opinion was that the restart would see Clare explode into action. The explosion failed to materialise and Cork finished convincing winners. The final score was Cork 2-15; Clare 0-10. Alan Browne was the scorer of the second goal. Other players to catch the eye were Brian Corcoran and Fergal McCormack.

Much was afterwards said and written about the apparent lack of seriousness with which the Clare management approached the match. I prefer to go along with someone close to the Clare scene, namely Séamus Hayes (*Clare Champion*), who assures us that none of it was true – 'Clare went to Thurles seeking victory but failed to match Cork's hunger and will to win throughout the field.' Two weeks later, on 17 May, at the same venue Cork and Waterford met in the final. Waterford's emergence surprised some people. Yet it was a team managed by former Cork star Gerald McCarthy and built around key players in vital areas. The presence of individuals such as Browne, Hartley, Greene, Frampton, McGrath, Kirwan and Flynn made it a very formidable outfit! Jimmy Barry-Murphy and his cohorts had also put together a good Cork team. It was a team which had lost only twice in two years, and one greatly enhanced by Cork's Under-21 All-Ireland Championship winning side of 1997 – a team managed by Bertie Óg Murphy. Could 1998 be the year in which self-esteem was to be restored to a county already steeped in hurling tradition? As the league final approached the significance of a win grew in stature – victory was essential. Jimmy Barry-Murphy and all associated with the team knew it – Cork expected!

By 5pm on the afternoon of 17 May, the hopes and dreams of Leesiders were fulfilled. A close, keenly contested match had been played during which Cork needed an Alan Browne goal ten minutes from time to set them on their way to glory. Like many teams before them, Waterford had their chances but failed to capitalise on them. As on previous occasions Brian Corcoran at centre-half back was at his brilliant best. Indeed the half-back line as a whole performed magnificently, so much so that the full-back line was rarely under pressure. It was a good day too for the forwards with each one of them getting his name on the score sheet. Special mention goes to Seán O'Farrell who scored Cork's all-important first goal. His scoring feat did not end there as he went on to score three late points. All in all it was a fine team performance and a just reward for the mentors who worked so hard to haul Cork hurling back from what seemed rock bottom. It was certainly a case of heartiest congratulations to all concerned. The final score was Cork 2-14; Waterford 1-13. A sweet victory for Cork and a delighted Jimmy Barry-Murphy, who praised his team for their dedication, and for restoring Cork's hurling pride.

The Cork team was: Ger Cunningham, Fergal Ryan, John Browne, Diarmuid O'Sullivan, Mark Landers, Brian Corcoran, Seán Óg Ó hAilpín, Pat Ryan, Michael Daly, Seanie McGrath, Fergal McCormack, Kieran Morrison, Seán O'Farrell, Alan Browne, and Joe Deane.

The Waterford team was: Brendan Landers, Tom Feeney, Seán Cullinane, Mark O'Sullivan, Stephen Frampton, Fergal Hartley, Brian Greene, Tony Browne, Peter Queally, Dan Shanahan, Ken McGrath, Dave Bennett, Michael White, Anthony Kirwan, and Paul Flynn.

THE CHAMPIONSHIP TRAIL

With the Church & General National Hurling League Trophy ensconced by the banks of the Lee, another date with destiny loomed for Jimmy Barry-Murphy's men. With the exception of a first-round championship win over Kerry in 1995, Cork hurlers had not won a single championship match since they defeated Down in the All-Ireland semi-final of 1992. In 1998 the championship trail began at the Gaelic Grounds, Limerick on Sunday 31 May. The venue had of late not been a happy hunting ground for Cork. In four out of the last five championship matches the Rebels had come away from the Treaty City empty handed! The fact that pundits burdened Jimmy Barry-Murphy's young team with the tag of favourites added to the pressure. It was generally accepted that Cork's opponents, Limerick, were not the force they were a few years previously. Nevertheless, a side with high calibre players such as Gary Kirby, Mike Houlihan, Mark Foley and the Carey brothers in its ranks was certain to relish a showdown on home territory. Against that background the now highly-acclaimed attacking skills of Cork's Seanie McGrath and Joe Deane, and the experience of equally accomplished defender Brian Corcoran, would come in for close scrutiny. Of course the daddy of them all, the man who had won every honour in the game, Cork's superb goalkeeper, Ger Cunningham, would take it all in his stride. Oddly enough the match outcome may have hinged on what was regarded as the dubious positioning of some players on the Limerick team. In particular the assigning of outstanding half-back player, Mark Foley, to centre-forward came in for hefty criticism.

What gave vent to the outcry was that Seanie McGrath, who would normally have been marked by Mark Foley, scored four valuable points from play in the opening fifteen minutes. To add fuel to fire, Brian Corcoran, Mark Foley's opposite number dominated during that period. Limerick did, however, come back strongly into the match, so much so that they built up a five-point lead. Then, when all seemed to be going well, Cork's Alan Browne got on the end of a Pat Ryan free and smartly kicked the sliotar past Joe Quaid into the Limerick net.

From that point on the Shannonsiders lead gradually dwindled and at the halfway mark only a point separated the teams. After the interval, a period of Cork domination led to the Rebels opening up an eight point gap. Pat Ryan was having a fine game at midfield and Joe Deane, who had been well curtailed by Stephen McDonagh for much of the match came good in the final twenty minutes. Then in the closing stages, at a time when the outcome seemed heavily weighted in Cork's favour, sloppy defending by the Leesiders let Limerick in for two goals. The score at the final whistle was Cork 1-20; Limerick 3-11. Importantly, apart from concentration losses towards the end of the match, the team had performed well, and there was reason to believe that the form shown in the National League might just stand up to championship fare. At least Cork had finally come out on the right side of a championship fixture. The mentors must have been encouraged by the continuing improvement in their young players. The Cork team lined out exactly as in the National League final. The Limerick team as it appeared on the match programme was: Joe Quaid, Stephen McDonagh, Pa Carey, Declan Nash, Dave Clarke, Ciarán Carey, Mark Foley, Mike Houlihan, Jack Foley, T.J. Ryan, Shane O'Neill, Mike Galligan, Barry Foley, Gary Kirby and Damien Quigley. Only Joe Quaid and the Carey brothers finished the match in their starting positions. Followers of the Leeside team all of a sudden had a spring to their step.

They would flock to Thurles on Sunday 21 June for the Munster semi-final meeting with All-Ireland champions Clare, in the words of the number one hit by Billie, 'Because we Want to'. The 1998 deeds of the Rebels thus far were sufficient to entice even those domiciled in north Antrim back to Semple Stadium. Loughgiel Shamrock's clubman, Paddy McIntyre, and myself set off in the early hours of what is widely regarded as the longest day of the year. The cathedral town had scarcely changed since my last visit some years previously. The buzz, the pubs, the bustle, and the various activities in Liberty Square were all as in days of yore. One thing though had changed, mingling with the red and white clad followers of Cork were saffron and blue bedecked Clare folk, instead of the more accustomed blue and gold of Tipperary's supporters.

On the stroke of 3.30 pm referee Willie Barrett set in motion a match which would either further enhance Clare's already mighty reputation, or alternatively install Jimmy Barry-Murphy's emerging fledglings as a team going places sooner than most expected. It was wind-assisted Cork that first settled. Alan Browne, without scoring, was getting the better of Clare's full-back Brian Lohan, and Fergal McCormack was at least unsettling star half-back player, Seanie McMahon. The Clare defence gave away frees at will which Joe Deane unerringly converted. At that point Cork seemed comfortable enough. As the

match wore on the Clare players began to impose themselves. Seanie McMahon became dominant and Brian
Lohan got to grips with Alan Browne. Suddenly, Ollie
Baker, Eamonn Taaffe and Niall Gilligan were creating and
taking scoring chances at ease. At half-time the score stood
at Cork 0-9; Clare 0-9. Clearly the Clare machine was now
firing on all cylinders.

On resumption, true to form, the Rebels refused to fold.
Ger Cunningham was called upon to make a few outstanding saves but full credit to the whole team, with seven
minutes of normal playing time to go, only two points separated the sides. Finally Clare's experience, strength, class
and determination told. In the closing stages we had to
admire what could only be described as an awesome display of score taking by the Banner County. The Corkmen
had given it their best shot and went away satisfied that
few teams of any era would have held Clare on the day.
There could be no argument about it – a superb Clare team
thoroughly deserved victory.

Frank Lohan had held Joe Deane to a single point from
play, Anthony Daly had blotted out Seanie McGrath and
Mr consistent, Brian Corcoran, wasn't given an inch in
which to operate. On that occasion maybe it was Another
Level, the name of the group responsible for the current
number one hit 'Freak Me' which was most appropriate.
As in the the first round match at Limerick, the Cork team
line-out remained unchanged. We concluded that if Jimmy
Barry-Murphy stayed on in charge the setback would be
temporary. The spring and early summer of 1999 would
reveal all.

The Clare team was: David Fitzgerald, Brian Quinn,
Brian Lohan, Frank Lohan, Liam Doyle, Seanie McMahon,
Colin Lynch, Ollie Baker, David Forde, Jamsie O'Connor,
P.J. O'Connell, Eamonn Taaffe, Alan Markham, and Niall
Gilligan.

HURLING BY THE BACKDOOR, POOR TIMING, REPLAYS, BUT
OFFALY BENEFITS
Clare went on to retain the Munster championship they
won in 1997 but only after the sternest test by a good

Waterford team. There was no winner at the first attempt. In the replay Clare took the spoils with a comfortable 2-16 to 0-10 win. As controversy continued surrounding the pros and cons of a system whereby the beaten finalists in Munster and Leinster re-entered the championship, Waterford and Offaly did just that. The Faithful County had gone down to the Noresiders in the Leinster final. In the All-Ireland quarter-finals played in Croke Park on 26 July, it was the 'back door' teams of Waterford and Offaly who advanced to the All-Ireland semi-finals by virtue of wins over Galway and Antrim. The scores were Waterford 1-20; Galway 1-10 and, Offaly 2-18; Antrim 2-9. The semi-final pairings were Offaly versus Clare, and Kilkenny versus Waterford. Kilkenny accounted for Waterford at Croke Park on 16 August but only by the narrowest of margins. The final score was Kilkenny 1-11; Waterford 1-10. The Clare versus Offaly duel led to a mini-marathon of hurling which began on 9 August and finished on 29 August. In all three matches were played. The first one ended in a draw, Offaly 1-13, Clare 1-13. It was followed by a match declared void because of a timekeeping error. The score was Clare 1-16; Offaly 2-10. At the third attempt Offaly were victorious, winning by three points. The final score was Offaly 0-16; Clare 0-13.

Not unlike the 1997 scenario when two Munster teams met in the All-Ireland final, in 1998 again a unique pairing of two Leinster teams, Kilkenny and Offaly, competed. The 'backdoor' re-entry to the championship came in for renewed criticism, and to further raise the hackles, Offaly became All-Ireland champions on Sunday 16 September when they defeated the team to which they had succumbed in the Leinster championship back on 5 July. Confused? Stranger than fiction some said!

Nevertheless, it was the September scoreline of Offaly 2-16; Kilkenny 1-13 which determined the All-Ireland Hurling champions of 1998. The title of a number one hit single back in April, 'It's Like That' by Run-DMC Vs Jason Nevins explains it all.

ASSEMBLY IN PLACE, YET VIOLENCE BRINGS NEW LEVEL OF
ABHORRENCE

While the hurling fraternity in this country and soccer's
World Cup enthusiasts around the globe were having the
time of their lives during the summer of 1998, what else
was happening? Well, for one thing France won the World
Cup. In Newtownhamilton, County Armagh on the eve of
25 June, the day Northern Ireland voters elected 108 members to an Assembly established under the Good Friday
Agreement, and endorsed by the 22 May referendum, a car
bomb caused widespread damage and injured a thirteen-
year-old boy. In July, when members of the Assembly met
for the first time at Stormont, Ulster Unionist Party Leader
David Trimble was elected First Minister, and SDLP man
Seamus Mallon became Deputy First Minister.

On the ground little had changed. Arson attacks on
Roman Catholic properties continued, and the now annual
Drumcree/Gervaghy Road related violence erupted
province wide. Indeed it led to the deaths of three children
whose home was attacked by petrol bombs. Sadly, as the
month of August came and went the people of this island
were left stunned by the callousness of those who chose to
plant bombs with a total disregard for life. A dissident
organisation calling itself the Real IRA was the main per-
petrator. First it was a car bomb at Banbridge, County
Down, where fortunately lives were not lost. On 15
August, a day now permanently etched on the minds of so
many, men of evil struck at the heart of Omagh, leaving 28
people dead. Included were men, women and children. A
further 200 victims of the atrocity were injured, some seriously. The aftermath of the Omagh tragedy, which later
claimed a further life, brought with it even more powerful-
ly than the Enniskillen outrage the realisation that the chief
victims of terrorism were innocent individuals; ordinary
people going about their business who were in no way
responsible for, nor involved in, political conflict. A glance
at the death list resulting from the dastardly deed speaks
for itself – a woman pregnant with twins, three schoolchildren from Donegal, Spanish visitors, and a twelve-
year-old cub scout. In the days, weeks and months which

followed the gross act of inhumanity, it seemed that the widespread revulsion coming from all quarters might inject new purpose and resolve into the ailing peace process.

Yet, even with the announcement of an INLA ceasefire, stumbling blocks held solid. Early prisoner release, power sharing, and no movement in the decommissioning of weapons continued to impede progress. There were times when the title of a July number one hit, 'Deeper Underground' by Jamiroquai seemed apt in the circumstances.

Those who took an interest in the chart toppers of the time may have been encouraged by contributions from the Spice Girls and Boyzone respectively – 'Viva Forever' and 'No Matter What'.

TRIALS AND TRIBULATIONS BUT YEAR ENDS ON A 'HIGH' FOR SOME

Running parallel to the events in our own country was a drama being played out in the United States. The now-familiar Monica Lewinsky, in her evidence to a grand jury, contradicted the sworn statement of President Clinton, who denied having sexual relations with her. Later the president admitted to an 'inappropriate physical relation'. Later still, while on a visit to Ireland, and at a time when the president faced increasing pressure from within the ranks of the Democratic Party, he further admitted, 'I made a bad mistake, its indefensible and I'm sorry'.

As autumn faded John Hume and David Trimble were jointly awarded the 1998 Nobel Peace Prize for their efforts to find a solution to the Northern Ireland troubles. In 1998, hurricane Mitch caused an estimated 10,000 deaths in Central America. In a single incident a mud slide engulfed 1,500 people. Hurricane George was responsible for a death toll which ran into hundreds, and created havoc in the Caribbean and parts of the United States.

In that part of the world too an event took place which would have been unthinkable ten years previously. It was the visit of Pope John Paul II to communist Cuba. An

estimated 50,000 people attended an open air Mass celebrated by the Pontiff.

What appeared to be a never-ending stream of number
one hits continued to resound. In September, first it was 'If
You Tolerate this Your Children Will Be Next' by Manic
Street Preachers, followed by All Saints, 'Bootie';
'Millennium' by Robbie Williams; and 'I Want You Back'
by Melanie B featuring Miss Elliott.

In November a high profile trial at the special criminal
court in Dublin ended with the conviction of Paul Ward for
murder in connection with the assassination of Veronica
Guerin. Veronica, one of the country's most prominent
journalists, died in June 1996. In spite of the thorny problem of decommissioning being far from resolved,
December saw Northern Ireland political leaders clinch a
deal on a new executive and cross-border bodies. It was
hailed by David Trimble as the most important step in the
peace process since the Good Friday Agreement.

South of the border, it was news of a £2,000,000 tax
claim against former Taoiseach, Charles Haughey, being
dropped by the Revenue Commissioners, which caused
uproar. As the penultimate year of the century drew to a
close, Baghdad was at the receiving end of a punishing air
offensive carried out by United States and British forces.
At the same time accusations of violence and homelessness
in Kosovo resulting from Serb aggression reached us
through the media on a daily basis. Local news told of
storms wreaking havoc in the west of Ireland, and a road
death toll of 454 people in the past year.

Appropriately, a proliferation of number one hit singles began in October with 'Rollercoaster' by B*Witched.
Before the end of the month, 'Girlfriend' by Billie, 'Gym
and Tonic' by Stardust, and 'Believe' by Cher each graced
top position. B*Witched returned in December with 'To
You I Belong'.

Personalities who lost their lives one way and another
during 1998 included: Mick McCarthy, Cork footballer;
Tommy Quaid, Limerick hurler; Noel Carroll, athlete; Tom
Craddock, golfer; Justin Fashanu, soccer player, Fred
David, snooker player; Flo Jo – Florence Griffith Joyner,

athlete; Billy Bremner, soccer player; John Hunt, mountaineer; Archie Moore, boxer; Paddy Clancy, singer; Frank Sinatra, singer and actor; Tammy Wynette, country singer; Dermot Morgan, actor and writer; Denis Joseph Fitzgerald – Den Joe, radio personality; Maurice O'Doherty, RTE newsreader; Sybil Connolly, fashion designer; Sir John Mills, actor; Gene Autry, the singing cowboy; Roy Rogers, the Lone Star Ranger; Reg Smythe, creator of Andy Capp; Fred Francis, scalextric inventor; Pol Pot, Cambodian notorious dictator; Enoch Powell, politician; and Joe Christie, reputed to have demolished Dublin's Nelson's Pillar.

Looking back on 1998 in the Republic of Ireland, the Celtic Tiger was said to have roared louder than ever. On the field of sport the lions share of plaudits went to the Under-18, and Under-16 soccer teams who excelled in becoming champions of Europe. Excelling too were athletes Sonia O'Sullivan and Catherina McKiernan. Sonia returned to form and won two gold medals at the European Championships, while Catherina became queen of the marathon, only narrowly missing out on the world record. It was also the year in which a postman was awarded £43,500 and costs when he took an action against his employers. He claimed that low level letter boxes had been responsible for a back problem he had suffered with since 1993. The Republic too made its mark on the drug scene. On one hand it had the fourth highest rate of cannabis-related arrests per capita in Europe, while on the other hand research chemists in Cork definitely made it big, and raised more than an eyebrow by developing a drug which hit pharmaceutical stores worldwide with a bang! Yes, it was of course Viagra! Could it have something to do with the fact that the largest space explosion ever recorded by astronomers occurred in 1998? What a success story on which to round off the year; no doubt further expansion is in the pipeline! Fittingly, the Spice Girls saw 1998 out with their number one hit, 'Goodbye'.

1999

An End Maybe, but Admiration and a Concert

From early January onwards, 1999 was labelled the year which marked the end, not only of a decade, or even a century, but a millennium. As if to register protest the latter days of 1998 were accompanied by hurricane-force winds in the midlands, north, and northwest of Ireland. Up to 160,000 householders were without power over the holiday period. Further evidence of the wind ferocity can be gauged from the fact that 1,800 Electricity Supply Board poles were knocked down.

In some ways 1998 may have been stormy for President Clinton of the United States, but when American's were asked to vote for their most admired man, the president topped the poll. By the same token, the First Lady, Mrs Clinton, was voted the most admired woman.

1999 was still young when Boyzone, the Irish band with six UK number one singles to its credit, thrilled 1,000 teenagers packed into Omagh Leisure Centre for a special tribute concert.

Ulster Joy, Snippets, NATO Decides, and a Pair of Irish Ladies

In the world of sport, Saturday 30 January was a red-letter day for followers of Ulster rugby. The thousands of northern fans who converged on Dublin for the European Rugby Cup final were amply rewarded when their team emerged victorious. A great day for Ulster and Irish rugby!

Snippets from abroad during February and March told of widespread violence across Kosovo with Serbs shelling and burning Albanian villages; a helicopter rescue in the French Alps which resulted in three skiers being plucked to safety having spent nine days in a makeshift igloo 3,000m up the mountain; intense bombing of Iraq's military targets by United States' aircraft; and a new

$79,000,000 space telescope which, according to NASA reports, failed to orbit five days after its launch.

Five had a number one hit with 'Keep On Movin'', followed by Geri Halliwell's chart topper, 'Lift Me Up' and Westlife's number one hit, 'Flying Without Wings'.

In March, devastating condemnation of incompetence, bad management and lack of political control led to the forced collective resignation of EU Commissioners. A conclusion drawn from a report into allegations of corruption and nepotism in the EU Commission stated, 'It is becoming difficult to find anyone who has the slightest sense of responsibility'.

Later in the month when thousands of ethnic Albanians were fleeing Kosovo because of Serb atrocities, NATO controversially decided that air strikes would commence against the Serb-led Yugoslavian war machine of President Slobodan Milosevic.

On a 'higher' note, after nineteen days aloft, a Swiss doctor and a British pilot crossed an invisible line on Africa's map and became the first to realise man's century-old dream of circling the world in a hot-air balloon.

Early April was a time of joy for Ireland's Kirsten Sheridan, because at Dresden Film Festival she won first prize in her category for the best short film. Sinead O'Connor was also in the news when she was ordained to the priesthood by dissenting bishop, Michael Cox. He became £150,000 richer in the process. Ms O'Connor explained she gave the money as 'an act of charity'.

THE HIGHS AND LOWS OF LATE SPRING AND EARLY SUMMER
When wind caused widespread damage to properties and uprooted trees in Ballygawley, County Sligo, Met Éireann believed a tornado had hit the village.

In Rome, Padre Pio was beatified by Pope John Paul II. The imposing ceremony in St Peter's Square was attended by more than 300,000 people, including 1,000 Irish pilgrims.

Early May marked Nelson Mandela's retirement from public life, while Dana, singer and former presidential candidate, announced her intention to run in the elections to

331

the European Parliament. Maybe there was a belated message for the electorate in Robbie William's number one hit, 'She's the One'.

Manchester United Football Club achieved European glory by winning the Champions League Cup. That success along with claiming the Premier League and the FA Cup completed a historic treble for one season – 1998/9.

Among the earliest summer visitors to Ireland were 138 Kosovan refugees. Given a free choice between coming to Ireland and living in peace at home, they would almost certainly have chosen the latter.

Yet, freedom was in the air, because that is what Gay Byrne and Hilary Clinton respectively received from the cities of Dublin and Galway. Around the same time the population of Galway city was reported to be growing at 450 per cent faster than the national rate.

Towards the end of May, figures issued by the government of the Irish Republic showed that the Flood and Moriarty tribunals had cost £6,000,000 to date. The amount may seem less substantial when placed in context of the £20,000,000 paid at Christies' New York spring sale for Van Gogh's, 'Canal with Washerwoman'.

June had arrived, the Munster hurling championship of 1999 had already taken its first steps but it would be midmonth before the red jerseys of Cork would adorn Semple Stadium. Another stadium, Croke Park, headquarters of Gaelic games, played host to around 30,000 people on Sunday 6 June. The occasion was not a hurling or football match but the one hundredth anniversary of the Pioneer Total Abstinence Association.

Meanwhile, South African, Cathy O'Dowd, became the first woman to scale Mount Everest from both its southern and more treacherous northern slopes; constructors of Russia's Mir space station decided to abandon the thirteen-year-old vessel and bring it down into the Pacific Ocean early in 2000; the career of Ireland's triple-winning Olympic swimming champion, Michelle de Bruin, appeared to have ended when the Court of Arbitration for Sport in Lausanne, Switzerland, rejected her appeal against a four-year ban imposed last summer by FINA, the Sports governing body; and the outcome of elections to the European Parliament held on 11 June resulted in Dana winning a seat in the Connaught-Ulster constituency.

THE UNFOLDING OF A CHAMPIONSHIP

My immediate interest was focused on the unfolding in the southern province of the new hurling season. On 22 May at Thurles, Kerry and Tipperary literally got the ball rolling. As expected the Premier County won (4-29 to 2-6). The likely outcome of the second Munster championship match between Waterford and Limerick was not so easy to predict. Waterford emerged victorious (1-16 to 1-15); a nervous one point win according to reports.

At the semi-final stage, first off the blocks were Clare and Tipperary. They met at Páirc Uí Chaoimh on Sunday 6 June in a match which produced some sparkling hurling from both sides. Tipperary seemed destined for the final but slipped up and Clare forced a draw (2-12 to 0-18). Cork and Waterford met in the second semi-final on Sunday 13 June at Thurles. The replay between Clare and Tipperary took place at Páirc Uí Chaoimh on Saturday 12 June.

I arrived at Páirc Uí Chaoimh just in time to witness the hurlers of Clare trounce Tipperary(1-21 to 1-11) in the Munster championship replay.

THE DAY THE SERIOUS STUFF BEGAN

It was the following Sunday that Cork's hurlers began their 1999 championship quest. Groups of people were already wandering about the streets when we arrived in Thurles at 10.30am. Of those we spoke to, few gave Cork more than an outside chance of beating Waterford. Seldom, if ever, had I experienced so many Cork followers who expected so little from their hurling team on Munster semi-final day. Throughout a mediocre National League campaign, umpteen players had been tried out but a settled side had not emerged. In the end of the day the youngest and, consequently the most inexperienced team ever to represent Cork in senior championship hurling were selected to face the might of a tried and talented Waterford side. Yes, Jimmy Barry-Murphy and his selectors, among them former stars, stood to have their very considerable reputations badly tarnished if their bold and courageous actions backfired.

Referee Aodán Mac Suibhne let battle commence at 3.30pm. There was little to choose between the teams in the first twenty minutes, during which time the scores were level on four occasions. Waterford had played with a certain assuredness but missed out on crucial scoring chances. However, from a Cork point of view all was well and the sceptics were beginning to take note.

It was clear that Jimmy Barry-Murphy's team was not going to be overwhelmed. As on so many previous occasions, it was Brian Corcoran who showed the way. Playing at centre-half back, he took control of that key area from the outset. Cork's midfield players, Mickey O'Connell and team captain Mark Landers, were fiercely competitive, and indeed were to impose themselves to the extent that they dominated. Tony Browne, who came into the match with a huge reputation, completely failed to match Mickey O'Connell. Indeed O'Connell's tremendous striking from far out the field was a feature of the first-half.

Mark Landers played a real captain's part with a fine display of strength and consistency. Early on Diarmuid O'Sullivan looked a little vulnerable against Waterford's ace full-forward, Paul Flynn, but he rode that storm to finish up having an outstanding game. The man between the posts, Donal Óg Cusack, was flawless, while Fergal Ryan and John Browne enhanced their reputations by the minute. To the right and left of the magnificent Brian Corcoran, Wayne Sherlock and Séan Óg Ó hAilpín were the essence of consistency and dependability. What of the forwards? From the start Fergal McCormack was effective. He found Stephen Frampton a handful, but worked hard with success in a vital sector of the field. Seanie McGrath and Timmy McCarthy tried hard but struggled to get into the game in the first-half. The supply of ball to Joe Deane was limited but he did look threatening when in possession.

Corner-forwards Ben O'Connor and Neil Ronan worked tirelessly, with Ben being the more effective of the two. For Waterford, Fergal Hartley, who was to retire injured at half-time, and Peter Queally both gave fine first-half performances. At the interval the score was Cork 0-10; Waterford 0-7. To date the revelation of the day was Cork's Mickey O'Connell. His work rate was phenomenal, and each of his attempted scores, whether from placed balls or play, regardless of distance, sailed straight over the bar. In spite of earlier negative expectations, one of the biggest crowds ever to follow the Rebels to Thurles for a provincial semi-final were perceivably pleased during the interval.

The restart brought with it a renewed determination from the Decies men. Ken McGrath, Stephen Frampton, Brian Flannery and Tom Feeney soon became prominent. At one stage only a single point separated the sides. However, the Corkmen showed their fighting spirit and, by the forty-seventh minute had the three-point margin restored. Brian Corcoran was not as influential as he had been early on but Diarmuid O'Sullivan was inspirational at full-back. Inspirational too was right-half forward, Timmy McCarthy, who had a marvellous second-half. His strong running at the Waterford defence caused a serious problem for the Decies mentors. A tricky period came for the Leesiders following a Paul Flynn goal in the fifty-sixth minute. It was followed by a Dan Shanahan point, leaving only the narrowest of margins separating the scores.

First to react for the Rebels was Mark Landers who again opened up a two-point gap. Waterford were not to score again until the last minute of the match. Cork's young charges had finished much the stronger of the two sides. The final score was Cork 0-24; Waterford 1-15.

The Cork team was: Donal Óg Cusack, Fergal Ryan, Diarmuid O'Sullivan, John Browne, Wayne Sherlock, Brian Corcoran, Séan Óg Ó hAilpín, Mark Landers (captain), Mickey O'Connell, Timmy McCarthy, Fergal McCormack, Seanie McGrath, Ben O'Connor, Joe Deane and Neil Ronan. The subs were: Kevin Murray for Ben O'Connor; Alan Browne for Seanie McGrath The scorers were: Mickey O'Connell 0-8 (0-2 frees, 0-1 65, 0-1 sideline); Joe Deane 0-7 (0-4 frees); Timmy McCarthy 0-3; Mark Landers 0-2, Brian Corcoran, Fergal McCormack, Ben O'Connor and Kevin Murray 0-1 each.

The Waterford team was: Brendan Landers, Tom Feeney, Séan Cullinane, Brian Flannery (captain), Peter Queally, Stephen Frampton, Brian Green, Tony Browne, Fergal Hartley, Dan Shanahan, Billy O'Sullivan, Ken McGrath, Michael White, Paul Flynn and Dave Bennett. The subs were: Pat Walsh for Fergal Hartley; Anthony Kirwan for Brian Greene; and Michael Malumphy for Dave Bennett. The scorers were: Paul Flynn 1-4 (1-3 frees); Ken McGrath 0-4 (0-1, 65); Dan Shanahan 0-3; Dave Bennett, Michael White, Stephen Frampton(free); and Michael Malumphy (free), 0-1 each. The 45,806 attendance had been entertained to a fine game of hurling.

Man-of-the-match selection could not have been easier. Mickey O'Connell, the young man from Midleton, had excelled in virtually all aspects of midfield play over 70 minutes. Jimmy Barry-Murphy's youthful charges had served notice that Cork hurling was back. The thoughts of Cork fans soon turned to the Munster final meeting with the Banner County, whose display against Tipperary in the replay was truly awesome.

THE RETURN TO THURLES

Sunday 4 July was showdown day at Thurles. A sell-out 54,554 crowd thronged Semple Stadium. Along with my son, John, we stopped off in Roscrea overnight on our way from Ballycastle. Never outside of Cork did we meet so many Rebel County well wishers and all of them staunch Tipperary supporters. How times had changed! Sunday morning in Thurles was the centre of the universe for the avid hurling followers of Cork and Clare. A magnificent atmosphere prevailed. Inside the Stadium it was like old times. The buzz, the magic, the colour, the apprehension. It was all there. As the young Corkmen and the more mature Claremen strode around in the pre-match parade on Munster final day, I experienced something which had been long absent. It was that unique shiver up the spine which culminates with the hair seeming to stand out in the back of your head – a shiver generated on such occasions by pride, passion and tension.

Soon all eyes were on referee Dickie Murphy as he

prepared to throw in the sliotar. Cork were first to score – a Joe Deane free. It was Jimmy Barry-Murphy's men who were first to gain the initiative even though the scores were level at one, three and four points. By half-time the Rebels had opened up a six point lead (1-10 to 0-7).

The Leesiders had indeed performed magnificently. Only the presence of Niall Quinn, Republic Of Ireland soccer international star, distracted us a little during the interval, as he stood nearby signing autographs for starry-eyed fans. Clare opened the second-half in the style we had become accustomed to. What had manager, Ger Loughnane, said in the dressing room? Over a 24-minute period the Banner County outscored Cork by 0-6 to 0-1! The whole scenario had changed! Clare's defence had noticeably tightened up. Liam Doyle in particular was covering right across the half-back line. Fergal McCormack brought some respite to the Corkmen but only temporarily because Clare soon added on a further three points without reply. Then it was Ben O'Connor who stopped the rot in the fifty-ninth minute to leave the score precariously fixed at Cork 1-12; Clare 0-13. In the closing twelve minutes of the match a never-say-die youthful Cork team rallied and showed the stern stuff they were made of. We saw a sterling defence complimented by the combined shooting power of Joe Deane and Ben O'Connor who between then added 0-3 to Cork's tally. In reply Niall Gilligan slotted over a single point for Clare. The 70 minutes were up, added on time was being played and the score was 1-14 to 0-14 in favour of Cork. Then what brought me the greatest relief of the day happened. From a difficult angle, well out the wing, Ben O'Connor sent the sliotar arrow-like over the bar. It was the insurance point – a four-point lead. Within a minute I was dancing like a ten-year-old on the seats of Semple Stadium. We had beaten Clare and we were Munster champions!!

The Cork team was identical to that which lined out against Waterford in the semi-final. The subs were: Pat Ryan for Mark Landers; Alan Browne for Neil Ronan; and Kevin Murray for Seanie McGrath. The scorers were: Joe Deane 1-4 0-4 frees), Mickey O'Connell 0-5 (0-2 frees, 0-1

65), Seanie McGrath 0-2, Ben O'Connor 0-2, Neil Ronan and Fergal McCormack 0-1 each. The Clare team was: David Fitzgerald, Frank Lohan, Brian Lohan, Brian Quinn, Liam Doyle, Sean McMahon, Anthony Daly (captain), Ollie Baker, Colin Lynch, Enda Flannery, David Forde, Alan Markham, Niall Gilligan, Ronan O'Hara, and Barry Murphy. The subs were: Danny Scanlan for Brian Quinn; John Reddan for Ollie Baker; and Conor Clancy for Ronan O'Hara. The scorers were: David Forde 0-3 (0-2 frees), Niall Gilligan 0-3, Ollie Baker 0-2, Ronan O'Hara, Sean McMahon (free), Alan Markham, Barry Murphy, Colin Lynch, and Danny Scanlan 0-1 each.

We reflected on the match and concluded that Cork's solid defence was the key component of the victory. Again Donal Óg Cusack was flawless. Not surprisingly, Fergal Ryan was a candidate for man-of-the-match. Beside him Diarmuid O'Sullivan and John Browne were towers of strength. Brian Corcoran did not have an awe-inspiring match by his standards but the displays of Wayne Sherlock and Seán Óg Ó hAilpín mirrored all that is good about this tenacious, battling Cork team. While Mickey O'Connell did not reach the dizzy heights of the previous match he was still tremendously effective. The same could be said of his midfield partner Mark Landers but it had to be remembered that their opposite numbers, Ollie Baker and Colin Lynch, are top performers. Indeed the loss of Ollie Baker through injury had a huge impact on the match. Cork's forwards were certainly a match for the highly-acclaimed Clare defence. Joe Deane, Seanie McGrath and Ben O'Connor always looked the part – competent, alert, compact and accurate. It wasn't one of Timmy McCarthy's best days but along with Neil Ronan and Fergal McCormack, he contributed to a fine Cork victory. Pat Ryan, Kevin Murray and Alan Browne who came on as substitutes, showed how important they are to the squad. Their input when Cork needed it most was vital.

THE FAITHFUL COUNTY BECKONED
On Sunday 8 August 1999 there was only one place for followers of Cork and Offaly hurling to be. It was at Croke

Park for the All-Ireland semi-final clash between the Munster champions and the current All-Ireland holders. It had been a long time since 1992 when the Rebels last graced Croke Park on All-Ireland hurling semi-final day. Jimmy Barry-Murphy's youthful team would again have to prove themselves when pitted against a vastly experienced and talented Offaly side. Doubts still lingered in the minds of some as to how they would fare in the heat of battle at Croke Park.

As in the Munster final, Dickie Murphy was the man with the whistle. At 3.30pm he duly obliged the 37,629 attendance by getting the match underway. Cork played into the teeth of a strong wind in the first-half. The Offalymen were first to exert pressure and as the half progressed there were times when the Rebels felt the pinch. Once again Cork were blessed to have Brian Corcoran on their side. He was there like a colossus in the middle of the defence, catching and clearing the sliotar with panache and determination, time after time. Such play was the tonic which inspired confidence in his teammates. Offaly's Johnny Dooley and his midfield partner Johnny Pilkington were causing major problems for Mickey O'Connell and Mark Landers. Yet the Corkmen continued to battle in the fashion we had now come to expect. At times both sides produced great hurling. By the interval Offaly had 0-10 on the scoreboard to Cork's 0-9. Joe Deane had scored a total of 0-7 (0-4 frees). Cork's remaining two scores came from Fergal McCormack and Seanie McGrath. In a five-minute spell immediately after the interval the young Cork forwards demonstrated their very considerable skills in a way that was to pay rich dividends. Back came the All-Ireland champions to reply with a defiance which was to make the match memorable. We were treated to the wondrous defensive play of the Whelahan brothers, Brian and Simon; the marksmanship of the Dooley brothers, Johnny and Joe; the magic of John Troy; the commanding full-back play of Kevin Kinihan; and the apparent leisurely style of hurling genius, Johnny Pilkington.

On the sixty-first minute when Johnny Dooley stroked over a point, the score stood at 0-16 to 0-14 in favour of

Offaly. By the sixty-sixth minute the scores were level thanks to the shooting talents of Kevin Murray and Joe Deane. The younger legs of the Rebels began to tell, and the now customary final assault was launched. It was an assault which resulted in three further points being added on without reply from Offaly. To their credit the Faithful County men battled to the final whistle. In spite of their efforts to force a goal, the immaculate Donal Óg Cusack stopped and cleared the sliotar which got behind the formidable defence in which Brian Corcoran, Fergal Ryan, Diarmuid O'Sullivan and John Browne were outstanding. The final score was Cork 0-19; Offaly 0-16.

Cork were through to the All-Ireland final! Cork's team lined out as in the previous championship matches. The subs were: Alan Browne for Neil Ronan; Kevin Murray for Timmy McCarthy; and Johnny Sheehan for Mickey O'Connell. The scorers were: Joe Deane 0-10 (0-7 frees), Fergal McCormack 0-2, Seanie McGrath 0-2, Ben O'Connor 0-2, Mickey O'Connell, Alan Browne and Kevin Murray 0-1 each. The Offaly team was: Stephen Byrne, Simon Whelahan, Kevin Kinahan, Martin Hanamy, Brian Whelahan (captain), Hubert Rigney, Kevin Martin, Johnny Dooley, Johnny Pilkington, Paudie Mulhare, John Ryan, Michael Duignan, John Troy, Joe Erritty and Joe Dooley. The subs were: Billy Dooley for Joe Erritty; and Gary Hanniffy for John Ryan. The scorers were: Johnny Dooley 0-5 (0-3 frees), Joe Dooley 0-2, John Troy 0-2, Johnny Pilkington 0-2, Paudie Mulhare, Michael Duignan, Billy Dooley, Brian Whelahan (free), and John Ryan 0-1 each.

GLORYO, GLORYO TO BOLD JIMMY'S YOUNG MEN
Sunday 12 September 1999 marked the return of a Cork hurling team to Croke Park on All-Ireland final day. It had been all of seven years, away back in 1992, since the Rebel County last competed for hurling's ultimate inter-county trophy – the Liam McCarthy Cup. Except for a few Cork true-blues, the young Rebels were given no chance. I failed to understand the extent to which Kilkenny were installed as favourites. To date, the Noresiders' major championship scalps had been Offaly and Clare. Cork had also beaten

those teams! It had to be maturity and experience which swayed the pundits, but why so? The Leesiders had already dealt with those assets in the current championship, not once, but trice.

We arrived in Dublin at 11am, and joined our Cork counterparts at the Sunnybank Hotel, a now long established meeting place for us on Croke Park days. Later as we made our way to the venue, the rain which had threatened for so long did eventually come. Undaunted, an attendance of 62,989 had gathered by the time referee Pat O'Connor of Limerick let battle commence. On a wet and slippery surface there was much huffing and puffing from both sides, but little in the way of scores. It took Cork eight minutes to hit the target, and Kilkenny a further twelve minutes. At that stage Mark Landers (0-1) and Timmy McCarthy (0-2) had Cork three point ahead. It was Henry Shefflin (0-1 free) who opened Kilkenny's account on the Noresiders tenth scoring attempt.

By half-time a total of 23 misses had spectators looking on in disbelief. The score was Kilkenny 0-5; Cork 0-4. So far it had not been an All-Ireland final for the purists.

Reflecting on the opening 35 minutes of play, again it was the resolve of Cork's defence which stood out. The magnificent Brian Corcoran had eclipsed John Power, Séan Óg Ó hAilpín had shown just how good he is by keeping Kilkenny's ace performer, D.J. Carey out of the game, and Wayne Sherlock hurled brilliantly after allowing Brian McEvoy a little leeway early on. In the rearguard, Donal Óg Cusack had done everything right, Fergal Ryan was having the game of his life, Diarmuid O'Sullivan had coped masterfully and John Browne, after a shaky start,soon settled. While Mark Landers had started well at mid-field, Mickey O'Connell found it hard to get into the game, and as the half progressed it was Andy Comerford and Denis Byrne who dominated. Forwards Timmy McCarthy, Fergal McCormack and young Neil Ronan worked hard with success. The fact that Neil Ronan was instrumental in making space for Fergal McCormack and in the setting up of Timmy McCarthy's first score did not go unnoticed. Of the inside trio, Seanie McGrath and Ben

O'Connor got more possession than Joe Deane. In the opening minute of the second-half Cork substitute Alan Browne hit over a great point.

Several positional changes in the Kilkenny team seemed to help their cause and four successive points without reply gave credence to that belief. By the fifty-first minute the Noresiders had opened up a four-point gap and Pat O'Neill was having his best spell at centre-half back. The character of Cork's young lions was now called upon as never before. This time they needed help from their mentors. It came in the form of Kevin Murray for the tiring Mark Landers and the decision to switch Timmy McCarthy to midfield. Within two minutes of his arrival on the pitch, Kevin Murray slotted over a desperately-needed Cork point. Timmy McCarthy now began to run menacingly at Kilkenny's defence, and suddenly we were seeing much more of Seanie McGrath's silken skills. The time had come for the young Corkmen to demonstrate the strong finish which had become their hallmark. They were not found wanting! From the last line of defence right through to the inside forwards they gave 100 per cent. The most exciting part of an otherwise lack lustre spectacle was at hand! Cork's talented forwards, greatly assisted by the unerring striking of Joe Deane, chipped away at Kilkenny's lead.

Seanie McGrath, with marvellous stick-work, clawed back three points and a now-rampant Timmy McCarthy laid claim to another. The sides were level! Ben O'Connor and Joe Deane put the Rebels two points ahead before Henry Shefflin struck back in the sixty-eight minute.

That was to be the last score of the match. With Cork at 0-13; Kilkenny 0-12 the long whistle sounded. Cork were All-Ireland hurling champions of 1999! Kilkenny's manager, Brian Cody, and his players were devastated. It was their second successive defeat at the final hurdle. But the Noresiders are big hearted men and rationally accepted that Cork had scored one point more than them. Once again the Cork team lined-out exactly as it had done since the first championship outing against Waterford back in June. The subs were: Alan Browne for Neil Ronan; and Kevin Murray for Mark Landers. The scorers were: Joe

Deane 0-3 (0-2 frees), Timmy McCarthy 0-3, Seanie McGrath 0-3, Mark Landers, Alan Browne, Kevin Murray and Ben O'Connor 0-1 each. The Kilkenny team was: James McGarry, Philip Larkin, Canice Brennan, Willie O'Connor, Michael Kavanagh, Pat O'Neill, Peter Barry, Andy Comerford, Denis Byrne (captain), D. J. Carey, John Power, Brian McEvoy, Ken O'Shea, Henry Shefflin, and Charlie Carter. The subs were: P.J. Delaney for John Power; and Niall Moloney for Charlie Carter. The scorers were: Henry Shefflin 0-5 (0-4 frees), Andy Comerford 0-2, Charlie Carter 0-2, John Power, Denis Byrne, and Brian McEvoy (sideline) 0-1 each.

There was much to reflect on in the wake of Cork's victory. The young team were most certainly a credit to themselves and the management team of Jimmy Barry-Murphy, Tom Cashman, Fred Sheedy, Seanie O'Leary, Johnny Crowley and Teddy Owens. If credit is to be fairly apportioned, I believe few would disagree that a large chunk of it should go to the man who had most to lose when earlier in the year he gambled by fielding a team with an average age of 22. Against Waterford in June the starting fifteen had amongst its ranks, Donal Óg Cusack, Wayne Sherlock, Mickey O'Connell, Timmy McCarthy, Neil Ronan and Ben O'Connor, each of whom were making their inter-county championship debuts. Yet, the same fifteen players started in each subsequent match. The confidence and unfailing belief which Jimmy Barry-Murphy placed in the young, never-say-die players had now been well and truly repaid. They had succeeded in enhancing the already awesome hurling folklore attributed to the great Corkman. The winning of the 1999 All-Ireland hurling championship was a personal triumph for the managerial skills of the former hurling and football maestro, Jimmy Barry-Murphy.

Jimmy Barry-Murphy left no one in doubt as to his depth of feelings and commitment when he opened his heart to the media – ' I'd have to say its the greatest day of my sporting life to see Cork back on top again'. As for the players, the team, the squad, what can one say? Magnificent! I feel obliged to mention the brilliant hurling talents of Brian Corcoran. He was ably assisted at any one time by fourteen other players each of whom has to be heartily congratulated. A special word has to be reserved for the leadership of team captain Mark Landers because his whole-hearted approach was inspirational. Let us not forget that Donal Óg Cusack made hurling history by becoming the first goalkeeper to retain a clean sheet in the provincial final, the All-Ireland semi-final and the final in the same year.

Back in Cork on the Monday night, 55,000 people turned out to welcome Jimmy Barry-Murphy and the Guinness All-Ireland Hurling champions of 1999 back home. A sea of flags, banners, hats and tops, turned the city-centre red. Yes, it had been a great year for the Rebel County's hurling followers.

So How Did Our Footballers Fare?

In a year when the hurlers of Cork went all the way in the championship, the Rebel County's footballers did their best to emulate them. They entered the championship fray as proud National League trophy holders with an easy win over Waterford at Dungarvan. The final score was Cork 3-23; Waterford 0-4. At Páirc Uí Rinn in June a semi-final meeting with Limerick resulted in the capitulation of the away side after a spirited first-half performance. The final score was Cork 4-13; Limerick 1-6. Ahead lay one of the big occasions in Munster's football calendar. It is a day with a particular gloss when Cork and Kerry are in opposition; it is the Munster final. On Sunday 18 July it was Kerry's turn to travel to Páirc Uí Chaoimh. Cork's team manager/coach was Larry Tompkins, the man who first appeared in a Cork jersey in 1987. Subsequently, he was hugely influential in the Rebel County getting to four All-Ireland finals in a row. He captained the All-Ireland winning side of 1990. He will continue to rate as one of the best centre-half forwards ever to play Gaelic football. Now in his third year in charge, he had built up a new look side which in May brought the National League trophy to Cork after an absence of ten years. Many observers saw the Cork versus Kerry Munster final clash as a defining moment for his young side.

On the day the team measured up to expectations. An

excellent second-half performance from the side captained by Philip Clifford of Bantry destroyed the Kingdom. The final score was Cork 2-10; Kerry 2-4. The Cork team and scorers: Kevin O'Dwyer, Ronan McCarthy, Séan Óg Ó hAilpín, Anthony Lynch, Ciarán O'Sullivan, Owen Sexton, Martin Cronin, Nicholas Murphy, Michael O'Sullivan (0-1), B.J. O'Sullivan, Joe Kavanagh (0-1), Pádraig O'Mahony (0-4), Philip Clifford (captain, 0-4), Don Davis, and Mark O'Sullivan. The subs and scorers were: Fachtna Collins (1-0) for B.J. O'Sullivan; and Fionán Murray (1-0) for Nicholas Murphy. The Kerry team and scorers: Declan O'Keeffe, Michael McCarthy, Barry O'Shea, Killian Burns, Tomás Ó Sé, Séamus Moynihan, Eamonn Breen, Dara Ó Sé, Donal Daly, John McGlynn (0-1), Liam Hassett, Dara Ó Cinnéide, John Crowley (captain, 0-2), Aodán MacGearailt (2-0), and Maurice Fitzgerald. The subs and scorer: Billy Ó Shea for Liam Hassett; William Kirby (0-1) for John McGlynn; and Mike Frank Russell for Aodán MacGearailt. It was a great day for Cork football and those associated with it, but none more than the young, talented Na Piarsaigh man, Séan Óg Ó hAilpín, who, in carrying on the great tradition of Cork dual players, collected a second senior Munster championship medal in the same year. Back the Cork fans came in force to Croke Park for the All-Ireland semi-final clash with Mayo. The Connacht champions had beaten Galway, the current All-Ireland holders, and came to Croke Park with renewed determination. Once again the Westerners were to disappoint by not realising their full potential on the day; a below par performance allowed Cork passage through to the All-Ireland final. The final score was Cork 2-12; Mayo 0-12. The Cork team and scorers: Kevin O'Dwyer, Ronan McCarthy, Séan Óg Ó hAilpín, Anthony Lynch, Ciaran O'Sullivan, Owen Sexton, Martin Cronin, Nicholas Murphy, Michael O'Sullivan, Micheál Cronin, Joe Kavanagh (0-1), Pádraig O'Mahony (0-3), Philip Clifford (captain, 0-4), Don Davis (0-2), and Mark O'Sullivan (0-1). The subs and scorer: Fachtna Collins for Micheál Cronin; Fionán Murray (1-1) for Pádraig O'Mahony; and B.J. O'Sullivan for Philip Clifford. The Mayo team and scorers: Peter Burke, Aidan Higgins, Kevin Cahill, Gordon Morley,

Fergal Costello, David Heaney, Alan Roche, James Nallen, David Brady (0-1), Kieran McDonald (0-3), Kenneth Mortimer (captain, 0-1), Colm McManaman (0-1), Maurice Sheridan (0-3), James Horan (0-3), and David Nestor. The subs were: Pat Fallon for Gordon Morley; John Casey for Kenneth Mortimer; and Liam McHale for David Nestor.

It was All-Ireland final day - football on this occasion. Sunday 26 September at Croke Park revived memories of the late 1980s and particularly of the famous day in 1990 when Cork completed the double. The double was again on the cards in 1999 and, as previously, Meath were the opponents. Cork's star hurling half-back Séan Óg Ó hAilpín was in line to emulate the feat of Teddy McCarthy by winning two All-Ireland senior medals in the same year. Alas, it was not to be! Instead, for the fourth time in twelve years, it was the mighty men of Meath who became champions. The match, attended by a crowd of 63,276, and well refereed by Mick Curley, was played in a sporting atmosphere, but did not reach classic status. The Leinster champions won despite failing to score from a penalty early in the second-half. Encouraged by Kevin O'Dwyer's save, Philip Clifford swung over a great point. It was followed by the most memorable moments of the match, when in the thirty-ninth minute Joe Kavanagh soloed and weaved his way through the Meath defence, played a quick one-two with Podsie O'Mahony, and duly dispatched the ball to the back of the net. Cork were in the lead, 1-6 to 1-5. Thoughts of the double loomed as Cork's supporters got behind their team. Lo and behold instead of driving home their advantage, the Corkmen resorted to a short-passing game, which to the exasperation of onlookers broke down again and again. It was painful to watch! Meath took full advantage of the inept play, and during that period outscored Cork by a 3 to 1 ratio - 0-6 to 0-2. The final score was Meath 1-11; Cork 1-8.

It was a disappointing result in a match which Cork could have won. Disappointment was greatest for the players and the management team of Larry Tompkins, Terry O'Neill, Conor Counihan, and Paddy Sheehan. Collectively they were the men who had worked so hard to reach the final. Meath team and scorers were: Cormac

O'Sullivan, Mark O'Reilly, Darren Fay, Cormac Murphy, Paddy Reynolds, Enda McManus, Hank Traynor, Nigel Crawford, John McDermott, Evan Kelly (0-3), Trevor Giles (0-4), Nigel Nestor, Ollie Murphy (1-0), Graham Geraghty (captain, 0-3) and Donal Curtis (0-1) The subs were: Richie Kealy for Nigel Nestor; Barry O'Callaghan for Hank Traynor; and Tommy Dowd for Evan Kelly.

Cork team and scorers were: Kevin O'Dwyer, Ronan McCarthy, Séan Óg Ó hAilpín, Anthony Lynch, Ciarán O'Sullivan, Owen Sexton, Martin Cronin, Nicholas Murphy, Michael O'Sullivan, Micheál Cronin, Joe Kavanagh (1-1), Pádraig O'Mahony (0-1), Philip Clifford (captain, 0-5), Don Davis, and Mark O'Sullivan (0-1). The subs were: Fionán Murray for Mark O'Sullivan; Fachtna Collins for Micheál Cronin; and Michael O'Donovan for Pádraig O'Mahony.

THE MONTH NOSTRADAMUS GOT IT WRONG AND AUGUST ARRIVED

Back in July, while many of us were absorbed in matters relating to hurling, news items which caught the eye were: 77 athletes from the Irish Republic took their honoured place among the nation's great sporting ambassadors at the opening of the Special Olympic Games in Raleigh, North Carolina; an announcement that Tory island off the Donegal coast was to get a secondary school; the world's first test-tube baby, Louise Brown, celebrated her twenty-first birthday; two Roman Catholic nuns in Colombia shot and killed an intruder; Manchester United and England football player, David Beckham and Posh Spice, Victoria Adams got married in Ireland; Dubliner Kevin McCrossan, in response to an order by a judge stood for four hours out-side the Allied Irish ATM on O'Connell Street, wearing a placard, on which the words – 'I apologise for urinating in O'Connell Street' were written; and a New York judge ruled women's breasts are no different than men's.

In early July, four airmen were killed when their Air Corps helicopter crashed near Tramore, County Waterford. The cause of the tragedy left investigators 'mys-tified'. Across the Atlantic on 18 July, a single-engine six-seater Piper Saratoga piloted by John F. Kennedy Jr plummeted into the sea off the coast of Massachusetts. On board were his wife and sister-in-law. The bodies of all three were later recovered from the sea bed.

It was in July too that an arson attack on an island homestead in Inishbofin resulted in the deaths of its occupants – three elderly ladies.

Thankfully the marching season in Northern Ireland reached its climax with little of the violence, death and destruction which had accompanied the Drumcree standoff in recent years. Yet the overall situation in the six-counties was far from good. A reported 158 men, women and children had been driven from their homes, shot or beaten since the beginning of 1999.

East Timor, half of a small South Pacific island 600 miles north of Australia and with a population of approximately 800,000 sounds as if it may well be one of those paradise islands advertised on a holiday brochure. The former Portuguese colony declared independence in 1975 and had lived in a state of conflict with the might of Indonesia ever since. In late 1975 Indonesia troops illegally invaded the island and forced East Timor to become an Indonesian province. In the interim Indonesia orchestrated tyranny against the resisting East Timor people had reportedly led to the deaths of over 200,000 civilians.

August's greatest claim to fame may have been the much published solar eclipse. People in this part of the world flocked to Cornwall in the south of England to get the best view, though the southwest of Ireland boasted of a 96 per cent totality.

The annual spate of natural disasters which in the first-half of the year appeared to be relatively few, began to make their presence felt as autumn approached. Headline makers were: an earthquake in Turkey which claimed in the region of 40,000 lives; a heatwave in the United States which contributed to the deaths of up to 200 people; and floods in South Korea which left at least ten dead and forced almost 11,500 people to flee submerged homes.

In Ireland: Brian Meehan was found guilty of the murder of journalist Veronica Guerin; Robbie Williams charmed 80,000 fans in brilliant sunshine at Slane Castle; the £65,000,000 Kildare by-pass, held up for six months at a cost of millions to protect a rare breed of snail, was about to get the all-clear; a summer school devoted to Bram Stoker, the creator of Dracula, claimed he may well have been an Irishman; and an Irish-related good news story from Brazil confirmed the Kerry Group opened a $20,000,000 plant in southern Brazil.

INTO THE LAST STRAIGHT

As the last straight of 1999 was about to be entered the East Timor crisis figured prominently. Mass murder and mayhem were among the terms used to describe what followed an election in which the electorate voted 78.5 per cent in favour of independence.

Pro-Indonesian militia resumed their campaign of terror. Thousands of civilians were murdered, terrorised, starved, and driven from their homes by armed thugs. Eventually President Habibie of Indonesia reluctantly agreed to let a UN peacekeeping force into East Timor.

Almost directly north of East Timor, off the coast of China and split by the Tropic of Cancer, is the island of Taiwan. On 22 September two major earth tremors hit Taiwan causing over 2,000 deaths and leaving 80,000 homeless.

As Cork's hurlers deservedly basked in the glory of their All-Ireland victory, the disturbing news of a savage attack which left Kilkenny's P.J. Delaney, a fellow hurler and contemporary unconscious, was reported. The incident, which took place outside a Thurles night club was abhorred nationwide.

It seemed that trouble and strife was destined to see the millennium out. Not even Christina Aguilera's number one hit 'Genie in a Bottle' helped. Now it was the turn of Chechnya. The story was a now familiar one – Chechnya wants independence from Russia, Russia says no, so war begins. Who suffers? The men, women and children who are forced to flee the ravages of war. They set out in their thousands with little food, clothes or money to seek refuge in nearby Ingushetia, a country struggling to feed its own people. The border crossings become sites of starvation and depravity.

'Jack Lynch Politician, Sportsman, 1917-1999', 'FAREWELL Honest Jack', 'Record six All-Ireland titles ensure legendary status', 'Last goodbye to the 'real taoiseach', 'A Nation Pays Tribute' – just some of the headlines which appeared following the death in October of Jack Lynch, the most favoured Cork son of all time. Contemporaries of the great man and people twenty years his junior will readily recall the deeds which made him legendary.

The mention of his name immediately triggers the vision of a great Cork hurler, truly one of the best. I remember being overcome by emotion at Semple Stadium, Thurles in 1984, when as part of the GAA centenary celebration, former hurling greats paraded on the pitch. Jack, the dual star of his day and the personification of Cork's sporting prowess, was given a tumultuous greeting by the crowd.

Moving from a sportsman of an era past to present day personalities, tennis enthusiasts will have noted that US Open champion Andre Agassi and retired ace Steffi Graf are now reportedly an 'item', while in the world of boxing a familiar surname, that of Ali, surfaced. Yes, the name does have a connection with the great Muhammad, it refers to his daughter Laila, who in her debut as professional women's heavyweight boxer, knocked out her opponent in the first-round.

In the Republic of Ireland, October was not a good time to be ill because the nurses went on strike. Huge nationwide backing in support of the strikers blamed the Government for the resulting chaos in hospitals.

The number one hit by Eiffel 65, 'Blue', may describe the feelings of dazed survivors and rescue workers who searched in freezing temperatures for signs of life in the rubble of Turkey's second devastating earthquake in less than three months. The quake, which shook the northwest of the country on 12 November resulted in 374 deaths and 3,000 injured.

In the Orissa region of eastern India a further natural

disaster struck with horrific consequences. A cyclone with a recorded wind speed of 162 miles per hour left up to 10,000 people dead, wiped out 1,000 villages and left around 2,000,000 people without homes or means of subsistence.

Egyptians too were to taste sorrow when a Boeing 767 plunged into the Atlantic close to the United States coastline. All 217 people on board Egypt Air Flight 990 died instantly.

There was however cause for celebration in some countries. Germany remembered the tenth anniversary of the Berlin Wall removal, whilst in Britain the crowning of Lennox Lewis as undisputed heavyweight boxing champion of the world was the occasion. China too had cause to celebrate because the massive Asian country joined the world's exclusive space club when it launched its first unmanned spacecraft. Australians, no strangers to sporting success, undoubtedly celebrated rugby's World Cup victory, and in the United States some property tycoons may well have had reason for glee when it was announced that Madison Avenue, New York is the world's most expensive street at a cost of $6,500 per square meter.

In Northern Ireland no one was celebrating just yet! After months of intense negotiation in which former United States' Senator George Mitchell played a major role, the future of the peace process ended up in the hands, or rather votes, of a divided Ulster Unionists Party. When the Ulster Unionist council voted on the review of the Good Friday agreement the pro-Northern Ireland Executive forming faction led by Mr David Trimble won the day. Power-sharing and devolution would become a reality but would not last if immediate decommissioning of some IRA weapons did not begin. Thereby hangs a tale!

Wamdue Project had a number one hit with 'King of my Castle' in mid-November, but before the month was out the popularity of Cliff Richard's 'Millennium Prayer' toppled it. The 'Prayer' was hit number 121 in the long and illustrious singing career of Sir Cliff.

The Celtic Tiger continued to roar. For the record: car sales in 1998 reached a record 145,000; the Central Statistics Office produced two sets of figures, one which showed that the number of couples employed had doubled in the ten years from 1986 to 1996, and the second which showed that in the last year about 10,000 British people came to live and work in Ireland; the Department of Justice too released statistics which showed a big upswing both in applications to the circuit court for divorce, and in the number of divorces granted; and President McAleese received an apology from the BBC.

A mother gave birth to triplets, one of whom was born outside her womb. According to Davor Jurkovic, consultant obstetrician, the chances of having such a pregnancy are one in 60,000,000; in 1998 the size of the hole in the ozone layer over Antarctica was the largest ever measured; a consultant dermatologist warned that people using sunbeds twice a week for more than two years could be at risk of developing skin cancer; human rights group Amnesty International called for an investigation into the disappearance of 3,000 Algerian citizens since 1993; in his speech on the occasion of the nineteenth anniversary of independence, the president of Zambia stated that 1,200 citizens of that country are dying of AIDS each week; according to findings by the International Labour Organisation in conjunction with the Tribhuvan University of Katmandu about 2,600,000 children between the ages of five and fourteen work in Nepal despite laws against child labour; German doctors were reported to have designed an artificial eye which blinks at the same time as the users healthy eye; the average British child was said to eat £103.35 worth of chocolate every year; a man who travelled 1,800 miles past his destination after falling asleep on an aircraft won a claim for damages against the airline that was transporting him; more than 37,000 Americans have insured themselves against being kidnapped – by aliens; and Monica Lewinsky said President Clinton was 'a good kisser'.

Among the young and not so young who departed this life in 1999 were: Jack Lynch, former Taoiseach and Cork GAA star; Ambrose Rodgers, Down and Ulster Gaelic football star; Siobhán O'Neill, Tyrone camogie star; Kevin Hassett, son of former Tipperary hurling star, Matt Hassett; Mrs Joan Fitzgerald, wife of former Taoiseach;

Rosemary Nelson, Human Rights lawyer; Neil Shanahan, motor racing driver; Lord Killanin (Michael Morris), former president of the International Olympic Committee; Cardinal Hume, Head of Roman Catholic Church in England; Jill Dando, television personality; William Payne Stewart, American golfer; Lena Zavaroni, singer/child star; Frankie Vaughan, singer; Dusty Springfield, singer; Oliver Reid, actor; George C. Scott, actor; and Viscount William Whitelaw, former Northern Ireland Secretary of State.

Cork county ended the millennium on a high note by winning the All-Ireland hurling championship with one of the youngest teams ever, capturing the Rose of Tralee crown, and having Clonakilty named the tidiest town in Ireland. Let's not forget our football team who went so close to showering further glory on the Rebel County.

2000

TRANSITION – OLD TO NEW

Perhaps we should have a new millennium more often! The enthusiasm generated by the arrival of the year 2000 might well justify such a modification! The transition of millennium to millennium was always likely to be special. So it proved to be! The world at large celebrated in unison as never before. Diversity of application saw firework displays on a scale hitherto unknown, bells rang out in record-breaking numbers and mankind feasted in a celebration to top all celebrations. Only one thing could have possibly derailed the bandwagon of merriment. It was Y2K, 'the millennium computer bug'. What a damp squib that turned out to be!

In the midst of all the jollity, one little girl was totally unaware of her history-making feat. She is Caroline Ann McGarr, the first baby born in the new millennium. The infant arrived one second past midnight at Dublin's Coombe hospital, thereby becoming Ireland's first citizen of the twenty-first century.

In the north of Ireland, along with the new millennium came a new dawn, hope for a new future. It came in the form of a power-sharing executive at Stormont and, the establishment of new All-Ireland political bodies.

On the world stage, perhaps the event which took most people by surprise was the resignation of Russia's President, Boris Yeltsin. Instead of what was expected to be a routine presidential New Year's message, an emotional Yeltsin deviated into a pronouncement of retirement and regret. So ended eight tempestuous years in office of a man who was often ill and sometimes unpredictable. Nevertheless, during his stewardship democracy was established in a country that had known only authoritarian rule for centuries.

Resignation was not on the agenda of popular music group Westlife. Instead with 'I Have a Dream'/'Seasons in

354

the Sun', they became the first act for over a year to stay at the number one spot for four weeks. Westlife's reign at the top of the singles chart ended when Manic Street Preachers with their hit called 'The Masses Against the Classes' took over in mid-January. A week later Britney Spears returned with her second number one single 'Born to Make You Happy'.

CARS AND POWER TROUBLES, A REAL TAOISEACH, BUT OH THOSE ABBREVIATIONS
On the first day of operation in early January, the National Car Test (NCT) in the Republic of Ireland, failed 79 per cent of vehicles examined. Some new car buyers found problems well removed from the NCT. There were no cars available for purchase! Demand outstripped supply to such an extent that in some cases a five-month wait became the order of the day. Indeed it was reported that Ireland's allocation of top of the range Mercedes CL, which retails at just over £110,000, sold out so quickly in January, that a new waiting list for next year's allocation had already begun.

The 'Tiger's' lungs must still be in fine fettle! If further evidence of the 'Tiger's' ability to roar was required, one had only to look towards a Government-expressed concern. It was the fear of major power cuts arising from the economic boom and its accompanying spiralling demand for electricity.

As the month came to a close, British soul diva Gabrielle knocked Britney Spears off the top spot with 'Rise'. Sadly, many were not in form to enjoy her music because a killer flu outbreak reached epidemic proportions. However, all was not doom and gloom, and it was pleasing to read that sufficient folk, healthy or otherwise, responded to a *Sunday Independent* telephone poll and voted Cork's 'real taoiseach', Jack Lynch, the best ever by a proverbial mile.

January is a quiet month on the GAA scene and as such journalists scrape around for headline stories. Like myself, some followers of the Association may initially have experienced difficulty with abbreviations such as

355

PAG and GPA. That the former referred to the GAA's Players Advisory Group, and latter to the Gaelic Players Association, soon became clear. Inevitably, disharmony between top exponents of our national games and the governing body of an association which has established itself as the premier sporting institution in our country, made for sad reading indeed.

A CRASH, A REFUSAL, BUT NUPTIALS, AN ARCHBISHOP AND TOPLESS IN KOBE

The arrival of February saw the new dawn and promise of a new future in Northern Ireland come crashing down. Reluctance by the Provisional IRA to decommission weapons was cited by Secretary of State, Peter Mandelson, as the reason for suspending the 72-day-old Stormont Assembly.

It was in February too that Trinity College, Dublin failed to be influenced by the Oasis number one hit tune 'Go Let It Out'. At least that's how it seemed, because the authorities of the august institution incensed local counsellors in Kells, County Meath, by refusing to return the Book of Kells to the town of its origin for a period of four weeks.

Disgruntlement in Kells perhaps but nothing of the kind over to the west in Knock. Not for the first time positive reporting came from the County Mayo village. This time it was the masterminding of twenty marriages in 1999 by two of its female residents.

Positive too was the appointment of Bishop Murphy-O'Connor as Archbishop of Westminster. A Corkman? With a name like Murphy-O'Connor he has to be! Around the same time appointments of a different kind were made in Kobe, Japan. There it was – topless female bank clerks.

MOZAMBIQUE, THE LEAGUE, A TRIAL, REFUGEES, ISTABRAQ AND RANGERS

As the month came to a close and All Saints made it to number one with 'Pure Shores', news of a flooding disaster in Mozambique attracted worldwide attention; thousands faced death as rising floodwaters threatened to sweep away people clinging to trees, rooftops, power pylons and dwindling patches of high ground.

Already the brand new year of the brand new millennium was beginning to show signs of slipping away. So much so that the early rounds of the Church and General National Hurling League were in progress. Cork, the All-Ireland champions started their campaign at Nowlan Park, Kilkenny on 20 February. The only absentee from the side which showered itself in glory during the 1999 championship was Seán Óg Ó hAilpín. His place was filled by Cobhman, Derek Barrett. Kilkenny emerged victors in what was described as 'a fine match'. The score was Kilkenny 1-13; Cork 0-12.

Cork's second outing on 12 March was a home match against a managerless Laois team which failed to provide meaningful opposition. The Rebels won a contest which was really all over at half-time by 4-21 to 0-11. Kevin Murray helped himself to a hat-trick of goals. Two weeks later, before an attendance of 15,000, the Corkmen took on Waterford. The Leesiders made full use of the five substitutions allowed but narrowly failed to get the better of a fine Decies team. Victory was sealed in the dying seconds of a hard-fought match when Dan Shanahan got on the end of a 75m Paul Flynn free and drove the sliotar past Donal Óg Cusack to the Cork net. The final score was Waterford 2-17; Cork 2-14.

Away from the hurling scene the media was obsessed by the Catherine Nevin murder trial. New allegations of affairs and intrigue accompanied almost every news item emanating from the hearing. It even diverted attention from the shameful, squalid and sickening facts which daily emerged from corruption trials involving public representatives, businesses, and individuals. Topical too was the subject of refugees, asylum seekers, and migrant workers. Plans to house refugees in 'floatels' caused tension within the government and beyond.

As Madonna topped the singles chart with 'American Pie', and one week later Chicane's, 'Don't Give Up', featuring Bryan Adams, did likewise, a famous racehorse was once again preparing for a mammoth test of resolve. Could 'Istabraq' win the Smurfit Champion Hurdle for the third successive year? Some, in fact the vast majority of horse racing enthusiasts believed that the 15/8 on favourite was life's only certainty. Well, on the day 'Istabraq' and jockey Charlie Swan made no mistake at the Cheltenham Festival when they had four lengths to spare over their nearest contenders. The proudest man at the Meeting must have been owner J.P. McManus.

In March, South Armagh's Crossmaglen Rangers GAA Club who had produced teams to win an unprecedented three All-Ireland Club football championships in four years were also proud. It is a tremendous achievement against all odds; one which showers enormous credit on all concerned. The Rangers have indeed become synonymous with victory at Croke Park on St Patrick's Day.

Gerri Halliwell's 'Bag It Up' hit number one and just one week later, Melanie C/Lisa L.E Lopes took over at the top with 'Never Be the Same Again'. Melanie C thus became the third Spice Girl to have a solo number one; Gerri has three and Melanie B one.

EXECUTION, U2 AND IRISH HAPPY, GALWAY'S LEAGUE AND SEAN AT THE HELM

While Gerri Halliwell and Melanie C were hitting the high spots an interesting event was about to take place in China. It was the annual session of the national legislature, the most important political event of the year. In order to mark the occasion a deputy provincial governor, one of the highest-level officials, was to be executed for his part in bribery and corruption. It was to be the Chinese leaders way of showing resolve to wipe out naked dishonesty!

Back in Ireland, though something completely different was about to take place – rock giants U2 were to be granted the freedom of Dublin. Stade de France was the venue for one of Irish rugby's finest 80 minutes, when on 20 March the Paris losing streak came to an end – a 28-year-long drought.

Losses on successive Sundays in late March and early April to Waterford and Tipperary respectively put paid to Cork's hopes of reaching the semi-finals of the Church & General Hurling League. Subsequent victories over Derry and Wexford were academic. Galway finally emerged as worthy winners of the national trophy with a fine win over Tipperary in the final.

Away from the field of play, Joe McDonagh's GAA presidential stint ended and Monaghanman Sean McCague took over from the former Galway hurling star.

THE NORTH, WORLD LEADERS, NEVIN, BIDDY, HORSES DEAD AND ALIVE!

In Northern Ireland the new Bloody Sunday Inquiry, expected to last for two years, kept journalists busy. Observations on the general political scene varied from warnings of more conflict to beliefs that the Good Friday Agreement was down but not out.

On the pop music front a sequence of debut singles had made it to number one, bringing the total to seven in as many weeks, and ending on the week beginning 16 April with 'Toca's Miracle' by Fragma. April forerunners were Westlife's, 'Fool Again', and Craig David's, 'Fill Me In'. Fragma remained at the top for a further week.

President Robert Mugabe of Zimbabwe made it clear to the country's white farmers in April that they should dance to his tune or leave. There were no threats issued in Russia when Vladimir Putin fitted like a glove into the position vacated by Boris Yeltsin in January.

In Ireland a murder trial received top media billing for almost four months. In its conclusion it took the jury an unprecedented four days to reach a verdict; Catherine Nevin was found guilty of the murder of her husband Tom. She was sentenced to life in prison.

'A Nest of Vipers', 'A Can of Worms', 'Cash in Plastic Bags' – headlines perhaps referring to aspects of the Nevin murder trial? No! Instead they alluded to revelations coming from enquiries at Dublin Castle into the corrupt dealings of some public representatives and their friends. Shame and dishonour abounded. Yet it was the departure of the very popular Biddy (Mary McAvoy) from top soap 'Glenroe' which caused far more furore.

On a Monday morning in April a news item which caused a few ears to perk up came over the airwaves – a

Kerryman believed he had found the head of kidnapped racehorse 'Shergar' wrapped in a sack a few miles from Tralee! Within days the Irish Equine Centre ended speculation by categorically stating that the head did not belong to the racehorse 'Shergar'. There were no mistakes surrounding the fate of another racehorse – 'Papillon'. In the winners enclosure at Aintree Racecourse on 9 April, and at Kill, County Kildare the following day scenes of unbridled ecstasy were witnessed when the Grand National winner ridden by Ruby Walsh and trained by his father, Ted, returned triumphant. The father and son combination mirrored the feat of another Irish duo, that of Tommy and Paul Carberry in 1999 when 'Bobbyjo' was first past the post.

No doubt the Walsh family identified with Britney Spears late April number one hit, 'Oops! I Did it Again'. On another sporting front the mighty men of Munster rugby made light of a Stade Francais challenge in the Heineken European Cup quarter-final at Thomond Park, on Saturday, 15 April.

BREAKTHROUGHS, A SECRET, FIREWORKS AND BRAVE GIRLS
Throughout May the world's trouble spots, sadly too numerous to mention, and each with its own specific reason for inflicting misery on people, showed little signs of problem resolution.

Perhaps there was some succour to be drawn from the fact that a breakthrough on decommissioning of arms by the Provisional IRA opened the way for a return of the Stormont Executive. A measure of optimism was also generated by the negotiated ending of Israel's 22-year occupation of southern Lebanon. It was in May too that Pope John Paul celebrated his eightieth birthday, and the Vatican made known its interpretation of the long-awaited Fatima secret. It was said to relate to the failed 1981 assassination attempt on the Pope. Mid-month brought with it the Netherlands' worst disaster since 1992. Then a plane crashed into a block of flats and left 43 people dead. This time it was a devastating explosion at a fireworks warehouse in the town of Enschede. It resulted in death, injury, and the incineration of 400 houses in fifteen streets.

Madison Avenue's number one hit 'Don't Call Me Baby' may well have reflected the thoughts of Strabane's Ruth Murphy when she became the first Ulster woman to join the Irish Navy. The boxing daughter of former world heavyweight champion Joe Frazier could have been in the same frame of mind when in four pro-career fights to date, Jacqui Frazier-Lade stopped all opponents inside the distance. She plans to keep fighting once a month until a match can be made with Laila Ali, the undefeated boxing daughter of Muhammad Ali.

Munster's rugby followers experienced both elation and agony in May. The elation was born on a glorious sunny day at Stade Lescure, Bordeaux, when their team defeated Toulouse, the aristocrats of French rugby. A place in the final of the Heineken European Cup was the prize! On that particular afternoon agony seemed a million miles away. Yet at Twickenham, in the final, a missed penalty with a minute to go gave victory to Northampton by the narrowest of margins. The final score read Northampton 9; Munster 8.

BUSINESS AS USUAL AT OLD TRAFFORD AND MUNSTER HURLING VENUES

It was business as usual at Old Trafford when Manchester United Football Club again became Premiership champions in front of a record 61,629 attendance. As Billie Piper's, 'Day and Night', made her the youngest female artist to have three number one hit records, the very serious business of the 2000 Guinness Hurling Championship was looming large on the horizon. In Munster, the youngest team in the country, Cork's All-Ireland champions flexed their muscles against Kerry.

At Fitzgerald Stadium, Killarney, the Leesiders had a very comfortable win, thus easing themselves into a Munster semi-final clash with Limerick. The final score was Cork 2-32; Kerry 0-4.

With a much closer final score of 0-17 to 0-14 Tipperary marked paid to Waterford's championship dreams. Clare would later test the mettle of the Premier County. As Cork's meeting with Limerick at Thurles on 4 June drew nigh, with Sonique's 'It Feels so Good' topping the singles chart gave reason for optimism.

For once the atmosphere in Liberty Square was somewhat subdued. With one exception, the Cork team fielded by Jimmy Barry-Murphy a year ago, and deemed by the critics at the time to be too young and too small, again lined out but this time they were All-Ireland champions. In the meantime questions had been answered and doubts erased. The Limerick side showed a blend of long-established top exponents of the game alongside several comparatively new faces. So was it to be all plain sailing for Cork? Far from it! New pressures had emerged for the young Leesiders, not least the tag of All-Ireland champions. Indeed a clearcut victory was expected and anything less would be seized on as lack of resolve in the wake of last year's success.

The final preliminary before the throw-in was the observance of a minutes silence in memory of former Limerick and Munster hurler Eddie Stokes who had recently passed away. The eyes of the 39,000 attendance were now on referee Aodán Mc Suibhne, who after a quick look at his watch let battle commence. Limerick's apparent tactic to knock Cork out of their rhythm early on paid dividends. As a result the men in green and white shared the opening exchanges with the Leesiders. However, the Rebels refused to be rattled and much of Limerick's too-fiery play led to giving away easy frees. Significantly, Seanie McGrath's twelfth minute goal considerably quenched the Shannonsider's fire. The highly-acclaimed Cork defence was once again to prove its worth, though one of Limerick's newcomers, James Butler, did trouble Cork's John Browne in the early stages of the match. Special mention has to go to Wayne Sherlock who broke Limerick's hearts with some marvellous hurling. At midfield Mickey O'Connell and Pat Ryan battled bravely but it was Limerick's Mike O'Brien who caught the eye. After 21 minutes of play Cork's forwards had opened up a seven-point lead. In spite of that they were being well martialled by the excellent defensive work of Stephen McDonagh, T.J. Ryan and Mark Foley. A five point half-time lead (1-8 to 0-

6) seemed comfortable enough for the Leesiders. Yet there was a niggling feeling that we had seen a slightly below par performance from the men in red.

Limerick's new-look defence took on an even more solid demeanour in the third quarter. Indeed it took the introduction of substitute Alan Browne to add weight to Cork's attack. By then a John Butler goal had left Limerick a mere two points adrift. A Timmy McCarthy point increased the Rebels lead but the Shannonsiders again lifted their challenge and subjected Cork's defence to fairly sustained pressure. Yet it has to be said that the Rebels did remain in control. That was due mainly to sterling defensive play in which Diarmuid O'Sullivan, John Browne and Wayne Sherlock excelled. It began to look as if Cork could handle whatever Limerick threw at them. When Pat Ryan, Alan Browne and Fergal Mc Cormack really began to make their presence felt that belief was reinforced. Then with eighteen minutes of normal time left, the irrepressible Seán Óg Ó hAilpín collected a T.J. Ryan lengthy clearance and dispatched it to Joe Deane who had moved inside the Limerick full-back line. Joe's brilliant first-time overhead flick to the net was a stroke of pure hurling genius. Immediately following that action, given the circumstances, a most magnanimous sporting gesture was made when Limerick's full-back, T.P. Ryan, congratulated the Corkman. The goal effectively decided the match. The final score was Cork 2-17; Limerick 1-11.

The Cork team was: Donal Óg Cusack, Fergal Ryan (captain), Diarmuid O'Sullivan, John Browne, Wayne Sherlock, Brian Corcoran, Seán Óg Ó hAilpín, Mickey O'Connell, Pat Ryan, Timmy McCarthy, Fergal McCormack, Neil Ronan, Seanie McGrath, Joe Deane and Ben O'Connor. Subs: Alan Browne for Neil Ronan; Ger O'Connor for Mickey O'Connell; Kevin Murray for Ben O'Connor; and Derek Barrett for Timmy McCarthy. Scorers: J. Deane 1-4 (0-3 frees); S. McGrath 1-2; P. Ryan 0-3 (0-1 free); F. McCormack and T. McCarthy 0-2 each; N. Ronan, B. O'Connor, W. Sherlock and K. Murray 0-1 each. The Limerick team was: Joe Quaid, Stephen McDonagh, T.J Ryan, Stephen Lucey, Brian Geary, Ollie Moran (captain),

Mark Foley, Mike O'Brien, James Moran, Shane O'Neill, Ciarán Carey, Mark Keane, James Butler, Brian Begley and Barry Foley. Subs: Clement Smith for Stephen Lucey; Dave Stapleton for Barry Foley, Dave Hennessy for Shane O'Neill; Mike Galligan for Dave Stapleton; and Willie Walsh for Clement Smith. Scorers: J. Butler 1-1; M. Keane 0-3 (0-2 65m, 0-1 free); B. Begley, C. Carey, M. O'Brien, M. Foley (free), C. Smith, J. Moran and D. Hennessy 0-1 each.

The second Guinness Munster Hurling Championship semi-final was played at Páirc Uí Chaoimh on 11 June. Tipperary easily disposed of Clare to set up a Munster final pairing of Cork and Tipperary. It had a ring about it which had been long craved for in some quarters.

JUNE HEADLINES BUT MOSTLY MUNSTER FINAL FARE

Making the news headlines in June were: the tragic deaths of 58 Chinese migrants whose bodies were discovered in a sealed container at the port of Dover; the return of Elian Gonzales from the United States to Cuba after a bitter seven-month battle over the fate of the castaway boy; the Still Life with Fruit and Pot by Paul Cezanne which fetched a cool £15 million at Christie's Auction Rooms in London; the Euro 2000 football tournament; and the fact that Murray Walker, the Formula One commentator, missed his first race in 50 years after breaking a hip.

Sonique's, 'It Feels so Good', which led us into the championship hurling in May, was still firmly installed at number one by mid-June. In fact Sonique held top spot for three consecutive weeks, making her the longest-running number one of the millennium. In the June weeks which followed 'You See the Trouble With Me' by Black Legend, and Kylie Minogue's 'Spinning Around' were the most favoured singles.

It was again almost time to head south for the Munster final at Thurles, on 2 July. On arrival in Thurles, with time to spare we dropped into the Cathedral of the Assumption where recently the funeral service of the late Raymond Smith had taken place. As I knelt there I recalled a man so steeped in the tradition of Munster hurling final day at Semple Stadium, that in his writings, he said he would happily die there on a sun drenched day with ideally Tipperary and Cork doing battle. 2 July 2000 had all those ingredients. As we moved into Liberty Square the atmosphere was electric. Tipperary fans were back in force. My own family connections from west Cork and the Careys of Mallow were out in force because of a vested interest in a member of Cork's minor hurling team. Brian Carey, the young man who wore the number eight jersey, is my grand-nephew. We were very proud of him! His presence on the team ensured that we took up our seats in the uncovered section of Ardán Ó Coinneáin well before the 1.30pm throw-in. As it turned out the match lacked any real competitive edge with Cork running out easy winners over Limerick.

So what did the senior match between Cork and Tipperary hold in store? Whatever else it was highly unlikely to lack a competitive edge! Tipperary came into the final on a high, fuelled by impressive wins over Waterford and Clare. There was every reason for optimism in the Premier County camp. As for Cork, the young Rebels overcame the challenge of Kerry and Limerick but there were times when they seemed to be off a cylinder or two. We had seen some brilliant individual performances but also some slightly indifferent ones. All-in-all there was no room for complacency.

In the midst of all the animated excitement Cork's captain Fergal Ryan and Tipperary's captain Tommy Dunne proudly led the way as the teams managed by all-time greats, Jimmy Barry-Murphy of Cork and Nicholas English of Tipperary, paraded in front of the flag-waving, empassioned capacity attendance. The red jerseys of Cork, the blue and gold of Tipperary, the air laden with anticipation, suspense at a maximum, and a sun-kissed setting; yes it was all there in abundance, ingredients which swell emotion to bursting point.

The waiting was over, referee Pat Horan assured himself that all was in order, and before we knew what was happening the match was in progress. First impressions were that the huge occasion had got to the players. A nervous start by both teams which only disappeared slowly was the hallmark of the opening period.

Scrappy, jittery hurling rather than controlled, confident stick-work resulted in a below par spectacle. Perhaps
Cork's most satisfactory performance came from Derek
Barrett at midfield. So influential was he that John Leahy,
Tipperary's most inspirational player in the previous
rounds of the championship, never managed to get into the
match. The Cobhman's input was a major plus for Jimmy
Barry-Murphy's side. A Tommy Dunne twelfth-minute
penalty saved on the line by full-back supreme Diarmuid
O'Sullivan did not dishearten the Premier County men
who, through Dunne, Corcoran, O'Meara and O'Neill con-
tinued to press forward. Once again Cork's defence
responded magnificently with Brian Corcoran, Diarmuid
O'Sullivan and Fergal Ryan majestic. Yet, Tipperary's
Eugene O'Neill finished to the net in the twenty-eighth
minute. The half-time score was Cork 0-8; Tipperary 1-5.
Interval reflections on the first-half implied that while the
Rebels' play occasionally looked scrappy, at no time were
they really troubled by a wasteful Tipperary attack.

Within seconds of the resumption Ben O'Connor, who
was to remain a constant threat throughout the second-
half, shot Cork into the lead. It was to be shortlived!
Premier County teams have a long tradition of grit and
determination – the 2000 version was no different. In a five-
minute spell they scored through Eddie Enright, Liam
Cahill and Eugene O'Neill to open up a two point margin.
Again though Jimmy Barry-Murphy's men showed why
they were All-Ireland champions. Up front Joe Deane and
Seanie McGrath, who were now at the receiving end of
more measured distribution, began to play ducks and
drakes with Tipperary's full-back line. At midfield, Pat
Ryan, who had replaced Mickey O'Connell, was having a
fine game. Cork seemed to be on their way to victory.

Then Tommy Dunne struck! A vital and superb goal for
the Premier County. As on previous occasions when the
Corkmen needed a confidence booster Alan Browne came
to the rescue; he restored Cork's lead with a well-taken
point. Drama was soon to follow when Tipperary were
awarded a penalty. This time it was John Leahy who

stepped up to take it. As with Tommy Dunne's effort in the first-half it was saved and cleared. That seemed to be the cue for Cork to finally dominate the match. With Joe Deane, Ben O'Connor, Timmy McCarthy, Seanie McGrath, Alan Browne, Seán Óg Ó hAilpín and Fergal Ryan at their best the Rebels popped over six points in quick succession.

Tipperary could only muster a single point in reply. Was that it all over? No, it was not! Imagine the excitement and heartstopping moments which followed when two minutes from the end of normal time Tommy Dunne scored another goal – an even better one than the first! Were the Tipperarymen dramatically to astound the large Cork following by snatching the Guinness Munster Hurling Championship of 2000? To say that our hearts were in our mouths when substitute Paul Kelly narrowed Cork's winning margin to a single point would be the understatement of the year. I closed my eyes as Donal Óg Cusack took the puck-out, hopefully listening for the long whistle.

It didn't come immediately and when I opened my eyes the sliotar was sailing over the Tipperary crossbar from the stick of Seanie McGrath. In what seemed like an eternity but could only have been seconds, the final whistle sounded. We had done it again! Jimmy Barry-Murphy's lads, who had been subjected to the sternest of tests came through in the end with flying colours. The final score was Cork 0-23; Tipperary 3-12.

Regardless of what the scribes had to say the contest did develop into a second-half thriller of epic proportions. It was the stuff that Munster hurling finals are made of. Perhaps one has to be a staunch believer in the unique occasion to fully appreciate its full significance. I don't remember who was selected as man-of-the-match. I might have given it to Tommy Dunne, but the commanding displays of Joe Deane and Séan Óg Ó hAilpín are vivid in my mind. Full marks too to Fergal McCormack who, in spite of a nasty head wound picked up early in the first-half continued to battle manfully up to the fifty-sixth minute.

The Cork team was: Donal Óg Cusack, Fergal Ryan (captain), Diarmuid O'Sullivan, John Browne, Wayne

Sherlock, Brian Corcoran, Séan Óg Ó hAilpín, Mickey O'Connell, Derek Barrett, Timmy McCarthy, Fergal McCormack, Alan Browne, Seanie McGrath, Joe Deane, and Ben O'Connor. Subs: Pat Ryan for Mickey O'Connell; Kevin Murray for Fergal McCormick. Scorers: J. Deane 0-10 (0-7 frees); B. O'Connor 0-3; S. McGrath 0-3; A. Browne 0-3; P. Ryan 0-2 (0-1 free); D. Barrett 0-1; Kevin Murray 0-1. The Tipperary team was: Brendan Cummins, Paul Ormonde, Philip Maher, Michael Ryan, John Carroll, David Kennedy, Eamonn Corcoran, Tommy Dunne (captain), John Leahy, Mark O'Leary, Eddie Enright, Brian O'Meara, Eugene O'Neill, Paul Shelley, and Paddy O'Brien. Subs: Liam Cahill for Paddy O'Brien; Michael Ryan (Templederry) for Mark O'Leary; Paul Kelly for Paul Shelley. Scorers: E. O'Neill 1-5 (0-4 frees); T. Dunne 2-0; B O'Meara 0-2; E Enright 0-2; J. O'Leary 0-1; L. Cahill 0-1; P. Kelly 0-1.

A MIXTURE OF EMOTION AND SNIPPETS OF NEWS

Elated by the afternoon of high drama at Semple Stadium, our euphoria was soon dampened when over the radio came the news that ace motorcycle legend Joey Dunlop had been killed at a race in Tallinn, Estonia. The shy, unassuming, five-times Formula One world champion from north Antrim had endeared himself to people all over the world. He was a champion too of the less fortunate inhabitants of Romania who, without fanfare, were benefactors of his unstinting charitable work. As we travelled north on that summer's evening drama too was unfolding at Rotterdam where the final of Euro 2000 between France and Italy was in progress. Italy were first to score but a ninetieth minute goal for France took the match into extra time. A brilliant goal by David Trezeguet sealed victory for France. It was a fitting end to what has been described as a compelling tournament.

40,000 spectators turned up at Berlin's Hoppegarten to witness Europe's first elephant race – an event which did not please animal protection activists, including film diva Brigitte Bardot; 60-year-old superstar Tina Turner informed thousands of her fans that she intended giving up live touring; Heinz announced its intention to start making green ketchup; ladies at Apollo Bay, Australia were asked not to bother the lifeguards except when drowning; loyalist protesters were pelting police at Drumcree; a man carrying a placard proclaiming 'The End of the World is Nigh' was knocked down and killed while crossing the road; in south-east India 20,000 were evacuated in a flood alert; and 'Sinndar' trained by John Oxx, and ridden by Johnny Murtagh, won the Irish Derby.

STEEPED IN SPORT

July, traditionally a month steeped in sport, was kind to 24-year-old American superstar Tiger Woods. He won the British Open Championship by a record score at St Andrews, Scotland. That victory etched another niche in the annals of golf by completing a career Grand Slam of all four Major titles – the British Open, the US Open, the USPG championship and, the Masters he captured at Augusta in 1997.

Another American who out-gunned all comers was 20-year-old tennis player Venus Williams. She became the first black lady to win the Wimbledon singles championship in 42 years. Her glory did not end there because along with her 18-year-old sister Serena she left an indelible mark on the Wimbledon tournament by adding the doubles trophy to the growing collection of family silverware. Though Pete Sampras made history by winning his seventh Wimbledon men's single title, the tournament is likely to be remembered more for the feats of the Williams girls.

July was also kind to another family. With 'Breathless', the Corrs topped the UK singles chart for the first time. The multi-million selling act knocked Eminem's, 'The Real Slim Shady' off the top. But the Corr's reign was shortlived. Ronan Keating with 'Life is a Rollercoaster' saw to that. Life may be a roller coaster but life at the top is also tough. For the fourth week in succession the number one spot changed hands; on that occasion to the winning combination of Five and Queen with 'We Will Rock You'. Then, just as the month drew to a close Craig David's, 'Seven Days' ruled supreme in the single chart.

EVIL, CONCORDE GRIEF AND 2/9 FAVOURITES

Unfortunately for some, the abiding memories of high summer did not revolve around sport, music, or happy times. Eight-year-old Sarah Payne from West Sussex, disappeared and her naked body was eventually found in undergrowth.

Air France's Concorde burst into flames shortly after take-off from Charles de Gaulle airport, Paris. Seconds later it crashed into a hotel in the town of Gonesse, killing all 109 on board and five bystanders on the ground.

As Robbie Williams secured his third solo number one with 'Rock D.J.', Cork's hurlers did not have Kilkenny's D.J. on their minds just yet, but surely it would be only a matter of time. The Leesiders were quoted at 2/9 to beat Offaly in the All-Ireland semi-final. Few argued against it! Offaly had gained re-entry to the championship by the 'backdoor', having been soundly thrashed by Kilkenny in the Leinster final. At the quarter-final stage of the All-Ireland series, apparent lack of heart and commitment against Derry begged the question as to whether Offaly were capable of mounting a meaningful challenge against Cork in the semi-final. The managerial tasks faced by team managers Jimmy Barry-Murphy of Cork and Pat Fleury of Offaly were diagonally opposite. The problem confronting the Rebel County's supremo was one of controlling complacency in a capable and confident camp, while his Faithful County counterpart had to draw on all his deep-set emotional ties and evident pride in his county's hurling heritage in order to motivate his men. At least that's how it seemed from the outside!

We took our seats in Croke Park on 6 August. Across the pitch a large opening with a building-site-like appearance, which will soon house a state-of-the-art new Hogan Stand, left the famous grounds somewhat devoid of its customary All-Ireland semi-final day ambience.

Having watched a very useful Cork minor team show the way with a 2-17 to 1-11 victory over Dublin, the time had come for the senior hurlers of Cork and Offaly to take the field. As excitement and anticipation mounted, to the relief of the 34,655 attendance, referee Willie Barrett got the ball rolling. The Rebels quickly got into their stride and registered three points without reply in as many minutes. Joe Deane and Seanie McGrath were causing havoc up front. As had been predicted by the pundits, Offaly were severely under pressure! The pundits though did not take into account that the Faithful County had men for the big occasion and, that when the chips were down those men would respond. Superbly led by team captain Johnny Dooley, other star performers began to make their presence felt in several areas of the pitch. Cork's dominance was suddenly halted and worryingly their usually immaculate score-taking forwards became seriously wayward. At half-time the Leesiders had a slender two-point lead. Top of discussions during the interval were the ten scoring opportunities missed by Cork compared to Offaly's two. But the lads would come good – a belief that was reinforced when within minutes of the restart the Leesiders extended their lead. Amazingly, they didn't score again for another eighteen minutes. Meanwhile, during virtually every one of those minutes, Offaly grew in stature. As the match wore on it became clear that it was to be Offaly's day; everything they did turned to gold. A whole team-full of stars emerged. Simon Whelahan was the brightest of them all. For the young Cork team we had seen performing so brilliantly over the past year little seemed to go right. To say that the Rebel County followers were bewildered and disappointed would not convey the depth of hurt felt. But as the saying goes, you can't win them all. The final score was Offaly 0-19; Cork 0-14.

A real possibility is, that in spite of repeated warnings from manager Jimmy Barry-Murphy, the All-Ireland champions did get caught in the psychological trap of over-confidence. True to form the Cork manager accepted defeat with dignity. He said, 'We were beaten by a better team on the day and we just have to get on with it'. That his confidence in the fine squad of hurlers he has assembled remains unshaken came when he added, 'But this is a very young team, they'll be back in Croke Park, I can guarantee that'. Cork's captain, Fergal Ryan, too had no doubt that Offaly played better hurling on the day. Interestingly,

Joe Dooley, without prompting, was quoted as saying, 'We had a bit of luck on the day too, anything we hit went over and you need that'.

The Cork team was: Donal Óg Cusack, Fergal Ryan (captain), Diarmuid O'Sullivan, John Browne, Wayne Sherlock, Brian Corcoran, Séan Óg Ó hAilpín, Pat Ryan, Timmy McCarthy, Fergal McCormack, Alan Browne, Seanie McGrath, Joe Deane and Ben O'Connor. Subs: Kevin Murray for Timmy McCarthy; Mickey O'Connell for Pat Ryan; and Neil Ronan for Fergal McCormack. Scorers: J. Deane 0-10 (0-6 frees); B. O'Connor, P. Ryan, D. Barrett, A. Browne, S. McGrath 0-1 each. The Offaly team was: Stephen Byrne, Simon Whelahan, Kevin Kinahan, Niall Claffey, Brian Whelahan, Joe Errity, Kevin Martin, Johnny Dooley (capt.), Ger Oakley, Johnny Pilkington, Gary Hanniffy, Brendan Murphy, Michael Duignan, John Ryan, and Joe Dooley. Subs: Paudie Mulhare for Michael Duignan; Cillian Farrell for Johnny Pilkington. Scorers: Johnny Dooley 0-7 (0-5 frees); J. Pilkington 0-4; G. Hanniffy 0-3; J. Dooley 0-2; G. Oakley, J. Ryan, B. Murphy 0-1 each.

On 13 August Kilkenny qualified for a place in a third All-Ireland final in a row when they defeated a gallant Galway side by a score of 2-19 to 0-17. No doubt the Noresiders will not want to go home empty handed another year, but I'm sure Offaly will have other ideas.

Unperturbed by the happenings at Croke Park, Melanie C's fourth solo single 'I Turn to You' went straight to number one. To date in 2000 short stays at the top was par for the course. Spiller ensured the trend continued by displacing Melanie C with 'Groovejet' (If this Ain't Love). Then up popped Madonna's long-awaited new single, 'Music', to depose Spiller.

MONSOON AND KURSH DISASTERS, ROAD CARNAGE, TIGER AND NICK FAME

Throughout much of August the aftermath of a natural disaster in the form of torrential monsoon rains brought death, suffering, misery, destruction and heartbreak to the people of north-east India. Possibly thousands were killed and more than two million left homeless as floods and landslides ravaged enormous tracts of land.

Yet it was a catastrophic accident at sea which made the largest headlines. For a reason not yet clear a Russian nuclear submarine, the *Kursk*, with a crew of 118, sunk in the Barents Sea, a part of the Arctic Ocean north of Norway. Sadly, follow-up rescue operations to save any sailors alive failed completely.

In Ireland, summer carnage on the roads was a number one killer. During a seven day period in August seventeen lives were lost.

Lives too were again being lost on the streets of Belfast. Infighting between loyalist activists hell-bent on control-ling areas of the city for the purpose of drug-trafficking, extortion and protection racketeering was at the heart of a feud which caused the return of British troop patrols.

As the month drew to a close, depending on whether one's interest lay with sport or television, a hero from each category stood out from the pack. From the world of sport it was a young American golfer of whom we heard much earlier in the summer – Tiger Woods. This time he raised his profile still further by completing the winning of three Majors in one year. In the world of television there was no contest; it was one Nick Bateman (Nasty Nick) of 'Big Brother', the British Channel 4 gameshow which became a phenomenon.

THE END IS INDEED NIGH!

For me the time has come to end a chronicle of memories, change and events all of which began in the early days of the dim and distant 1950s. Recalling the personalities and deeds of our great hurlers, some now gone to their final resting place, has touched me enormously.

As for changes in the ways-of-life only those who have lived through it can possibly understand the magnitude of the transformations. There isn't a single aspect of society which has remained untouched.

Perhaps the one development which has touched the lives of all is the explosive growth in technology. Mobile phones, personal computers and satellite television are just three examples of technological advances which have become part of our everyday lives. Nowhere is the increase in technology exemplified more than in the use of the Internet. Five years ago it was used mainly by the United States Government and academics, today it is the most incredible communications medium the world has ever seen.

On this September day, with the Boy band A1 perched at the top of the singles chart with 'Take on Me', let me recall some of life's personalities who saw in the new millennium before departing this life for good: Brendan Donnelly, Ulster and Antrim hurler; Gerry Fitzgerald, Limerick hurler and referee; Eddie Stokes, Munster and Limerick hurler; Alfie O'Brien, Clare hurler; Vincent Twomey, Cork hurler (back to back All-Ireland minor 1970-1971); Tadhgie Lyne, Kerry footballer; Phil Crowe, Irish rugby international; Frank Patterson, Irish tenor; Tony Doyle, actor; Raymond Smith, journalist; Michael Ferris, T.D.; Jonathan Philbin Bowman, writer; Charles Schulz, cartoonist; Dame Barbara Cartland, writer; Cardinal John O'Connor; Sir John Gielgud, actor; Sir Alec Guinness, actor; Douglas Fairbanks Jnr, actor; Walter Matthau, actor; and Sir Robin Day, broadcaster.

Sadly my beloved Rebels missed out on the Guinness All-Ireland Senior Hurling Championship final of 2000. Frankly, on 10 September I did not readily gravitate towards Croke Park. The impetus which tipped the balance was the presence of my grand-nephew Brian Carey on the Cork team to play Galway in the All-Ireland minor hurling final.

It was a fine, mild, even warm afternoon at the capital, where inside the stadium the supporters of Kilkenny and Offaly swamped the meagre smattering of Cork and Galway followers.

The minor match turned out to be high scoring without being hugely entertaining. The young men of Galway emerged winners. Superior forward play, especially excellent point-taking throughout the match, was the key factor in a well deserved victory.

As I passively observed the various pre-match activities to the one-hundred-and-twelfth senior All-Ireland hurling final, it occurred to me that something unusual might be going on. The difference was, on other days I had eyes only for men wearing red jerseys! That the President of Ireland was introduced to the crowd and teams had somehow passed me by. I had scant recollection of previously seeing the President of the GAA on the pitch either!

Those happenings were always too close to the throw-in, when the flow of adrenalin blurs all but thoughts relating to players. However, the parade which is unique and special to our games did make an impact – the men of Kilkenny and Offaly respectively led by team captains Willie O'Connor and Johnny Dooley.

The now familiar figure of referee Willie Barrett was at hand to set in motion a match which Kilkenny would dominate from beginning to end; a match too which surely would silence any critics D.J. Carey may have had. By the time the Young Ireland's clubman had helped himself to a goal and contributed enormously to further goals by Henry Shefflin and Charlie Carter, nothing short of a miracle could have brought Offaly back into the match. At the interval, in spite of Offaly's eighteen scoring chances to Kilkenny's fifteen, the score was Kilkenny 3-8; Offaly 0-7. We had seen a first-half when, try as they might, the Offalymen, magnificently led by the talented and ever-green Johnny Dooley, could not come to terms with the firepower of the aforementioned Kilkenny trio. The focused Noresiders seemed capable of scoring a goal each time Offaly even remotely threatened their position of superiority.

At the beginning of the second-half a straight swap between ace wing-back Brian Whelahan and star corner-forward Michael Duignan failed to change the course of the match. The introduction of substitute and former all-star John Troy met with a similar fate. Not even a fifty-ninth minute goal by the indefatigable Johnny Pilkington gave the Offalymen a realistic hope of salvaging a match which was by then well out of reach.

We had seen a fine Kilkenny team effort. Players such as Willie O'Connor, Phil Larkin, Eamon Kennedy, Peter Barry, Andy Comerford, Denis Byrne, John Power, John Hoyne and the devastating full-forward line of Charlie

Carter, D.J. Carey and Henry Shefflin all starred on the day. When Willie Barrett brought the match to a close the score read Kilkenny 5-15; Offaly 1-14.

The Kilkenny team was: James McGarry, Michael Kavanagh; Noel Hickey, Willie O'Connor (captain), Phil Larkin, Eamon Kennedy, Peter Barry, Andy Comerford, Brian McAvoy, Denis Byrne, John Power, John Hoyne, Charlie Carter, D.J.Carey, and Henry Shefflin.

It was a disappointing outing for Offaly's followers and management. Neutrals were not impressed either but it was a great day for Kilkenny's fans and of course team manager Brian Cody.

The third attempt by the Cats in as many years finally saw the McCarthy Cup on its way to the Marble City. Few, if any, by the banks of the Nore will spend time reflecting on the quality of the match. The McCarthy Cup is like gold dust; it comes infrequently and, only at the end of a long road hallmarked by sweat and toil.

Dare we hope for a swift return of the famous trophy to Leeside in 2001? Yes, I believe our chances are well within the odds-on category.

Meanwhile congratulations to Kilkenny, the 2000 All-Ireland senior hurling champions.